YOU ARE HERE.

**NATIONAL
GEOGRAPHIC
KiDS**

World
Atlas

**Fourth
Edition**

NATIONAL GEOGRAPHIC

SCHOLASTIC INC.

Table of Contents

FRONT OF THE BOOK

GETTING STARTED	**6**
How to Use This Atlas	6
UNDERSTANDING MAPS	**8**
Exploring Your World	8
Kinds of Maps	10
How to Read a Map	12
PLANET EARTH	**14**
Earth in Space	14
Earth in Motion	16
THE PHYSICAL WORLD	**18**
Physical Map	18
The Land	20
World Climate	22
Factors Influencing Climate	24
World Vegetation	26
Environmental Hot Spots	28
Natural Disasters	30
THE POLITICAL WORLD	**32**
Political Map	32
World Population	34
Population Trends	36
World Languages & Literacy	38
World Religions	40
World Economies	42
World Trade	44
World Water	46
World Food	48
World Energy & Minerals	50

NORTH AMERICA 52

PHYSICAL & POLITICAL MAPS	**54**
ABOUT THE CONTINENT	**56**
CANADA	**60**
UNITED STATES	**62**
MEXICO & CENTRAL AMERICA	**64**
Belize	
Costa Rica	
El Salvador	
Guatemala	
Honduras	
Mexico	
Nicaragua	
Panama	
WEST INDIES & THE BAHAMAS	**66**
Antigua & Barbuda	
Bahamas	
Barbados	
Cuba	
Dominica	
Dominican Republic	
Grenada	
Haiti	
Jamaica	
St. Kitts & Nevis	
St. Lucia	
St. Vincent & the Grenadines	
Trinidad & Tobago	

SOUTH AMERICA 68

PHYSICAL & POLITICAL MAPS	**70**
ABOUT THE CONTINENT	**72**
NORTHWESTERN SOUTH AMERICA	**76**
Bolivia	
Colombia	
Ecuador	
Peru	
Venezuela	
NORTHEASTERN SOUTH AMERICA	**78**
Brazil	
Guyana	
Suriname	
SOUTHERN SOUTH AMERICA	**80**
Argentina	
Chile	
Paraguay	
Uruguay	

EUROPE 82

PHYSICAL & POLITICAL MAPS	**84**
ABOUT THE CONTINENT	**86**
NORTHERN EUROPE	**90**
Denmark	
Estonia	
Finland	
Iceland	
Latvia	
Lithuania	
Norway	
Sweden	
WESTERN EUROPE	**92**
Andorra	
Austria	
Belgium	
France	
Germany	
Ireland	
Italy	
Liechtenstein	
Luxembourg	
Malta	
Monaco	
Netherlands	
Portugal	
San Marino	
Spain	
Switzerland	
United Kingdom	
Vatican City	
EASTERN EUROPE	**94**
Belarus	
Czech Republic	
Hungary	
Moldova	
Poland	
Slovakia	
Ukraine	
BALKANS & CYPRUS	**96**
Albania	
Bosnia and Herzegovina	
Bulgaria	
Croatia	
Cyprus	
Greece	
Kosovo	
Macedonia	
Montenegro	
Romania	
Serbia	
Slovenia	
EUROPEAN RUSSIA	**98**

South America:
Llama, page 73

North America: Grand Canyon, page 56

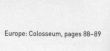

Europe: Colosseum, pages 88–89

ASIA 100

PHYSICAL & POLITICAL MAPS	102
ABOUT THE CONTINENT	104
ASIAN RUSSIA	108
CENTRAL ASIA	110
Kazakhstan	
Kyrgyzstan	
Mongolia	
Tajikistan	
Turkmenistan	
Uzbekistan	
EAST ASIA	112
China	
Japan	
North Korea	
South Korea	
EASTERN MEDITERRANEAN	114
Armenia	
Azerbaijan	
Georgia	
Israel	
Jordan	
Lebanon	
Syria	
Turkey	
SOUTHWEST ASIA	116
Bahrain	
Iran	
Iraq	
Kuwait	
Oman	
Qatar	
Saudi Arabia	
United Arab Emirates	
Yemen	
SOUTH ASIA	118
Afghanistan	
Bangladesh	
Bhutan	
India	
Maldives	
Myanmar	
Nepal	
Pakistan	
Sri Lanka	
SOUTHEAST ASIA	120
Brunei	
Cambodia	
Laos	
Malaysia	
Philippines	
Singapore	
Thailand	
Vietnam	
INDONESIA & TIMOR-LESTE	122

AFRICA 124

PHYSICAL & POLITICAL MAPS	126
ABOUT THE CONTINENT	128
NORTH AFRICA	132
Algeria	
Egypt	
Libya	
Morocco	
Tunisia	
WEST AFRICA	134
Benin	
Burkina Faso	
Cameroon	
Cape Verde	
Cote d'Ivoire	
Equatorial Guinea	
Gabon	
Gambia	
Ghana	
Guinea	
Guinea-Bissau	
Liberia	
Mali	
Mauritania	
Niger	
Nigeria	
Sao Tomé & Principe	
Senegal	
Sierra Leone	
Togo	
EAST AFRICA	136
Burundi	
Central African Republic	
Chad	
Congo	
Democratic Republic of the Congo	
Djibouti	
Eritrea	
Ethiopia	
Kenya	
Rwanda	
Somalia	
South Sudan	
Sudan	
Tanzania	
Uganda	
SOUTHERN AFRICA	138
Angola	
Botswana	
Comoros	
Lesotho	
Madagascar	
Malawi	
Mauritius	
Mozambique	
Namibia	
Seychelles	
South Africa	
Swaziland	
Zambia	
Zimbabwe	

AUSTRALIA, NEW ZEALAND, & OCEANIA 140

PHYSICAL & POLITICAL MAPS	142
ABOUT THE REGION	144
AUSTRALIA & NEW ZEALAND	148
OCEANIA	150
Federated States of Micronesia	
Fiji	
Kiribati	
Marshall Islands	
Nauru	
Palau	
Papua New Guinea	
Samoa	
Solomon Islands	
Tonga	
Tuvalu	
Vanuatu	

ANTARCTICA 152

| ABOUT THE CONTINENT | 154 |

Antarctica: Penguins, page 154

THE OCEANS 156

Investigating the Oceans	158
Pacific Ocean	160
Atlantic Ocean	162
Indian Ocean	164
Arctic Ocean	166

BACK OF THE BOOK

FLAGS & FACTS	168
GAMES	176
GLOSSARY	186
GEO FACTS & FIGURES	189
OUTSIDE WEBSITES	191
INDEX: PLACE-NAMES	191
INDEX: OCEAN FEATURES	205
ILLUSTRATIONS CREDITS	207

Australia, New Zealand, & Oceania: Maori man, page 144

Africa: Mother and child, page 129

GETTING STARTED

How To Use This Atlas

This atlas is a window on your planet. Through it you can explore the world. To learn about maps, use the first section, Understanding Maps. Next, basic facts about Earth as a planet are presented in the section called Planet Earth. The section Physical World includes world maps that focus on different aspects of nature and the environment. The Political World contains world maps about how humans live on the planet. In the pages that follow, the maps, photographs, and essays are arranged by continent and region. You can look up specific places or just browse. Remember, it's your planet—learn it, love it, explore it!

"YOU ARE HERE"
Locator globes help you see where one area is in relation to others. On regional pages (shown here), the area covered by the main map is yellow on the globe, and its continent is green. On pages with continent maps, the locator globe shows the whole continent in yellow. The surrounding land is brown.

116 SOUTHWEST ASIA

THIS CONTINENT
ASIA

THE BASICS

STATS

Largest country
Saudi Arabia 756,985 sq mi
(1,960,582 sq km)
Smallest country
Bahrain 277 sq mi (717 sq km)
Most populous country
Iran 78,868,000
Least populous country
Bahrain 1,336,000
Predominant language
Arabic, Farsi (modern-day Persian), Kurdish
Predominant religion
Islam
Highest GDP per capita
Qatar $98,900
Lowest GDP per capita
Yemen $2,500
Highest life expectancy
Bahrain, Qatar 79 years
Highest literacy rate
Qatar 96%

GEO WHIZ

Rub' al Khali (Empty Quarter), the world's largest sand desert, covers 226,000 square miles (583,000 sq km), an area larger than France.

More than 4,000 years ago, the Sumerians built the first cities in the world on the plain between the Tigris and Euphrates Rivers in what is now Iraq.

The ancient Romans called Yemen "Arabia Felix," meaning "Happy Arabia."

Five times a day, every day, Muslims all over the world face the city of Mecca, in Saudi Arabia, to pray. Mecca is the birthplace of the prophet Muhammad, the founder of Islam.

Iran drilled the first oil wells in the region in 1908.

Causeways connect Bahrain Island—the largest of the 33 islands that make up the country of Bahrain—to two others and to the mainland of Saudi Arabia.

Southwest Asia

This region, made up largely of deserts and mountains, includes the countries of the Arabian Peninsula and those that border the Persian Gulf. Islam is the dominant religion in each, and the two holiest places for Muslims—Mecca and Medina—are here. Arabic is the principal language everywhere but Iran, where most people speak Farsi. While water has been the most important natural resource here for millennia, global attention has focused in recent decades on the region's oil wealth. With the majority of the world's reserves found here, oil has brought outside influences and military conflict. Long a cradle of civilization, Southwest Asia continues to hold the world's attention.

⬤ **GIRL TALK.** Young Iranian girls get together at a film festival in Tehran. The scarves they are wearing are part of the Islamic dress code hijab, which says that women and girls must cover their heads and dress modestly.

⬤ **HE'S GOT THE BEAT.** This Omani drummer plays at a dance in the Arabian Sea port of Qurayyat. Though modernizing in many ways, Oman works hard to preserve its traditional culture.

⬤ **DIFFERENT WORLDS.** A contrast between horse and horsepower, this roadside meeting in Qatar also displays both traditional Arab and Western clothing styles. This Persian Gulf country preserves a rich history of Arabian horse breeding and continues to produce champions.

REGIONAL OIL RESERVES

Saudi Arabia
262.6*
Venezuela
211.2
Canada
175.2
Iran
137.0
Iraq
115.0
Kuwait
104.0
United Arab Emirates
97.8
Russia
60.0
Libya
46.4

*Figures are for oil reserves, in billions of barrels, 2011

Saudi Arabia leads the region and the world in oil reserves and production, but four other countries in Southwest Asia also rank near the top.

STATS & FACTS
At the left-hand edge of each continent opener and regional page is a bar that includes basic information about the subject. This feature is a great first stop if you're writing a report.

CHARTS & GRAPHS
Each region includes a chart or graph that shows information visually.

74 ABOUT THE CONTINENT

SOUTH AMERICA
more about
South America

ABOUT THE CONTINENT **75**

SOUTH AMERICA

WHERE THE PICTURES ARE

WHERE ARE THE PICTURES?
If you want to know where a picture in the regional sections of this atlas was taken, look for the map in the photo essay. Find the label that describes the picture you're curious about, and follow the line to its location.

Maps use symbols to stand for political and physical features. At right is the key to the symbols used in this atlas. If you are wondering what you're looking at on a map, check here.

INDEX AND GRID

Look through the index for the place-name you want. Next to it is a page number, a letter, and another number. Go to the page. Draw imaginary lines from the letter along the side of the map and the number along the top. Your place will be close to where the lines meet.

Río Muni (region),
  Equatorial Guinea **135** F7
Rivera, Uruguay **81** D4
Riverside, California
  (U.S.) **62** E2
Riviera (region), Europe
  84 F3
Rivne, Ukraine **95** D6
Riyadh, Saudi Arabia
  117 E4

COLOR BARS

Every section of this atlas has its own color. Look for the color on the Contents pages and across the top of every page in the atlas. Within that color bar, you'll see the name of the section and the title for each topic or map. These color bars are a handy way to find the section you want.

North America

South America

Europe

Asia

Africa

Australia, New Zealand, & Oceania

Antarctica

SOUTHWEST ASIA | 117

THE CONTINENT:
ASIA

◑ **LOST AND FOUND.** Thousands of treasures dating from ancient Mesopotamia were destroyed, lost, or stolen during the invasion of Iraq in April 2003. This ring is among the few items recovered.

BLACK SEA
GEORGIA
TURKEY
ARMENIA
AZERBAIJAN
CASPIAN SEA
TURKMENISTAN
KURDISTAN
Khoy
Orūmīyeh
Marand
Tabriz
Ardabil
Bojnūrd
Qūchān
Mashhad
Tall 'Afar
Dahūk
Nīnawā
Zanjān
Qazvīn
Karaj
Elburz Mts.
Rasht
Sabzevār
Neyshābūr
KHORASAN
AFGHANISTAN
Mosul
Kirkūk
Arbīl
Sulaymānīyah
Sanandaj
Tehrān
Damāvand
18,605 ft
5,671 m
Dasht-e Kavīr
(Salt Desert)
Gonābād
SYRIA
Sāmarrā
Tikrīt
Kermānshāh
Hamadān
Qom
Kāshān
Sāveh
ZAGROS MOUNTAINS
IRAQ
Ar Ramādī
Baghdād
Al Fallūjah
Karbalā'
Dezfūl
Arāk
Isfahan
Yazd
Bīrjand
Zābol
IRAN
JORDAN
SYRIAN DESERT
Al Hillah
An Najaf
Al Kūfah
Al Kūt
Qomsheh
Rafsanjān
Zāhedān
Al Qurayyāt
Ur
Al 'Amārah
Kermān
Bam
Zābol
'Ar'ar
Sakākah
An Nāṣirīyah
Ahvāz
FARS
Behbahān
Sā'īdābād
Jīroft
Al Jawf
Al Baṣrah
Ābādān
Shīrāz
Fasā
Tārom
Īrānshahr
An Nafūd
KUWAIT
Būshehr
Man Dasht
Persepolis
Al Kuwayt
Jahrom
Ḥā'il
Ḥafar al Bāṭin
Bandar-e 'Abbās
Strait of
Hormuz
Angohrān
BALUCHISTAN
Buraydah
Unayzah
Al Jubayl
Ra's al-Khaimah
Chāh Bahār
PAKISTAN
Ad Dammām
BAHRAIN
OMAN
SAUDI
Manama
Al Mubarraz
Sharjah
GULF OF OMAN
Medina
Riyadh
QATAR
Dubai
ARABIA
Yanbu' al Baḥr
Jabal Tuwayq
United Arab
Emirates
Ibri
Nizwa
Suhār
Jeddah
Al Hillah
Al Khalj
Ibri
Muscat
Mecca
At Tā'if
ARABIAN
PENINSULA
Al Hadīdah
(meteorite craters)
Khalūf
Qurayyāt
Sūr
Al Qunfudhah
Rub al Khali
(Empty Quarter)
Duqm
Masira
OMAN
Abhā
Khamis
Mushayt
ZUFAR
ARABIAN
SEA
Abū 'Arīsh
Najrān
Mirbāt
Jīzān
Ṣa'dah
Salālah
Ḥawf
Nishtūn
ERITREA
YEMEN
Sanaa
Nishtūn
Al Hudaydah
Dhamār
Ḥaḍramawt
Ash Shiḥr
Ta'izz
Ibb
Rida'
Al Mukallā
Laḥij
ETHIOPIA
Aden
Socotra
(YEMEN)
DJIBOUTI
GULF OF ADEN
SOMALIA

TROPIC OF CANCER

RED SEA
MEDITERRANEAN SEA
LEBANON
ISRAEL
AL HIJAZ
SUDAN
Ṭabūk

Map Key
◉ Country capital
••• City or town
...... Boundary

300 miles
0
0   300 kilometers
Two-Point Equidistant Projection

COLOR BARS (continued)

BAR SCALE

If you want to find out how far it is from one place on a map to another, use the scale. A bar scale appears on every map. It shows how distance on paper relates to distance in the real world.

• • •	City / Town	791 ft +
241 m	Mountain peak with elevation above sea level	⊬⊬ Waterfall	Dry / Salt Lake
★	Country capital			⊸⊢ Dam	Glacier
◉	State / Provincial capital	-282 ft .
-86 m	Low point with elevation below sea level	⊔⊔⊔ Canal	Swamp
◆	Small country	....	Defined boundary	⋏⋏⋏ Ice Shelf	Sand
∴	Ruin	... ...	Undefined boundary	⌒ Reef	Tundra
■	Point of Interest	....	Claimed boundary	⌒ Lake	Lava
		⌒	River	⌒ Intermittent Lake	Below sea level

Exploring Your World

Earth is a big place. Even from space you can't see it all at one time. But with a map, you can see the whole world or just a part of it. Thanks to the Internet, you can download programs that allow you to experience Earth from space, pick a place you want to explore, and zoom closer and closer until you are "standing" right there! These screenshots (right) take you from space to Chicago at the click of a mouse. You can even find a satellite view of your house (see below).

Compare the computer-enhanced satellite images with the maps on the opposite page, and you will see how the same places can be shown in very different ways. You will want to explore all these ways to really get to know your world.

COMPUTER ENHANCED VIEWS OF...

THE WORLD

CONTINENT & COUNTRY

Chicago

REGION & STATE

Chicago

METROPOLITAN AREA

Chicago

CITY & SKYLINE

FIND YOUR HOUSE

This image from SkylineGlobe shows the National Geographic offices in Washington, D.C. To see your house, go to www.skylineglobe.com, one of several websites that allow you to view satellite imagery of the world.

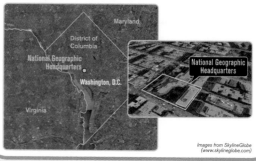

Maryland

District of Columbia

National Geographic Headquarters

Washington, D.C.

National Geographic Headquarters

Virginia

Images from SkylineGlobe (www.skylineglobe.com)

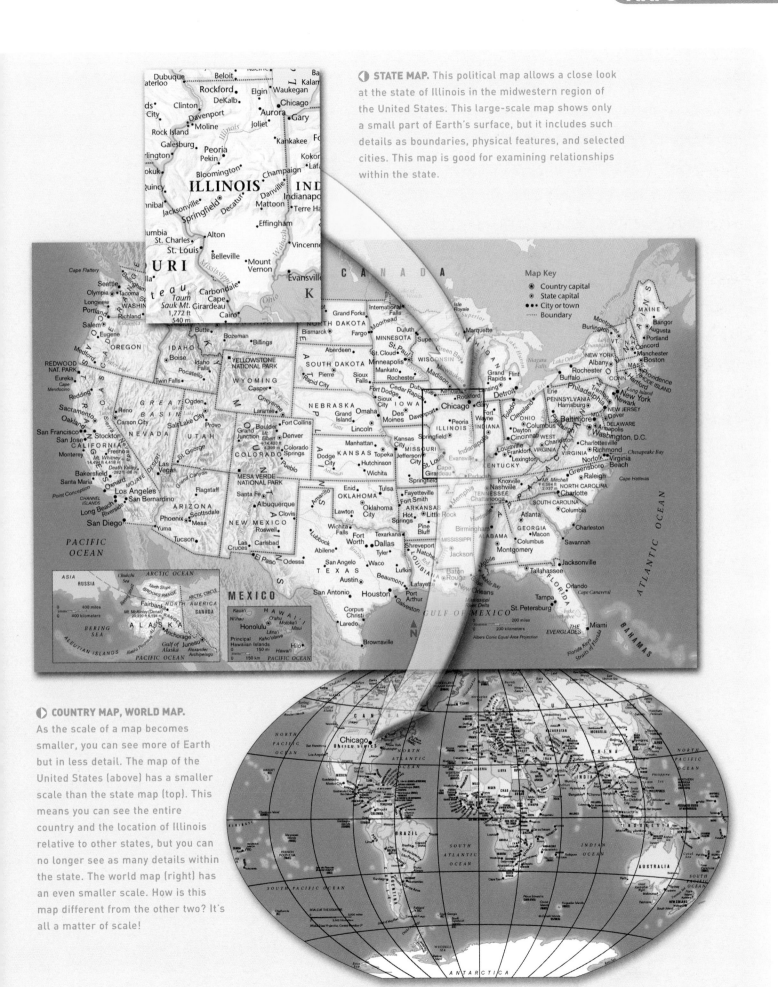

STATE MAP. This political map allows a close look at the state of Illinois in the midwestern region of the United States. This large-scale map shows only a small part of Earth's surface, but it includes such details as boundaries, physical features, and selected cities. This map is good for examining relationships within the state.

Map Key
⊛ Country capital
⊛ State capital
● City or town
---- Boundary

COUNTRY MAP, WORLD MAP.
As the scale of a map becomes smaller, you can see more of Earth but in less detail. The map of the United States (above) has a smaller scale than the state map (top). This means you can see the entire country and the location of Illinois relative to other states, but you can no longer see as many details within the state. The world map (right) has an even smaller scale. How is this map different from the other two? It's all a matter of scale!

Kinds of Maps

Maps are special tools that geographers use to tell a story about Earth. Some maps show physical features, such as mountains or vegetation. Maps also show climates or natural hazards and other things we cannot easily see. Other maps illustrate different human features on Earth—political boundaries, urban centers, and economic systems.

Maps are not perfect. A globe is a scale model of Earth with accurate relative sizes and locations. Because maps are flat, they involve distortions of size, shape, and direction. Also, cartographers— people who create maps—make choices about what information to include. Because of this, it is important to study many different types of maps to learn the complete story of Earth.

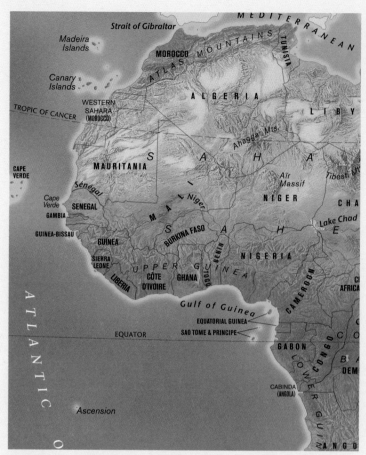

PHYSICAL MAPS. Earth's natural features—landforms, water bodies, and vegetation—are shown on physical maps. The map above uses color and shading to illustrate mountains, lakes, rivers, and deserts in western Africa. Country names and borders are added for reference, but they are not natural features.

MAP PROJECTIONS. To create a map, cartographers transfer an image of the round Earth to a flat surface, a process called projection. All projections involve distortion. For example, an interrupted projection (top map) shows accurate shapes and relative sizes of land areas, but oceans have gaps. Other types of projections are cylindrical, conic, or azimuthal—each with certain advantages, but all with some distortion.

MAKING MAPS

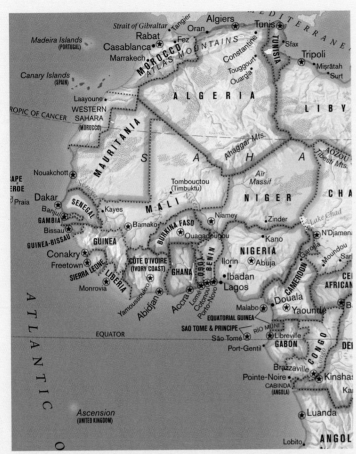

⬭ **POLITICAL MAPS.** These maps represent human characteristics of the landscape, such as boundaries, cities, and place-names. Natural features are added only for reference. On the map above, capital cities are represented with a star inside a circle, while other cities are located with black dots.

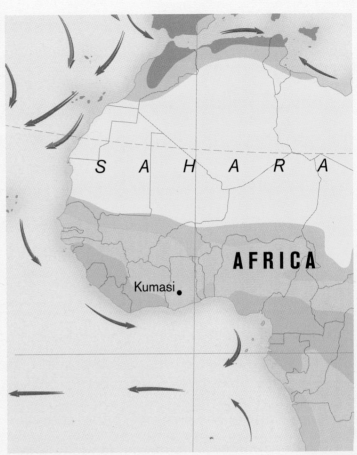

⬭ **THEMATIC MAPS.** Patterns related to a particular topic, or theme, such as population distribution, appear on these maps. The map above displays the region's climate zones, which range from tropical wet (bright green) to tropical wet and dry (light green) to semiarid (dark yellow) to arid or desert (light yellow).

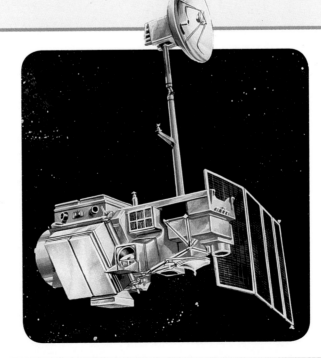

Long ago, cartographers worked with pen and ink, carefully hand-crafting maps based on explorers' observations and diaries. Today, mapmaking is a high-tech business. Cartographers use Earth data stored in "layers" in a Geographic Information System (GIS) and special computer programs to create maps that can be easily updated as new information becomes available. The cartographers at left are changing country labels on a map of the Balkans.

Satellites in orbit around Earth act as eyes in the sky, recording data about the planet's land and ocean areas. The data is converted to numbers that are transmitted back to computers that are specially programmed to interpret the data. They record it in a form that cartographers can use to create maps.

How to Read a Map

Every map has a story to tell, but first you have to know how to read the map.

Maps are useful for finding places because every place on Earth has a special address called its absolute location. Imaginary lines, called latitude and longitude, create a grid that makes finding places easy because every spot on Earth has a unique longitude and latitude. In addition, special tools, called Global Positioning Systems (GPS), communicate with orbiting satellites to determine absolute location.

Maps are also useful for determining distance and direction. Maps have a scale, often a bar scale or a verbal scale, that shows the relationship between distance on the map and distance on Earth. Maps often have a compass rose to show direction. Many people think north is at the top of a map, but this is not always true. The compass rose indicates north for each map.

Maps represent other information by using a language of symbols. Knowing how to read these symbols provides access to a wide range of information. To find out what each symbol means, you must use the map key. Think of the map key as your secret decoder, identifying information represented by each symbol on the map.

▶ LATITUDE AND LONGITUDE. Latitude and longitude lines help us determine locations on Earth. Lines of latitude run west to east, parallel to the Equator (below, left). These lines measure distance in degrees north or south, from the Equator (0° latitude) to the North Pole (90°N) or to the South Pole (90°S). One degree of latitude is approximately 70 statute miles (113 km).

Lines of longitude run north to south, meeting at the Poles (below, right). These lines measure distance in degrees east or west from 0° longitude (prime meridian) to 180° longitude. The prime meridian runs through Greenwich, England.

Latitude

Longitude

▶ ABSOLUTE LOCATION. The imaginary grid composed of lines of latitude and longitude helps us locate places on a map. Suppose you are playing a game of global scavenger hunt. The clue says the prize is hidden at absolute location 30°S, 60°W. You know that the first number is south of the Equator, and the second is west of the prime meridian. On the map at right, find the line of latitude labeled 30°S. Now find the line of longitude labeled 60°W. Trace these lines with your fingers until they meet. Identify this spot. The prize must be located in central Argentina (see arrow, right).

UNDERSTANDING MAPS

90°N (North Pole)
75°N
60°N
45°N
30°N
15°N
0° (Equator)
15°S
30°S
45°S
60°E
75°E
90°E
105°E
120°E
135°E

SYMBOLS

There are three main types of map symbols: points, lines, and areas. Points, which can be either dots or small icons, represent the location or the number of things, such as schools, cities, or landmarks. Lines are used to show boundaries, roads, or rivers and can vary in color or thickness. Area symbols use patterns or color to show regions, such as a sandy area or a neighborhood.

POINT
A point symbol, a black dot, indicates a city, such as Omdurman.

LINE
Sudan's country boundary appears as a line symbol: a dotted line with a colored edge.

AREA
Sandy places, such as parts of the Saharan desert, are shown by a tan, speckled area.

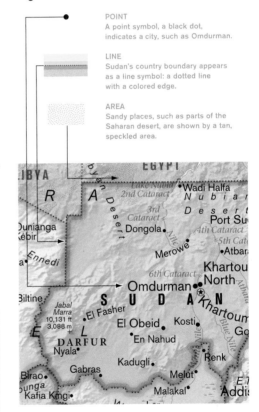

SCALE & DIRECTION

The scale on a map can be shown as a fraction, as words, or as a line or bar. It relates distance on the map to distance in the real world. Sometimes the scale identifies the type of map projection. Maps may include an arrow or compass rose to indicate north on the map. Maps in this atlas are oriented north, so they do not use a north indicator.

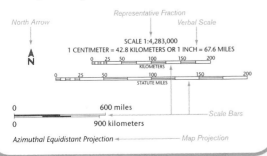

Representative Fraction
Verbal Scale
North Arrow

SCALE 1:4,283,000
1 CENTIMETER = 42.8 KILOMETERS OR 1 INCH = 67.6 MILES

0 25 50 100 150 200
KILOMETERS

0 25 50 100 150 200
STATUTE MILES

Scale Bars

0   600 miles
0   900 kilometers

Azimuthal Equidistant Projection   Map Projection

⏺ **APPLYING WHAT YOU'VE LEARNED.**
Now that you know how to read a map, can you find places on the maps in this atlas? What about Sapporo in the eastern Asian country of Japan? The index at the back of this atlas tells you that Sapporo is on "page 113 B10." Along the edges of the map are letters and numbers. Place one finger on the B at the side and another finger on the 10 at the top. Now trace straight across from the B and down from the 10. Sapporo is where your fingers meet!

Earth in Space

Earth, the planet we call home, is part of a cosmic family called the solar system. It is one of the planets that revolve around a giant solar nuclear reactor that we call the sun.

The extreme heat and pressure on the sun cause atoms of hydrogen to combine in a process called fusion, producing new atoms of helium and releasing tremendous amounts of energy. The sun is the essential source of energy that makes life on Earth possible. It provides us with light and warmth.

Time on Earth is defined by our relationship to the sun. It takes Earth, following a path called an orbit, approximately 365 days—one year—to make one full revolution around the sun. As Earth makes its way around the sun, it also turns on its axis, an imaginary line that passes between the Poles. This motion, called rotation, occurs once every 24 hours and results in day and night.

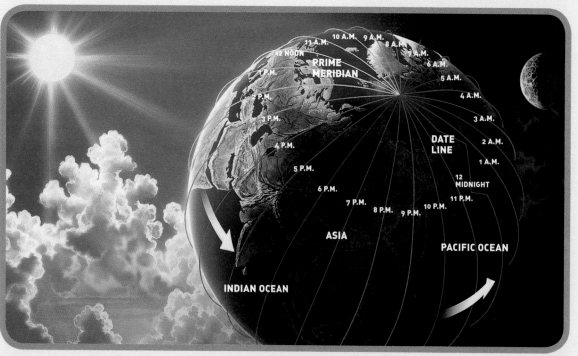

◖ **TIME ZONES.** Long ago, when people lived in relative isolation, they measured time by the position of the sun overhead. That meant that noon in one place was not the same as noon in a place 100 miles (160 km) to the west. Later, with the development of long-distance railroads, people needed to coordinate time. In 1884, a system of 24 standard time zones was adopted. Each time zone reflects the fact that Earth rotates west to east 15 degrees each hour. Time is counted from the prime meridian, which runs through Greenwich, England.

Callisto

Titan

Triton

Jupiter

Saturn

Uranus

Charon

Haumea

Neptune

Pluto

Makemake

Eris

Note: Art shows relative sizes of the sun and planets, but distances are not to scale.

SOLAR SYSTEM. The sun and its family of planets are located near the outer edge of the Milky Way, a giant spiral galaxy. Earth is the third planet from the sun and one of the four "terrestrial" planets. These planets—Mercury, Venus, Earth, and Mars—are made up of solid rocky material. Beyond these inner planets are the four gas giants—Jupiter, Saturn, Uranus, and Neptune. Recently, astronomers—scientists who study space—have named a new category called "dwarf" planets that includes Pluto, Ceres, Eris, Haumea, and Makemake. More of these dwarf planets may soon be identified. Many planets, including Earth, have one or more moons orbiting them. The art above names a few: Io, Callisto, Titan, Triton, and Charon.

ENVELOPE OF AIR. Earth is enclosed within a thick layer of air called the atmosphere. Made up of a mix of nitrogen, oxygen, and other gases, the atmosphere provides us with the life-giving air that we breathe. It also protects us from dangerous radiation from the sun. Weather systems move through the atmosphere, redistributing heat and moisture and creating Earth's climates.

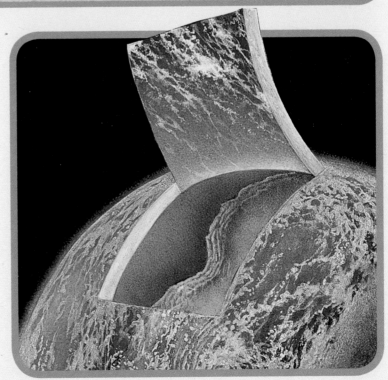

Earth in Motion

If we could step into a time machine and travel 500 million years into the past, we probably would not recognize Earth. Back then, most of the landmasses we call continents were joined together in a single giant landmass called Pangaea. So how did the continents break away from Pangaea and move to their current positions? Where will they be in another 500 million years?

Deep within Earth, pressure and heat cause rocks of the mantle to become partially molten, but near Earth's surface a thin shell of solid rock forms the crust. Currents of heat rise and fall within the mantle, causing the crust to break into large pieces, called plates, which very slowly move about on Earth's surface. These powerful forces are at work today, creating and destroying land features and reshaping Earth's surface.

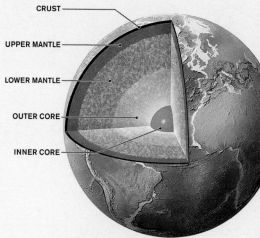

◖ CRUST IN MOTION. Earth's major plates are outlined in red on the map at right. Plate edges are the most active parts, with volcanoes and earthquakes (yellow dots on the map) resulting from plates moving together or grinding past each other.

CRUST
UPPER MANTLE
LOWER MANTLE
OUTER CORE
INNER CORE

◠ A LOOK WITHIN. The distance from Earth's surface to its center is 3,963 miles (6,377 km). There are four layers: a thin, rigid crust; the rocky mantle (upper and lower); the outer core, which is a layer of molten iron; and finally the inner core, which is solid iron.

CONTINENTS ON THE MOVE

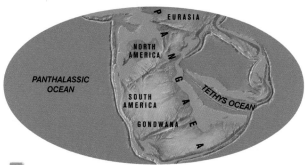

1 PANGAEA. About 240 million years ago, Earth's landmasses were joined together in one supercontinent that extended from Pole to Pole.

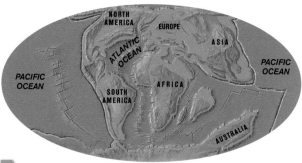

3 EXTINCTION. About 65 million years ago an asteroid smashed into Earth, creating the Gulf of Mexico (red * on map). This impact may have resulted in the extinction of half the world's species, including the dinosaurs—one of several major extinctions.

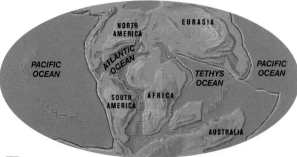

2 BREAKUP. By 94 million years ago, Pangaea had broken apart into landmasses that would become today's continents. Dinosaurs roamed Earth during this period of warmer climates.

4 ICE AGE. By 18,000 years ago, the continents had drifted close to their present positions, but most far northern and far southern lands were buried beneath huge glaciers.

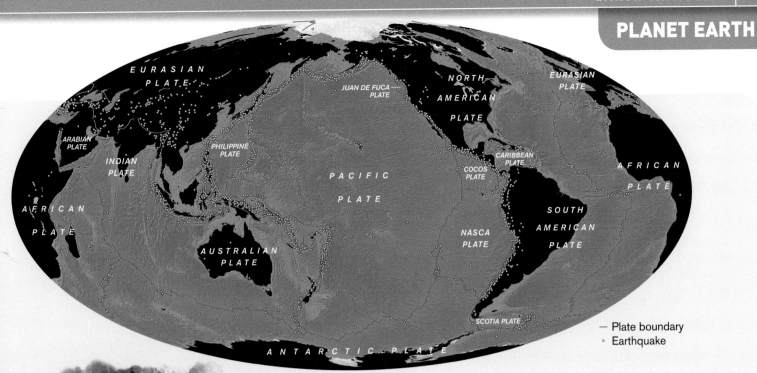

EURASIAN PLATE

ARABIAN PLATE

INDIAN PLATE

PHILIPPINE PLATE

JUAN DE FUCA PLATE

NORTH AMERICAN PLATE

EURASIAN PLATE

AFRICAN PLATE

AFRICAN PLATE

PACIFIC PLATE

COCOS PLATE

CARIBBEAN PLATE

SOUTH AMERICAN PLATE

NASCA PLATE

AUSTRALIAN PLATE

SCOTIA PLATE

ANTARCTIC PLATE

— Plate boundary
∘ Earthquake

Earth Shapers

Earth's features are constantly undergoing change—being built up, destroyed, or just rearranged. Plates are in constant, very slow motion. Some plates collide, others pull apart, and still others slowly grind past each other. As the plates move, mountains are uplifted, volcanoes erupt, and new land is created.

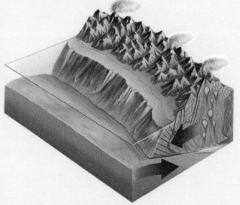

VOLCANOES form when molten rock, called magma, rises to Earth's surface. Some volcanoes occur as one plate pushes beneath another plate. Other volcanoes result when a plate passes over a column of magma, called a hot spot, rising from the mantle.

SUBDUCTION occurs when an oceanic plate dives under a continental plate. This often results in volcanoes and earthquakes, as well as mountain building.

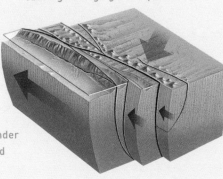

FAULTING happens when two plates grind past each other, creating large cracks along the edges of the plates. A famous fault is the San Andreas, in California, where the Pacific and North American plates meet, causing damaging earthquakes.

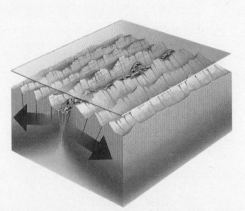

SPREADING results when oceanic plates move apart. The ocean floor cracks, magma rises, and new crust is created. The Mid-Atlantic Ridge spreads a few centimeters—about an inch—a year, pushing Europe and North America farther apart.

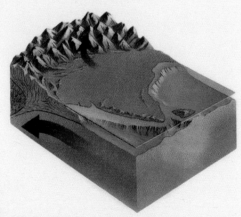

COLLISION of two continental plates causes plate edges to break and fold, creating mountains, Earth's highest landforms. The Himalaya are the result of the Indian plate colliding with the Eurasian plate, an ongoing process that began 50 million years ago.

The Physical World

Earth is dominated by large landmasses called continents—seven in all—and by an interconnected global ocean that is divided into four parts by the continents. More than 70 percent of Earth's surface is covered by oceans; the remaining 30 percent is made up of land areas.

Different landforms give variety to the surface of the continents. The Rockies and Andes mark the western edge of North and South America, and the Himalaya tower above southern Asia. The Plateau of Tibet forms the rugged core of Asia, while the Northern European Plain extends from the North Sea to the Ural Mountains. Much of Africa is a plateau, and dry plains cover large areas of Australia. Beneath massive ice sheets, mountains rise more than 16,000 feet (4,877 m) in Antarctica.

Mountains and trenches make the ocean floors as varied as any continent (see pages 156–167). A mountain chain called the Mid-Atlantic Ridge runs the length of the Atlantic Ocean. In the western Pacific Ocean, trenches drop to depths greater than 35,000 feet (10,668 m).

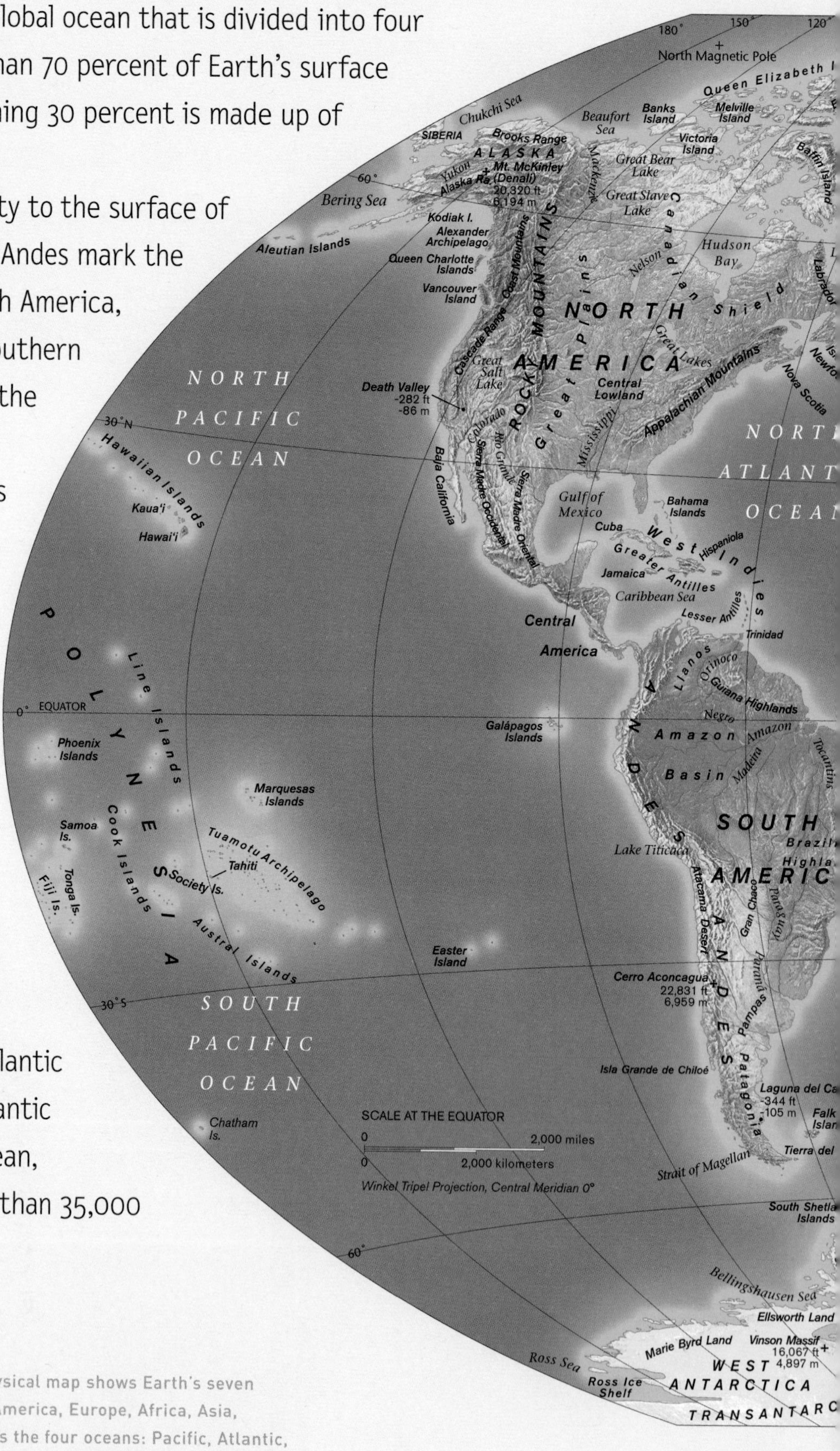

🌑 **LAND AND WATER.** This world physical map shows Earth's seven continents—North America, South America, Europe, Africa, Asia, Australia, and Antarctica—as well as the four oceans: Pacific, Atlantic, Indian, and Arctic. Some people regard the area from Antarctica to 60°S, where the oceans merge, as a fifth ocean called the Southern Ocean.

SCALE AT THE EQUATOR

0 — 2,000 miles

0 — 2,000 kilometers

Winkel Tripel Projection, Central Meridian 0°

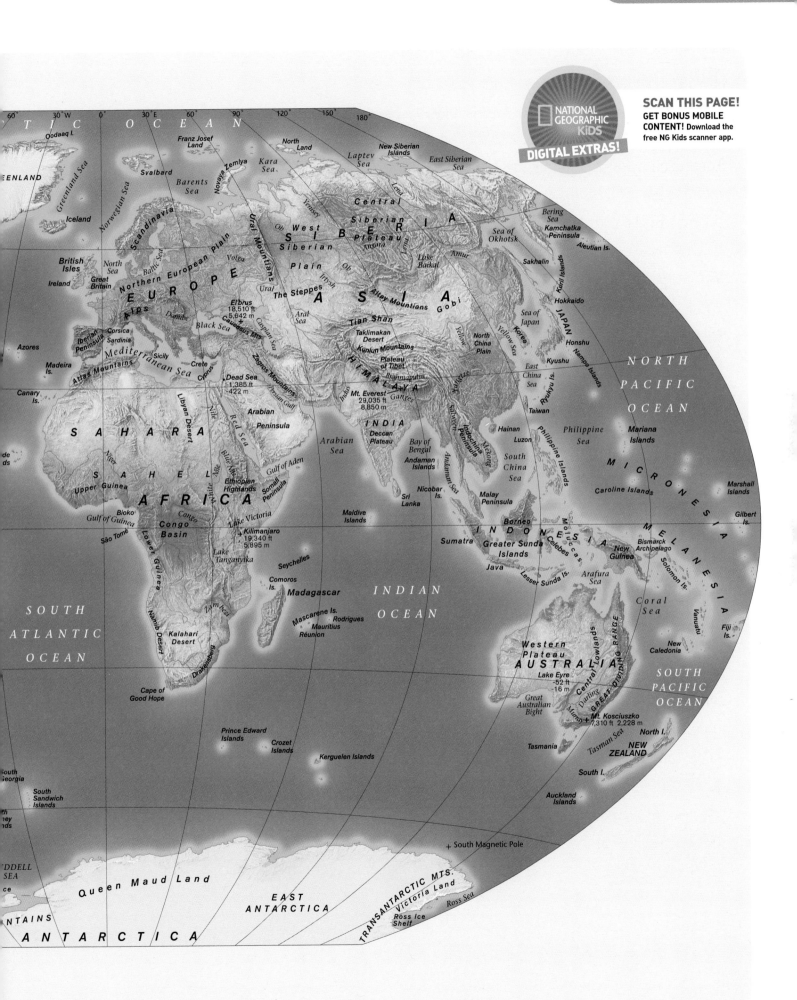

NATIONAL GEOGRAPHIC KiDS
DIGITAL EXTRAS!

SCAN THIS PAGE!
GET BONUS MOBILE
CONTENT! Download the
free NG Kids scanner app.

60°   30° W   0°   30° E   60°   90°   120°   150°   180°

TIC OCEAN

Oodaaq I.

GREENLAND

Greenland Sea

Iceland

Franz Josef Land

North Land

New Siberian Islands

Laptev Sea

East Siberian Sea

Svalbard

Novaya Zemlya

Kara Sea

Barents Sea

Norwegian Sea

Scandinavia

Central Siberian Plateau

Bering Sea

Kamchatka Peninsula

British Isles

North Sea

Baltic Sea

Northern European Plain

Ob

West Siberian Plain

Yenisey

S I B E R I A

Angara

Lena

Sea of Okhotsk

Ireland

Great Britain

EUROPE

Volga

Ural Mountains

Ob

Irtysh

Lake Baikal

Amur

Aleutian Is.

Sakhalin

Kuril Islands

Hokkaido

Alps

Danube

Ural

The Steppes

A S I A

Altay Mountains

Gobi

Sea of Japan

JAPAN

Azores

Iberian Peninsula

Corsica

Sardinia

Sicily

El'brus 18,510 ft 5,642 m

Aral Sea

Tian Shan

Honshu

Madeira Is.

Atlas Mountains

Mediterranean Sea

Crete

Cyprus

Black Sea

Caucasus Mts.

Caspian Sea

Zagros Mountains

Taklimakan Desert

Kunlun Mountains

Plateau of Tibet

HIMALAYA

North China Plain

Yellow

Yellow Sea

Korea

Kyushu

Nampo Islands

NORTH PACIFIC OCEAN

Canary Is.

Dead Sea -1,385 ft -422 m

Persian Gulf

Indus

Mt. Everest 29,035 ft 8,850 m

Ganges

Brahmaputra

Yangtze

East China Sea

Ryukyu Is.

Taiwan

SAHARA

Libyan Desert

Nile

Red Sea

Arabian Peninsula

Arabian Sea

I N D I A

Deccan Plateau

Bay of Bengal

Salween

Indochina Peninsula

Mekong

Hainan

South China Sea

Philippine Islands

Philippine Sea

Mariana Islands

M I C R O N E S I A

Marshall Islands

SAHEL

Niger

Blue Nile

Gulf of Aden

Ethiopian Highlands

Somali Peninsula

Andaman Islands

Andaman Sea

Malay Peninsula

Caroline Islands

Upper Guinea

AFRICA

Sri Lanka

Nicobar Is.

Maldive Islands

Gilbert Is.

Bioko

Gulf of Guinea

Congo Basin

Lake Victoria

Kilimanjaro 19,340 ft 5,895 m

Sumatra

Borneo

Greater Sunda Islands

I N D O N E S I A

Moluccas

Celebes

New Guinea

Bismarck Archipelago

M E L A N E S I A

São Tomé

Lower Guinea

Lake Tanganyika

Seychelles

Java

Lesser Sunda Is.

Arafura Sea

Solomon Is.

Vanuatu

Fiji Is.

SOUTH ATLANTIC OCEAN

Namib Desert

Zambezi

Comoros Is.

Madagascar

Mascarene Is.

Rodrigues

Mauritius

Réunion

I N D I A N OCEAN

Coral Sea

New Caledonia

SOUTH PACIFIC OCEAN

Kalahari Desert

Drakensberg

Cape of Good Hope

Western Plateau

AUSTRALIA

Lake Eyre -52 ft -16 m

Central Lowlands

Darling

GREAT DIVIDING RANGE

Great Australian Bight

Murray

Mt. Kosciuszko 7,310 ft 2,228 m

North I.

Tasman Sea

NEW ZEALAND

Prince Edward Islands

Crozet Islands

Kerguelen Islands

Tasmania

South I.

South Georgia

South Sandwich Islands

Auckland Islands

South Magnetic Pole

WEDDELL SEA

Queen Maud Land

EAST ANTARCTICA

TRANSANTARCTIC MTS.

Victoria Land

Ross Sea

NTAINS

ANTARCTICA

Ross Ice Shelf

The Land

A closer look at Earth's surface reveals many varied forms and features that make each place unique. The drawing (right) captures 41 natural and human-made features in an imaginary landscape that shows how these different land and water features relate to each other. For example, a large moving "river" of ice, called a glacier, descends from a high mountain range. A river passes through a valley and empties into a gulf. And a harbor, built by people, creates safe anchorage for ships.

Features such as these can be found all over the world because the same forces are at work wherever you might go. Internal forces such as volcanoes and the movement of the plates of Earth's crust are constantly creating and building up new landforms, while external forces such as wind, water, and ice continuously wear down surface features.

Earth is dynamic—constantly changing, never the same.

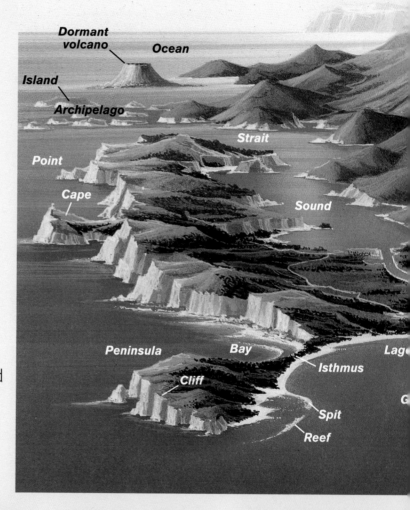

RIVER

As a river moves through flatlands, it twists and turns. Above, the Rio Los Amigos winds through a rain forest in Peru.

CANYON

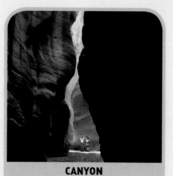

Steep-sided valleys called canyons are created mainly by running water. Buckskin Gulch (above) is the deepest slot canyon in the American Southwest.

DESERT

Deserts are a land feature created by climate, specifically by a lack of water. Above, a camel caravan crosses the Sahara, in North Africa.

OASIS

Occasionally, water rises from deep below a desert, creating a refuge that supports trees and sometimes crops, as in this oasis in Africa.

Mountain peak

Mountain range

Glacier

Iceberg

Basin

Desert

Mesa

Oasis

Divide

Plateau

Waterfall

Valley

Escarpment

Lake

Canal

Canyon

Plain

River

Fork

Delta

Hills

Harbor

Tributary

Breakwater

A NAME FOR EVERY FEATURE

Land has a vocabulary all its own, each name identifying a specific feature of the landscape. A cape, for example, is a broadish chunk of land extending out into the sea. It is not pointed, however, for then it would be a point. Nor does it have a narrow neck. A sizable cape or point with a narrow neck is a peninsula. The narrow neck is an isthmus. Such specific identifiers have proven useful over the centuries. In the early days of exploration, even the simplest maps showed peninsulas, bays, and straits. Sailors used these landmarks to reach safe harbor or avoid disastrous encounters.

◑ **EXPLORING THE LANDSCAPE.** How many land and water features can you identify in the imaginary landscape at left? Definitions for these terms can be found in the glossary on pages 186–188.

MOUNTAIN

Mountains are Earth's tallest landforms, and Mount Everest (above) rises highest of all at 29,035 feet (8,850 m) above sea level.

GLACIER

Glaciers—"rivers" of ice—such as Alaska's Hubbard (above), move slowly from mountains to the sea. Global warming may be shrinking them.

VALLEY

Valleys, cut by running water or moving ice, may be broad and flat or narrow and steep, such as the Indus River Valley in Ladakh, India (above).

WATERFALL

Waterfalls form when a river reaches an abrupt change in elevation. Above, Kaieteur Falls, in Guyana, descends 800 feet (244 m).

World Climate

Weather is the condition of the atmosphere—temperature, precipitation, humidity, wind—at a given place at a given time. Climate, however, is the average weather for a particular place over a long period of time. Different places on Earth have different climates, but climate is not a random occurrence. It is a pattern that is controlled by factors such as latitude, elevation, prevailing winds, temperature of ocean currents, and location on land relative to water. Climate is generally constant, but many are concerned that human activity may be causing a change in the patterns of climate.

THE BASICS

According to the National Oceanic and Atmospheric Administration (NOAA), 2010 ranks first as the hottest year on record, followed by 1998. The global annual temperature for combined land and ocean surfaces was 1°F (.6°C) above the average established between 1880 and 2004.

Ice cores taken from Antarctica and Greenland have enabled scientists to gain detailed information about the history of Earth's climate and its atmosphere—especially the presence of greenhouse gases—dating back thousands of years.

Data collected by satellite imagery suggest that the Sahara, Earth's largest desert, had a wet climate that supported vast forests some 12,000 years ago. Extremely dry conditions did not begin until about 5,000 years ago.

According to climatologists, Earth had what is called the Little Ice Age, which lasted from the 17th century to the late 19th century. During that time, temperatures were cold enough to cause glaciers to advance.

🌐 **CLIMATE GRAPHS.** Temperature and precipitation data provide a snapshot of the climate at a particular place. This information can be shown in a special type of graph called a climate graph (see below). Average monthly temperatures (scale on the left side of the graphs) are represented by the lines at the tops of the colored areas, while average monthly precipitation totals (scale on the right side of the graphs) are reflected in the bars. For example, the graph for Belém, Brazil, shows a constant warm temperature with abundant rainfall year-round. In contrast, the graph for Fairbanks, Alaska, shows a cool, variable temperature with only limited precipitation.

Map labels: Resolute. Fairbanks. Subarctic Current. North Pacific Drift. ROCKY MOUNTAINS. NORTH AMERICA. Des Moines. Labrador Current. Gulf Stream. North Atlantic Drift. California Current. Monterrey. Gulf of Mexico. Hawaiian Islands. TROPIC OF CANCER. North Equatorial Current. PACIFIC OCEAN. ATLANTIC OCEAN. Equatorial Countercurrent. EQUATOR. South Equatorial Current. AMAZONIA. Belém. SOUTH AMERICA. Peru Current. ANDES. TROPIC OF CAPRICORN. Falkland Current. Antarctic Peninsula.

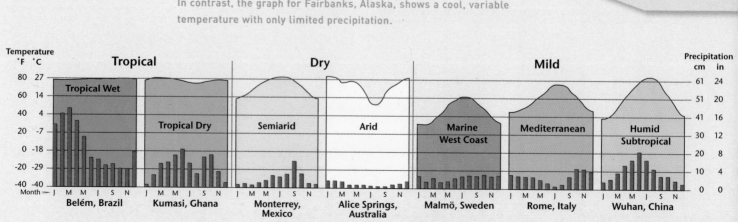

Temperature °F °C	Tropical	Dry	Mild	Precipitation cm in

Tropical Wet — Belém, Brazil
Tropical Dry — Kumasi, Ghana
Semiarid — Monterrey, Mexico
Arid — Alice Springs, Australia
Marine West Coast — Malmö, Sweden
Mediterranean — Rome, Italy
Humid Subtropical — Wuhan, China

Temperature scale: 80 27 / 60 14 / 40 4 / 20 -7 / 0 -18 / -20 -29 / -40 -40

Precipitation scale: 61 24 / 51 20 / 41 16 / 30 12 / 20 8 / 10 4 / 0 0

Month — J M M J S N (repeated for each graph)

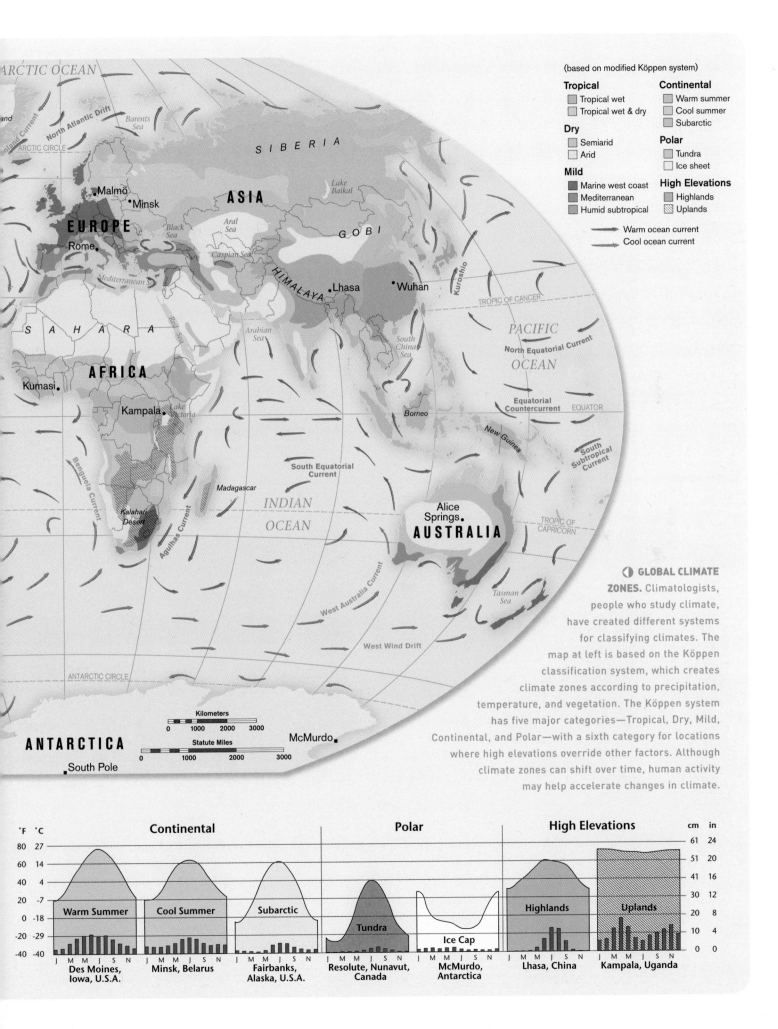

(based on modified Köppen system)

Tropical
- Tropical wet
- Tropical wet & dry

Dry
- Semiarid
- Arid

Mild
- Marine west coast
- Mediterranean
- Humid subtropical

Continental
- Warm summer
- Cool summer
- Subarctic

Polar
- Tundra
- Ice sheet

High Elevations
- Highlands
- Uplands

→ Warm ocean current
→ Cool ocean current

◖ **GLOBAL CLIMATE ZONES.** Climatologists, people who study climate, have created different systems for classifying climates. The map at left is based on the Köppen classification system, which creates climate zones according to precipitation, temperature, and vegetation. The Köppen system has five major categories—Tropical, Dry, Mild, Continental, and Polar—with a sixth category for locations where high elevations override other factors. Although climate zones can shift over time, human activity may help accelerate changes in climate.

Continental

Warm Summer — Des Moines, Iowa, U.S.A.
Cool Summer — Minsk, Belarus
Subarctic — Fairbanks, Alaska, U.S.A.

Polar

Tundra — Resolute, Nunavut, Canada
Ice Cap — McMurdo, Antarctica

High Elevations

Highlands — Lhasa, China
Uplands — Kampala, Uganda

°F °C — 80 27 / 60 14 / 40 4 / 20 -7 / 0 -18 / -20 -29 / -40 -40

cm in — 61 24 / 51 20 / 41 16 / 30 12 / 20 8 / 10 4 / 0 0

J M M J S N

Factors Influencing Climate

Earth's climate is a bit like a big jigsaw puzzle. To understand it, you need to fit all the pieces together, because climate is influenced by a number of different, but interrelated factors. These include latitude, topography (shape of the land), elevation above sea level, wind systems, ocean currents, and distance from large bodies of water. Climate has always affected the way we live, but scientists now believe that the way we live may also be affecting climate. Pollution from industries and motor vehicles may be contributing to global warming. And this could be causing Earth's climate to change.

TOPOGRAPHY. Mountain ranges are natural barriers to the movement of air. In North America, prevailing westerly winds carry air full of moisture from the Pacific Ocean to the West Coast. As air rises over the Coast Ranges, light precipitation falls. Farther inland, the much taller Sierra Nevada range triggers heavy precipitation as air rises higher. On the leeward side of the Sierra Nevada, sinking air warms, clouds evaporate, and dry "rain shadow" conditions prevail. As winds continue across the interior plateau, the air remains dry because there is no significant source of moisture.

Windward (wet)   Leeward (dry)

Pacific Ocean   Wind

Coast Ranges   Sierra Nevada

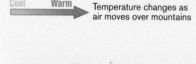

Cool — Warm   Temperature changes as air moves over mountains

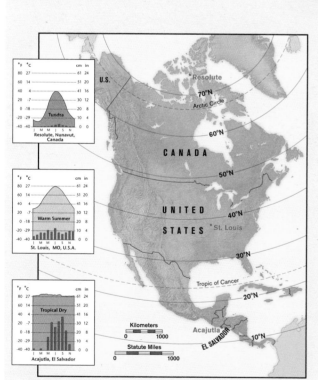

LATITUDE. Energy from the sun drives global climates. Latitude—distance north or south of the Equator—affects the amount of solar energy received. Places near the Equator (see Acajutla, El Salvador, above) have warm temperatures year-round. As distance from the Equator increases (see St. Louis, U.S.A., and Resolute, Canada, above), average temperatures decline, and cold winters become more pronounced.

ELEVATION. In general, climate conditions become cooler as elevation increases. Since cooler air holds less moisture, less precipitation falls. As temperature and moisture conditions change, vegetation also changes. In the mountain diagram (right), dense mixed forest grows near the base of the mountain on the windward side. As elevation increases and temperatures decline, the mixed forest changes to all evergreen, followed by alpine meadows, until finally the mountain's rocky peaks are covered by snow and ice. As air moves down the leeward slope of the mountain, it warms and evaporates moisture, causing the leeward side to be drier and have less vegetation.

WINDWARD

Cold winds over warm water
Cool onshore ocean winds
Desert winds
Warm onshore ocean winds

DIGGING OUT. Arctic winds roar across Canada, picking up moisture from the Great Lakes (see purple arrows on map, left). As the moisture-laden air crosses over the frozen land, temperatures fall and heavy precipitation—called lake effect snow—buries cars and roads, as shown here in Oswego, New York, U.S.A.

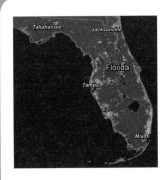

WARM CURRENT.
The Gulf Stream, a warm ocean current averaging 50–93 miles (80–150 km) wide, sweeps up the East Coast of North America (see red arrow on map above). One branch continues across the North Atlantic Ocean and above the Arctic Circle. In this color-enhanced satellite image (left), the Gulf Stream looks like a dark red river moving up the coast. This "river" of warm water influences climate along its path, bringing moisture and mild temperatures to the East Coast of the United States and causing ice-free ports above the Arctic Circle in Europe.

LEEWARD

GLOBAL WARMING

Earth's climate history has been a story of ups and downs, with warm periods followed by periods of bitter cold. The early part of the 20th century was marked by colder than average temperatures (see graph below), followed by a period of gradual and then steady increase in temperature. Scientists are concerned that the current warming trend may be more than a natural cycle. Evidence indicates that human activity is adding to the warming. One sign of change is melting glaciers in Greenland and Antarctica. If glaciers continue to melt, areas of Florida (shown above in red) and other coastal land will be underwater.

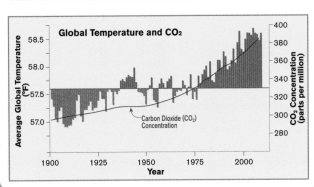

World Vegetation

Natural vegetation—plants that would grow under ideal circumstances at a particular place—depends on several factors. The climate is very important, as is the quality and type of soil that is available. Therefore, vegetation often reflects patterns of climate. (Compare the vegetation map at right with the world climate map on pages 22–23.) Forests thrive in places with ample precipitation; grasses are found in places with less precipitation or with only seasonal rainfall; and xerophytes—plants able to survive lengthy periods with little or no water—are found in arid areas that receive very little precipitation on a yearly basis. Grasses and shrubs cover almost half of Earth's land.

TEMPERATE BROADLEAF FOREST

Broadleaf trees that grow in mid-latitude areas with mild temperatures, such as this one in Shenandoah National Park in Virginia, U.S.A., are deciduous, meaning they lose their leaves in winter. Many such forests have been cleared for cropland.

DESERT AND DRY SHRUB

Deserts, areas that receive less than 10 inches (25 cm) of rainfall a year, have vegetation that is specially adapted to survive under dry conditions, such as these dry shrubs and cacti growing in the Sonora Desert in Arizona, U.S.A.

TUNDRA

With only two to three months of temperatures above freezing, tundra plants are mostly dwarf shrubs, short grasses, mosses, and lichens. Much of Canada's Yukon has tundra vegetation, which turns red as winter approaches.

CONIFEROUS FOREST

Needleleaf trees with cones to protect their seeds from bitter winters grow in cold climates with short summers, such as British Columbia, Canada. These trees are important in lumber and papermaking industries.

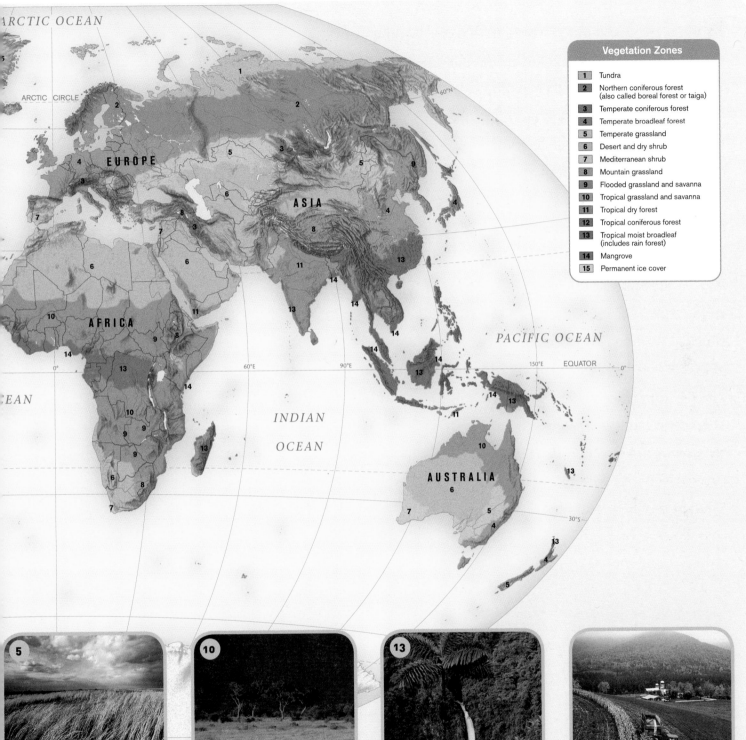

ARCTIC OCEAN

ARCTIC CIRCLE

EUROPE

ASIA

AFRICA

PACIFIC OCEAN

INDIAN

OCEAN

AUSTRALIA

EQUATOR

Vegetation Zones

1	Tundra
2	Northern coniferous forest (also called boreal forest or taiga)
3	Temperate coniferous forest
4	Temperate broadleaf forest
5	Temperate grassland
6	Desert and dry shrub
7	Mediterranean shrub
8	Mountain grassland
9	Flooded grassland and savanna
10	Tropical grassland and savanna
11	Tropical dry forest
12	Tropical coniferous forest
13	Tropical moist broadleaf (includes rain forest)
14	Mangrove
15	Permanent ice cover

5

TEMPERATE GRASSLAND

Grasslands, such as this tall-grass prairie in southwestern Missouri, U.S.A., are found in areas where precipitation is too low to support forests. Many temperate grasslands have been converted to cropland for grain production.

10

TROPICAL GRASSLAND

Tall grasses and scattered trees that can survive a hot, dry season dominate low latitude grasslands, also called savannas. Africa's grasslands are home to game animals, such as this male lion crossing the savanna in Botswana.

13

RAIN FOREST

A waterfall tumbles over a cliff in the Costa Rican rain forest. Rain forest trees can grow to be as much as 200 feet (61 m) above the forest floor. The overlapping branches of the tallest trees keep sunlight from reaching the forest floor.

CROPLAND

People remove natural vegetation in many places to create fields to grow crops to feed both people and animals. Here, a farmer in the Catskill Mountains of New York uses a mechanized harvester to cut corn to feed his dairy cattle.

Environmental Hot Spots

Around the world, people are putting more and more pressure on the environment by dumping pollutants into the air and water and by removing natural vegetation to extract mineral resources or to turn the land into cropland for farming. In more developed countries, industries create waste and pollution; farmers use fertilizers and pesticides that run off into water supplies; and motor vehicles release exhaust fumes into the air. In less developed countries, forests are cut down for fuel or to clear land for farming; grasslands are turned into deserts as farmers and herders overuse the land; and expanding urban areas face problems of water quality and sanitation.

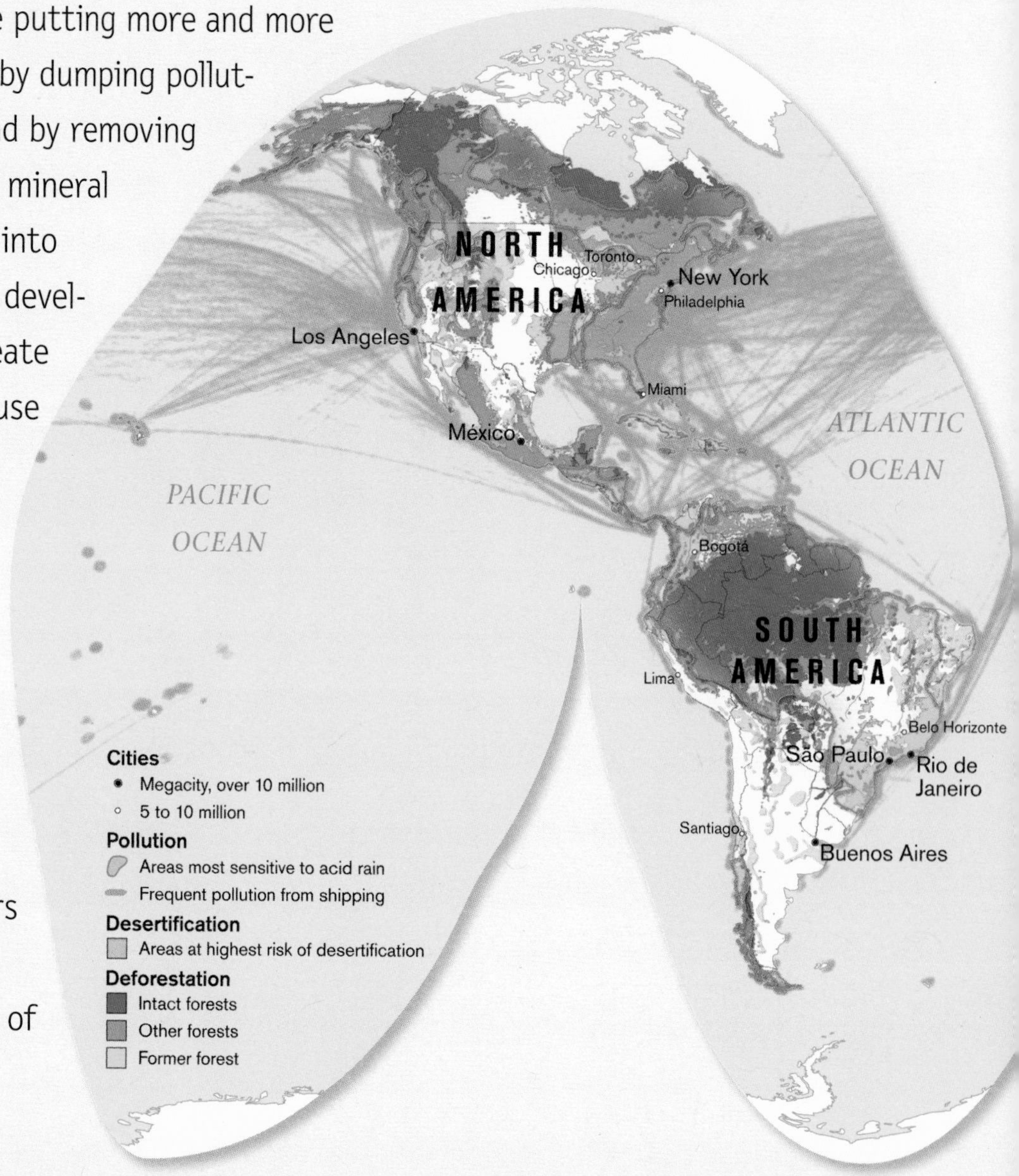

NORTH AMERICA

Toronto
Chicago
New York
Philadelphia
Los Angeles
Miami
México

ATLANTIC OCEAN

PACIFIC OCEAN

Bogotá

SOUTH AMERICA

Lima

Belo Horizonte
São Paulo
Rio de Janeiro

Santiago

Buenos Aires

Cities
- • Megacity, over 10 million
- ○ 5 to 10 million

Pollution
- Areas most sensitive to acid rain
- Frequent pollution from shipping

Desertification
- Areas at highest risk of desertification

Deforestation
- Intact forests
- Other forests
- Former forest

ENDANGERED

Human activity poses the greatest threat to Earth's biodiversity— its rich variety of species. Loss of habitat puts many species, including those at right, at great risk. Experts estimate that species are becoming extinct at a rate 100 to 1,000 times higher than would be caused by natural loss.

Monarch Butterfly

Giant Tree Frog

California Condor

Asian Elephant

Rafflesia Flower

Napoleon Wrasse Fish

POLLUTION

Poor air quality is a serious environmental problem. Industrial plants are a major source of pollution. Smoke containing particles that contribute to acid rain is released from a factory in Poland (above).

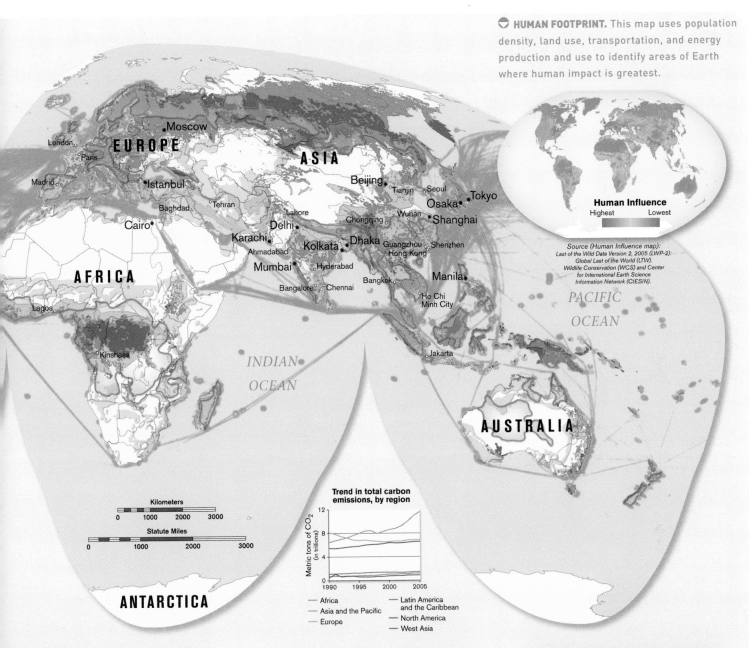

HUMAN FOOTPRINT. This map uses population density, land use, transportation, and energy production and use to identify areas of Earth where human impact is greatest.

Human Influence
Highest   Lowest

Source (Human Influence map):
Last of the Wild Data Version 2, 2005 (LWP-2):
Global Last of the World (LTW).
Wildlife Conservation (WCS) and Center
for International Earth Science
Information Network (CIESIN).

EUROPE
Moscow
London
Paris
Madrid
Istanbul
Baghdad
Tehran
Cairo

ASIA
Beijing
Tianjin
Seoul
Tokyo
Osaka
Shanghai
Wuhan
Chongqing
Delhi
Lahore
Karachi
Ahmadabad
Kolkata
Dhaka
Guangzhou
Hong Kong
Shenzhen
Mumbai
Hyderabad
Bangalore
Chennai
Bangkok
Manila
Ho Chi
Minh City

AFRICA
Lagos
Kinshasa

INDIAN
OCEAN

PACIFIC
OCEAN

Jakarta

AUSTRALIA

ANTARCTICA

Kilometers
0   1000   2000   3000

Statute Miles
0   1000   2000   3000

Trend in total carbon emissions, by region

Metric tons of CO_2 (in trillions)

12

8

4

0

1990   1995   2000   2005

— Africa
— Asia and the Pacific
— Europe
— Latin America and the Caribbean
— North America
— West Asia

DEFORESTATION

Loss of forest cover, such as on this hillside in Malaysia, contributes to a buildup of carbon dioxide in the atmosphere, as well as to a loss of biodiversity. This is a frequent problem in the tropics.

DESERTIFICATION

Villagers in Mauritania, Africa, shovel sand away from their schoolhouse. In semiarid areas, which receive limited and often unreliable rainfall, land that is overgrazed or overcultivated can become desertlike.

DAMAGED REEFS

Coral reefs, such as this one in the Indian Ocean near the Maldives, can be damaged by increases in ocean temperatures. If a reef dies, a habitat for the many marine creatures that live there is lost.

Natural Disasters

Every world region has its share of natural disasters—the menacing mix just varies from place to place. The Ring of Fire—grinding tectonic plate boundaries that follow the coasts of the Pacific Ocean—shakes with volcanic eruptions and earthquakes. Coastal lives and livelihoods can be swept away by quake-caused tsunamis. The U.S. heartland endures blizzards in winter and dangerous tornadoes that can strike in spring, summer, or fall. Tropical cyclones batter many coastal areas with ripping winds, torrents of rain, and huge storm surges along their deadly paths.

NORTH AMERICA

Tri-State Tornado (1925)

Hurricane Sandy (2012)

ROCKY MOUNTAINS

Hawaiian Islands

Galveston Hurricane (1900)

Hurricane Katrina (2005)

ATLANTIC OCEAN

PACIFIC OCEAN

Hurricane Mitch (1998)

ANDES

SOUTH AMERICA

Kilometers
0 1000 2000 3000

Statute Miles
0 1000 2000 3000

Winkel Tripel Projection

KINDS OF DISASTERS

Earthquake
A shaking of Earth's crust caused by a volcanic eruption or by the release of energy along a fault in the crust

Tornado
A violently rotating column of air that touches Earth's surface during intense thunderstorm activity

Tropical Cyclone
A huge weather system, fueled by warm water, that can become a rotating storm packing winds of at least 74 miles per hour (119 kph); called hurricanes in the Atlantic Ocean and eastern Pacific, cyclones in the Bay of Bengal and Indian Ocean, and typhoons in the western Pacific

Tsunami
Ocean waves caused by an undersea earthquake or by a volcanic eruption

Volcanic Eruption
The upward movement and usually forceful release of molten material and gases from Earth's interior onto the surface

TORNADO. A funnel cloud roars across open country near Campo, Colorado, U.S.A. More of these storms occur in "Tornado Alley" (see map) than anywhere else on Earth.

TROPICAL CYCLONE. In late October 2012, "Superstorm" Sandy slammed into the U.S. East Coast, bringing widespread destruction and flooding that forced some people to evacuate their home in rafts.

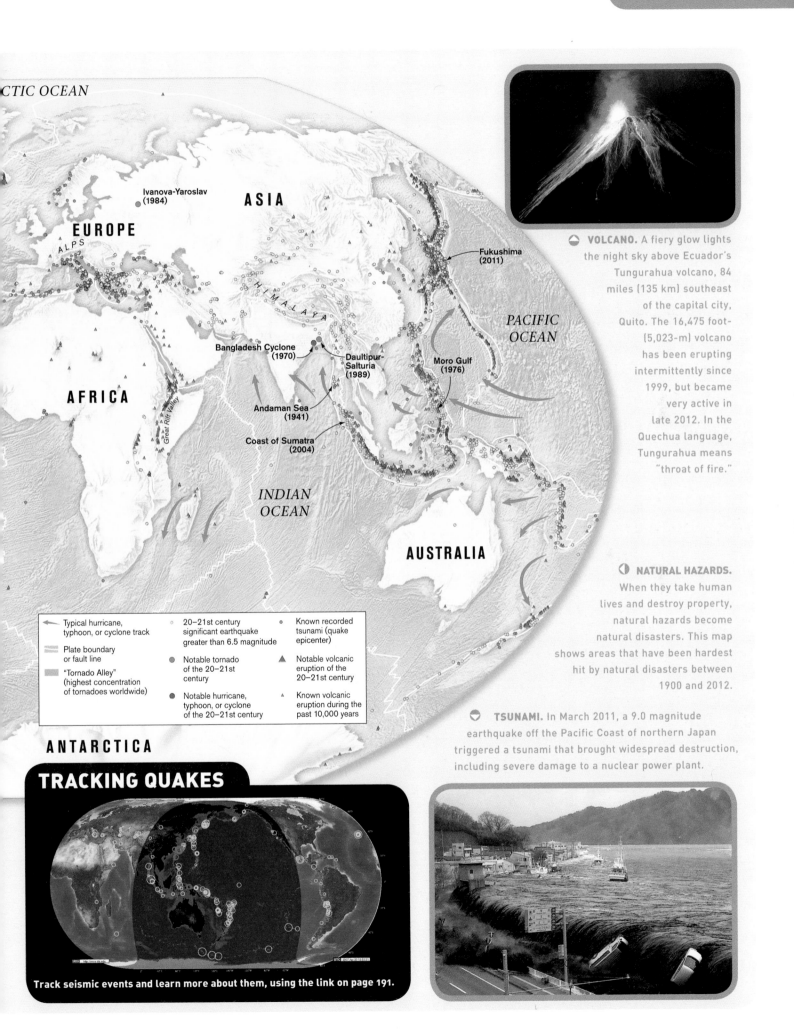

CTIC OCEAN

Ivanova-Yaroslav (1984)

ASIA

EUROPE

ALPS

Fukushima (2011)

H I M A L A Y A

PACIFIC OCEAN

AFRICA

Bangladesh Cyclone (1970)

Daultipur-Salturia (1989)

Moro Gulf (1976)

Great Rift Valley

Andaman Sea (1941)

Coast of Sumatra (2004)

INDIAN OCEAN

AUSTRALIA

Typical hurricane, typhoon, or cyclone track

20–21st century significant earthquake greater than 6.5 magnitude

Known recorded tsunami (quake epicenter)

Plate boundary or fault line

Notable tornado of the 20–21st century

Notable volcanic eruption of the 20–21st century

"Tornado Alley" (highest concentration of tornadoes worldwide)

Notable hurricane, typhoon, or cyclone of the 20–21st century

Known volcanic eruption during the past 10,000 years

ANTARCTICA

TRACKING QUAKES

IRIS

UTC

Track seismic events and learn more about them, using the link on page 191.

VOLCANO. A fiery glow lights the night sky above Ecuador's Tungurahua volcano, 84 miles (135 km) southeast of the capital city, Quito. The 16,475 foot-(5,023-m) volcano has been erupting intermittently since 1999, but became very active in late 2012. In the Quechua language, Tungurahua means "throat of fire."

NATURAL HAZARDS. When they take human lives and destroy property, natural hazards become natural disasters. This map shows areas that have been hardest hit by natural disasters between 1900 and 2012.

TSUNAMI. In March 2011, a 9.0 magnitude earthquake off the Pacific Coast of northern Japan triggered a tsunami that brought widespread destruction, including severe damage to a nuclear power plant.

using the link on page 191.

POLITICAL WORLD

The Political World

Earth's land area is mainly made up of seven giant continents, but people have divided much of the land into smaller political units called countries. Australia is a continent with a single country, and Antarctica is set aside for scientific research. But the other five continents include almost 200 independent countries. The political map (right) shows boundaries—imaginary lines agreed to by treaties—that separate countries. Some boundaries, such as the one between the United States and Canada, are very stable and have been recognized for many years. Other boundaries, such as the one between Ethiopia and Eritrea in northeast Africa, are relatively new and still disputed.

Countries come in all shapes and sizes. Russia and Canada are giants. Other countries, such as Luxembourg in western Europe, are small. Some countries are long and skinny—look at Chile in South America! Still other countries—like Indonesia and Japan in Asia—are made up of groups of islands. The political map is a clue to the diversity that makes Earth so fascinating.

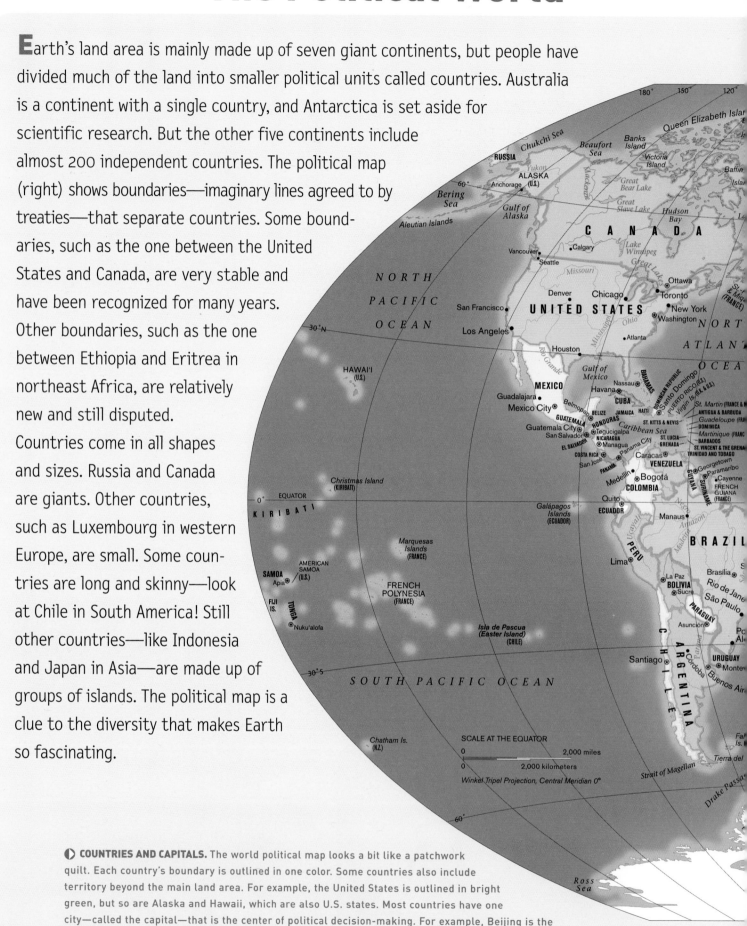

⬤ **COUNTRIES AND CAPITALS.** The world political map looks a bit like a patchwork quilt. Each country's boundary is outlined in one color. Some countries also include territory beyond the main land area. For example, the United States is outlined in bright green, but so are Alaska and Hawaii, which are also U.S. states. Most countries have one city—called the capital—that is the center of political decision-making. For example, Beijing is the capital of China. But a few countries have more than one capital, such as La Paz and Sucre in Bolivia. The capital of each country is marked with a star inside a circle. Many other major cities are also shown.

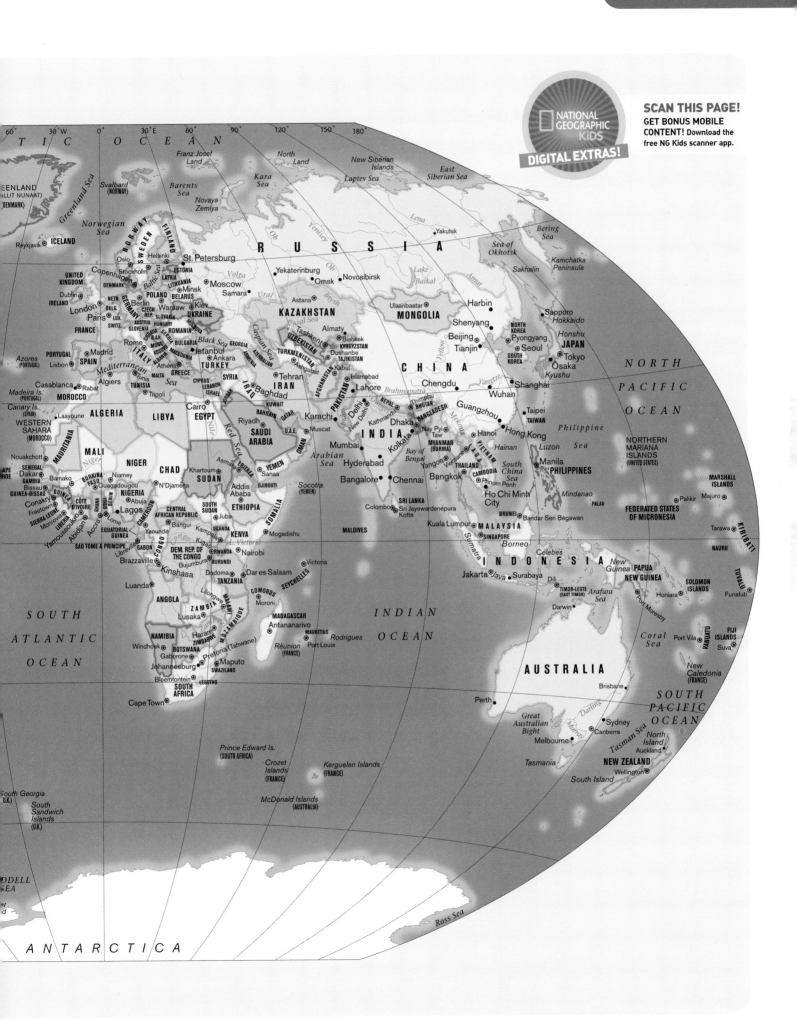

NATIONAL GEOGRAPHIC KiDS
DIGITAL EXTRAS!

SCAN THIS PAGE!
GET BONUS MOBILE
CONTENT! Download the
free NG Kids scanner app.

POLITICAL WORLD

World Population

How big is a billion? It's hard to imagine. But Earth's population is 7.1 billion and rising, with more than a billion living in both China and India. And more than 60 million people are added to the world each year. Most population growth occurs in the less developed countries of Asia, Africa, and Latin America, while some countries in Europe are hardly increasing at all. Population changes can create challenges for countries. Fast-growing countries with young populations need food, housing, and schools. Countries with low growth rates and older populations need workers to sustain their economies.

MOST POPULOUS COUNTRIES

(mid-2012 data)	
1. China	1,350,378,000
2. India	1,259,721,000
3. United States	313,858,000
4. Indonesia	240,990,000
5. Brazil	194,334,000
6. Pakistan	180,428,000
7. Nigeria	170,124,000
8. Bangladesh	152,875,000

MOST CROWDED COUNTRIES

Population Density (People per sq mi/sq km; 2010 data)	
1. Monaco	45,000 / 18,000
2. Singapore	19,288 / 7,447
3. Bahrain	4,709 / 1,818
4. Malta	3,414 / 1,318
5. Maldives	2,745 / 1,060
6. Vatican City	4,180 / 2,090
7. Bangladesh	2,673 / 1,032
8. Mauritius	1,650 / 637

◗ **DENSITY.** Demographers, people who study population, use density to measure how concentrated population is. For example, the population density of Egypt is almost 200 people per square mile (77 per sq km). This assumes that the population is evenly spread throughout the country, but this is not the case in Egypt. Almost all of the people live along the banks of the Nile River. Likewise, Earth's population is not evenly spread across the land. Some places, like central Australia, are almost empty, whereas others, such as Europe or India, are very crowded.

◗ **CITY DWELLERS.** More than half the world's people have shifted from rural areas to urban centers, with some countries adding more than 100 million to their urban populations between 1950 and 2015 (see map, right). In more developed countries, about 75 percent of the population is urban, compared with just 46 percent in less developed countries. But the fastest growing urban areas are in less developed countries, where thousands flock to cities, such as Dhaka, Bangladesh (photo, far right), in search of a better life. By 2015 there could be as many as 22 cities with populations of 10 million or more.

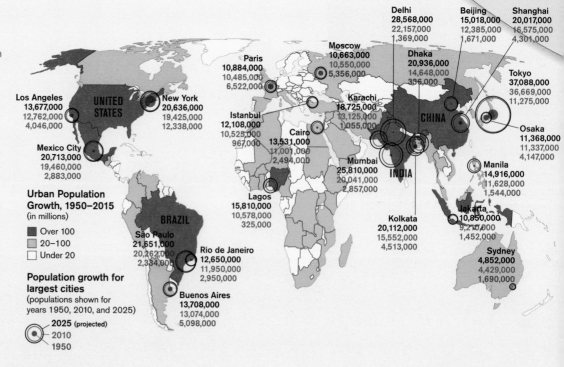

Los Angeles–Long Beach–Santa Ana   Dallas–Fort Worth

Mexico City

PACIFIC OCEAN

Urban Population Growth, 1950–2015
(in millions)

- Over 100
- 20–100
- Under 20

Population growth for largest cities
(populations shown for years 1950, 2010, and 2025)

- 2025 (projected)
- 2010
- 1950

Los Angeles
13,677,000
12,762,000
4,046,000

UNITED STATES

New York
20,636,000
19,425,000
12,338,000

Mexico City
20,713,000
19,460,000
2,883,000

Paris
10,884,000
10,485,000
6,522,000

Moscow
10,663,000
10,550,000
5,356,000

Delhi
28,568,000
22,157,000
1,369,000

Beijing
15,018,000
12,385,000
1,671,000

Shanghai
20,017,000
16,575,000
4,301,000

Dhaka
20,936,000
14,648,000
336,000

Tokyo
37,088,000
36,669,000
11,275,000

Istanbul
12,108,000
10,525,000
967,000

Cairo
13,531,000
11,001,000
2,494,000

Karachi
18,725,000
13,125,000
1,055,000

CHINA

Osaka
11,368,000
11,337,000
4,147,000

Mumbai
25,810,000
20,041,000
2,857,000

INDIA

Manila
14,916,000
11,628,000
1,544,000

BRAZIL

São Paulo
21,651,000
20,262,000
2,334,000

Lagos
15,810,000
10,578,000
325,000

Rio de Janeiro
12,650,000
11,950,000
2,950,000

Kolkata
20,112,000
15,552,000
4,513,000

Jakarta
10,850,000
9,210,000
1,452,000

Buenos Aires
13,708,000
13,074,000
5,098,000

Sydney
4,852,000
4,429,000
1,690,000

50	100	150	200	250	300	350	400	450	500	550	600	650	700	750	800	850	900	950

Year

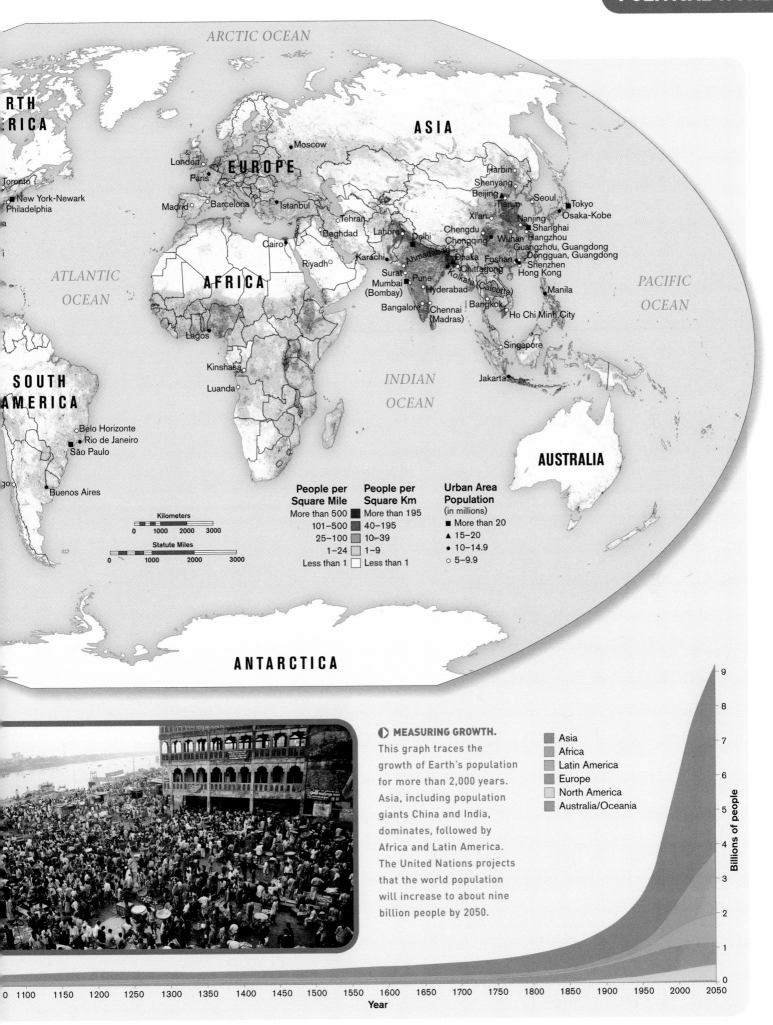

ARCTIC OCEAN

RTH
RICA

ASIA

•Moscow

London○
Paris○

EUROPE

Harbin○
Shenyang•
Beijing•
Tianjin○ Seoul
Xi'an○ Nanjing• ■Tokyo
Chengdu• Shanghai Osaka-Kobe
Chongqing○ Wuhan○ Hangzhou
Guangzhou, Guangdong
Dongguan, Guangdong
Shenzhen
Hong Kong

Toronto○
■New York-Newark
Philadelphia

Madrid○ ○Barcelona •Istanbul

Tehran○
Baghdad○ Lahore○ •Delhi
Cairo○ Riyadh○ Karachi•
Ahmadabad• Dhaka Foshan
Surat○ Chittagong
Mumbai Pune○ Kolkata
(Bombay) Hyderabad• (Calcutta)

ATLANTIC
OCEAN

AFRICA

Manila

PACIFIC
OCEAN

Bangalore○
Chennai
(Madras)

Bangkok
Ho Chi Minh City

Lagos•

SOUTH
AMERICA

Kinshasa•
Luanda○

INDIAN
OCEAN

Jakarta•

Singapore○

Belo Horizonte○
●Rio de Janeiro
São Paulo■

AUSTRALIA

go○

•Buenos Aires

People per Square Mile	People per Square Km	Urban Area Population (in millions)
More than 500	More than 195	■ More than 20
101–500	40–195	▲ 15–20
25–100	10–39	● 10–14.9
1–24	1–9	○ 5–9.9
Less than 1	Less than 1	

Kilometers
0 1000 2000 3000

Statute Miles
0 1000 2000 3000

ANTARCTICA

9
8
7
6

◖ MEASURING GROWTH.
This graph traces the
growth of Earth's population
for more than 2,000 years.
Asia, including population
giants China and India,
dominates, followed by
Africa and Latin America.
The United Nations projects
that the world population
will increase to about nine
billion people by 2050.

Asia
Africa
Latin America
Europe
North America
Australia/Oceania

5
4
3
2
1
0

Billions of people

0 1100 1150 1200 1250 1300 1350 1400 1450 1500 1550 1600 1650 1700 1750 1800 1850 1900 1950 2000 2050
Year

Population Trends

Population growth rates are slowing, total fertility rates are declining, and populations are aging. Nevertheless, world population will continue to increase for many years to come because the base population is so large. Almost 60 million people are added, on average, to the world's population each year, 90 percent of whom are born in less developed countries where poverty is greatest. In more affluent countries, life expectancy is higher and populations are aging. By 2050, almost one-quarter of the world's population will be 60 years of age or older.

United States
78 years
1.9
6.1

PACIFIC OCEAN

HIGHEST FERTILITY RATE

(average number of children born to a woman in her lifetime, 2012 data)

1. Niger	7.1
2. Somalia	6.4
3. Burundi	6.4
4. Mali	6.3
5. Angola	6.3
6. Dem. Rep. of the Congo	6.3
7. Zambia	6.3
8. Afghanistan	6.2

LOWEST FERTILITY RATE

(2012 data)

1. Latvia	1.1
2. Singapore	1.2
3. Andorra	1.2
4. Bosnia and Herzegovina	1.2
5. San Marino	1.2
6. South Korea	1.2
7. Hungary	1.2
8. Moldova	1.3

LONGEST LIFE EXPECTANCY

(average expected life span, both sexes, in years 2011 data)

1. Japan	83
2. San Marino	83
3. Australia	82
4. Spain	82
5. Israel	82
6. France	82
7. Switzerland	82
8. Sweden	82

SHORTEST LIFE EXPECTANCY

(2011 data)

1. Afghanistan	44
2. Zimbabwe	46
3. Guinea-Bissau	48
4. Swaziland	49
5. Zambia	49
6. Dem. Rep. of the Congo	49
7. Lesotho	49
8. Central African Republic	50

◖ POPULATION GROWTH.
This map shows projected population change (%) over the next 40 years. Much of Europe, Russia, and Japan face a decline in population due to low birth rates and women waiting longer to have children. Countries in Africa can expect to see an opposite trend as fertility rates remain high.

Map Symbols

■ **Life expectancy** (symbol equals 10 years, both sexes)

♟ **Infant mortality** (symbol equals 10 deaths per 1,000 live births)

♟ **Fertility rate** (average number of children born to women in a given population; symbol equals 1 child)

74
1.9
20

POPULATION PYRAMIDS

The population of a country can be shown in a bar graph in which age and sex groups are stacked up (males, left; females, right). This creates a country profile that helps predict future trends. Countries with high birth rates and high percentages of young people, such as Nigeria, are shaped like pyramids, which suggests continued growth. Countries, such as Italy, whose birth rates are below the replacement fertility rate of 2.1 children per couple, show bulges in the higher age brackets, but a narrow base, which indicates population decline.

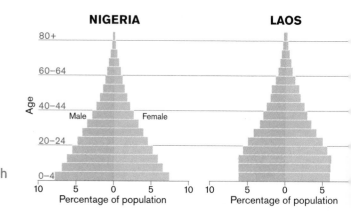

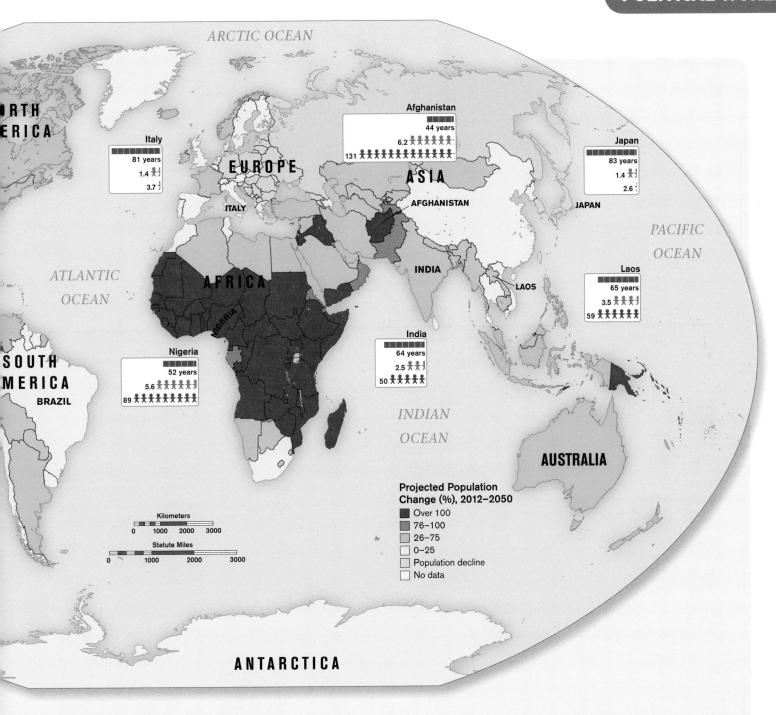

ARCTIC OCEAN

NORTH AMERICA

EUROPE

ASIA

Afghanistan
44 years
6.2
131

ITALY

AFGHANISTAN

Italy
81 years
1.4
3.7

Japan
83 years
1.4
2.6

JAPAN

PACIFIC OCEAN

ATLANTIC OCEAN

AFRICA

NIGERIA

INDIA

LAOS

Laos
65 years
3.5
59

SOUTH AMERICA

BRAZIL

Nigeria
52 years
5.6
89

India
64 years
2.5
50

INDIAN OCEAN

AUSTRALIA

Projected Population Change (%), 2012–2050

- Over 100
- 76–100
- 26–75
- 0–25
- Population decline
- No data

Kilometers
0 1000 2000 3000

Statute Miles
0 1000 2000 3000

ANTARCTICA

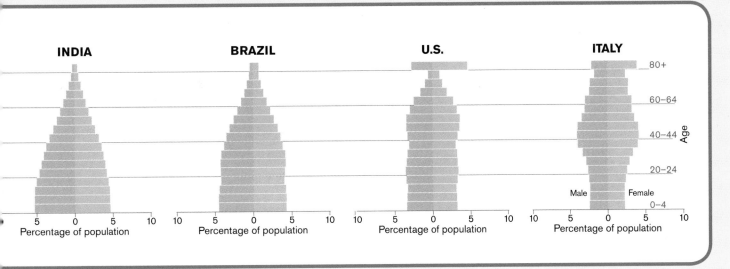

INDIA

5   0   5   10
Percentage of population

BRAZIL

10   5   0   5   10
Percentage of population

U.S.

10   5   0   5   10
Percentage of population

ITALY

80+

60–64

40–44

Age

20–24

Male   Female
0–4

10   5   0   5   10
Percentage of population

POLITICAL WORLD

World Languages & Literacy

Earth's 7.1 billion people live in 195 independent countries, but they speak more than 5,000 languages. Some countries, such as Japan, have one official language. Other countries have many languages, such as India, where 23 are official. Experts believe that humans may once have spoken as many as 10,000 languages, but that number has dropped by one-half and is still declining.

Literacy is the ability to read and write in one's native language. High literacy rates are associated with more developed countries. But literacy is also a gender issue, since women in less developed countries often lack access to education (see pages 42–43).

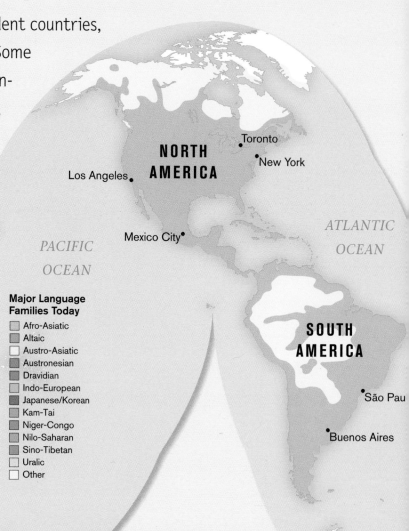

NORTH AMERICA

Toronto
New York
Los Angeles
Mexico City

PACIFIC OCEAN

ATLANTIC OCEAN

SOUTH AMERICA

São Pau
Buenos Aires

Major Language Families Today
- Afro-Asiatic
- Altaic
- Austro-Asiatic
- Austronesian
- Dravidian
- Indo-European
- Japanese/Korean
- Kam-Tai
- Niger-Congo
- Nilo-Saharan
- Sino-Tibetan
- Uralic
- Other

LEADING LANGUAGES

Some languages have only a few hundred speakers, but 23 languages stand out with more than 50 million speakers each. Earth's population giant, China, has 845 million speakers of Mandarin, more than double the next largest group of language speakers. Colonial expansion, trade, and migration account for the spread of the other most widely spoken languages. With growing use of the Internet, English is becoming the language of the technology age.

Population of first language speakers (in millions)

Language	Speakers
Chinese (Mandarin)	845
Spanish	329
English	328
Arabic	221
Hindi	182
Bengali	181
Portuguese	178
Russian	144
Japanese	122
German	90

Languages

◯ **EDUCATION AND LITERACY.** These Nenet boys in Siberia spend hours learning the national language—Russian—but this may result in the loss of their native language. Literacy can lead to good jobs in the future for these boys and improved economic success for their country.

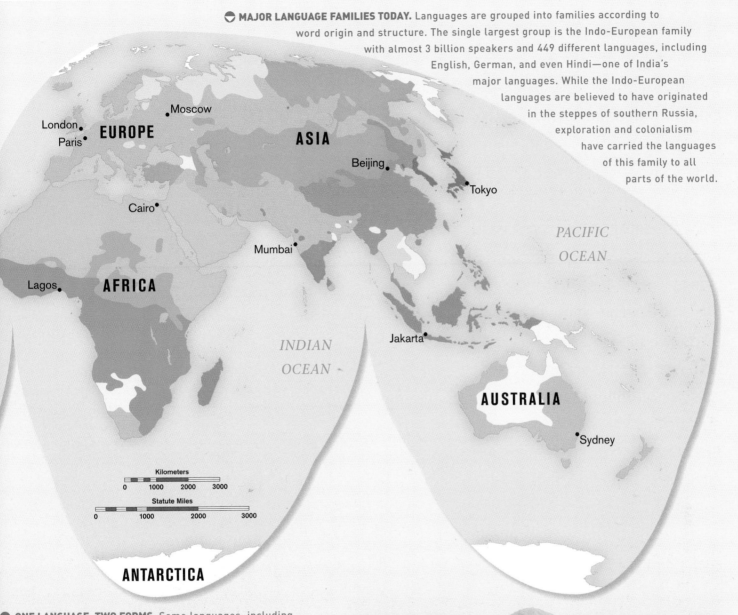

◐ **MAJOR LANGUAGE FAMILIES TODAY.** Languages are grouped into families according to word origin and structure. The single largest group is the Indo-European family with almost 3 billion speakers and 449 different languages, including English, German, and even Hindi—one of India's major languages. While the Indo-European languages are believed to have originated in the steppes of southern Russia, exploration and colonialism have carried the languages of this family to all parts of the world.

London
Paris
EUROPE
Moscow
ASIA
Beijing
Tokyo
Cairo
Mumbai
PACIFIC OCEAN
AFRICA
Lagos
INDIAN OCEAN
Jakarta
AUSTRALIA
Sydney

Kilometers
0 1000 2000 3000

Statute Miles
0 1000 2000 3000

ANTARCTICA

◐ **ONE LANGUAGE, TWO FORMS.** Some languages, including Chinese, use characters instead of letters. The Golden Arches provide a clue to the meaning of the characters on the restaurant sign. Many signs, such as the one in the foreground, also show words in pinyin, a spelling system that uses the Western alphabet.

◐ **UNIVERSAL LANGUAGE.** The widespread use of technology—for example, the electronic games that hold the attention of these children in France—has crossed the language barrier. Computers, the Internet, and electronic communication devices use a universal language that knows no national borders.

World Religions

Rooted in people's attempts to explain the unknown, religion takes many forms. Some belief systems, such as Christianity, Islam, and Judaism, are monotheistic, meaning that followers believe in just one supreme being. Others, like Hinduism, Shintoism, and most native belief systems, are polytheistic, believing in many gods.

All of the major religions have their origins in Asia, but they have spread around the world. Christianity, with the largest number of followers, has three divisions—Roman Catholic, Eastern Orthodox, and Protestant. Islam, with about one-fifth of all believers, has two main divisions—Sunni and Shia. Hinduism and Buddhism together account for almost another one-fifth of believers. Judaism, dating back some 4,000 years, is the oldest of all the major monotheistic religions.

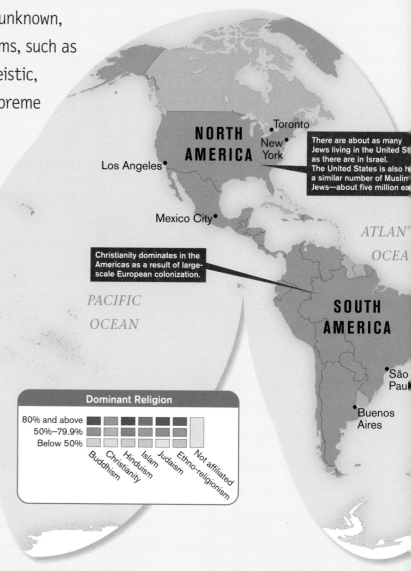

NORTH AMERICA

Toronto
New York
Los Angeles
Mexico City

There are about as many Jews living in the United St as there are in Israel. The United States is also h a similar number of Muslim Jews—about five million ea

ATLAN
OCEA

Christianity dominates in the Americas as a result of large-scale European colonization.

PACIFIC OCEAN

SOUTH AMERICA

São Pau
Buenos Aires

Dominant Religion

80% and above		
50%–79.9%		
Below 50%		

Buddhism · Christianity · Hinduism · Islam · Judaism · Ethno-religionism · Not affiliated

BUDDHISM

Founded about 2,500 years ago in northern India by a Hindu prince named Gautama Buddha, Buddhism spread throughout East and Southeast Asia. Buddhist temples house statues, such as the Mihintale Buddha (above) in Sri Lanka.

CHRISTIANITY

Based on the teachings of Jesus Christ, a Jew born some 2,000 years ago in the area of modern-day Israel, Christianity has spread worldwide and actively seeks converts. Followers in Switzerland (above) participate in a procession with lanterns and crosses.

HINDUISM

Dating back more than 4,000 years, Hinduism is practiced mainly in India. Hindus follow sacred texts known as the Vedas and believe in reincarnation. During the festival of Diwali, Hindus light candles (above) to symbolize the victory of good over evil.

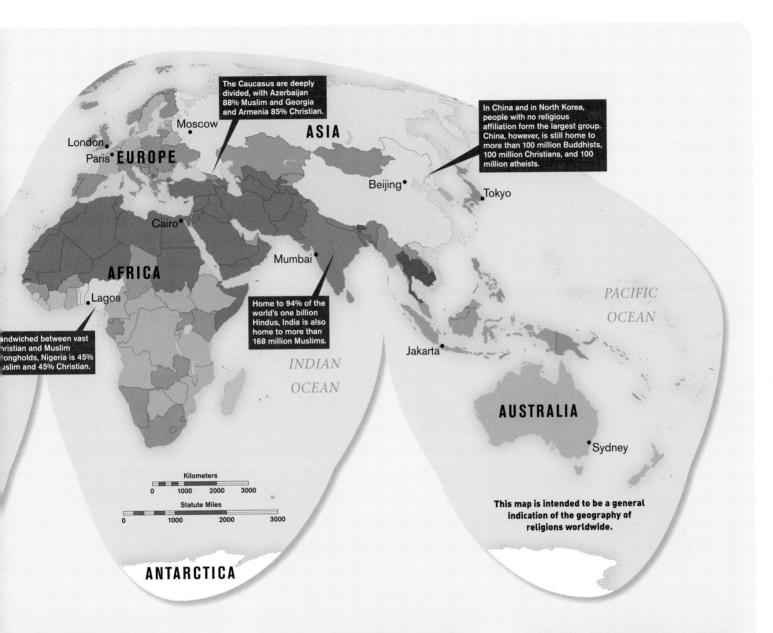

The Caucasus are deeply divided, with Azerbaijan 88% Muslim and Georgia and Armenia 85% Christian.

In China and in North Korea, people with no religious affiliation form the largest group. China, however, is still home to more than 100 million Buddhists, 100 million Christians, and 100 million atheists.

Sandwiched between vast Christian and Muslim strongholds, Nigeria is 45% Muslim and 45% Christian.

Home to 94% of the world's one billion Hindus, India is also home to more than 168 million Muslims.

Moscow

London
Paris **EUROPE**

ASIA

Beijing

Tokyo

Cairo

AFRICA

Lagos

Mumbai

PACIFIC OCEAN

Jakarta

INDIAN OCEAN

AUSTRALIA

Sydney

This map is intended to be a general indication of the geography of religions worldwide.

ANTARCTICA

Kilometers
0 1000 2000 3000

Statute Miles
0 1000 2000 3000

ISLAM

Muslims believe that the Koran, Islam's sacred book, records the words of Allah (God) as revealed to the Prophet Muhammad around A.D. 610. Believers (above) circle the Kabah in the Haram Mosque in Mecca, the spiritual center of the faith.

JUDAISM

The traditions, laws, and beliefs of Judaism date back to Abraham, its founder, and to the Torah, the first five books of the Old Testament. Followers (above) pray before the Western Wall, which stands below Islam's Dome of the Rock in Jerusalem.

RELIGIOUS FOLLOWERS

Hinduism 14.0%
Nonreligious 16.0%
Buddhism 6.0%
Chinese traditional 6.0%
Other 4.0%
Christianity 33.0%
Islam 21.0%

Most people identify with a major religion. Some are nonreligious.

POLITICAL WORLD

World Economies

A country's economy can be divided into three parts, or sectors—agriculture, industry, and services. Sometimes a fourth sector dealing with information and knowledge is added. The map shows that the economies of the United States and Western Europe are dominated by the service sector. These economies enjoy a high GDP (Gross Domestic Product) per capita—the value of goods and services produced each year, averaged per person in each country. In contrast, some economies in Africa and Asia still depend mostly on agriculture, which generates a low GDP per capita.

HIGHEST GDP PER CAPITA*	
1. Luxembourg	$104,196
2. Norway	$102,249
3. Qatar	$99,839
4. Switzerland	$76,598
5. Australia	$69,582
6. United Arab Emirates	$65,755
7. Sweden	$55,969
8. Denmark	$55,150
9. United States	$52,805
10. Canada	$52,088

LOWEST GDP PER CAPITA*	
1. Democratic Republic of the Congo	$251
2. Malawi	$262
3. Burundi	$317
4. Niger	$434
5. Central African Republic	$451
6. Madagascar	$458
7. Liberia	$470
8. Ethiopia	$518
9. Guinea-Bissau	$529

*All data as of 2013.

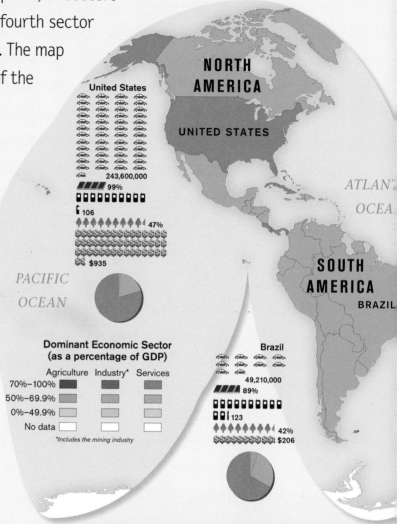

NORTH AMERICA

UNITED STATES

United States
243,600,000
99%
106
47%
$935

ATLANTIC OCEAN

SOUTH AMERICA
BRAZIL

PACIFIC OCEAN

Dominant Economic Sector
(as a percentage of GDP)

	Agriculture	Industry*	Services
70%–100%			
50%–69.9%			
0%–49.9%			
No data			

*Includes the mining industry

Brazil
49,210,000
89%
123
42%
$206

🖱 **INFORMATION.** Computers and other technologies have opened employment opportunities dealing with information and knowledge creation. These college students in the United Kingdom learn skills in an Information Technology lab that will prepare them for 21st-century jobs.

🔧 **INDUSTRY.** A man assembles a hybrid Prius car on an automated assembly line in a Toyota factory in Japan. Manufacture of cars is an important industrial activity and a key part of the global economy.

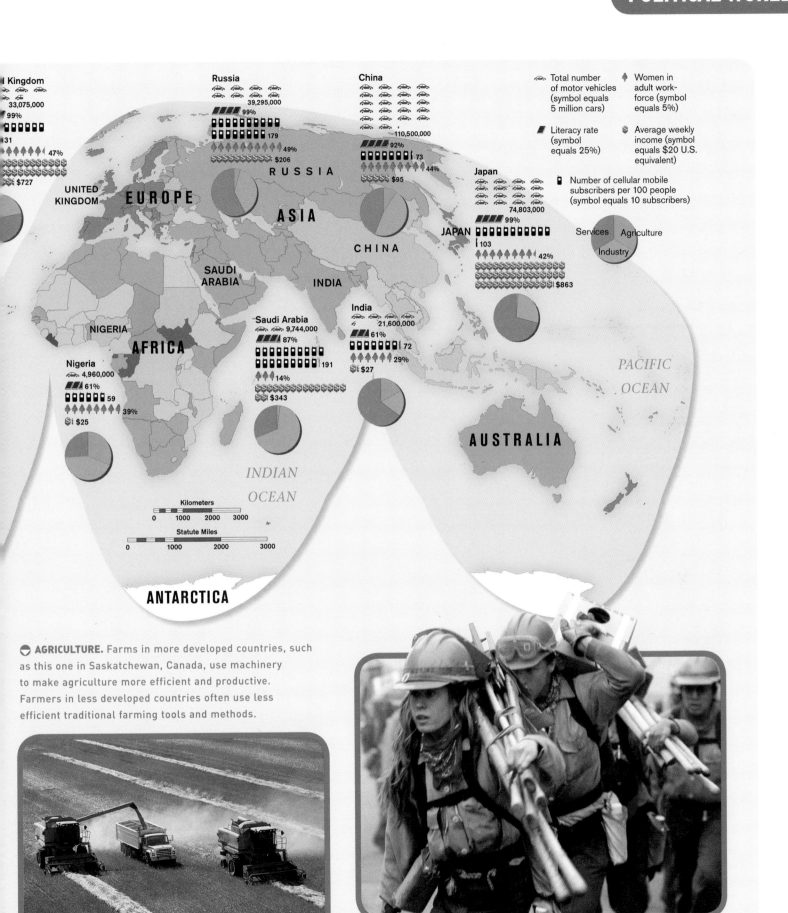

Kingdom
33,075,000
99%
31
47%
$727

Russia
39,295,000
99%
179
49%
$206

China
110,500,000
92%
73
44%
$95

Total number of motor vehicles (symbol equals 5 million cars)

Women in adult work-force (symbol equals 5%)

Literacy rate (symbol equals 25%)

Average weekly income (symbol equals $20 U.S. equivalent)

Number of cellular mobile subscribers per 100 people (symbol equals 10 subscribers)

Japan
74,803,000
99%
103
42%
$863

Services   Agriculture

Industry

UNITED KINGDOM

EUROPE

RUSSIA

ASIA

CHINA

SAUDI ARABIA

INDIA

NIGERIA

AFRICA

Saudi Arabia
9,744,000
87%
191
14%
$343

India
21,600,000
61%
72
29%
$27

Nigeria
4,960,000
61%
59
39%
$25

PACIFIC OCEAN

AUSTRALIA

INDIAN OCEAN

Kilometers
0   1000   2000   3000

Statute Miles
0   1000   2000   3000

ANTARCTICA

AGRICULTURE. Farms in more developed countries, such as this one in Saskatchewan, Canada, use machinery to make agriculture more efficient and productive. Farmers in less developed countries often use less efficient traditional farming tools and methods.

SERVICES. People employed in the service sector, such as these national forest firefighters in Washington State, U.S.A., use their skills and training to provide services rather than products. Teachers, lawyers, and store clerks, among others, are also part of the service sector.

World Trade

World trade has expanded at a rapid rate in the decades since the end of World War II in 1945. In fact, trade has grown much faster than world production. Some countries, such as the United States, have complex economies that involve trading many different products, especially manufactured goods. But many less developed countries (see map at right) rely on only a few products—sometimes even just one product—to generate trade income. In recent years, commercial services, such as financial and information management, have expanded and become an important part of world trade.

▶ **TRADE.** The map (right) shows the richest and poorest economies around the world. The wealth of economies can be measured in terms of Gross National Income (GNI) per person—that is, income derived from economic activity. The arrows on the map show the movement and volume of trade among different world regions.

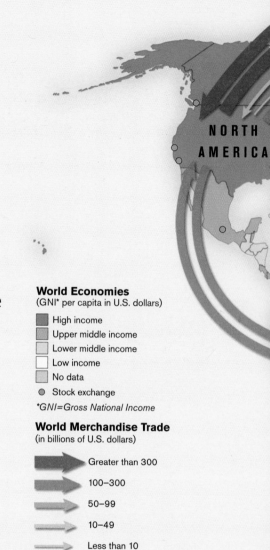

NORTH AMERICA

World Economies
(GNI* per capita in U.S. dollars)

■	High income
■	Upper middle income
■	Lower middle income
□	Low income
■	No data
●	Stock exchange

*GNI=Gross National Income

World Merchandise Trade
(in billions of U.S. dollars)

➤	Greater than 300
➤	100–300
➤	50–99
➤	10–49
➤	Less than 10

TOP MERCHANDISE EXPORTERS

(2011 data, billion U.S. $)	
1. China	$1,898
2. United States	$1,480
3. Germany	$1,472
4. Japan	$823
5. Netherlands	$661
6. France	$596
7. South Korea	$555
8. Italy	$523
9. Russia	$522

TOP MERCHANDISE IMPORTERS

(2011 data, billion U.S. $)	
1. United States	$2,266
2. China	$1,743
3. Germany	$1,254
4. Japan	$855
5. France	$714
6. United Kingdom	$638
7. Netherlands	$599
8. Italy	$557
9. South Korea	$524

TOP COMMERCIAL SERVICE EXPORTERS

(2011 data, billion U.S. $)	
1. United States	$581
2. United Kingdom	$274
3. Germany	$253
4. China	$182
5. France	$167
6. Japan	$142
7. Spain	$140
8. India	$137
9. Netherlands	$134

TOP COMMERCIAL SERVICE IMPORTERS

(2011 data, billion U.S. $)	
1. United States	$395
2. Germany	$289
3. China	$237
4. United Kingdom	$170
5. Japan	$166
6. France	$143
7. India	$124
8. Netherlands	$118
9. Ireland	$114

MAIN TRADING NATIONS

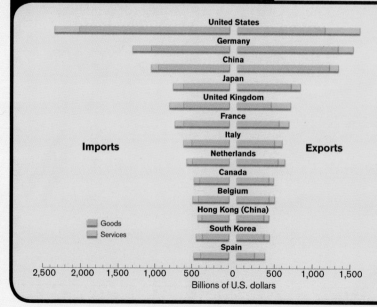

United States
Germany
China
Japan
United Kingdom
France
Italy
Netherlands
Canada
Belgium
Hong Kong (China)
South Korea
Spain

Imports | Exports

■ Goods
■ Services

2,500 2,000 1,500 1,000 500 0 500 1,000 1,500
Billions of U.S. dollars

The United States, Germany, and China dominate world trade. They protect their economies by imposing quotas and taxes that limit trade in products, such as agriculture and textiles, from other countries. Member countries of the World Trade Organization are negotiating to reduce trade barriers so that all countries can compete in the world economy.

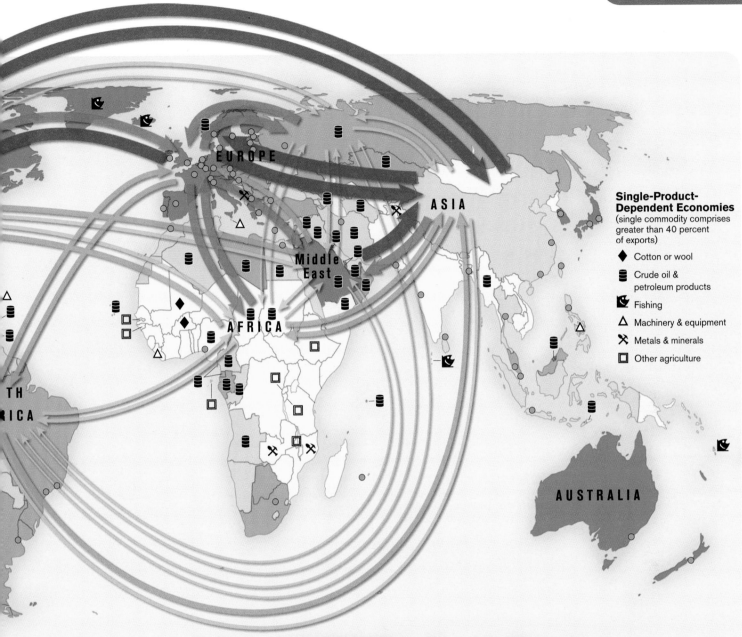

EUROPE

ASIA

Middle
East

AFRICA

TH
RICA

AUSTRALIA

**Single-Product-
Dependent Economies**
(single commodity comprises
greater than 40 percent
of exports)

◆ Cotton or wool

▮ Crude oil &
petroleum products

Fishing

△ Machinery & equipment

✕ Metals & minerals

☐ Other agriculture

TRADE AGREEMENTS.

de within regions is
easing. Neighboring
ntries, such as the countries
he European Union, agree to
r each other trade benefits
can improve the economy
he whole region. Such
eements allow products,
kers, and money to move
e easily among member
ntries. However, these
eements may also prevent
e with nonmember countries
may be able to provide
ducts at a lower cost.

NORTH
AMERICA

EUROPE

ASIA

AFRICA

SOUTH
AMERICA

AUSTRALIA

Major Regional Trade Agreements

APEC - Asia-Pacific
Economic Cooperation

ASEAN - Association of
Southeast Asian Nations

APEC & ASEAN

COMESA - Common
Market for Eastern and
Southern Africa

ECOWAS - Economic
Community of West
African States

EU - European Union

MERCOSUR - Southern
Common Market

NAFTA & APEC - North
American Free Trade
Agreement

SAPTA - South Asian
Preferential Trade
Arrangement

World Water

Water is Earth's most precious resource. Although more than two-thirds of the planet is covered by water, fresh water, which is needed by plants and animals—including humans—is only about 2.5 percent of all the water on Earth. Much of this is trapped deep underground or frozen in ice sheets and glaciers. Of the small amount of water that is fresh, less than one percent is available for human use.

The map at right shows each country's access to renewable freshwater supplies. Watersheds are large areas that drain into a particular river or lake.

Unfortunately, human activity often puts great stress on watersheds. For example, in Brazil, plans are being made to build large dams on the Amazon. This will alter the natural flow of water in this giant watershed. In the United States, heavy use of chemical fertilizers and pesticides has created toxic run-off that threatens the health of the Mississippi watershed.

Access to clean fresh water is critical for human health. But in many places, safe water is scarce due to population pressure and pollution.

WATER FACTS

Rivers that have been dammed to generate electricity are the source of almost 90 percent of Earth's renewable energy resources.

North America's Great Lakes hold about 20 percent of Earth's available fresh water.

If all the glaciers and ice sheets on Earth's surface melted, they would raise the level of Earth's oceans by about 230 feet (70 m). It is estimated that during the last ice age, when glaciers covered about one-third of the land, sea level was 400 feet (122 m) lower than it is today.

Desalination is the process of removing salt from ocean water so that it can be used for irrigation, water for livestock, and for drinking. Most of the world's desalination plants are in the arid countries of the Arabian Peninsula.

Because of the water cycle, Earth has roughly the same amount of water now as it has had for two billion years.

If all the world's water were placed in a gallon jug, the fresh water available for humans to use would equal only about one tablespoon.

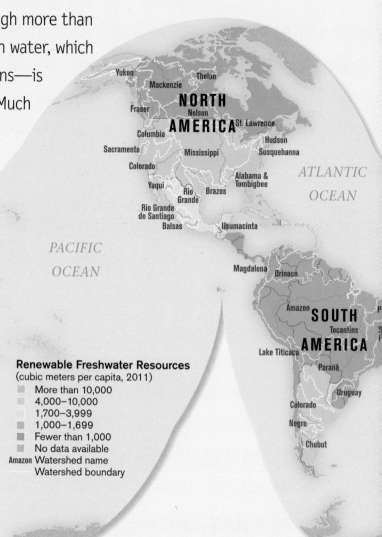

Renewable Freshwater Resources
(cubic meters per capita, 2011)
- More than 10,000
- 4,000–10,000
- 1,700–3,999
- 1,000–1,699
- Fewer than 1,000
- No data available
- Amazon Watershed name
- Watershed boundary

BIG SPLASH! Water sports are a favorite recreational activity, especially in hot places such as Albuquerque, New Mexico, U.S.A., where these young people cool down in a giant wave pool.

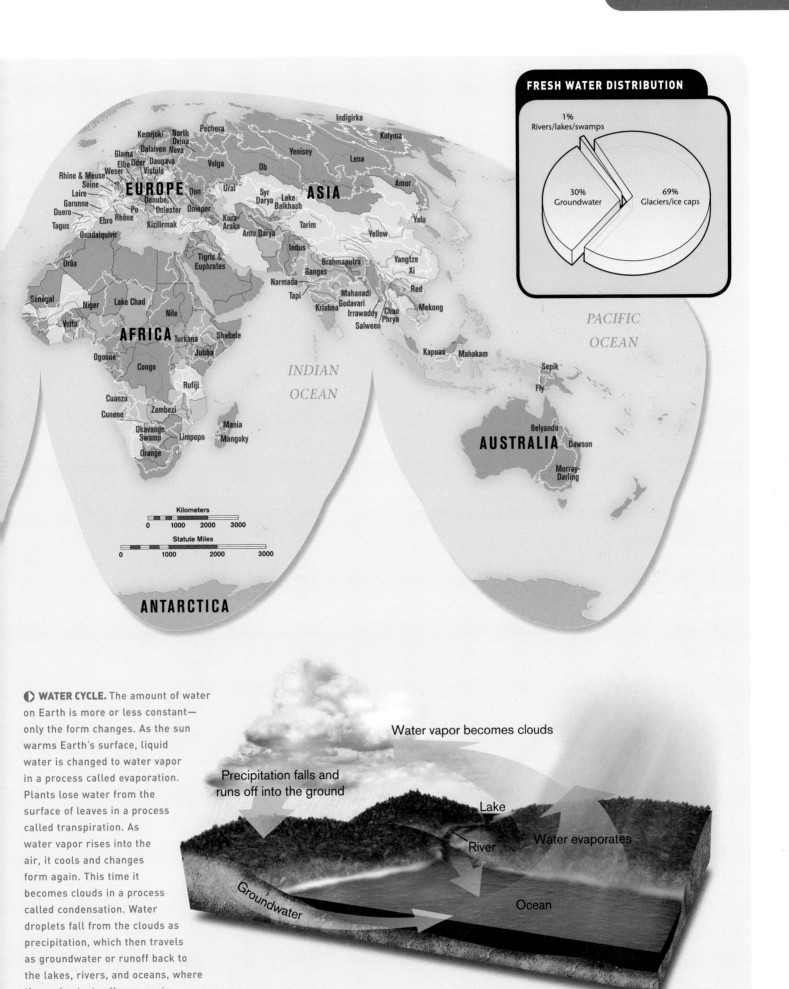

FRESH WATER DISTRIBUTION

1%
Rivers/lakes/swamps

30%
Groundwater

69%
Glaciers/ice caps

EUROPE

Kemijoki
North
Dvina
Glama
Dalalven Neva
Elbe Oder Daugava
Rhine & Meuse
Weser Vistula
Seine
Loire
Garonne
Duero
Tagus Ebro Rhône
Guadalquivir
Po
Danube
Dniester
Dnieper
Don
Ural

Pechora

Indigirka

Kolyma

Yenisey

Lena

Amur

Volga

Ob

ASIA

Syr
Darya
Lake
Balkhash

Kura-
Araks

Amu Darya

Tarim

Yellow

Yalu

Kizilirmak

Tigris &
Euphrates

Indus

Brahmaputra
Ganges

Yangtze
Xi

Narmada

Tapi

Mahanadi
Godavari
Krishna
Irrawaddy
Salween

Red

Mekong

Chao
Phrya

AFRICA

Orâa

Sénégal

Niger
Lake Chad

Nile

Volta

Turkana

Shebele

Ogooué

Congo

Jubba

Cuanza

Rufiji

Cunene

Zambezi

Okavango
Swamp
Orange
Limpopo

Mania
Mangoky

Kapuas

Mahakam

Sepik

Fly

PACIFIC
OCEAN

INDIAN
OCEAN

AUSTRALIA

Belyando
Dawson

Murray-
Darling

Kilometers
0   1000   2000   3000

Statute Miles
0   1000   2000   3000

ANTARCTICA

WATER CYCLE. The amount of water on Earth is more or less constant—only the form changes. As the sun warms Earth's surface, liquid water is changed to water vapor in a process called evaporation. Plants lose water from the surface of leaves in a process called transpiration. As water vapor rises into the air, it cools and changes form again. This time it becomes clouds in a process called condensation. Water droplets fall from the clouds as precipitation, which then travels as groundwater or runoff back to the lakes, rivers, and oceans, where the cycle starts all over again.

Water vapor becomes clouds

Precipitation falls and
runs off into the ground

Lake

Water evaporates

River

Groundwater

Ocean

World Food

Earth produces enough food for all its inhabitants but not everyone gets enough to eat. It's a matter of distribution. Agricultural regions, shown in the map at right, are unevenly spread around the world, and it is sometimes difficult to move food supplies from areas of surplus to areas of great need. Africa, in particular, has regions where hunger and malnourishment rob people of healthy, productive lives.

In recent decades, food production has increased, especially production of meat and cereals, such as corn, wheat, and rice. They dominate the calorie supply of people, especially in Africa and Asia. But increased yields of grain require intensive use of fertilizers and irrigation, which are not only expensive but also possibly a threat to the environment.

Agricultural Extent
Nonagricultural land

100% Cropland — 100% Grazing land

HARVEST BY FISHING COUNTRY

The world's yearly catch of ocean fish is more than four times what it was in 1950. The most heavily harvested areas are in the North Atlantic and western Pacific Oceans. Overfishing is becoming a serious problem. At least seven of the most-fished species are considered to be at their limit. Aquaculture—raising fish and seaweed in controlled ponds—accounts for 40 percent of the fish people eat. This practice began some 4,000 years ago in China, where it continues today, accounting for about two-thirds of the country's total output. Fish are among the most widely traded food products, with 75 percent of the total catch sold on the international market each year.

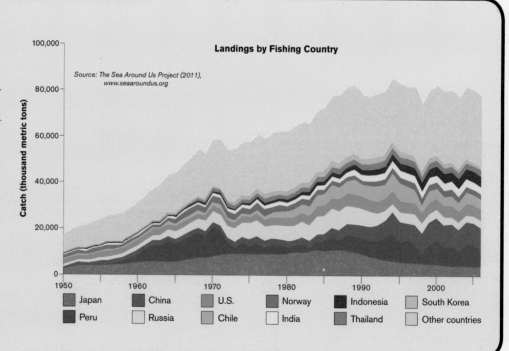

Landings by Fishing Country

Source: The Sea Around Us Project (2011), www.seaaroundus.org

Catch (thousand metric tons)

Japan • China • U.S. • Norway • Indonesia • South Korea
Peru • Russia • Chile • India • Thailand • Other countries

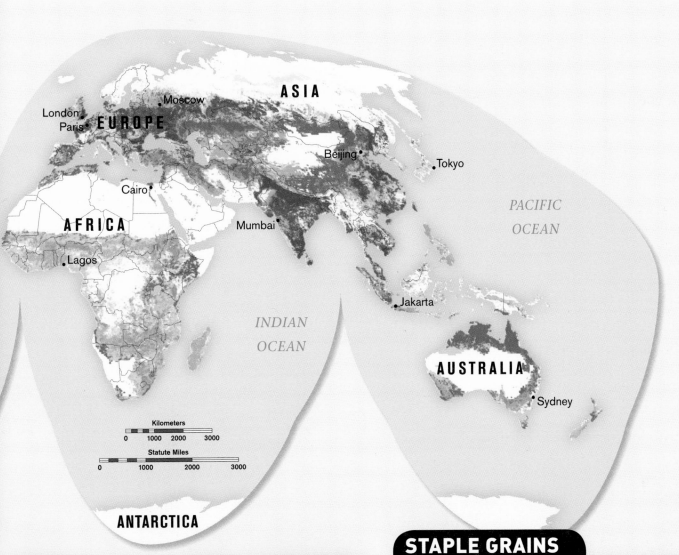

ASIA

Moscow

London
Paris

EUROPE

Beijing

Tokyo

PACIFIC OCEAN

Cairo

AFRICA

Mumbai

Lagos

Jakarta

INDIAN OCEAN

AUSTRALIA

Sydney

Kilometers
0 1000 2000 3000

Statute Miles
0 1000 2000 3000

ANTARCTICA

⬤ **CASTING NETS.** Fishermen in Orissa, India, cast their nets on the Birupa River. Fish is an important source of protein in their diets. Any surplus catch can be sold in the local market.

STAPLE GRAINS

CORN. A staple in prehistoric Mexico and Peru, corn (or maize) is native to the New World. By the time Columbus's crew first tasted it, corn was already a hardy crop in much of North and South America.

WHEAT. One of the two oldest grains (barley is the other), wheat was important in ancient Mediterranean civilizations. Today, it is the most widely cultivated grain. Wheat grows best in temperate climates.

RICE. Originating in Asia many millennia ago, rice is the staple grain for about half the world's people. It is a labor-intensive plant that grows primarily in paddies (flooded fields) and thrives in the hot, humid tropics.

World Energy & Minerals

Almost everything people do—from cooking to powering an airplane—requires energy. But energy comes in different forms. Traditional energy sources, still used by many people in the developing world, include burning dried animal dung and wood. Industrialized countries and urban centers around the world rely on coal, oil, and natural gas—called fossil fuels because they formed from decayed plant and animal material accumulated from long ago. Fossil fuel deposits, either in the ground or under the ocean floor, are unevenly distributed on Earth (see map, right), and many countries frequently cannot afford them.

Carbon dioxide from the burning of fossil fuels as well as other emissions may be contributing to global warming. Concerned scientists are looking at new ways to harness renewable sources of energy, such as water, wind, and sun.

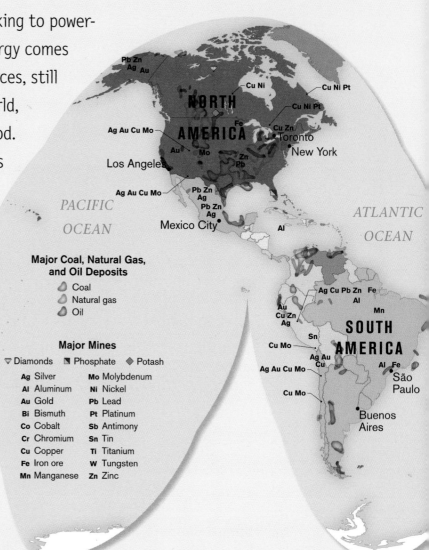

Major Coal, Natural Gas, and Oil Deposits

- Coal
- Natural gas
- Oil

Major Mines

▽ Diamonds   ◥ Phosphate   ◆ Potash

Ag Silver		**Mo** Molybdenum	
Al Aluminum		**Ni** Nickel	
Au Gold		**Pb** Lead	
Bi Bismuth		**Pt** Platinum	
Co Cobalt		**Sb** Antimony	
Cr Chromium		**Sn** Tin	
Cu Copper		**Ti** Titanium	
Fe Iron ore		**W** Tungsten	
Mn Manganese		**Zn** Zinc	

OIL, GAS, AND COAL

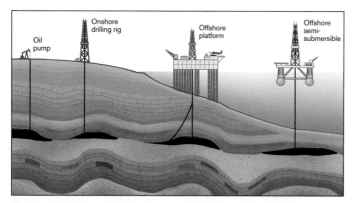

⬭ **DRILLING FOR OIL AND GAS.** The type of equipment used depends on whether the oil or natural gas is in the ground or under the ocean. This illustration shows some of the different kinds of onshore and offshore drilling equipment.

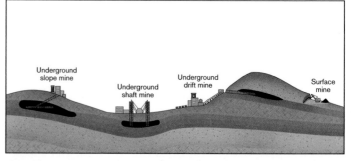

⬭ **COAL MINING.** The mining of coal made the industrial revolution possible, and coal still remains a major energy source. Work that was once done by people using picks and shovels now relies heavily on mechanized equipment. This diagram shows some of the various kinds of mines currently in use.

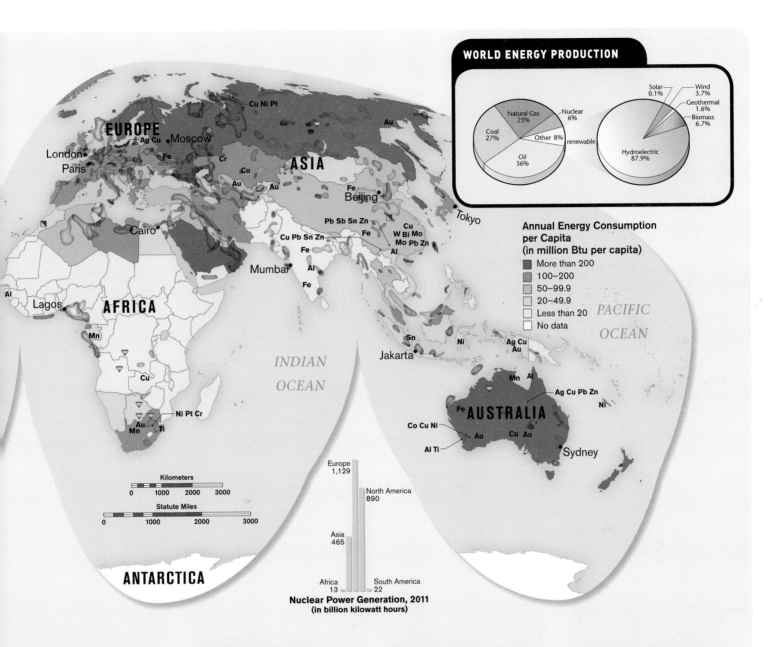

WORLD ENERGY PRODUCTION

Natural Gas 23%
Nuclear 6%
Coal 27%
Other 8%
renewable
Oil 36%

Solar 0.1%
Wind 3.7%
Geothermal 1.6%
Biomass 6.7%
Hydroelectric 87.9%

Annual Energy Consumption per Capita
(in million Btu per capita)

- More than 200
- 100–200
- 50–99.9
- 20–49.9
- Less than 20
- No data

EUROPE
London
Paris
Moscow
Ag Cu
Fe
Cu Ni Pt
Au
ASIA
Cr
Cu
Au
Au
Fe
Beijing
Pb Sb Sn Zn
Cu
W Bi Mo
Mo Pb Zn
Al
Fe
Tokyo
Cu Pb Sn Zn
Fe
Mumbai
Al
Fe
Cairo
AFRICA
Al
Lagos
Mn
Cu
INDIAN OCEAN
Sn
Ni
Jakarta
Ag Cu Au
PACIFIC OCEAN
Ni Pt Cr
Au
Mn
Ti
Mn
Al
AUSTRALIA
Fe
Ag Cu Pb Zn
Ni
Co Cu Ni
Au
Cu Au
Al Ti
Sydney
ANTARCTICA

Kilometers
0 1000 2000 3000
Statute Miles
0 1000 2000 3000

Europe 1,129
North America 890
Asia 465
Africa 13
South America 22
Nuclear Power Generation, 2011
(in billion kilowatt hours)

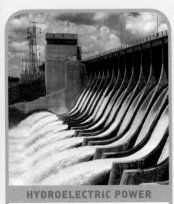

HYDROELECTRIC POWER

Hydroelectric plants, such as Santiago del Estero in Argentina (above), use dams to harness running water to generate clean, renewable energy.

GEOTHERMAL POWER

Geothermal power, originating from groundwater heated by magma, provides energy for this power plant in Iceland. Swimmers enjoy the warm, mineral-rich waters of a lake created by the power plant.

SOLAR POWER

Solar panels on Samso Island in Denmark capture and store energy from the sun, an environmentally friendly alternative to the use of fossil fuels.

WIND POWER

Strong winds blowing through California's, U.S.A., mountain passes spin the blades of windmills on an energy farm, powering giant turbines that generate electricity for the state.

THE CONTINENT:
NORTH AMERICA

Highest point
Mount McKinley (Denali), Alaska
20,320 ft (6,194 m)

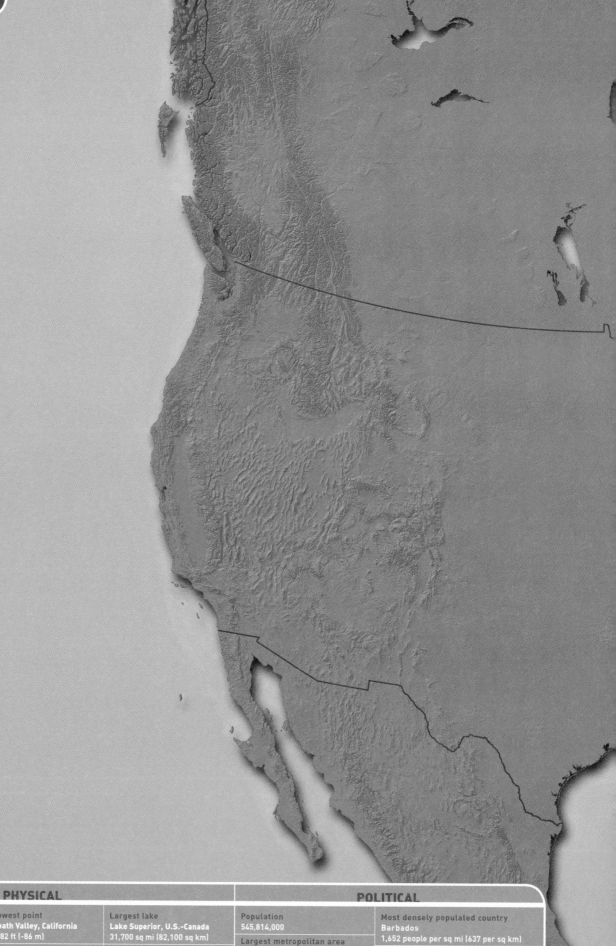

PHYSICAL

Land area
9,449,000 sq mi (24,474,000 sq km)

Highest point
Mount McKinley (Denali), Alaska
20,320 ft (6,194 m)

Lowest point
Death Valley, California
-282 ft (-86 m)

Longest river
Mississippi-Missouri,
United States
3,710 mi (5,971 km)

Largest lake
Lake Superior, U.S.-Canada
31,700 sq mi (82,100 sq km)

POLITICAL

Population
545,814,000

Largest metropolitan area
Mexico City, Mexico
Pop. 19,319,000

Largest country
Canada
3,855,101 sq mi (9,984,670 sq km)

Most densely populated country
Barbados
1,652 people per sq mi (637 per sq km)

Economy
Farming: cattle, grains, cotton, sugar
Industry: machinery, metals, mining
Services

North America

North America

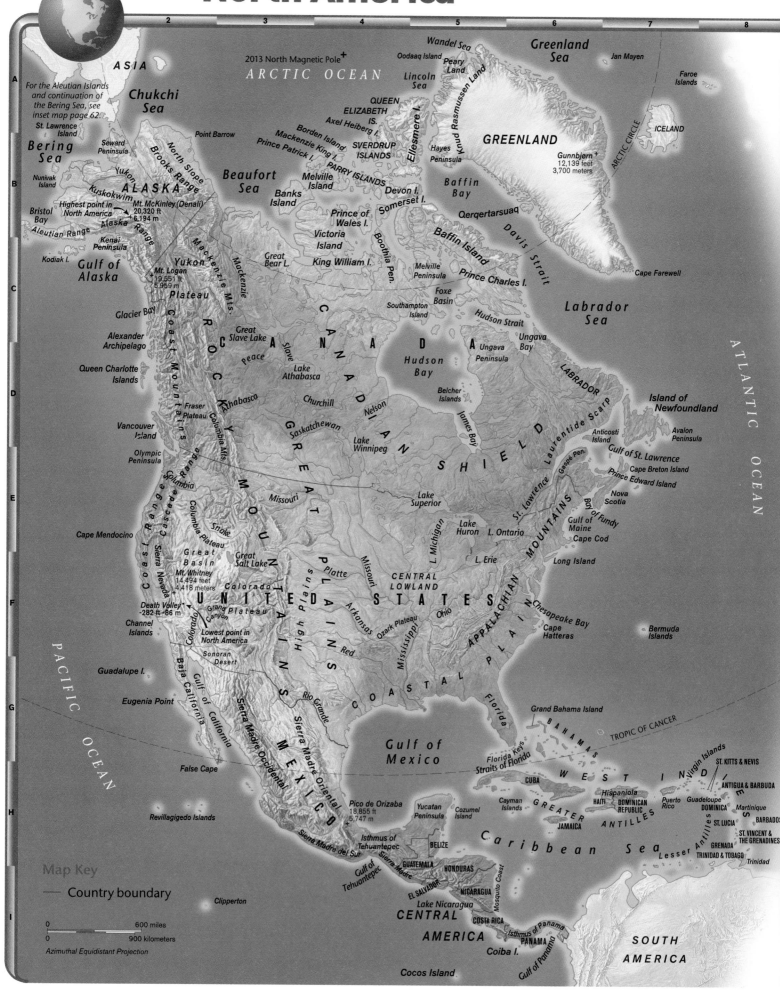

2   3   4   5   6   7   8

ASIA

Chukchi Sea

ARCTIC OCEAN

2013 North Magnetic Pole +

Wandel Sea

Greenland Sea

Jan Mayen

Oodaaq Island
Peary Land

Lincoln Sea

Knud Rasmussen Land

Faroe Islands

For the Aleutian Islands and continuation of the Bering Sea, see inset map page 62.

St. Lawrence Island

QUEEN ELIZABETH IS.

Axel Heiberg I.

Ellesmere I.

GREENLAND

ICELAND

ARCTIC CIRCLE

Bering Sea

Point Barrow

Borden Island

Mackenzie King I.

Prince Patrick I.

SVERDRUP ISLANDS

PARRY ISLANDS

Hayes Peninsula

Gunnbjørn +
12,139 feet
3,700 meters

Nunivak Island

Seward Peninsula

North Slope

Brooks Range

Beaufort Sea

Melville Island

Banks Island

Devon I.

Baffin Bay

ALASKA

Yukon

Kuskokwim

Bristol Bay

Highest point in North America

Mt. McKinley (Denali)
20,320 ft
6,194 m

Alaska Range

Prince of Wales I.

Great Bear L.

Victoria Island

Somerset I.

Boothia Pen.

King William I.

Melville Peninsula

Baffin Island

Prince Charles I.

Qertertasuaq

Davis Strait

Cape Farewell

Aleutian Range

Kenai Peninsula

Mt. Logan
19,551 ft
5,959 m

Yukon

Mackenzie Mts.

Mackenzie

Foxe Basin

Labrador Sea

Kodiak I.

Gulf of Alaska

Plateau

Southampton Island

Hudson Strait

ATLANTIC OCEAN

Glacier Bay

Great Slave Lake

Peace

Slave

C A N A D A

Ungava Peninsula

Ungava Bay

Alexander Archipelago

Fraser Plateau

Athabasca

Columbia Mts.

Lake Athabasca

Saskatchewan

Churchill

Nelson

Hudson Bay

Belcher Islands

LABRADOR

Island of Newfoundland

Vancouver Island

Rocky Mountains

Coast Mountains

Lake Winnipeg

G R E A T

S H I E L D

C A N A D I A N

James Bay

Laurentide Scarp

Anticosti Island

Gaspé Pen.

Gulf of St. Lawrence

Avalon Peninsula

Olympic Peninsula

Columbia

Columbia Plateau

Missouri

M O U N T A I N S

Lake Superior

L. Michigan

Lake Huron

L. Ontario

St. Lawrence

Cape Breton Island

Prince Edward Island

Nova Scotia

Bay of Fundy

Gulf of Maine

Cape Mendocino

Cascade Range

Coast Range

Snake

Great Basin

Great Salt Lake

P L A I N S

Platte

Missouri

CENTRAL LOWLAND

L. Erie

APPALACHIAN MOUNTAINS

Cape Cod

Long Island

Sierra Nevada

Mt. Whitney
14,494 feet
4,418 meters

Colorado Plateau

U N I T E D   S T A T E S

High Plains

Arkansas

Ohio

Chesapeake Bay

Bermuda Islands

Death Valley
-282 ft -86 m

Grand Canyon

Ozark Plateau

Mississippi

Cape Hatteras

Channel Islands

Lowest point in North America

Colorado

Red

C O A S T A L   P L A I N

Guadalupe I.

Sonoran Desert

Rio Grande

Florida

Grand Bahama Island

TROPIC OF CANCER

Eugenia Point

Baja California

M E X I C O

Sierra Madre Occidental

Gulf of California

Sierra Madre Oriental

B A H A M A S

PACIFIC OCEAN

False Cape

Gulf of Mexico

Florida Keys

Straits of Florida

CUBA

W E S T

Virgin Islands

ST. KITTS & NEVIS

ANTIGUA & BARBUDA

Guadeloupe

DOMINICA

Martinique

Revillagigedo Islands

Pico de Orizaba
18,855 ft
5,747 m

Yucatan Peninsula

Cozumel Island

Cayman Islands

G R E A T E R

A N T I L L E S

Hispaniola

HAITI
DOMINICAN REPUBLIC

Puerto Rico

I N D I E S

ST. LUCIA

BARBADOS

JAMAICA

Sierra Madre del Sur

Isthmus of Tehuantepec

BELIZE

Caribbean Sea

Lesser Antilles

ST. VINCENT & THE GRENADINES

GRENADA

TRINIDAD & TOBAGO

Trinidad

Gulf of Tehuantepec

Sierra Madre

GUATEMALA

HONDURAS

Mosquito Coast

EL SALVADOR

NICARAGUA

Map Key

— Country boundary

0   600 miles
0   900 kilometers

Azimuthal Equidistant Projection

Clipperton

C E N T R A L

A M E R I C A

Lake Nicaragua

COSTA RICA

PANAMA

Isthmus of Panama

Gulf of Panama

Coiba I.

SOUTH AMERICA

Cocos Island

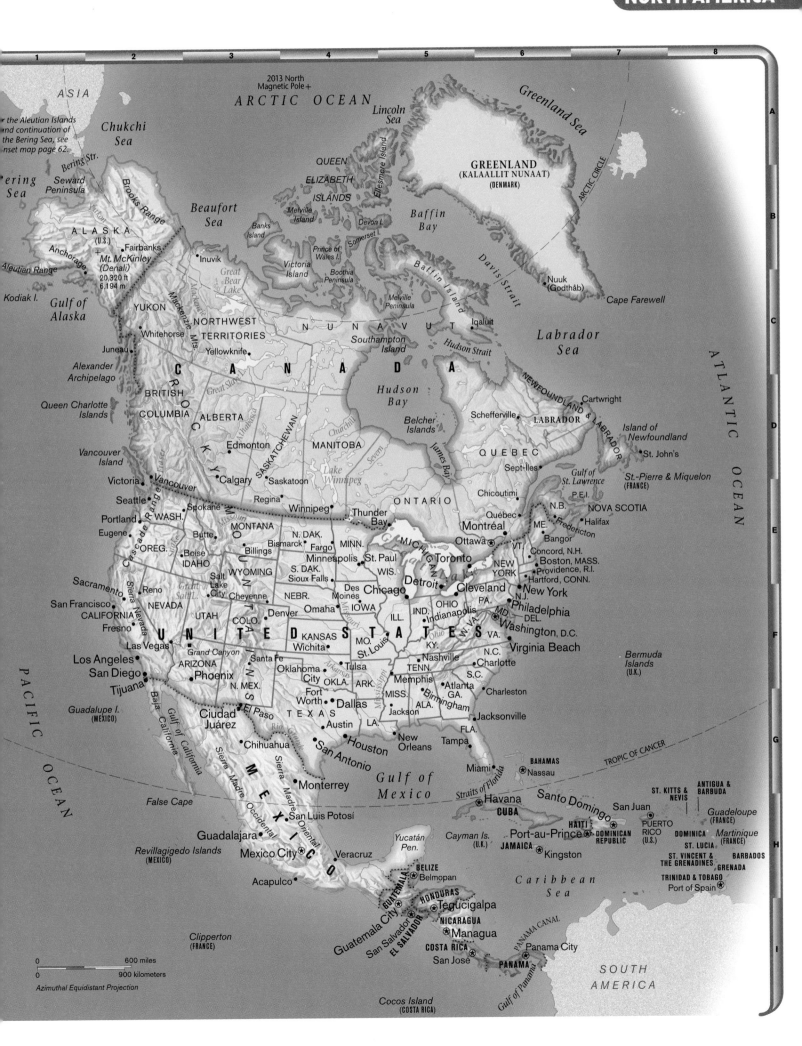

ASIA

2013 North Magnetic Pole +

ARCTIC OCEAN

Greenland Sea

the Aleutian Islands and continuation of the Bering Sea, see inset map page 62.

Chukchi Sea

Bering Str.

Lincoln Sea

GREENLAND
(KALAALLIT NUNAAT)
(DENMARK)

ering Sea

Seward Peninsula

Brooks Range

Beaufort Sea

QUEEN ELIZABETH ISLANDS

Ellesmere Island

ARCTIC CIRCLE

Yukon

Banks Island

Melville Island

Devon I.

Baffin Bay

ALASKA
(U.S.)

Fairbanks

Anchorage

Mt. McKinley
(Denali)
20,320 ft
6,194 m

Prince of Wales I.

Victoria Island

Boothia Peninsula

Melville Peninsula

Nuuk
(Godthåb)

Aleutian Range

Kodiak I.

Gulf of Alaska

YUKON

Great Bear Lake

Mackenzie Mts.

NORTHWEST TERRITORIES

Whitehorse

Yellowknife

Inuvik

Southampton Island

Iqaluit

Hudson Strait

Cape Farewell

Labrador Sea

ATLANTIC OCEAN

Juneau

Alexander Archipelago

CANADA

R
O
C
K
Y

Great Slave L.

Hudson Bay

Queen Charlotte Islands

BRITISH COLUMBIA

ALBERTA

Athabasca

SASKATCHEWAN

MANITOBA

Belcher Islands

NEWFOUNDLAND & LABRADOR

Cartwright

LABRADOR

Vancouver Island

Fraser

Edmonton

Calgary

Saskatoon

Lake Winnipeg

Severn

James Bay

QUEBEC

Schefferville

Island of Newfoundland

St. John's

Victoria

Vancouver

Seattle

Spokane

Regina

Winnipeg

Thunder Bay

ONTARIO

Churchill

Chicoutimi

Québec

Gulf of St. Lawrence

St.-Pierre & Miquelon
(FRANCE)

P.E.I.

N.B.

NOVA SCOTIA

Sept-Îles

Portland

WASH.

Butte

MONTANA

N. DAK.

MINN.

MICHIGAN

Montréal

Ottawa

ME.

Fredericton

Halifax

Bangor

Eugene

OREG.

Boise

IDAHO

Billings

Bismarck

Fargo

Minneapolis

St. Paul

WIS.

Toronto

NEW YORK

VT.

Concord, N.H.

Boston, MASS.

Providence, R.I.

Hartford, CONN.

Sacramento

Reno

WYOMING

Salt Lake City

Cheyenne

S. DAK.

Sioux Falls

Des Moines

Chicago

Detroit

Cleveland

PA.

New York

N.J.

San Francisco

NEVADA

UTAH

COLO.

Denver

Omaha

NEBR.

IOWA

ILL.

IND.

OHIO

Indianapolis

W. VA.

Philadelphia

MD.

DEL.

Washington, D.C.

Fresno

CALIFORNIA

Sierra Nevada

Grand Canyon

KANSAS

MO.

St. Louis

KY.

VA.

Virginia Beach

Las Vegas

Santa Fe

Wichita

Nashville

TENN.

Charlotte

N.C.

Los Angeles

ARIZONA

Phoenix

N. MEX.

Oklahoma City

OKLA.

Tulsa

ARK.

Memphis

Atlanta

GA.

S.C.

Charleston

San Diego

Tijuana

Baja California

El Paso

Fort Worth

Dallas

TEXAS

MISS.

ALA.

Birmingham

Bermuda Islands
(U.K.)

Guadalupe I.
(MEXICO)

Ciudad Juárez

Chihuahua

Rio Grande

Austin

LA.

Jackson

Jacksonville

FLA.

PACIFIC OCEAN

Gulf of California

Sierra Madre Occidental

San Antonio

Houston

New Orleans

Tampa

Monterrey

Gulf of Mexico

Miami

BAHAMAS

Nassau

TROPIC OF CANCER

False Cape

San Luis Potosí

MEXICO

Sierra Madre Oriental

Straits of Florida

Havana

CUBA

Santo Domingo

San Juan

PUERTO RICO
(U.S.)

ST. KITTS & NEVIS

ANTIGUA & BARBUDA

Guadalajara

Revillagigedo Islands
(MEXICO)

Mexico City

Veracruz

Yucatán Pen.

Cayman Is.
(U.K.)

Port-au-Prince

HAITI

DOMINICAN REPUBLIC

DOMINICA

Guadeloupe
(FRANCE)

Martinique
(FRANCE)

Acapulco

BELIZE

Belmopan

JAMAICA

Kingston

ST. LUCIA

ST. VINCENT & THE GRENADINES

BARBADOS

GRENADA

Caribbean Sea

TRINIDAD & TOBAGO

Port of Spain

GUATEMALA

Guatemala City

HONDURAS

Tegucigalpa

San Salvador

EL SALVADOR

NICARAGUA

Managua

0   600 miles

0   900 kilometers

Azimuthal Equidistant Projection

Clipperton
(FRANCE)

COSTA RICA

San José

PANAMA CANAL

Panama City

PANAMA

Gulf of Panama

SOUTH AMERICA

Cocos Island
(COSTA RICA)

North America
LAND OF CONTRASTS

From the windswept tundra of Alaska, U.S.A., to the rain forest of Panama, the third largest continent stretches 5,500 miles (8,850 km), spanning natural environments that support wildlife from polar bears to jaguars. Over thousands of years, Native American groups spread across these varied landscapes. But this rich mosaic of cultures largely disappeared with the onslaught of European fortune hunters and land seekers. While abundant resources and fast-changing technology have brought prosperity to Canada and the United States, other countries wrestle with the most basic needs. Promise and problems abound across this contrasting realm of 23 countries and 546 million people.

◓ **STORY IN THE ROCKS.** Slanting sun rays reveal layers in the rocks of the Grand Canyon. Each rock layer—oldest on the canyon floor, youngest at the canyon's rim—tells us about Earth's changing history.

◑ **DRESSED TO CELEBRATE.** This boy in Mexico's southern state of Chiapas wears traditional clothing, including a brightly colored string tie and a broad-brimmed sombrero with elaborate stitching around the edge.

HOLD TIGHT. These daring rafters are running the roaring rapids of the Kicking Horse River in British Columbia, Canada's westernmost province. Rivers tumbling down the steep slopes of the Rocky Mountains provide many recreational opportunities.

STREET MUSIC.
People from around the world visit New Orleans, Louisiana, U.S.A., to hear jazz musicians fill the air with their music.

NIGHT SONG.
This coyote sends his mournful howl into the dark Montana night. Members of the dog family, coyotes originated in the southwestern United States but are now found through-out North America—even in urban areas.

THE CONTINENT:
NORTH AMERICA

more about
North America

⬤ **DWELLINGS FROM THE PAST.** Between A.D. 1000 and A.D. 1300 native people known as Ancestral Puebloans built cliff dwellings called pueblos, such as this one in Mesa Verde, Colorado, U.S.A.

⬤ **MAYA TREASURE.** The Pyramid of the Magician marks the ruins of Uxmal on the Yucatán Peninsula. Nearly four million people of Maya descent still live in southern Mexico and Central America.

◑ **FROZEN SUMMER.** Because it lies so far north, even summers are cold in Greenland. Here, local people navigate their boat among icebergs in waters off the village of Augpilagtoq.

◑ HIGH FLYER. A young Kutchin boy sails off a snowbank on snowshoes in Canada's Yukon. The Kutchin, an Athabascan tribe, live in the forested lands of eastern Alaska and western Canada. The name Kutchin means "people."

⬤ SWIMMING FREE. A variety of fish swim among colorful corals in the clear blue waters of the Caribbean Sea. Tropical waters are the habitat for many species of fish.

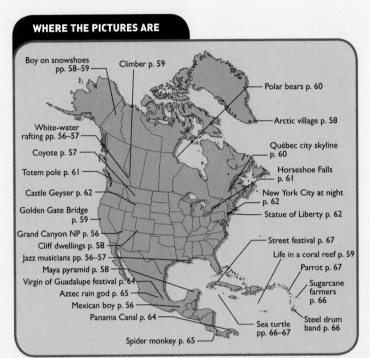

WHERE THE PICTURES ARE

- Boy on snowshoes pp. 58–59
- Climber p. 59
- Polar bears p. 60
- Arctic village p. 58
- White-water rafting pp. 56–57
- Québec city skyline p. 60
- Coyote p. 57
- Horseshoe Falls p. 61
- Totem pole p. 61
- New York City at night p. 62
- Castle Geyser p. 62
- Statue of Liberty p. 62
- Golden Gate Bridge p. 59
- Grand Canyon NP p. 56
- Street festival p. 67
- Cliff dwellings p. 58
- Life in a coral reef p. 59
- Jazz musicians pp. 56–57
- Parrot p. 67
- Maya pyramid p. 58
- Sugarcane farmers p. 66
- Virgin of Guadalupe festival p. 64
- Aztec rain god p. 65
- Mexican boy p. 56
- Steel drum band p. 66
- Panama Canal p. 64
- Sea turtle pp. 66–67
- Spider monkey p. 65

⬤ DON'T LOOK DOWN. Clinging to a sheer rock face, a young woman demonstrates great skill as she scales a steep cliff in Banff National Park in Canada. Covering more than 2,500 square miles (6,475 sq km) in the Canadian Rockies, Banff is a major tourist attraction.

⬤ WESTERN GATEWAY. The Golden Gate Bridge marks the entrance to San Francisco Bay. Beyond the bridge, captured above in the warm glow of twilight, is the California port city named after the bay.

THE CONTINENT:
NORTH AMERICA

THE BASICS

STATS

Area
3,855,101 sq mi (9,984,670 sq km)

Population
34,860,000

Predominant languages
English, French (both official)

Predominant religion
Christianity (Roman Catholic, Protestant)

GDP per capita
$40,500

Life expectancy
81 years

Literacy rate
99%

GEO WHIZ

Canada ranks second behind Saudi Arabia in largest oil reserves, thanks to the oil contained in the Athabasca tar sands in northern Alberta.

The Inuit territory of Nunavut has issued license plates in the shape of a polar bear for cars, motorcycles, and snowmobiles.

Canada is a constitutional monarchy, with Britain's Queen Elizabeth II as its head of state.

Montreal is the second most populous French-speaking city in the world, after Paris, France.

Canada's many bays, inlets, and islands give it the longest coastline of any country: 151,023 miles (243,042 km).

Geologists believe Réservoir Manicouagan in Quebec may have been created by the impact of a meteorite more than 200 million years ago.

Canada

Topped only by Russia in area, Canada has just 35 million people—fewer than live in the U.S. state of California. Ancient rocks yield abundant minerals. Lakes and rivers in Quebec are tapped for hydropower, and wheat farming and cattle ranching thrive across the western Prairie Provinces. Vast forests attract loggers, and mountain slopes provide a playground for nature lovers. Enormous deposits of oil sands lie waiting for technology to find a cheap way to convert them to hundreds of billions of barrels of oil. Most Canadians live within a hundred miles (161 km) of the U.S. border. Here, too, are its leading cities: Asia-focused Vancouver, ethnically diverse Toronto, capital Ottawa, and French-speaking Montreal.

◗ SILENT WATCHERS. Polar bears, North America's largest land carnivores, are adapted to the extreme Arctic environment around Cape Churchill in northern Manitoba. It is estimated that as many as 15,000 polar bears live in Canada.

LONGEST COASTLINE

Canada	151,023 miles (243,042 km)
Indonesia	33,998 miles (54,716 km)
Russia	23,397 miles (37,653 km)
Philippines	22,549 miles (36,289 km)
Japan	18,486 miles (29,751 km)
Australia	16,006 miles (25,760 km)
Norway	15,626 miles (25,148 km)
United States	12,380 miles (19,924 km)
New Zealand	9,404 miles (15,134 km)
China	9,010 miles (14,500 km)

Canada has the longest coastline in the world, and at more than 150,000 miles (243,000 km) it far surpasses the length of coastline of any other country.

◗ FRENCH ENCLAVE. Chateau Frontenac sparkles in Quebec City's nighttime skyline. Settled by the French in the early 1600s, the province of Quebec has maintained close ties to Europe and to its French heritage.

ARCTIC CIRCLE

Tu

ALASKA (U.S.)

Inuv

MACKENZIE

YUKON

Mt. Logan
19,551 ft
5,959 m

St. Elias Mts.

SELWYN MTS.

Haines
Junction

Whitehorse

Yukon

PACIFIC OCEAN

QUEEN CHARLOTTE IS.

Prince Rupert

Dawson Creek

ROCKY

BRITISH

Prince George

M

COLUMBIA

Fraser

Campbell River

Vancouver Island

Kamloops

Nanaimo

Kelowna

O

U

N

T

Victoria

Vancouver

◖ **KNOWING WHO WE ARE.** Native people of the Pacific Northwest preserve their family stories and legends in massive carved poles called totems, such as this one in Stanley Park in Vancouver, British Columbia.

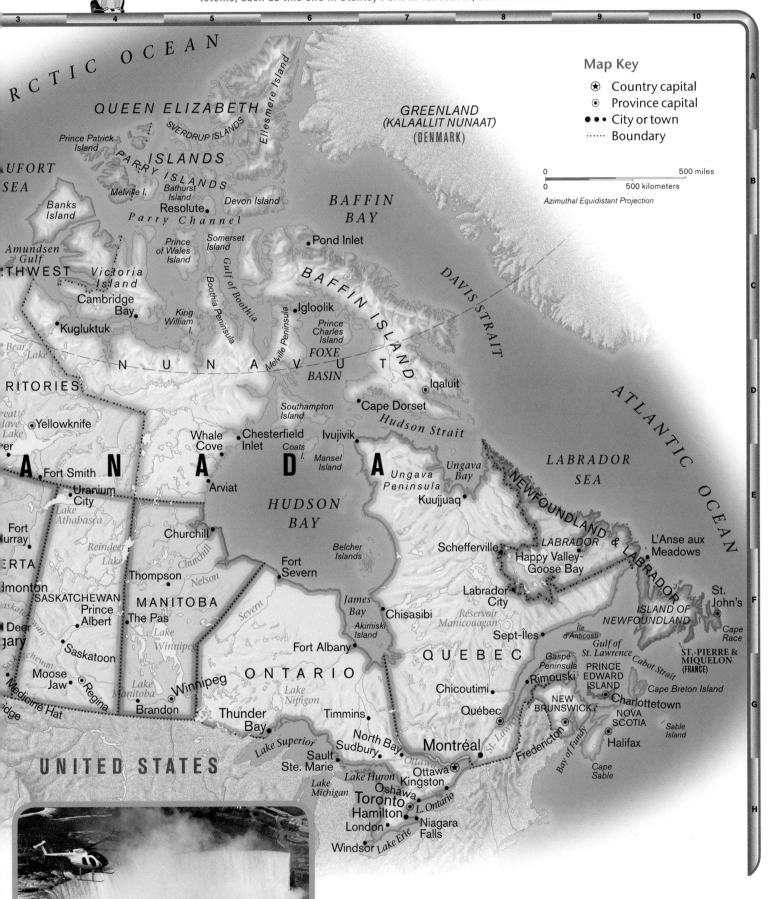

Map Key

⊛ Country capital
◉ Province capital
••• City or town
······ Boundary

0 — 500 miles
0 — 500 kilometers
Azimuthal Equidistant Projection

ARCTIC OCEAN

QUEEN ELIZABETH

Prince Patrick Island

ISLANDS

SVERDRUP ISLANDS

Ellesmere Island

GREENLAND
(KALAALLIT NUNAAT)
(DENMARK)

PARRY ISLANDS

Melville I. *Bathurst Island* *Devon Island*

AUFORT SEA

Banks Island

Resolute

Parry Channel

BAFFIN BAY

•Pond Inlet

Amundsen Gulf

THWEST

Victoria Island

Cambridge Bay

Prince of Wales Island

Somerset Island

Gulf of Boothia

Boothia Peninsula

BAFFIN ISLAND

DAVIS STRAIT

•Kugluktuk

King William I.

Melville Peninsula

•Igloolik

Prince Charles Island

Bear Lake

N   U   N   A   V   U   T

FOXE BASIN

ATLANTIC OCEAN

RITORIES

Southampton Island

•Iqaluit

•Cape Dorset

Hudson Strait

eat ave Lake er

•Yellowknife

Whale Cove

Chesterfield Inlet

Ivujivik•

Coats I.

Mansel Island

LABRADOR SEA

A   N   A   D   A

•Fort Smith

•Arviat

Ungava Peninsula

Ungava Bay

NEWFOUNDLAND & LABRADOR

L'Anse aux Meadows

•Uranium City

HUDSON BAY

•Kuujjuaq

LABRADOR

Lake Athabasca

Fort urray

ERTA

Churchill•

Belcher Islands

•Scheffervile

Happy Valley-Goose Bay

St. John's

monton

Thompson

Churchill

Fort Severn

Nelson

Labrador City

ISLAND OF NEWFOUNDLAND

Deer gary

SASKATCHEWAN

Prince Albert

MANITOBA

The Pas

Reindeer Lake

Severn

James Bay

Chisasibi•

Réservoir Manicouagan

Cape Race

Saskatoon

Lake Winnipeg

Akimiski Island

Sept-Îles•

Île d'Anticosti

Gulf of St. Lawrence

Cabot Strait

ST.-PIERRE & MIQUELON (FRANCE)

Moose Jaw

Regina

Lake Manitoba

Fort Albany•

QUEBEC

Gaspé Peninsula

Cape Breton Island

Medicine Hat

Brandon

Winnipeg•

ONTARIO

Chicoutimi•

Rimouski•

PRINCE EDWARD ISLAND

ridge

Thunder Bay

Lake Nipigon

Timmins•

Québec

NEW BRUNSWICK

Charlottetown•

NOVA SCOTIA

Sable Island

UNITED STATES

Lake Superior

Sudbury•

North Bay

Montréal

St. Lawrence

Fredericton•

Halifax•

Sault Ste. Marie

Lake Huron

Ottawa⊛

Bay of Fundy

Cape Sable

Lake Michigan

Toronto

Oshawa

Kingston•

Hamilton

L. Ontario

London•

Niagara Falls

Windsor•

Lake Erie

◖ **ICE-AGE REMNANT.** The Niagara River, which formed as glaciers of the last ice age began to melt, cascades over Canada's Horseshoe Falls. The falls, which stretch across the border between Canada and the United States, are a major tourist attraction.

THE CONTINENT:
NORTH AMERICA

THE BASICS

STATS

Area
3,794,083 sq mi (9,826,630 sq km)

Population
313,858,000

Predominant languages
English, Spanish

Predominant religion
Christianity (Protestant,
Roman Catholic)

GDP per capita
$48,300

Life expectancy
78 years

Literacy rate
99%

GEO WHIZ

Florida is known as the lightning capital of the United States. Sea breezes from the Gulf of Mexico and the Atlantic Ocean collide over the warm Florida peninsula, producing thunderstorms and the lightning associated with them.

Hawai'i is politically part of the United States but geographically part of the Polynesian cultural region of Oceania.

At 379 feet (115 m), Hyperion, a coast redwood in California's Redwood National Forest, is the world's tallest living tree. It is more than 70 feet (21 m) higher than the Statue of Liberty.

Lake Michigan is the only one of the Great Lakes located entirely within the United States. Each of the other four lakes spans the U.S.-Canada border.

In 2006, 18 whooping crane chicks made a historic migration from Wisconsin to Florida following an ultralight aircraft as part of Operation Migration.

United States

From "sea to shining sea" the United States is blessed with a rich bounty of natural resources. Mineral treasures abound—oil, coal, iron, and gold—and its croplands are among the most productive in the world. Americans have used— and too often overused—this storehouse of raw materials to build an economic base unmatched by any other country. An array of high-tech businesses populate the Sunbelt of the South and West. By combining its natural riches and the creative ideas of its ethnically diverse population, this land of opportunity has become a leading global power.

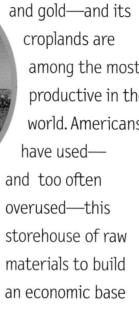

◖ **STAPLE CROP.**
Approximately 80 million acres (32.4 million ha) are planted in corn in the U.S. Most of the crop is used as livestock feed.

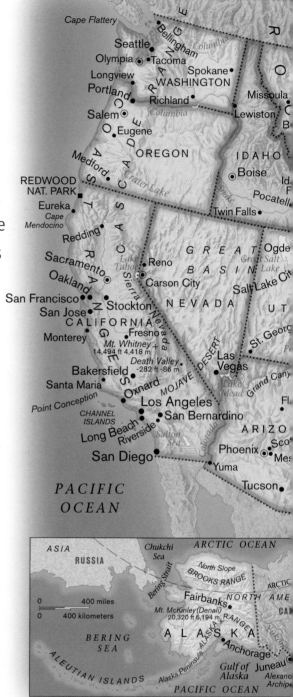

◖ **WORLD CITY.** The lights of Manhattan glitter around New York City's Chrysler Building. The city's influence as a financial and cultural center extends across the United States and around the world.

◖ **LETTING OFF STEAM.** Castle Geyser is just one of many active geological features in Yellowstone National Park in Wyoming. The park is part of a region that sits on top of a major tectonic hot spot.

⚫ **LADY LIBERTY.** The Statue of Liberty, a gift from France, stands in New York City's harbor. The statue has become a symbol of hope for millions of immigrants coming to the United States in search of a better life.

C A N A D A

Lake of the Woods

Isle Royale

Lake Superior

MINNESOTA

Minot
Grand Forks
International Falls
Moorhead
NORTH DAKOTA
Bismarck ⊙
Fargo
Duluth
Marquette
Superior
Green Bay

Billings

ONTANA
an

Aberdeen
SOUTH DAKOTA
St. Cloud
St. Paul
Minneapolis
Mankato
Rochester
WISCONSIN
Milwaukee
Madison
Kenosha

M I C H I G A N

Lake Huron

Lake Michigan

Grand Rapids
Flint
Lansing
Detroit

Niagara Falls

Lake Ontario

Montpelier
Burlington
Lake Champlain
N.H.
NEW YORK
Albany
Rochester
Buffalo

M A I N E
Bangor
Augusta
Portland
Concord
Manchester
Boston
MASS.
Providence
RHODE ISLAND
CONN. Hartford

LOWSTONE
IONAL PARK

YOMING
Casper

Pierre
Rapid City
Sioux Falls
Fort Dodge
Cedar Rapids
Dubuque
I O W A
Sioux City
Des Moines
Davenport
Rockford
Aurora
Chicago
Gary
Fort Wayne
Toledo
Cleveland
Erie
PENNSYLVANIA
Harrisburg

Pittsburgh
Philadelphia
Trenton
Newark
New York
Long Island
NEW JERSEY

Cheyenne
Laramie

NEBRASKA
Grand Island
Omaha
Lincoln
Peoria
ILLINOIS
Springfield
INDIANA
Indianapolis
Dayton
Cincinnati
Columbus
OHIO
Baltimore
Annapolis
MD.
DELAWARE
Dover
Washington, D.C.

Boulder
Fort Collins
Denver
Mt. Elbert
+14,433 ft
4,399 m
Colorado Springs
rand
nction
C
OLORADO
Pueblo

Manhattan
KANSAS
Topeka
Dodge City
Hutchinson
Wichita

Kansas City
MISSOURI
Jefferson City
St. Louis
Springfield
Cape Girardeau
Evansville
Paducah
Louisville
Frankfort
Lexington
KENTUCKY
WEST VIRGINIA
Charleston
Charlottesville
Richmond
VIRGINIA
Norfolk
Virginia Beach
Chesapeake Bay

MESA VERDE
ATIONAL PARK
nta Fe ⊙

Albuquerque
Clovis
MEXICO
Roswell

Carlsbad
El Paso

Enid
OKLAHOMA
Lawton
Oklahoma City
Tulsa
Fayetteville
Fort Smith
ARKANSAS
Little Rock
Hot Springs
Pine Bluff
Memphis
Huntsville
Chattanooga
Knoxville
Nashville
TENNESSEE
Mt. Mitchell
+6,684 ft
2,037 m
NORTH CAROLINA
Greensboro
Raleigh
Charlotte
Charleston
SOUTH CAROLINA
Columbia
Cape Hatteras

Amarillo
Lubbock
Wichita Falls
Fort Worth
Abilene
Dallas
Texarkana
Tyler
Shreveport
Natchez
Jackson
MISSISSIPPI
Birmingham
ALABAMA
Columbus
Montgomery
GEORGIA
Atlanta
Macon
Savannah
Charleston

TEXAS
San Angelo
Waco
Austin ⊙
San Antonio
Houston
Beaumont
Lufkin
LOUISIANA
Lafayette
Baton Rouge
New Orleans
Port Arthur
Galveston
Biloxi
Mobile
Mobile Bay
Mississippi River Delta
Jacksonville
Tallahassee
FLORIDA
Orlando
Cape Canaveral
Tampa
St. Petersburg
Lake Okeechobee
Miami
THE EVERGLADES

Corpus Christi
Laredo
Brownsville

G U L F   O F   M E X I C O

Florida Keys
Straits of Florida

B A H A M A S

A T L A N T I C   O C E A N

H A W A I ' I
Honolulu
O'ahu
Moloka'i
Maui
Lāna'i
Kaho'olawe
Hilo
Hawai'i
iian Islands
150 mi
150 km
PACIFIC OCEAN

For location of Alaska and Hawai'i, see map page 32.

Map Key

⊛ Country capital
⊙ State capital
••• City or town
······ Boundary

0 —————— 200 miles
0 —————— 200 kilometers

Albers Conic Equal-Area Projection

NATION OF IMMIGRANTS

Figures represent the number of immigrants obtaining legal permanent resident status in 2011

Mexico 143,446
China 87,016
India 69,013
Philippines 57,011
Dominican Republic 46,109
Cuba 36,452

From its founding, the United States has attracted people from other lands. Today, most immigrants come from Latin America and Asia.

THE CONTINENT:
NORTH AMERICA

THE BASICS

STATS

Largest country
Mexico
758,449 sq mi (1,964,375 sq km)

Smallest country
El Salvador
8,124 sq mi (21,041 sq km)

Most populous country
Mexico
116,100,000

Least populous country
Belize
326,000

Predominant languages
English, Spanish, Mayan, various
Amerindian languages

Predominant religion
Christianity (Roman Catholic, Protestant)

Highest GDP per capita
Mexico
$14,700

Lowest GDP per capita
Nicaragua
$3,200

Highest life expectancy
Costa Rica, Panama
78 years

Highest literacy rate
Costa Rica
95%

GEO WHIZ

Mexico takes its name from the word
Mexica, another name for the Aztec, the
last of the indigenous cultures to rule
Mexico before it fell to Spanish conquer-
ors in 1521.

Scientists believe that the crater of the
comet that struck Earth 65 million years
ago, causing the dramatic climate changes
that led to the extinction of the dinosaurs,
is at Chicxulub, on the Yucatán Peninsula.

Coral colonies growing along much of
the coast of Belize form the longest barrier reef in the Western Hemisphere and
the second longest in the world, after
Australia's Great Barrier Reef.

Vampire bats, which are only about the size
of an adult person's thumb, drink the blood
of other animals to survive. They are found
throughout Central America.

A new set of locks on the Panama Canal
will allow ships with 2.5 times the cargo
capacity of ships now traveling the canal
to take this shortcut between the Atlantic
and Pacific Oceans.

◗ **CELEBRATION.**
Traditional costumes
and musical instruments
combine with Christian
beliefs during the annual
Virgin of Guadalupe festival, observed throughout
Mexico. The festival marks
the appearance of the Virgin
Mary to a peasant in 1531.

Mexico & Central America

⬢ **VITAL LINK.** As many as 14,000
vessels, 5 percent of global trade,
use the Panama Canal each year
to pass between the Atlantic and
Pacific Oceans.

Mexico and most
Central American coun-
tries share a backbone
of mountains, a legacy
of powerful Native
American empires, and a
largely Spanish colonial
history. Once-abundant
rain forests now are largely
gone. Mexico dwarfs its seven
Central American neighbors
in area, population, and natural resources. Its economy boasts
a rich diversity of agricultural crops, highly productive oil fields,
a growing manufacturing base, as well as strong trade with the
United States and Canada. Overall, Central American countries rely
on agricultural products such as bananas and coffee, though tourism
is increasing. Modern-day Mexico and Central America struggle to fulfill the
hopes of growing populations, some of whom search for better lives by migrating—both legally and illegally—north to the United States.

Tijuana
Ensenada
Mexicali
Nogale
Herm
Guaymas
Ciuc
Obreg
Los Mo
La Paz
False Cape

BAJA CALIFORNIA
Gulf of California

◗ **MYTHS AND LEGENDS.** The powerful Aztec Empire dominated much of Mexico and Central America from 1427 to 1521. The Aztecs worshipped many gods, including Tlaloc (shown here), the god of rain and fertility.

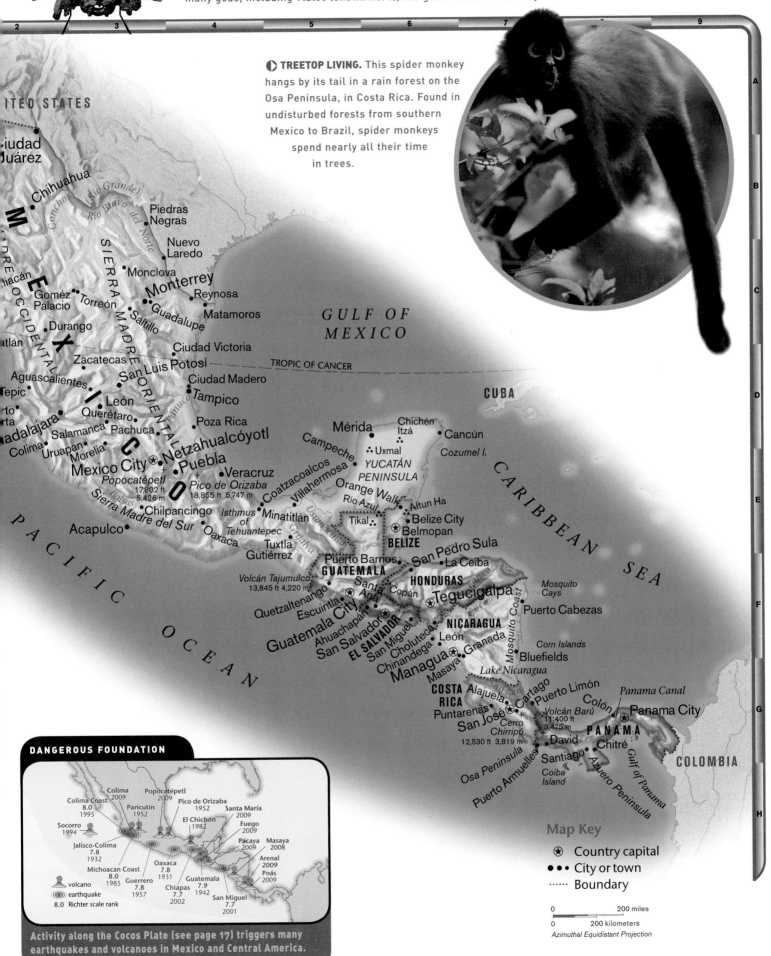

◗ **TREETOP LIVING.** This spider monkey hangs by its tail in a rain forest on the Osa Peninsula, in Costa Rica. Found in undisturbed forests from southern Mexico to Brazil, spider monkeys spend nearly all their time in trees.

2   3   4   5   6   7   8   9

A
B
C
D
E
F
G
H

UNITED STATES

Ciudad Juárez
Chihuahua
(Rio Grande)
Conchos
Río Bravo del Norte
Piedras Negras
Nuevo Laredo
Monclova
Monterrey
Reynosa
Gomez Palacio
Torreón
Guadalupe
Matamoros
Saltillo
Durango
Culiacán
Mazatlán
SIERRA MADRE OCCIDENTAL
MEXICO
SIERRA MADRE ORIENTAL
Ciudad Victoria
Zacatecas
San Luis Potosí
Ciudad Madero
TROPIC OF CANCER
Tampico
Aguascalientes
Tepic
Puerto Vallarta
León
Querétaro
Poza Rica
Guadalajara
Salamanca
Pachuca
Pánuco
Colima
Uruapan
Morelia
Mexico City
Netzahualcóyotl
Puebla
Popocatépetl
17,802 ft
5,426 m
Veracruz
Pico de Orizaba
18,855 ft 5,747 m
Coatzacoalcos
Villahermosa
Balsas
Sierra Madre del Sur
Chilpancingo
Isthmus of Tehuantepec
Minatitlán
Acapulco
Oaxaca
Tuxtla Gutiérrez
Usumacinta
Grijalva

GULF OF MEXICO

CUBA

Mérida
Chichén Itzá
Cancún
Campeche
Uxmal
YUCATÁN PENINSULA
Cozumel I.
Orange Walk
Río Azul
Altun Ha
Tikal
Belize City
Belmopan
BELIZE
San Pedro Sula
Puerto Barrios
La Ceiba
GUATEMALA
Volcán Tajumulco
13,845 ft 4,220 m
Santa Ana
Copán
HONDURAS
Tegucigalpa
Mosquito Cays
Quetzaltenango
Escuintla
Guatemala City
Puerto Cabezas
Ahuachapán
San Miguel
NICARAGUA
Mosquito Coast
San Salvador
Choluteca
León
EL SALVADOR
Chinandega
Masaya
Granada
Corn Islands
Managua
Bluefields
Masaya
Lake Nicaragua
COSTA RICA
Alajuela
Cartago
Puerto Limón
Colón
Panama Canal
Puntarenas
San José
Volcán Barú
11,400 ft
3,475 m
Panama City
Cerro Chirripó
12,530 ft 3,819 m
David
PANAMA
Chitré
Osa Peninsula
Santiago
Coiba Island
Azuero Peninsula
Gulf of Panama
Puerto Armuelles

CARIBBEAN SEA

COLOMBIA

PACIFIC OCEAN

Map Key
⊛ Country capital
•●• City or town
······ Boundary

0   200 miles
0   200 kilometers
Azimuthal Equidistant Projection

DANGEROUS FOUNDATION

Colima 2009
Popocatépetl 2009
Colima Coast 8.0 1995
Paricutín 1952
Pico de Orizaba 1952
Santa María 2009
Socorro 1994
El Chichón 1982
Fuego 2009
Jalisco-Colima 7.8 1932
Pacaya 2009
Masaya 2008
Michoacan Coast 8.0 1985
Oaxaca 7.8 1931
Arenal 2009
Guerrero 7.8 1957
Guatemala 7.9 1942
Poás 2009
Chiapas 7.7 2002
🌋 volcano
San Miguel 7.7 2001
◉ earthquake
8.0 Richter scale rank

Activity along the Cocos Plate (see page 17) triggers many earthquakes and volcanoes in Mexico and Central America. The strongest in the last 100 years are shown here.

THE CONTINENT:
NORTH AMERICA

West Indies & the Bahamas

THE BASICS

STATS

Largest country
Cuba
42,803 sq mi (110,860 sq km)

Smallest country
St. Kitts and Nevis
104 sq mi (269 sq km)

Most populous country
Cuba
11,200,000

Least populous country
St. Kitts and Nevis
54,000

Predominant languages
Spanish, English, French, French patois

Predominant religion
Christian (Roman Catholic, Protestant, and others)

Highest GDP per capita
Bahamas
$30,400

Lowest GDP per capita
Haiti
$1,200

Highest life expectancy
Cuba
78 years

Highest literacy rate
Cuba, Barbados
100%

GEO WHIZ

Voodoo, a religion that combines elements of West African spiritualism and the worship of Roman Catholic saints, is common in Haiti, the Dominican Republic, Cuba, Jamaica, and the Bahamas.

On the seafloor just off San Salvador, in the Bahamas, there is a bronze monument marking the site where Christopher Columbus is believed to have anchored his ship in 1492.

Pico Duarte (10,417 ft/3,175 m), on the island of Hispaniola, is the highest peak in the Caribbean.

Boiling Lake, in Morne Trois Pitons National Park on Dominica, is one of the world's largest thermal lakes.

Grenada, which is nicknamed the Spice Island, is one of the world's chief sources of nutmeg, mace, and other spices.

RHYTHM OF THE TROPICS. When traditional drums were banned in Trinidad in 1884, plantation workers looked for new instruments, including 55-gallon (208-L) oil drums, which were the origin of today's steel drums or "pans."

This region of tropical islands stretches from the Bahamas, off the eastern coast of Florida, to Trinidad and Tobago, off the northern coast of South America. The Greater Antilles—Cuba, Jamaica, Hispaniola, and U.S. territory Puerto Rico—account for nearly 90 percent of the region's land area and most of its 42 million people. A necklace of smaller islands called the Lesser Antilles plus the Bahamas make up most of the rest of this region. Lush vegetation, warm waters, and scenic beaches attract tourists from across the globe. While these visitors bring much needed income, most people in this region remain poor.

WHITE GOLD. Sugarcane is an important economic resource throughout the Caribbean. This woman carries freshly cut cane on her head in a field in Barbados.

FUN IN THE SUN

Figures represent tourist arrivals, 2011

Dominican Republic	Cuba	Jamaica	Bahamas	Aruba	Barbados	U.S. Virgin Islands	Martinique	St. Maarten	Curaçao
4,306,000*	2,688,000	1,952,000	1,344,000	871,000	568,000	536,000	495,000	424,000	390,000

These island countries are the region's most popular destinations for tourists seeking sandy beaches, blue waters, and warm breezes.

◗ **RARE BIRD.** The red-necked Amazon, or Jaco, parrot is found only on the Caribbean island of Dominica, where it lives on flowers, seeds, and fruits native to the island's forests. A Jaco pair typically raises two chicks each year.

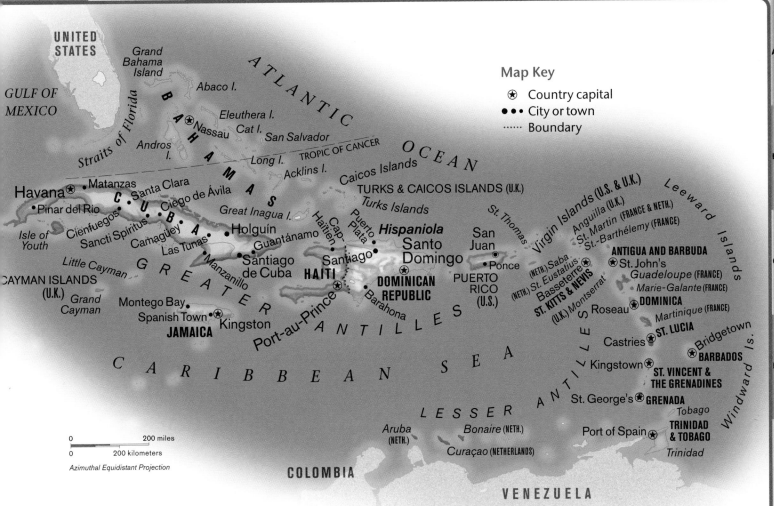

1 2 3 4 5 6 7 8

UNITED STATES

GULF OF MEXICO

Grand Bahama Island

Abaco I.

ATLANTIC

Eleuthera I.

Nassau
Cat I.
San Salvador

Straits of Florida

Andros I.

Long I. TROPIC OF CANCER

OCEAN

Acklins I.

Caicos Islands

Havana
Matanzas
Santa Clara
Pinar del Río
Ciego de Ávila
Cienfuegos
Sancti Spíritus
Camagüey
Isle of Youth
Las Tunas
Holguín
Guantánamo

C U B A

Great Inagua I.

TURKS & CAICOS ISLANDS (U.K.)
Turks Islands

St. Thomas

Virgin Islands (U.S. & U.K.)
Anguilla (U.K.)
St. Martin (FRANCE & NETH.)
St.-Barthélemy (FRANCE)

Leeward Islands

Little Cayman

CAYMAN ISLANDS (U.K.)
Grand Cayman

G R E A T E R

Manzanillo

Santiago de Cuba

Cap-Haïtien

Puerto Plata

Santiago

Hispaniola
Santo Domingo

San Juan
Ponce

PUERTO RICO (U.S.)

(NETH.) Saba
(NETH.) St. Eustatius
Basseterre
ST. KITTS & NEVIS
(U.K.) Montserrat

ANTIGUA AND BARBUDA
St. John's
Guadeloupe (FRANCE)
Marie-Galante (FRANCE)

Roseau
DOMINICA
Martinique (FRANCE)

Montego Bay
Spanish Town
Kingston

JAMAICA

Port-au-Prince

HAITI

DOMINICAN REPUBLIC

Barahona

A N T I L L E S

L E S S E R

Castries
ST. LUCIA

Bridgetown
BARBADOS

A N T I L L E S

Windward Is.

C A R I B B E A N   S E A

Kingstown
ST. VINCENT & THE GRENADINES

St. George's
GRENADA

Tobago

Aruba (NETH.)

Bonaire (NETH.)

Curaçao (NETHERLANDS)

Port of Spain
TRINIDAD & TOBAGO
Trinidad

Port of Spain

COLOMBIA

VENEZUELA

Map Key
⊛ Country capital
••• City or town
······ Boundary

0 200 miles
0 200 kilometers
Azimuthal Equidistant Projection

A

B

C

D

E

◗ **WATER WORLD.** The clear waters of the Caribbean allow face-to-face interaction with sea life, such as this green sea turtle. Adult sea turtles can remain underwater for two hours without breathing.

◗ **CELEBRATION.** Stilt walkers in brightly colored costumes tower above this street in Old Havana, Cuba, during the annual celebration of Carnival. Introduced by Catholic colonizers from Spain, this festival occurs prior to the beginning of the religious season of Lent.

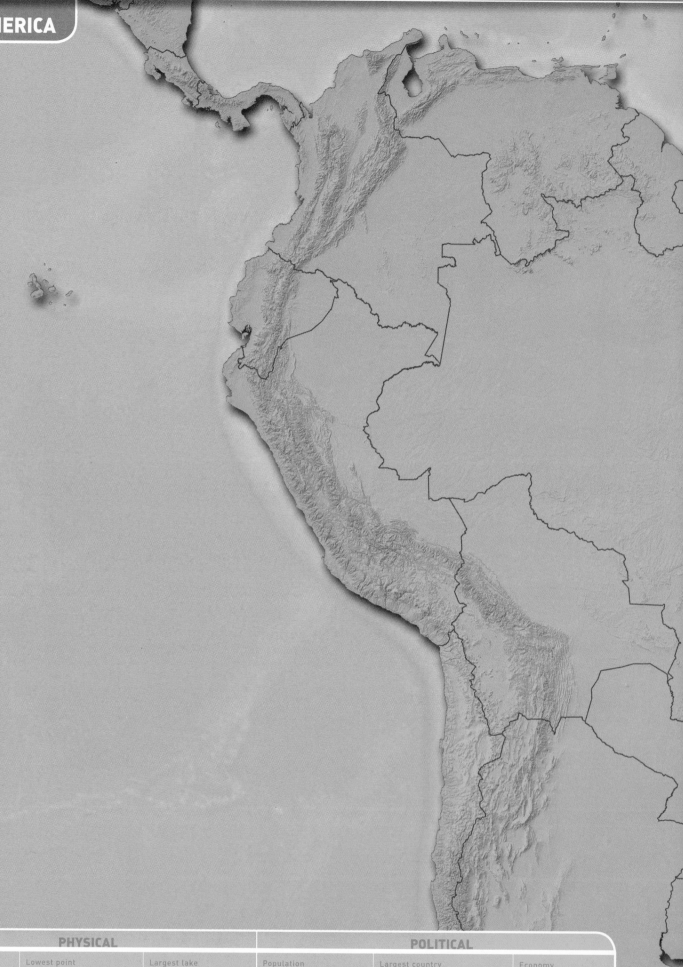

PHYSICAL			POLITICAL		
Land area **6,880,000 sq mi (17,819,000 sq km)**	Lowest point **Laguna del Carbón, Argentina -344 ft (-105 m)**	Largest lake **Lake Titicaca, Bolivia-Peru 3,200 sq mi (8,290 sq km)**	Population **396,938,000** Largest metropolitan area **São Paulo, Brazil: Pop. 19,960,000**	Largest country **Brazil** **3,300,169 sq mi (8,547,403 sq km)** Most densely populated country **Ecuador** **137 people per sq mi (52 per sq km)**	Economy **Farming: cattle, coffee, fruit** **Industry: mining, oil, manufacturing** **Services**
Highest point **Cerro Aconcagua, Argentina 22,831 ft (6,959 m)**	Longest river **Amazon 4,000 mi (6,437 km)**				

South America

South America

2　3　4　5　6　7　8

CARIBBEAN SEA

NORTH
AMERICA

Lake
Maracaibo

Orinoco

VENEZUELA

Angel Falls
Total drop
3,212 ft 979 m

GUYANA

GUIANA HIGHLANDS

SURINAME

FRENCH
GUIANA
(FRANCE)

COLOMBIA

Malpelo
Island

L
L
A
N
O
S

Galápagos
Islands

ECUADOR

Negro

Amazon

Marajó
Island

EQUATOR

A　M　A　Z　O　N

Marañón

Amazon

Madeira

Tapajós

Xingu

São Francisco

Ucayali

Purus

Teles Pires

Tocantins

S　e　l　v　a　s

B　A　S　I　N

P
E
R
U

B　R　A　Z　I　L

BRAZILIAN

HIGHLANDS

Lake
Titicaca

BOLIVIA

Altiplano

Pantanal

Paraguay

Salar de Uyuni

PARAGUAY

Iguazú
Falls

PACIFIC
OCEAN

TROPIC OF CAPRICORN

Atacama Desert

Gran Chaco

Paraná

ATLANTIC OCEAN

San Félix Island

San Ambrosio Island

Uruguay

A
N
D
E
S

Juan Fernández Islands

Cerro
Aconcagua
22,831 ft
6,959 m
Highest point in
South America

URUGUAY

River Plate

A
R
G
E
N
T
I
N
A

P
A
M
P
A
S

Negro

Valdés Peninsula

Map Key

— Country boundary

Isla Grande
de Chiloé

C
H
I
L
E

Taitao
Peninsula

Gulf of
San Jorge

Lowest point in
South America

Laguna del Carbón
-344 ft -105 m

0 ——— 600 miles
0 ——— 900 kilometers
Azimuthal Equidistant Projection

Wellington Island

P
A
T
A
G
O
N
I
A

FALKLAND ISLANDS
(ISLAS MALVINAS)

Strait of Magellan

TIERRA DEL FUEGO

Cape Horn

South Georgia

1 2 3 4 5 6 7 8

CARIBBEAN SEA

NORTH AMERICA

A

Santa Marta
Barranquilla
Cartagena
Maracaibo
Lake Maracaibo
Barquisimeto
Valencia
Maracay
Caracas
Ciudad Guayana
Cúcuta
Bucaramanga
San Cristóbal
Medellín
VENEZUELA
Georgetown
GUYANA
Paramaribo
SURINAME
Cayenne
FRENCH GUIANA
(FRANCE)
Angel Falls
GUIANA HIGHLANDS
Manizales
Ibagué
COLOMBIA
Bogotá
Cali
Boa Vista
Amapá
Malpelo Island
(COLOMBIA)
B
Boundary claimed by Suriname
EQUATOR
Esmeraldas
Pasto
Negro
Amazon
Marajó Island
Belém
Quito
ECUADOR
Guayaquil
Cuenca
Iquitos
Manaus
Santarém
São Luís
Parnaíba
Galápagos Islands
(ECUADOR)
Amazon (Solimões)
Madeira
Tapajós
Fortaleza
C
Marañón
Selvas
Purus
Xingu
Marabá
Teresina
Piura
Chiclayo
Trujillo
Chimbote
BASIN
Rio Branco
Porto Velho
Teles Pires
Natal
João Pessoa
Campina Grande
Recife
Ucayali
PERU
BRAZIL
Tocantins
Maceió
Aracaju
PACIFIC OCEAN
Callao
Lima
Machu Picchu
Ayacucho
Cusco
Titicaca
Trinidad
BRAZILIAN
Feira de Santana
Salvador
(Bahia)
Ilhéus
São Francisco
D
Arequipa
La Paz
BOLIVIA
Santa Cruz
Cochabamba
Oruro
Sucre
Goiânia
Brasília
HIGHLANDS
Arica
Altiplano
Pantanal
Campo Grande
Uberlândia
Uberaba
Governador Valadares
Belo Horizonte
Iquique
Salar de Uyuni
Tarija
PARAGUAY
Paraguay
São José do Rio Preto
Ribeirão Preto
Nova Iguaçu
E
TROPIC OF CAPRICORN
Antofagasta
Salta
Gran Chaco
Asunción
Iguazú Falls
Londrina
Campinas
São Paulo
Santos
Rio de Janeiro
San Miguel de Tucumán
Resistencia
Corrientes
Curitiba
San Félix Island
(CHILE)
San Ambrosio Island
Paraná
Passo Fundo
Florianópolis
F
La Serena
Córdoba
Santa Fe
Uruguaiana
Santa Maria
Porto Alegre
Cerro Aconcagua
22,831 ft
6,959 m
Rosario
URUGUAY
Valparaíso
Santiago
Mendoza
PAMPAS
Buenos Aires
La Plata
Montevideo
River Plate
Juan Fernández Islands
(CHILE)
Talca
ARGENTINA
G
Concepción
Mar del Plata
Temuco
Negro
Bahía Blanca
Puerto Montt
Viedma
Valdés Peninsula
CHILE
H
Isla Grande de Chiloé
Comodoro Rivadavia
Gulf of San Jorge
Taitao Peninsula
PATAGONIA
0   600 miles
0   900 kilometers
Azimuthal Equidistant Projection
Wellington I.
Laguna del Carbón
-344 ft -105 m
Stanley
FALKLAND ISLANDS (ISLAS MALVINAS)
(UNITED KINGDOM)
Rio Gallegos
I
Strait of Magellan
Punta Arenas
TIERRA DEL FUEGO
Ushuaia
Cape Horn
South Georgia
(U.K.)

ATLANTIC OCEAN

South America

A MIX OF OLD AND NEW

South America stretches from the warm waters of the Caribbean to the frigid ocean around Antarctica. Draining a third of the continent, the mighty Amazon carries more water than the world's next ten biggest rivers combined. Its basin contains the planet's largest rain forest. The Andes tower along the continent's western edge from Colombia to southern Chile. The Amerindian peoples who lived in the Andes were no match for the gold-seeking Spanish who arrived in 1532. The Spanish, along with the Portuguese, ruled most of the continent for almost 300 years. Centuries of ethnic blending have woven Amerindian, European, African, and Asian heritage into South America's rich cultural fabric.

SILENT STALKER. The jaguar is the largest member of the cat family native to the Americas. The largest populations of this at-risk species are found in the southern Amazon basin.

ROYAL CITY. Built by an Inca ruler between 1460 and 1470, Machu Picchu reveals the Inca's skill as stone masons. Massive blocks of granite were carved so carefully that all seams fit tightly without the use of mortar.

⬤ **SOUTHERN METROPOLIS.** A 1,300-foot (396-m)-high block of granite called Sugar Loaf dominates the harbor of Brazil's second largest city, Rio de Janeiro. Rio was Brazil's capital until 1960 and remains the country's most popular tourist destination.

◖ **NATURAL HERITAGE.** Extending 2.5 miles (4 km) along the border between Brazil and Argentina, Iguazú Falls, which means "great water" in the local Guarani language, is clouded in mist as the water drops 296 feet (90 m) into the Iguazú River.

◖ **MOUNTAIN BUDDIES.** An Aymara woman, with her llama, follows a traditional mountain lifestyle in the Andes of Peru.

more about
South America

⬤ **GLEAMING SANDS.** The white sands of Rio de Janeiro's 2.5-mile (4-km)-long Copacabana and Leme Beaches are among the most famous in the world, attracting tourists year-round. The beaches, which are now lined with upscale hotels that overlook Guanabara Bay, were once the site of thriving fishing villages.

⬤ **ICY COLD.** Rising to an elevation of almost 11,000 feet (3,353 m), Mount Fitz Roy in southern Argentina's Patagonia region presents major challenges to adventurous climbers who must contend with strong winds and bitter cold.

◗ **QUIET VIGIL.** A young Pinare Indian sits beside a rushing stream in Venezuela, holding his traditional spear ready to catch a fish. Many groups of native people live in relative isolation from the modern world.

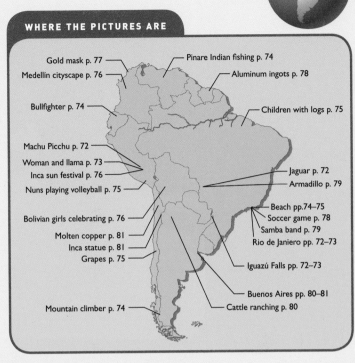

WHERE THE PICTURES ARE

Gold mask p. 77
Medellín cityscape p. 76
Bullfighter p. 74
Machu Picchu p. 72
Woman and llama p. 73
Inca sun festival p. 76
Nuns playing volleyball p. 75
Bolivian girls celebrating p. 76
Molten copper p. 81
Inca statue p. 81
Grapes p. 75
Mountain climber p. 74

Pinare Indian fishing p. 74
Aluminum ingots p. 78
Children with logs p. 75
Jaguar p. 72
Armadillo p. 79
Beach pp. 74–75
Soccer game p. 78
Samba band p. 79
Rio de Janiero pp. 72–73
Iguazú Falls pp. 72–73
Buenos Aires pp. 80–81
Cattle ranching p. 80

⬤ **JUICY HARVEST.** Grapes hang in heavy clusters ready for picking in a vineyard near Santiago, Chile. Second only to Italy, Chile produces almost one-quarter of the world's supply of fresh grapes. Grapes are Chile's leading fresh-fruit export.

⬤ **BREAK TIME.** Colonization of South America by Spain and Portugal in the 16th century brought a new religion—Roman Catholicism—to the region. Here, Catholic nuns in Arequipa, Peru, take a break from prayers to engage in a game of volleyball.

⬤ **ENVIRONMENTAL TRAGEDY.** These giants of the rain forest dwarf two children in the Amazon village of Paragominas in Brazil. Harvesting such trees provides income for villagers but poses a serious long-term threat to the environment.

◑ **EL TORRO!** Introduced to South America during the Spanish colonization, bullfighting is a popular sport and the focus of many festivals. Here, in Cayambe, Ecuador, a matador flashes his red cape before the bull.

THE BASICS

STATS

Largest country
Peru
496,224 sq mi (1,285,216 sq km)

Smallest country
Ecuador
109,483 sq mi (283,560 sq km)

Most populous country
Colombia
47,415,000

Least populous country
Bolivia
10,836,000

Predominant languages
Spanish, Amerindian languages
and dialects, English

Predominant religion
Christianity (Roman Catholic)

Highest GDP per capita
Venezuela
$12,600

Lowest GDP per capita
Bolivia
$4,800

Highest life expectancy
Ecuador
76 years

Highest literacy rate
Peru, Venezuela
93%

GEO WHIZ

On the llanos of Venezuela, capybaras, the world's largest rodents, are stalked and killed by anacondas, snakes weighing as much as 550 pounds (250 kg).

Some of the world's finest emeralds come from Colombia. Emeralds were sacred stones to the Inca, and some of the mines that ancient people worked are still a source of quality gemstones.

The world's only marine iguanas are among the unique animal species that live on the Galápagos, a volcanic chain of islands in the Pacific that belongs to Ecuador.

Bolivia's Madidi National Park is home to more plant and animal species than any other preserve in South America.

Northwestern South America

Like a huge letter "C," five countries crest the continent's northwest—Venezuela, Colombia, Ecuador, Peru, and Bolivia. Each has a seacoast, except for

⚲ **HAIL THE SUN.** The ancient Inca celebrated the new year in June with the festival of Inti Raymi. The tradition continues today in Cusco, Peru, with the Festival of the Sun, when the celestial body is honored through music and dance.

landlocked Bolivia. Dominated by the volcano-studded Andes range, the region contains huge rain forests in the upper Amazon and Orinoco River basins. Colombia and Venezuela share an extensive tropical grassland called Los Llanos. Though Spanish conquistador Pizarro defeated the Inca in the 16th century, Quechua, the Inca language, is still spoken by millions of Amerindians living in the altiplanos—high plateaus of

the Andes. Rich oil resources are centered around Lake Maracaibo, in Venezuela. Many people in the region are poor, and drug wars have caused political instability, but recent democratic successes offer some hope for the future.

⚲ **FOLKLORE CENTER.** Founded as a mining town, Oruro, Bolivia, is a UNESCO cultural heritage site. Each November a weeklong festival celebrates traditional Andean culture with ancient dances, music, and rituals.

⚲ **OLD MEETS NEW.** Against a backdrop of skyscrapers, a modern urban train speeds past the old government palace in Medellín, Colombia. Known as a center of illegal drug trafficking, the city has worked hard to change its image, introducing economic and social changes that have improved safety.

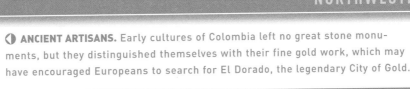

◀ ANCIENT ARTISANS. Early cultures of Colombia left no great stone monuments, but they distinguished themselves with their fine gold work, which may have encouraged Europeans to search for El Dorado, the legendary City of Gold.

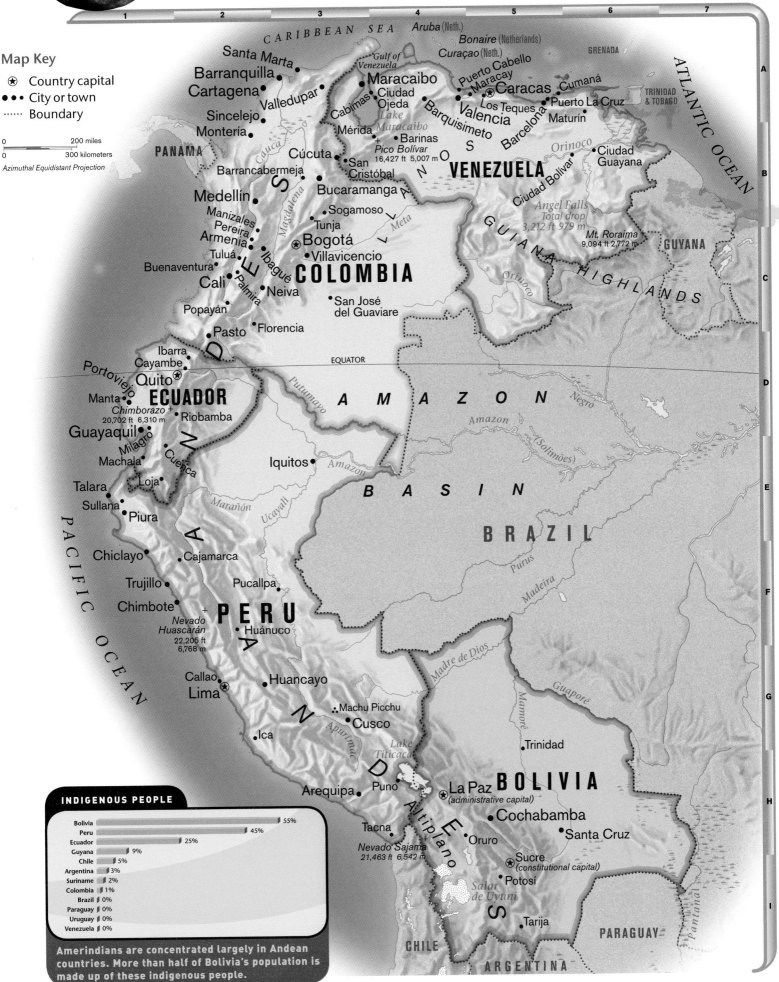

Map Key

⊛ Country capital
••• City or town
····· Boundary

0 — 200 miles
0 — 300 kilometers
Azimuthal Equidistant Projection

INDIGENOUS PEOPLE

Bolivia	55%
Peru	45%
Ecuador	25%
Guyana	9%
Chile	5%
Argentina	3%
Suriname	2%
Colombia	1%
Brazil	0%
Paraguay	0%
Uruguay	0%
Venezuela	0%

Amerindians are concentrated largely in Andean countries. More than half of Bolivia's population is made up of these indigenous people.

CARIBBEAN SEA

Aruba (Neth.)
Bonaire (Netherlands)
Curaçao (Neth.)
GRENADA
TRINIDAD & TOBAGO

Santa Marta
Barranquilla
Cartagena
Valledupar
Sincelejo
Montería
Gulf of Venezuela
Maracaibo
Ciudad Ojeda
Cabimas
Lake Maracaibo
Mérida
Puerto Cabello
Maracay
Caracas
Cumaná
Los Teques
Puerto La Cruz
Valencia
Barcelona
Maturín
Barquisimeto
Barinas

PANAMA
Cúcuta
Barrancabermeja
San Cristóbal
Pico Bolívar 16,427 ft 5,007 m
VENEZUELA

Medellín
Manizales
Pereira
Armenia
Tuluá
Ibagué
Buenaventura
Cali
Palmira
Popayán
Pasto
Neiva
Bucaramanga
Sogamoso
Tunja
⊛ Bogotá
Villavicencio
COLOMBIA
San José del Guaviare
Florencia

Magdalena
Cauca
Meta
Orinoco
Ciudad Guayana
Ciudad Bolívar
Angel Falls Total drop 3,212 ft 979 m
Mt. Roraima 9,094 ft 2,772 m
GUYANA
GUIANA HIGHLANDS

ATLANTIC OCEAN

Ibarra
Cayambe
Portoviejo
Quito ⊛
Manta
ECUADOR
Chimborazo 20,702 ft 6,310 m
Riobamba
Guayaquil
Milagro
Machala
Cuenca
Loja
Talara
Sullana
Piura

EQUATOR
Putumayo
A M A Z O N
Amazon
Negro
(Solimões)
B A S I N
BRAZIL

Iquitos
Amazon
Marañón
Ucayali

Chiclayo
Cajamarca
Trujillo
Chimbote
Nevado Huascarán 22,205 ft 6,768 m
PERU
Pucallpa
Huánuco

Purus
Madeira
Madre de Dios

Callao
Lima ⊛
Huancayo
Machu Picchu
Cusco
Ica
Lake Titicaca
Trinidad
Mamoré
Guaporé

Arequipa
Puno
La Paz ⊛ *(administrative capital)*
BOLIVIA
Cochabamba
Santa Cruz
Tacna
Oruro
Nevado Sajama 21,463 ft 6,542 m
Altiplano
Sucre ⊛ *(constitutional capital)*
Potosí
Salar de Uyuni
Tarija

A N D E S

PACIFIC OCEAN

CHILE
ARGENTINA
PARAGUAY
Pantanal

1 2 3 4 5 6 7
A B C D E F G H I

THE CONTINENT:
SOUTH AMERICA

THE BASICS

STATS

Largest country
Brazil
3,300,169 sq mi (8,547,403 sq km)

Smallest country
Suriname
63,037 sq mi (163,265 sq km)

Most populous country
Brazil
194,334,000

Least populous country
Suriname
542,000

Predominant languages
Portuguese, English, Dutch, Hindi

Predominant religions
Christianity (Roman Catholic, Protestant),
Hindu, Islam

Highest GDP per capita
Brazil, Suriname
$11,800

Lowest GDP per capita
Guyana
$7,600

Highest life expectancy
Brazil
73 years

Highest literacy rate
Guyana
92%

GEO WHIZ

Guyana has as many as 300 species of catfish, roughly a quarter of the total number
living in South America. Locals hunt them
and other fish for the international aquar-
ium trade by probing hollow tree trunks
submerged on river bottoms.

Paramaribo, Suriname's capital, is a melting pot of Dutch, Chinese, Hindu, East
Indian, and Javanese cultures. Dutch is the
only official language.

Brazil covers almost half of South
America's land area. It is the world's largest Portuguese-speaking country and the
largest Catholic country.

The Pantanal, the world's largest freshwater wetland, is almost ten times the size
of the Florida Everglades. It is formed by
the seasonal flooding of several rivers in
southwestern Brazil.

Northeastern South America

🔊 **GOAL!** Maracanã Stadium in Rio de Janeiro is packed
with enthusiastic soccer fans. Brazil has a long history of
producing world-class soccer players and strong teams—
winning the coveted World Cup five times.

Brazil dominates the region
as well as the continent in size
(it is the world's fifth largest
country in area) and population (half of South America's
397 million people live here).
Leading cities São Paulo and
Rio de Janeiro are among
the world's largest, and the
country's vast agricultural
lands make it a top global
exporter of coffee, soybeans,
beef, orange juice, and sugar.

The vast Amazon rain forest, once a dense wilderness of unmatched biodiversity, is now threatened by farmers, loggers, and miners. To Brazil's north
are lands colonized by the British, Dutch, and French—now sparsely settled
Guyana, Suriname, and French Guiana, a French overseas department where
the European Space Agency maintains its Spaceport, a launch site for explo-
rations beyond Earth. Formerly known as the Guianas, these lands are populated by a mix of people with African,
South Asian, and European heritage.

🔘 **BAUXITE TO ALUMINUM.** By exploiting rich deposits of bauxite, the ore from which aluminum is
made, and inexpensive hydropower, the small
country of Suriname produces aluminum ingots for
export, such as these headed for global markets.

VAST WATERSHED

The United States
at the same scale
as South America

Amazon Basin

South America

The Amazon River basin, which includes more than 2.6
million square miles (6.7 million sq km), would cover
much of the contiguous United States.

THE SIX-BANDED ARMADILLO, found throughout the dry grass-land areas of northeastern South America, lives on plants and insects. Also known as the yellow armadillo, it is unlike others of its species in that it remains active during the day.

Map Key

★ Country capital

••• City or town

······ Boundary

0 _____ 400 miles

0 _____ 400 kilometers

Azimuthal Equidistant Projection

ATLANTIC OCEAN

VENEZUELA

Georgetown
Paramaribo
GUYANA
SURINAME
Cayenne
FRENCH GUIANA (FRANCE)

Orinoco

GUIANA HIGHLANDS

Boa Vista

COLOMBIA

Boundary claimed by Suriname Macapá EQUATOR

Pico da Neblina
9,888 ft
3,014 m

Negro

Marajó Island Belém São Luís

A M A Z O N

Itacoatiara _Amazon_

Manaus Paragominas Parnaíba Fortaleza

Putumayo _(Solimões)_

Tefé Parintins Altamira Tucuruí Codó Sobral

Coari Santarém Marabá Caxias Teresina

Amazon _Tapajós_ Imperatriz

S e l v a

B A S I N Araguaína Crato Natal

Purus _Madeira_ João Pessoa

Cruzeiro do Sul Olinda Recife

Porto Velho B R A Z I L Jaboatão

Rio Branco Ariquemes Palmas Petrolina Arapiraca Maceió

Madre de Dios Ji-Paraná (Rondônia) Gurupi Feira de Santana Aracaju

Alta Floresta Barreiras Alagoinhas

PERU _Juruena_ Alvorado B R A Z I L I A N Salvador (Bahia)

Guaporé _Mamoré_ Jequié Itabuna

Teles Pires Várzea Grande Cuiabá Brasília Vitória da Conquista Ilhéus

Lake Titicaca Rondonópolis Anápolis _São Francisco_ H I G H L A N D S

BOLIVIA Goiânia Teófilo Otoni

Araguaia Uberlândia Governador Valadares

Paraguay Belo Horizonte Linhares

CHILE São José do Rio Preto Ribeirão Preto Juiz de Vitória

Campo Grande São José dos Campos Fora Vila Velha

Paraná São Paulo Nova Iguaçu Duque de Caxias

P A R A G U A Y Londrina Guaratinguetá Niterói

TROPIC OF CAPRICORN Santo André Santos Rio de Janeiro

Iguazú Falls

ARGENTINA Curitiba Paranaguá

Joinville

Paraná Florianópolis

Uruguay Caxias do Sul Criciúma

Santa Maria Novo Hamburgo

Canoas Porto Alegre

Patos Lagoon

Pelotas

URUGUAY

NATIONAL RHYTHM. Samba, often called Brazil's national music, combines the music traditions of the country's popula-tions—Amerindian, Portuguese, and African. Here a samba band practices on Rio de Janeiro's Ipanema Beach.

THE CONTINENT:
SOUTH AMERICA

THE BASICS

Largest country
Argentina
1,073,518 sq mi (2,780,400 sq km)

Smallest country
Uruguay
68,037 sq mi (176,215 sq km)

Most populous country
Argentina
40,829,000

Least populous country
Uruguay
3,381,000

Predominant languages
Spanish, Guarani, English, Italian, German, French

Predominant religion
Christianity (Roman Catholic, Protestant)

Highest GDP per capita
Argentina
$17,700

Lowest GDP per capita
Paraguay
$6,200

Highest life expectancy
Chile
78 years

Highest literacy rate
Uruguay
98%

GEO WHIZ

Guanacos, a member of the camel family that is most numerous in the Patagonia region of Chile and Argentina, keeps enemies at bay by spitting at them.

The Itaipú Dam, which spans the Paraná River between Brazil and Paraguay, is currently the world's largest operating hydroelectric power plant.

Guarani is the name of a people native to Paraguay, the country's basic unit of money, and one of its two official languages. Spanish is the other.

Argentinians eat 150 pounds (68 kg) of beef per person each year, making the country the world's largest per capita consumer of this meat.

Chile's Chuquicamata mine is among the world's largest open-pit copper mines.

Southern South America

Four countries make up this region, which is sometimes called the Southern Cone because of its shape. Long north-south distances in Chile and Argentina result in varied environments. Chile's Atacama Desert in the north contrasts with much cooler, moister lands in the country's south, where there are fjords and glaciers. Nine of ten Chileans live in Middle Chile, in and around booming Santiago. Similarly, most neighboring Argentinians live in the central Pampas region, where wheat and cattle flourish on the fertile plains. Farther south lie the arid, windswept plateaus of Patagonia. Landlocked Paraguay is small in comparison, less urbanized, and one of South America's poorest countries. Compact Uruguay is smaller still, but it possesses a strong agricultural economy, including cattle- and sheep-raising.

◖ **COWBOYS OF THE PAMPAS.**
Cattle are herded by gauchos, the Argentine term for cowboys. The country's extensive grass-covered plains support grain and cattle production on ranches called estancias.

◖ **GATEWAY CITY.** Skyscrapers in the modern skyline rise above Buenos Aires, capital of Argentina and second largest metropolitan area in South America. Situated on the Rio de la Plata, the city was established in 1536 by Spanish explorers. Its port is one of the busiest in South America.

GLOBAL BEEF EXPORTS

2009 data

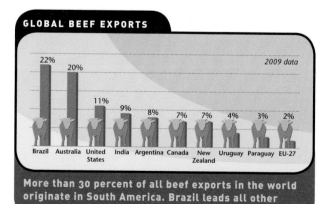

Brazil	Australia	United States	India	Argentina	Canada	New Zealand	Uruguay	Paraguay	EU-27
22%	20%	11%	9%	8%	7%	7%	4%	3%	2%

More than 30 percent of all beef exports in the world originate in South America. Brazil leads all other countries, with almost a quarter of all exports.

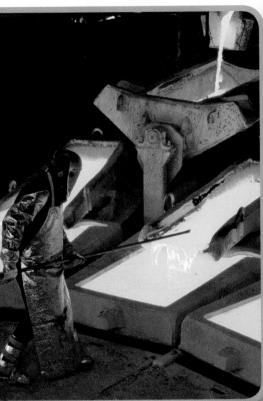

◑ **INCA TREASURE.** Near the frozen summit of Argentina's Cerro Llullaillaco, second highest active volcano in the world, archaeologists excavated Inca ruins and uncovered well-preserved mummies and 20 clothed statues, such as the one at left.

◔ **DESERT RICHES.** Molten copper is poured into molds at a refinery near Chuquicamata, the world's largest copper deposit, located in northern Chile's Atacama Desert. Chile accounts for about 35 percent of the world's copper production.

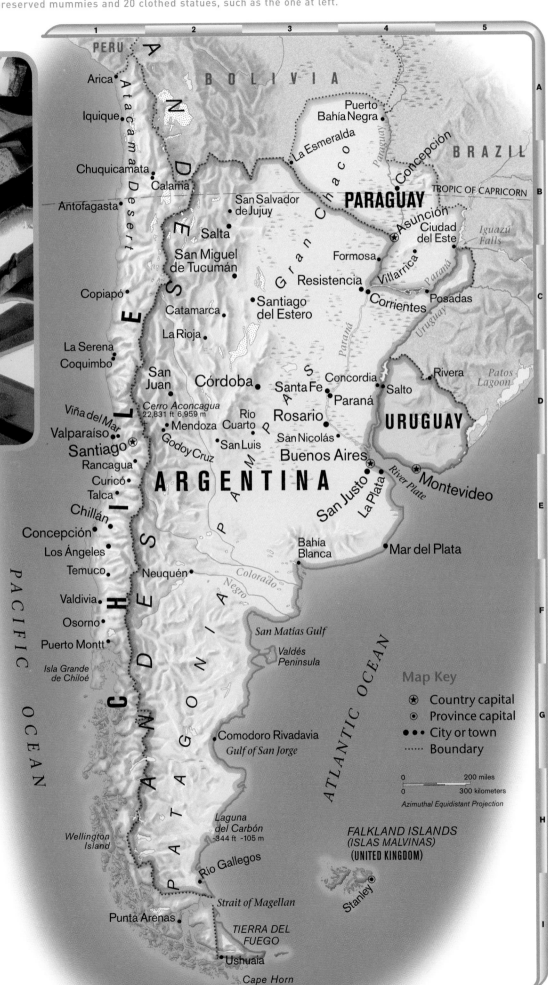

PERU

BOLIVIA

BRAZIL

Arica

Iquique

Puerto
Bahía Negra

La Esmeralda

TROPIC OF CAPRICORN

Chuquicamata

Calama

PARAGUAY

Concepción

Antofagasta

San Salvador
de Jujuy

Asunción

Ciudad
del Este

*Iguazú
Falls*

Salta

Formosa

Villarrica

San Miguel
de Tucumán

Resistencia

Copiapó

Catamarca

Santiago
del Estero

Corrientes

Posadas

La Rioja

La Serena

Coquimbo

San
Juan

Córdoba

Concordia

Rivera

*Patos
Lagoon*

Santa Fe

Paraná

Salto

Cerro Aconcagua
22,831 ft 6,959 m

Río
Cuarto

Rosario

URUGUAY

Viña del Mar

Mendoza

San Nicolás

Valparaíso

San Luis

Godoy Cruz

Buenos Aires

Santiago

Montevideo

Rancagua

ARGENTINA

San Justo

La Plata

River Plate

Curicó

Talca

Chillán

Bahía
Blanca

Mar del Plata

Concepción

Los Ángeles

Temuco

Neuquén

Colorado

PACIFIC

Negro

Valdivia

Osorno

Puerto Montt

San Matías Gulf

*Isla Grande
de Chiloé*

*Valdés
Peninsula*

ATLANTIC OCEAN

OCEAN

Map Key

⊛ Country capital

⊙ Province capital

••• City or town

••••• Boundary

Comodoro Rivadavia

Gulf of San Jorge

0   200 miles
0   300 kilometers
Azimuthal Equidistant Projection

*Laguna
del Carbón
-344 ft -105 m*

*Wellington
Island*

FALKLAND ISLANDS
(ISLAS MALVINAS)
(UNITED KINGDOM)

Río Gallegos

Stanley

Strait of Magellan

Punta Arenas

*TIERRA DEL
FUEGO*

Ushuaia

Cape Horn

THE CONTINENT:
EUROPE

THE CONTINENT:	PHYSICAL			POLITICAL		
Land area 3,841,000 sq mi (9,947,000 sq km)	**Lowest point** Caspian Sea -92 ft (-28 m)	**Largest lake** **entirely in Europe** Ladoga, Russia 6,835 sq mi (17,703 sq km)		**Population** 740,965,000	**Largest country entirely in Europe** Ukraine 233,090 sq mi (603,700 sq km)	**Economy** Farming: vegetables, fruit, grains
Highest point El'brus, Russia 18,510 ft (5,642 m)	**Longest river** Volga, Russia 2,290 mi (3,685 km)			**Largest metropolitan area** Moscow, Russia Pop. 10,523,000	**Most densely populated country** Monaco 45,000 people per sq mi (18,000 per sq km)	Industry: chemicals, machinery Services

Europe

Europe

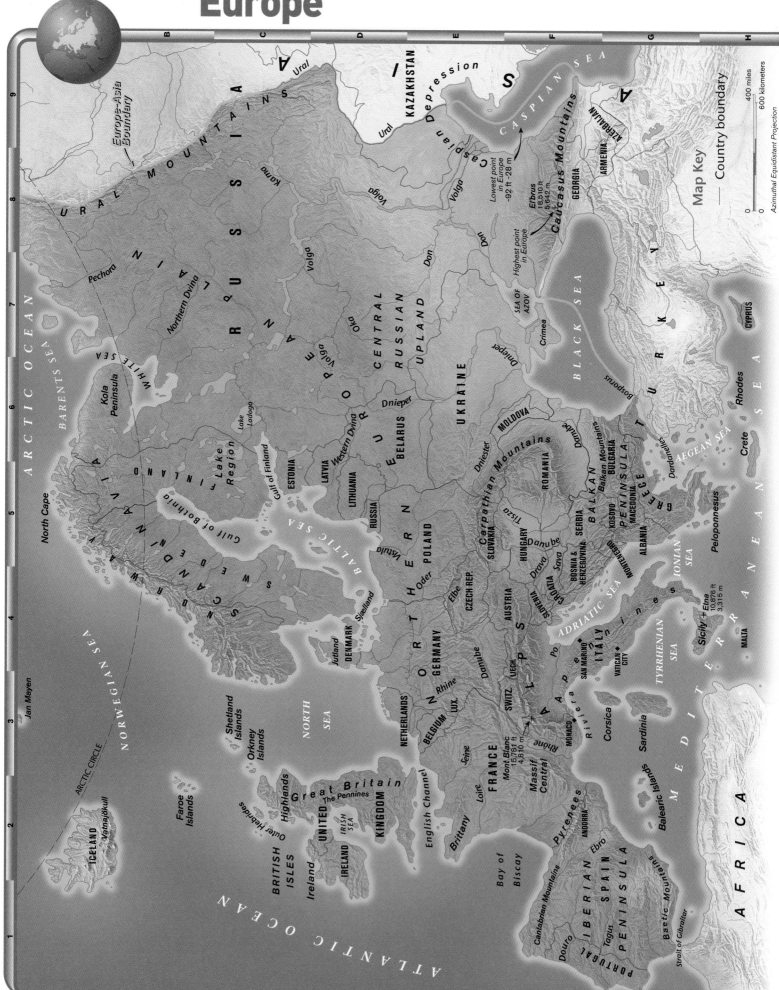

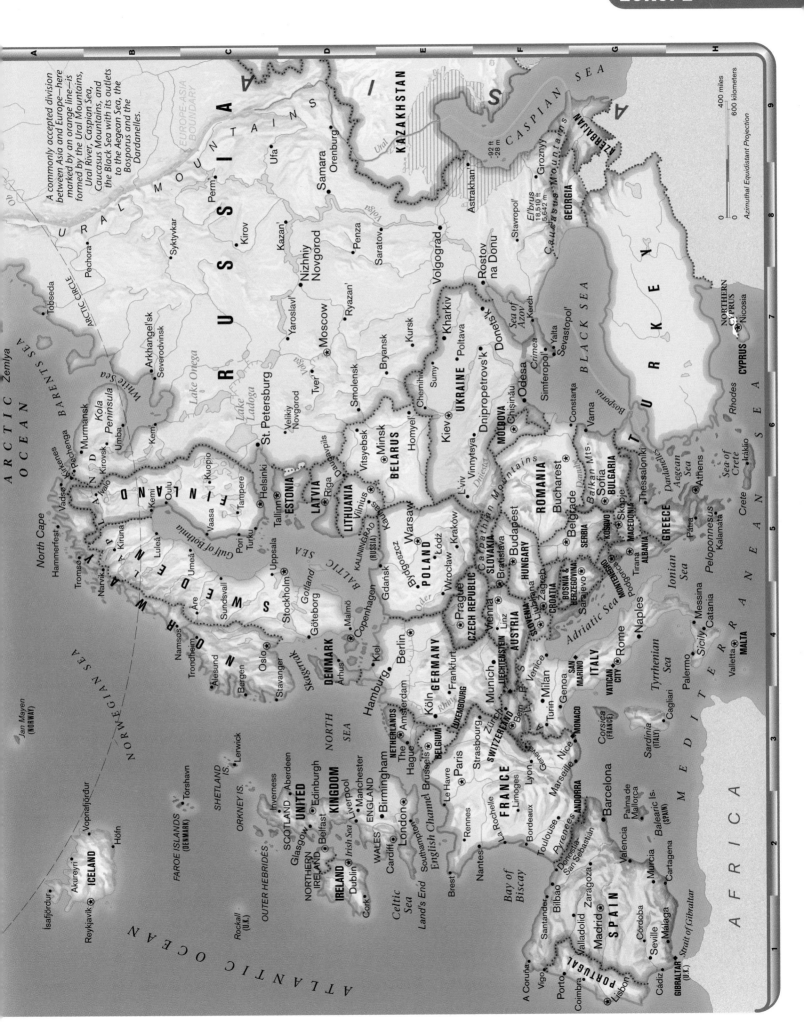

Europe

SMALL SPACES, DIVERSE PLACES

Acluster of islands and peninsulas jutting west from Asia, Europe is bordered by two oceans and more than a dozen seas, which are linked to inland areas by canals and navigable rivers such as the Rhine and Danube. The continent boasts a bounty of landscapes. Sweeping west from the Urals is the fertile Northern European Plain. Rugged uplands form part of Europe's western coast, while the Alps shield Mediterranean lands from frigid northern winds. Here, first Greek and then Roman civilizations laid Europe's cultural foundation. Its colonial powers built wealth from vast empires, while its inventors and thinkers revolutionized world industry, economy, and politics. Today, the 27-member European Union seeks to unite the continent's diversity.

◔ **WIND POWER.** A traditional windmill stands silent in Spain, calling to mind scenes from the classic Spanish novel *Don Quixote*. Modern windmills are used to generate electricity and pump water.

◔ **CHEERY GREETINGS.** Laughing children clown for the camera in Klaipeda, Lithuania. Klaipeda is the northernmost ice-free port on the eastern coast of the Baltic Sea.

◖ **ROCKY SENTINEL.** Towering 14,693 feet (4,478 m) in elevation, the Matterhorn, on the border between Switzerland and Italy, is one of Europe's most famous mountains. Frequent avalanches on its steep slopes pose challenges for mountain climbers.

◓ **WATCHFUL GUARDIAN.** A gargoyle stares out across the Paris skyline from a ledge of Notre Dame Cathedral. Gargoyles were first used in Gothic architecture as waterspouts but later were decorative additions meant to ward off evil spirits.

◓ **WINDOW ON THE PAST.** The brightly painted houses of Nyhavn (New Harbor), once the homes and ware-houses of wealthy Copenhagen merchants, are now shops and restaurants and one of the city's most popular tourist attractions.

more about
Europe

◓ **AGELESS TIME.** This famous astronomical clock, built in 1410 in Prague, Czech Republic, has an astronomical dial on top of a calendar dial. Together, they keep track of time as well as the movement of the sun, moon, and stars.

◐ **CLIFF DWELLERS.** The town of Positano clings to the rocky hillside along Italy's Amalfi coast. In the mid-19th century, more than half the town's population emigrated, mainly to the United States. The economy today is based on tourism.

◓ **SEABIRDS OF THE NORTH.** Colorful Atlantic puffins perch on a grass-covered cliff in Iceland, Europe's westernmost country. These unusual birds are skilled fishers but have difficulty becoming airborne and often crash upon landing.

◓ **CITY AT NIGHT.** A winged victory statue atop the Metropolis Building, a classic example of early 20th-century architecture, appears to watch the evening traffic on the Gran Via in Madrid, Spain.

◖ **GLIMPSE OF THE PAST.** Rome's Colosseum is a silent reminder of a once powerful empire that stretched from the British Isles to Persia (now Iran). The concrete, stone, and brick structure combined classic Greek and Roman architectural styles and could seat as many as 50,000 people.

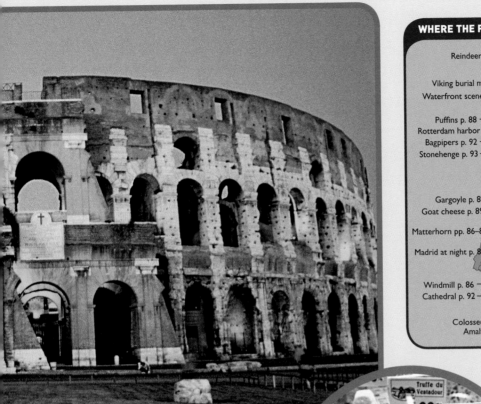

WHERE THE PICTURES ARE

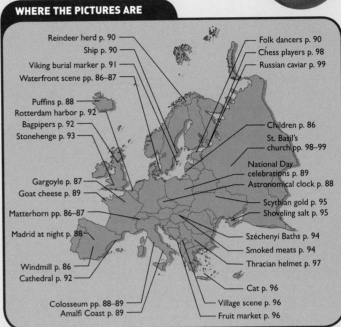

Reindeer herd p. 90
Ship p. 90
Viking burial marker p. 91
Waterfront scene pp. 86–87
Puffins p. 88
Rotterdam harbor p. 92
Bagpipers p. 92
Stonehenge p. 93
Gargoyle p. 87
Goat cheese p. 89
Matterhorn pp. 86–87
Madrid at night p. 88
Windmill p. 86
Cathedral p. 92
Colosseum pp. 88–89
Amalfi Coast p. 89

Folk dancers p. 90
Chess players p. 98
Russian caviar p. 99
Children p. 86
St. Basil's church pp. 98–99
National Day celebrations p. 89
Astronomical clock p. 88
Scythian gold p. 95
Shoveling salt p. 95
Széchenyi Baths p. 94
Smoked meats p. 94
Thracian helmet p. 97
Cat p. 96
Village scene p. 96
Fruit market p. 96

◖ **LUNCHTIME!** Varieties of creamy, fresh goat cheese are displayed in a market in the Brittany region of northern France.

◐ **NATIONAL PRIDE.** Young women carry banners in a parade marking Poland's National Day. Celebrated each year on May 3, it is the anniversary of the 1997 proclamation of the Polish Constitution.

THE CONTINENT:
EUROPE

THE BASICS

STATS

Largest country
Sweden 173,732 sq mi (449,964 sq km)

Smallest country
Denmark 16,640 sq mi (43,098 sq km)

Most populous country
Sweden 9,514,000

Least populous country
Iceland 320,000

Predominant languages
Russian, Polish, Swedish, Danish, Finnish, Norwegian, Lithuanian, Latvian, Estonian, Icelandic

Predominant religion
Christianity (Lutheran, Roman Catholic, Orthodox)

Highest GDP per capita
Norway $102,300

Lowest GDP per capita
Latvia $16,800

Highest life expectancy
Iceland, Sweden
81 years

Highest literacy rate
Estonia, Finland, Iceland, Latvia, Lithuania, Norway
100%

GEO WHIZ

Finland has more than 185,000 lakes. In fact, the southeastern part of the country is called the Lake Region.

The national symbol of Denmark is a statue of Hans Christian Andersen's Little Mermaid, in Copenhagen's harbor.

Vatnajökull, in Iceland, is the largest glacier in Europe.

According to Finnish folklore, Father and Mother Christmas live with their helpers on a mountain called Korvatunturi, in the country's Lapland region.

During Iceland's Thorrablot winter festival, locals celebrate by eating a Viking dish of rotten Greenland shark meat.

Legoland theme park, in Billund, Denmark, features miniature cities, models of famous landmarks such as the Taj Mahal, Statue of Liberty, and Mount Rushmore, and more—all made from some 33 million Lego blocks.

Northern Europe

This entire region lies in latitudes similar to Canada's Hudson Bay, but the warm North Atlantic Drift current moderates temperatures in western parts of the region, from volcanically active Iceland to Denmark and Norway. The area's better farmlands lie in southern Sweden and the breezy lowlands of Denmark. Lightly populated but mostly urban, Northern Europe is home to slightly more than 32 million people. Sweden is the largest and most populous country. Forested, lake-dotted Finland shares a long border with Russia. Estonia, Latvia, and Lithuania—the so-called Baltic States—were republics of the Russian-dominated Soviet Union, which ceased to exist in 1991.

NORDIC HERDERS. The Sami, indigenous people of northern Europe, herd their reindeer across the borders of Norway, Sweden, Finland, and Russia. Some use snowmobiles instead of horses.

MIGHTY WARSHIP. In 1628 the warship *Vasa* sank in the cold waters of Stockholm Harbor on its maiden voyage. After 333 years it was raised and reconstructed.

COLORFUL TRADITION.
Costumed folk dancers perform traditional dances at an open-air museum in Tallinn, Estonia.

NORTHERN FISHERIES

Norway	Iceland	Denmark	Sweden	Lithuania	Latvia	Finland	Estonia
2,524,437*	1,141,869	777,752	203,413	172,692	163,213	154,592	97,421

*Figures are in tons, 2009

Large schools of fish thrive in the cold waters off northern Europe. Norway harvests the most, bringing in more than 2.5 million tons of fish annually.

THE CONTINENT:
EUROPE

◀ **MARKER FROM THE PAST.** A stone memorial marks the burial site of Viking warriors in Sweden. Although their main activities were farming and trade, Vikings are better known for their ships and their fierce raids on towns across Europe.

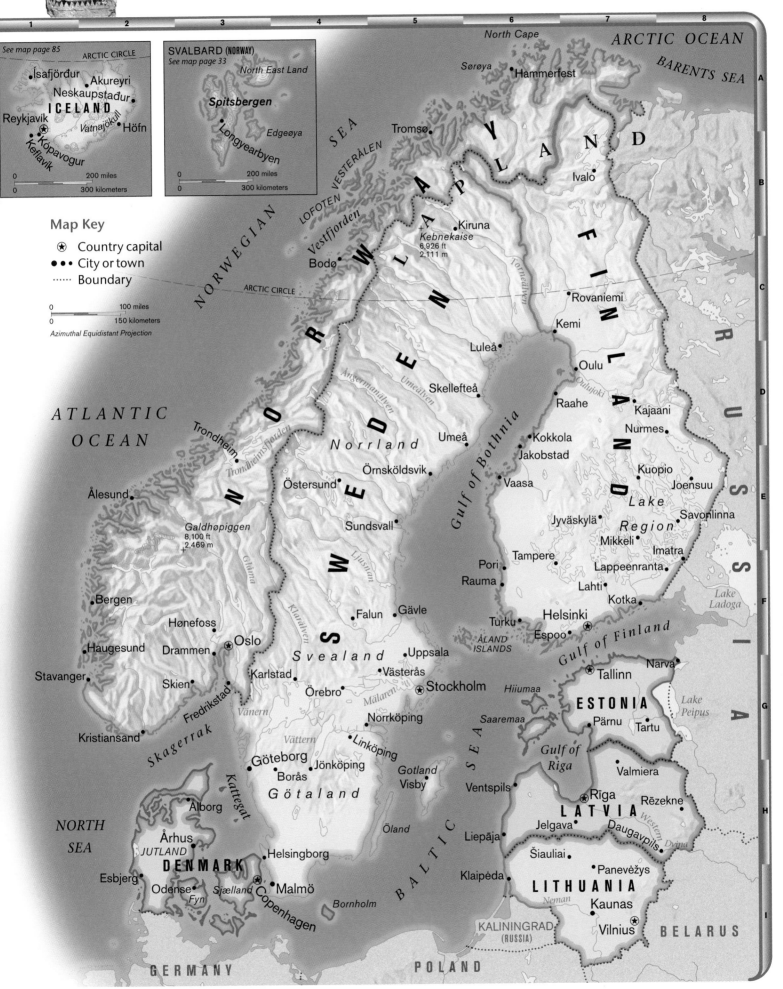

See map page 85

ARCTIC CIRCLE

Ísafjörður
Akureyri
Neskaupstaður
ICELAND
Reykjavik
Vatnajökull · Höfn
Kópavogur
Keflavik

0 —— 200 miles
0 —— 300 kilometers

SVALBARD (NORWAY)
See map page 33

North East Land

Spitsbergen

Longyearbyen · Edgeøya

0 —— 200 miles
0 —— 300 kilometers

Map Key

⊛ Country capital
••• City or town
······ Boundary

0 —— 100 miles
0 —— 150 kilometers
Azimuthal Equidistant Projection

North Cape

ARCTIC OCEAN

BARENTS SEA

Søroya · Hammerfest

Tromsø

Ivalo

LOFOTEN · VESTERÅLEN

Vestfjorden

Bodø

Kiruna
Kebnekaise
6,926 ft
2,111 m

ARCTIC CIRCLE

Torneälven

Rovaniemi

Kemi

ATLANTIC OCEAN

NORWEGIAN SEA

Trondheim

Trondheimsfjorden

Ålesund

Galdhøpiggen
8,100 ft
2,469 m

Bergen

Hønefoss

Haugesund
Drammen · ⊛ Oslo
Stavanger

Skien

Fredrikstad

Kristiansand

Skagerrak

Ångermanälven

Umeälven

Norrland

Östersund

Sundsvall

Ljusnan

Klarälven

Glåma

Falun · Gävle

Svealand

Karlstad
Örebro
Vänern
Vättern

Göteborg
Borås
Jönköping

Götaland

Skellefteå

Umeå
Örnsköldsvik

Gulf of Bothnia

Luleå

Oulu
Oulujoki

Raahe

Kokkola
Jakobstad

Vaasa

Pori
Rauma

FINLAND

Kajaani
Nurmes

Kuopio
Joensuu

Lake Region

Jyväskylä
Savonlinna
Mikkeli
Imatra

Tampere
Lappeenranta

Lahti
Kotka

Turku
Helsinki ⊛
Espoo

ÅLAND ISLANDS

Uppsala
Västerås

⊛ Stockholm

Norrköping

Linköping

Gotland
Visby

Öland

Mälaren

Hiiumaa

Saaremaa

BALTIC SEA

Gulf of Finland

Tallinn ⊛
Narva

ESTONIA
Pärnu
Tartu

Lake Peipus

Gulf of Riga

Valmiera

Rīga ⊛
Rēzekne

LATVIA
Jelgava
Daugavpils
Western Dvina

Liepāja

Šiauliai

Klaipėda
Panevėžys

LITHUANIA
Neman

Kaunas

Vilnius ⊛

KALININGRAD (RUSSIA)

BELARUS

Lake Ladoga

R U S S I A

NORTH SEA

Ålborg

Århus
JUTLAND

Kattegat

Helsingborg

DENMARK
Esbjerg
Odense
Fyn
Sjælland · Malmö
Copenhagen ⊛

Bornholm

GERMANY

POLAND

N O R W A Y

S W E D E N

L A P L A N D

THE BASICS

STATS

Largest country
France 210,026 sq mi (543,965 sq km)

Smallest country
Vatican City 0.2 sq mi (0.4 sq km)

Most populous country
Germany 81,825,000

Least populous country
Vatican City 836

Predominant languages
German, French, English, Italian, Spanish, Dutch, Portuguese

Predominant religion
Christianity (Roman Catholic, Protestant)

Highest GDP per capita
Luxembourg $104,200

Lowest GDP per capita
Malta $25,600

Highest life expectancy
Spain, France, Switzerland, Sweden 82 years

Highest literacy rate
Andorra, Liechtenstein, Luxembourg, Vatican City
100%

GEO WHIZ

Fossil hunters discovered a new species of dinosaur in northern Spain in 2006. Measuring up to 120 feet (37 m) and weighing 48 tons (44 t), *Turiasaurus riodevemsis* is the largest dinosaur ever found in Europe.

The catacombs of Paris, which date from Roman times, contain the skeletons of some six million people, including some victims of the French Revolution.

Antwerp, Belgium, is the center of the world's diamond industry.

The ears on several rhinoceros images in France's Chauvet cave look so much like a certain fast-food chain's Golden Arches that researchers have nicknamed them McEars.

Portugal is the world's leading producer of cork.

Mount Etna, on Italy's island of Sicily, is known as the home of Zeus, ruler of all Greek gods. It is also Europe's highest active volcano.

Western Europe

Eighteen countries crowd this diverse region, which has enjoyed a central role in world affairs for centuries while suffering the results of devastating wars. The past half-century has seen bitter rivals become wiser allies, with today's European Union growing out of the need to rebuild economic and political stability after World War II. Fertile soil in the many river valleys across the Northern European Plain and on Mediterranean hillsides gives rise to abundant harvests of a wide variety of crops. France leads in agricultural production and area, while Germany is the most populous country. These and other countries in this region face a population problem unlike that seen in most other regions: a decline in numbers.

MONUMENT TO FAITH. The towering spires of La Sagrada Familia (The Holy Family) rise above Barcelona, Spain. This massive Roman Catholic church has been under construction for more than a century.

HIGHLAND TUNE. Bagpipers in formal dress parade through the streets of Edinburgh, Scotland. Bagpipes may have arrived with Roman invaders, but today they are most associated with the Scottish Highlands.

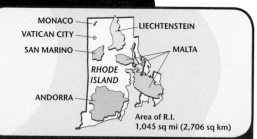

HOW BIG IS A COUNTRY?

MONACO
VATICAN CITY
SAN MARINO
LIECHTENSTEIN
MALTA
RHODE ISLAND
ANDORRA

Area of R.I.
1,045 sq mi (2,706 sq km)

Europe's six smallest countries (see pages 169–171 for areas) would fit inside Rhode Island, the smallest U.S. state, with room to spare.

MODERN SPAN. Tall red arches support the Willem Bridge across the Maas River in Rotterdam, Netherlands. The Maas, which flows into the North Sea, is a major trade and transport artery, linking the Netherlands to the rest of Europe.

CELTIC POWER. These rock pillars are part of Stonehenge, a puzzling arrangement of stones on the plains of southern England. Erected more than 5,000 years ago, Stonehenge is believed to be associated with sun worship.

200 miles
300 kilometers
Azimuthal Equidistant Projection

Map Key
★ Country capital
◉ Province capital
• • • City or town
········ Boundary

FINLAND
ESTONIA
NORWAY
SWEDEN
Shetland Islands
Orkney Islands
Rockall (UNITED KINGDOM)
NORTH SEA
BALTIC SEA
POLAND
DENMARK

ATLANTIC OCEAN
Outer Hebrides
Inner Hebrides
Inverness
SCOTLAND Aberdeen
Perth Dundee
Glasgow Edinburgh
Londonderry
NORTHERN IRELAND
Belfast
IRELAND Isle of Man
Limerick Dublin Liverpool Leeds KINGDOM
IRISH SEA Kingston upon Hull
Waterford Manchester Sheffield
Cork Birmingham Nottingham
WALES ENGLAND
Cardiff London
CELTIC SEA
Bristol Thames
Plymouth Brugge
Southampton
ENGLISH CHANNEL Strait of Dover
Channel Islands (U.K.)
Brest Caen Paris
Rennes Le Mans Orléans
Angers Tours
Nantes Loire

Kiel Rostock
Oldenburg Lübeck
Groningen Hamburg
Bremen Berlin
NETHERLANDS Hannover Magdeburg
The Hague Amsterdam Bielefeld
Utrecht Dortmund Leipzig
Rotterdam Essen Erfurt Dresden
Antwerp Köln GERMANY Chemnitz
BELGIUM Bonn Frankfurt CZECH REPUBLIC
Charleroi LUXEMBOURG Mainz Mannheim Nürnberg
Amiens Luxembourg Karlsruhe SLOVAKIA
Le Havre Rouen Metz Stuttgart Augsburg Linz
Reims Nancy Strasbourg Freiburg Munich Vienna
Besançon Basel AUSTRIA
Dijon Lausanne Zürich LIECHTENSTEIN Salzburg HUNGARY
Bern SWITZERLAND Innsbruck Graz
Vichy Geneva Bolzano SLOVENIA
FRANCE Lyon Mont Blanc 15,781 ft 4,810 m Trento Trieste
Limoges Matterhorn 14,691 ft 4,478 m Verona Venice CROATIA
Clermont-Ferrand Milan Padova
MASSIF CENTRAL St-Étienne Turin Ferrara Bologna BOSNIA & HERZEGOVINA
Nîmes Modena
Bordeaux Genoa Florence SAN MARINO
Aix-en-Provence Pisa Perugia Ancona
BAY OF BISCAY Montpellier Avignon MONACO Pescara
Donostia-San Sebastián Nice
Santander Bilbao Toulouse Marseille LIGURIAN SEA Terni ITALY Foggia Bari
Gijón Perpignan Toulon Bastia Rome Taranto
A Coruña Pamplona ANDORRA CORSICA VATICAN CITY Salerno Lecce
Oviedo León Vitoria-Gasteiz Andorra la Vella Sabadell Ajaccio Naples Gulf of Taranto
Vigo Santiago de Compostela Burgos Lleida Martaró Vesuvius 4,203 ft 1,281 m
Braga Bragança Valladolid Zaragoza Tarragona Barcelona Cosenza IONIAN SEA
Porto Viseu Salamanca BALEARIC SEA Minorca SARDINIA TYRRHENIAN SEA
Coimbra Madrid Castelló de la Plana Majorca
PORTUGAL Toledo Valencia Palma de Mallorca BALEARIC ISLANDS Messina Reggio di Calabria
Lisbon SPAIN Albacete Sassari Palermo Taormina
Setúbal Badajoz Alicante Cagliari Marsala SICILY Catania
SIERRA MORENA Murcia Cartagena MEDITERRANEAN Syracuse
Córdoba Jaén Alicante
Huelva Seville Granada Almería Valletta
Jerez Málaga MALTA
Cádiz
Algeciras GIBRALTAR (U.K.) ALBORAN SEA
Ceuta (SPAIN)
Strait of Gibraltar Melilla (SPAIN)
MOROCCO ALGERIA TUNISIA SEA

SERBIA
MONTENEGRO
ALBANIA
ADRIATIC SEA
APPENNINES
PYRENEES
ALPS

THE BASICS

STATS

Largest country
Ukraine 233,090 sq mi (603,700 sq km)

Smallest country
Moldova 13,050 sq mi (33,800 sq km)

Most populous country
Ukraine 45,556,000

Least populous country
Moldova 4,114,000

Predominant languages
Ukrainian, Russian, Polish, Hungarian, Czech, Belarusian, Slovak, Moldovan

Predominant religions
Christianity (Roman Catholic, Orthodox, Protestant), Judaism, Islam

Highest GDP per capita
Czech Republic $27,100

Lowest GDP per capita
Moldova $3,400

Highest life expectancy
Czech Republic 77 years

Highest literacy rate
Poland, Slovakia, Belarus, Ukraine 100%

GEO WHIZ

The Wieliczka salt mine has been in operation since the 13th century. Known as the underground salt cathedral of Poland, it features historical, religious, and mythical figures, chambers, chapels, and an exhibit about how salt is mined, all carved in salt.

The Pinsk Marshes, one of Europe's largest wetlands, covers thousands of square miles in southern Belarus and northwestern Ukraine. In 1970 the area was chosen as the site of the Chernobyl Nuclear Power Plant, largely because few people lived there and it had ready access to water. An explosion closed the power plant in 1986, and much of the area is still uninhabitable due to radioactive contaminants.

Budapest did not become a united city until 1873. Until that time there were two cities—Buda on the west bank of the Danube and Pest on the east. The first bridge between the cities was built in the mid-1800s by Count Istvan Széchenyi.

The so-called Velvet Revolution was the nonviolent uprising against the Communist government of Czechoslovakia in 1989 that led to the creation of two new countries: the Czech Republic and Slovakia.

Eastern Europe

⬤ **TIME TO EAT.** Smoked sausages and bacon, ready for purchase in the market, are an important part of the diet in the countries of eastern Europe.

Eastern Europe stretches from the Baltic Sea southeast to the Black Sea. Before 1991, Ukraine, Belarus, and Moldova were part of the Soviet Union, with the region's other countries largely under its control. A small, separated segment of Russia is still nearby: Kaliningrad. Much of the region has a continental climate similar to that of the U.S. Midwest. Nearly the size of Texas, Ukraine is the region's largest country in both population and area. Like Poland, it holds rich agricultural and industrial resources. Warsaw is the region's largest city, while the historic charms of Prague and Budapest make them popular tourist stops. With the exceptions of Hungarians and Moldovans, most people in these lands are linked by branches of Slavic language and ethnicity.

◗ **HEALING WATERS.**
Budapest's Széchenyi Baths, built between 1909 and 1913, are famous for their medicinal thermal waters, discovered in 1879. A total of 15 baths, as well as saunas and steam rooms, are housed in buildings decorated with sculptures and mosaics by Hungary's leading artists.

◀ **ANCIENT GOLD.** This skillfully crafted gold collar, called a pectoral, was found in a Scythian burial mound in Ukraine. The Scythians occupied the area from modern Ukraine into Russia from the eighth century B.C. to the second century A.D.

COMMUNICATION CHALLENGE

West Slavic 20%	**Polish** (40.0 million speakers) **Czech** (9.5 million speakers) **Slovak** (5.0 million speakers)
South Slavic 10%	**Bulgarian** (9.1 million speakers) **Bosnian** (2.2 million speakers) **Serbian** (7.0 million speakers) **Slovene** (2.0 million speakers) **Macedonian** (2.1 million speakers) **Croatian** (5.5 million speakers)
East Slavic 70%	**Belarusian** (8.6 million speakers) **Russian** (144.0 million speakers) **Ukrainian** (37.0 million speakers)

Slavic languages of Eastern Europe share a common origin, but they have evolved into a dozen distinctly different languages.

LATVIA
LITHUANIA
KALININGRAD (RUSSIA)
Olsztyn
Białystok
Warsaw
Brest
Lublin
elce
Rzeszów
rnów
Košice
Uzhhorod
lc
Nyíregyháza
Debrecen
ROMANIA

Vitsyebsk
Orsha
Barysaw
Mahilyow
Hrodna
⊛ Minsk
BELARUS
Baranavichy
Babruysk
Pinsk
Homyel'
Pinsk Marshes
Mazyr
Chernihiv
Chernobyl'
Luts'k
Rivne
Zhytomyr
⊛ Kiev
Bila Tserkva
L'viv
Ternopil'
UKRAINE
Khmel'nyts'kyy
Ivano-Frankivs'k
Vinnytsya
Cherkasy
Kam'yanets'-Podil's'kyy
Kirovohrad
Oleksandriya
Chernivtsi
Bălţi
MOLDOVA
Chişinău
Tiraspol
Mykolayiv
Odesa

Western Dvina
Dnieper
Sumy
Dniester
Dnieper
RUSSIA
Kharkiv
Poltava
Slov"yans'k
Lysychans'k
Kramators'k
Kadivka
Kostyantynivka
Luhans'k
Alchevs'k
Krasnyy Luch
Horlivka
Yenakiyeve
Donets'k
Makiyivka
Dniprodzerzhyns'k
Kryvyy Rih
Zaporizhzhya
Dnipropetrovs'k
Nikopol'
Melitopol'
Mariupol'
Berdyans'k
Kherson
Dnieper
SEA OF AZOV
Kerch
CRIMEA
Yevpatoriya
Simferopol'
Sevastopol'
Yalta
BLACK SEA
Kremenchuk

Danube
Prut
Dniester
CARPATHIAN MOUNTAINS

Map Key
⊛ Country capital
••• City or town
⋯⋯ Boundary

0 ———— 200 miles
0 ———— 300 kilometers
Azimuthal Equidistant Projection

◀ **MOUNTAIN OF SALT.**
These men shovel salt at a storage depot in Crimea, Ukraine. Salt is a traditional symbol of friendship in Ukraine.

THE BASICS

STATS

Largest country
Romania 92,043 sq mi (238,391 sq km)

Smallest country
Cyprus 3,572 sq mi (9,251 sq km)

Most populous country
Romania 21,408,000

Least populous country
Montenegro 622,000

Predominant languages
Romanian, Greek, Serbian, Croatian, Bulgarian, Albanian, Turkish, English

Predominant religions
Christianity (various Orthodox, Roman Catholic), Islam

Highest GDP per capita
Slovenia $28,800

Lowest GDP per capita
Kosovo $6,500

Highest life expectancy
Greece 80 years

Highest literacy rate
Slovenia
100%

GEO WHIZ

Along the coast of Croatia there are huge fish farms where bluefin tuna are raised, making the country an important supplier of this highly edible, very popular fish.

The Dalmatian, a popular breed of dog, is named for its region of origin: Dalmatia, along the Adriatic coast of the Balkan Peninsula.

Dracula tours abound in Romania, home of Vlad Dracula (also known as Vlad the Impaler), who ruled the region between the Danube and the Transylvanian Alps in the 15th century.

The famous Lipizzan horses of the Spanish Riding School in Vienna, Austria, trace their ancestry and their name back more than 400 years to a horse farm in Lipica, Slovenia.

Nicosia (Lefkosia) is the capital of both the independent Republic of Cyprus and the Rebublic of Northern Cyprus, which is under Turkish control.

Balkans & Cyprus

The Balkans—named for a Bulgarian mountain range—make up a rugged land with a rough history. Ethnic and religious conflict have long troubled the area. Since 1991, seven new countries have emerged from the breakup of Yugoslavia (see inset on page 97). Kosovo is the most recent. The storied Danube River winds east across the Balkans, separating Bulgaria from Romania, the region's largest country in both area and population. Rimmed by four seas—the Black, Aegean, Ionian, and Adriatic—the Balkans, particularly Greece, have a long maritime history. With more than 3.7 million people, Greece's capital, Athens, is the largest city in the region. In 2004, Cyprus, which has been uneasily divided for three decades into Turkish and Greek sections, joined the European Union along with Greece.

⬭ **TRADITIONAL LIFE.** Villagers walk down a cobbled street in Gusinje, a rural town in northeastern Montenegro. A place of rugged mountains, Montenegro is one of the countries that emerged from the former Yugoslavia.

⬭ **LAZY DAYS.** A cat stretches out along a whitewashed wall on the Greek island of Thíra. The blue dome in the background is part of a Greek Orthodox church.

⬭ **COLORFUL BOUNTY.** An open-air fruit market overflows with grapes, plums, apples, and other produce that thrive in the moderate climate of the Mediterranean region. Warm, dry summers and cool, rainy winters provide ideal growing conditions for a variety of fruits, many of which had their origins in the region.

❂ **ANCIENT WARRIORS.** Soldiers and horsemen from Thrace, an ancient territory in present-day Bulgaria and Greece, wore masks as they rode into battle. Often serving as paid fighters in other armies, the Thracians were allies of Troy in Homer's *Iliad*.

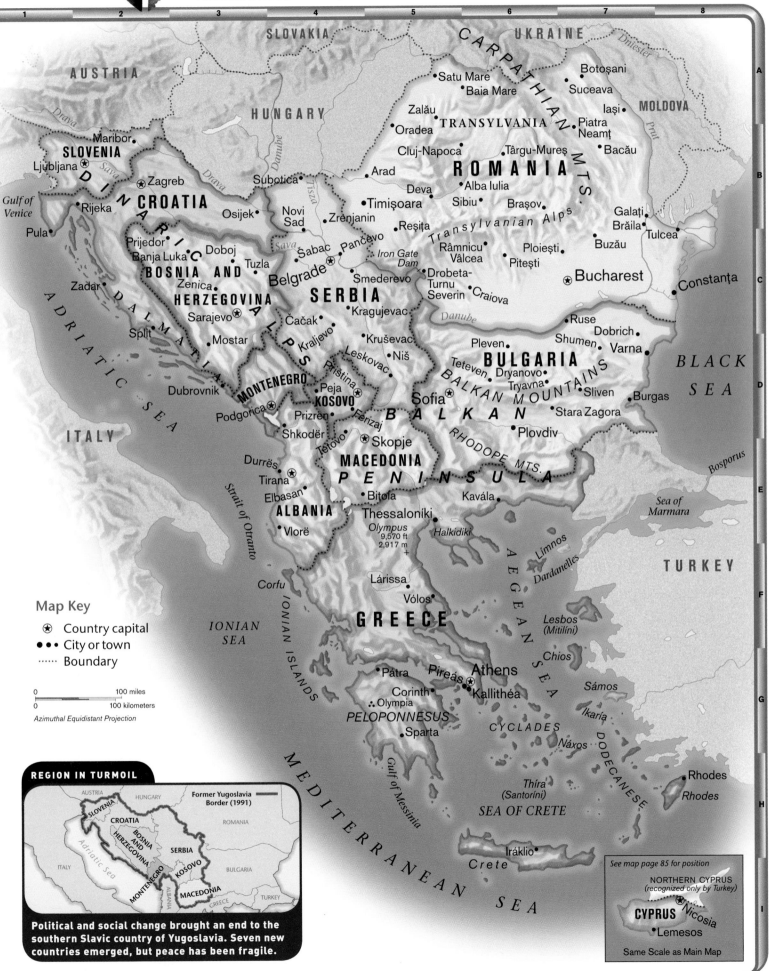

SLOVAKIA

UKRAINE

Dniester

AUSTRIA

HUNGARY

CARPATHIAN MTS.

• Satu Mare
• Baia Mare

• Botoşani

• Suceava

• Iaşi

MOLDOVA

Drava

• Zalău

TRANSYLVANIA

• Piatra
Neamţ

Prut

SLOVENIA

• Maribor

⊛ Zagreb

Sava

• Oradea

• Cluj-Napoca

• Târgu-Mureş

• Bacău

⊛ Ljubljana

CROATIA

Drava

Subotica •

• Arad

• Alba Iulia

ROMANIA

• Rijeka

D
I
N
A
R
I
C

• Osijek

Novi
Sad

• Deva

• Sibiu

• Braşov

• Galaţi

*Gulf of
Venice*

• Zrenjanin

• Timişoara

Transylvanian Alps

• Brăila

• Pula

Prijedor •

• Doboj

• Reşiţa

• Râmnicu
Vâlcea

• Ploieşti

• Buzău

• Tulcea

Banja Luka •

• Tuzla

Sava

Šabac •

• Pančevo

*Iron Gate
Dam*

• Pitești

BOSNIA AND

• Zenica

Smederevo •

Drobeta-
Turnu
Severin

• Bucharest ⊛

• Zadar

D
A
L
M
A
T
I
A

HERZEGOVINA

⊛ Sarajevo

Belgrade ⊛

SERBIA

• Kragujevac

• Craiova

Danube

• Constanţa

• Split

• Mostar

• Čačak

• Kruševac

• Ruse

• Dobrich

A
D
R
I
A
T
I
C

• Kraljevo

• Niš

• Pleven

• Shumen

• Varna

• Leskovac

BULGARIA

MONTENEGRO

Priština ⊛

• Teteven

• Dryanovo

**BLACK
SEA**

S
E
A

Dubrovnik •

KOSOVO

Peja •

• Tryavna

• Sliven

Podgorica ⊛

• Prizren

Ferizaj •

Sofia ⊛

B
A
L
K
A
N

• Stara Zagora

• Burgas

• Shkodër

• Tetovo

Skopje ⊛

RHODOPE

• Plovdiv

Durrës •

MACEDONIA

MTS.

ITALY

Tirana ⊛

P E N I N S U L A

Bosporus

• Elbasan

• Bitola

• Kavála

ALBANIA

• Vlorë

Thessaloníki •

AEGEAN

*Sea of
Marmara*

*Strait
of
Otranto*

Olympus
9,570 ft
2,917 m
+

• Halkidikí

• Límnos

TURKEY

Dardanelles

Corfu

• Lárissa

• Vólos

SEA

• Lesbos
(Mitilíni)

GREECE

• Chios

Map Key

⊛ Country capital

• • • City or town

‥‥‥ Boundary

I
O
N
I
A
N

I
S
L
A
N
D
S

**IONIAN
SEA**

• Pátra

Piraés •

⊛ Athens

• Kallithéa

• Sámos

• Ikaría

DODECANESE

• Corinth

‥ Olympia

PELOPONNESUS

• Sparta

C
Y
C
L
A
D
E
S

• Náxos

0   100 miles
0   100 kilometers

Azimuthal Equidistant Projection

*Gulf of
Messinia*

*Thíra
(Santoríni)*

• Rhodes

Rhodes

SEA OF CRETE

M
E
D
I
T
E
R
R
A
N
E
A
N

• Iráklio

Crete

S
E
A

REGION IN TURMOIL

Former Yugoslavia
Border (1991) ▬▬▬

AUSTRIA

HUNGARY

SLOVENIA

ROMANIA

CROATIA

Adriatic Sea

**BOSNIA
AND
HERZEGOVINA**

SERBIA

BULGARIA

ITALY

MONTENEGRO

KOSOVO

MACEDONIA

ALBANIA

GREECE

TURKEY

Political and social change brought an end to the southern Slavic country of Yugoslavia. Seven new countries emerged, but peace has been fragile.

See map page 85 for position

NORTHERN CYPRUS
(recognized only by Turkey)

CYPRUS

⊛ Nicosia

• Lemesos

Same Scale as Main Map

European Russia

THE BASICS

STATS*

Area
6,592,850 sq mi (17,075,400 sq km)

Population
143,165,000

Predominant languages
Russian, minority languages

Predominant religions
Christianity (Russian Orthodox), Islam

GDP per capita
$16,700

Life expectancy
66 years

Literacy rate
100%

*Note: These figures are for all of Russia.
For Asian Russia, see pages 108–109.

GEO WHIZ

St. Petersburg's many canals and hundreds of bridges have earned it the nickname Venice of the North.

The fertile Northern European Plain, which stretches west from the Urals, is home to most of Russia's population and industry, whereas most of its mineral resources lie east of the Urals in the Asian portion of the country.

Two of the world's most famous ballet companies are in Russia: the Kirov in St. Petersburg and the Bolshoi in Moscow.

Arkhangel'sk, founded in 1584, is Russia's oldest Arctic port. The rich timber resources that surround it and make up the bulk of its exports have been nicknamed "green gold."

The official residence of the President of Russia is inside a walled fortress known as the Kremlin in downtown Moscow. The site on which the Kremlin stands has been continuously occupied since 2000 B.C.

During the Soviet era (1920–1991), the city Nizhniy Novgorod was named Gorky after author Maxim Gorky. "Gorky" is a Russian word meaning "bitter."

Soviet dictator Josef Stalin used the GUM department store, located on Moscow's Red Square, to display propaganda posters and the body of his wife, who committed suicide in 1932.

◖ CHECKMATE! Bystanders watch intently as one player prepares to make his move in this chess game in a park in St. Petersburg. In Russia, chess is a national pastime, popular with people from all walks of life.

Home to four-fifths of Russia's 143 million people, European Russia contains most of the world's largest country's agriculture and industry. Here also is Moscow, its capital and Europe's largest city. Far to the north, Murmansk provides a year-round seaport—a gift of the warming currents of the North Atlantic Drift. This large, funnel-shaped portion of Russia, which spans 1,600 miles (2,575 km) from the icy Arctic to the imposing Caucasus Mountains, is home to the Volga, Europe's longest river, and Mount El'brus (18,510 ft/5,642 m), its highest peak. The Caucasus, together with the mineral-rich Urals, form a natural boundary between Europe and Asia. Although parts of Azerbaijan and Georgia in the south and Kazakhstan in the east span the continental boundary, only Russia is counted as part of Europe. To read about Asian Russia, see pages 108–109.

EUROPE'S GREAT RIVERS

Volga	3,685 km (2,290 mi)
Danube	2,888 km (1,795 mi)
Dnieper	2,290 km (1,423 mi)
Rhine	1,320 km (820 mi)
Elbe	1,091 km (678 mi)
Vistula	1,047 km (651 mi)
Tagus	1,038 km (645 mi)
Loire	1,012 km (629 mi)
Rhône	800 km (497 mi)
Po	652 km (405 mi)

Europe's rivers, many linked by canals, form a transportation network that connects the continent's people and places to each other and the world beyond.

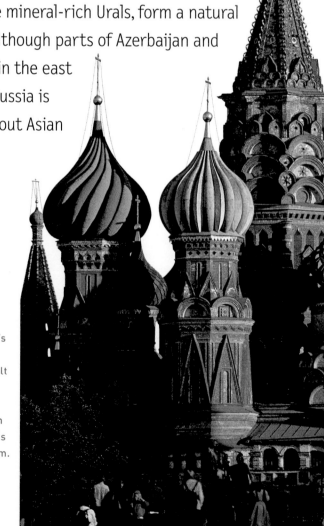

◖ CATHEDRAL ON THE SQUARE. The onion dome–topped towers of St. Basil's are a key landmark on Moscow's Red Square. Built between 1555 and 1561 to commemorate successful military campaigns by Ivan the Terrible, the building is rich in Christian symbolism.

◑ RUSSIAN DELICACY. Caviar, a distinctly Russian luxury food item, is the eggs (called roe) of sturgeon fish caught in the Caspian Sea. The eggs are aged in a salty brine before being packaged in cans (left) for shipment around the world.

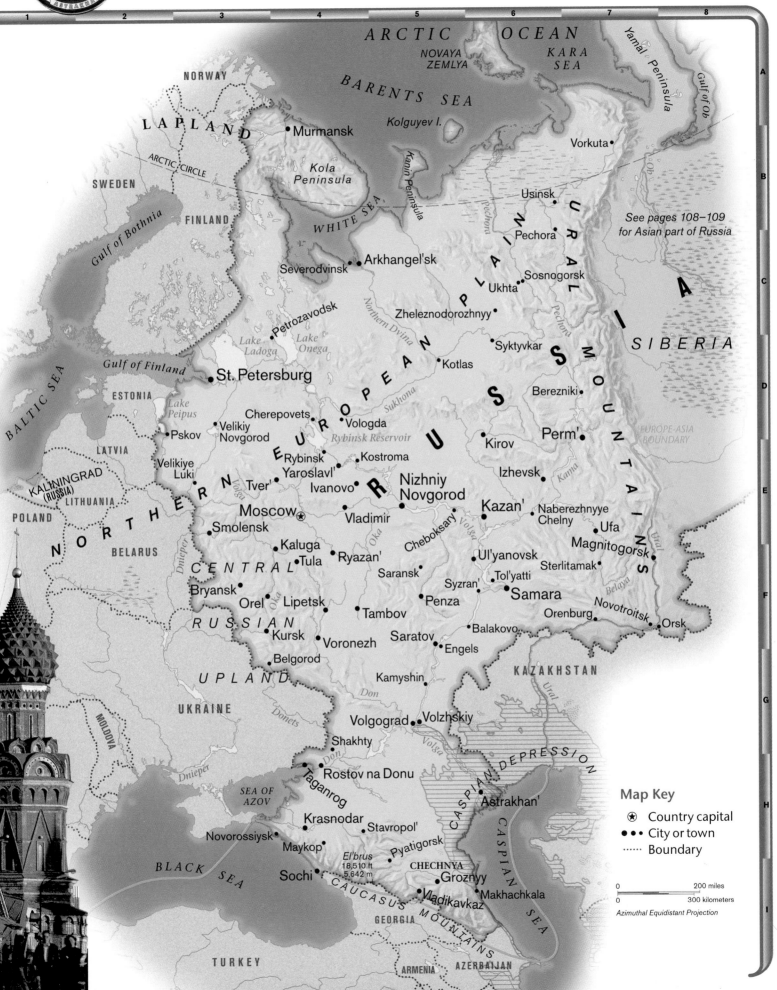

ARCTIC OCEAN

NOVAYA ZEMLYA

KARA SEA

Yamal Peninsula

Gulf of Ob

BARENTS SEA

Kolguyev I.

NORWAY

LAPLAND

Murmansk

Vorkuta

Kola Peninsula

Kanin Peninsula

Usinsk

ARCTIC CIRCLE

SWEDEN

FINLAND

WHITE SEA

Pechora

Pechora

URAL

See pages 108–109 for Asian part of Russia

Gulf of Bothnia

Severodvinsk

Arkhangel'sk

Ukhta

Sosnogorsk

PLAIN

Petrozavodsk

Zheleznodorozhnyy

Syktyvkar

MOUNTAINS

SIBERIA

Lake Ladoga

Lake Onega

Northern Dvina

Kotlas

Gulf of Finland

BALTIC SEA

St. Petersburg

Bere31niki

Perm'

EUROPE-ASIA BOUNDARY

ESTONIA

Lake Peipus

Cherepovets

Vologda

Sukhona

Kirov

Pskov

Velikiy Novgorod

Rybinsk Reservoir

Izhevsk

Kama

LATVIA

Velikiye Luki

Rybinsk

Kostroma

R

U

S

Perm'

KALININGRAD (RUSSIA)

Tver'

Yaroslavl'

Ivanovo

Nizhniy Novgorod

Kazan'

Naberezhnyye Chelny

Ufa

LITHUANIA

Moscow

Vladimir

Volga

Cheboksary

Volga

Magnitogorsk

POLAND

Smolensk

Oka

Ul'yanovsk

Sterlitamak

NORTHERN EUROPEAN RUSSIA

Kaluga

Ryazan'

Saransk

Syzran'

Tol'yatti

Belaya

Tula

Penza

Samara

Novotroitsk

BELARUS

CENTRAL

Bryansk

Orel

Oka

Lipetsk

Tambov

Saratov

Orenburg

Orsk

RUSSIAN

Kursk

Voronezh

Balakovo

Ural

Belgorod

Saratov

Engels

UPLAND

Kamyshin

KAZAKHSTAN

Don

UKRAINE

Donets

Volga

Volgograd

Volzhskiy

MOLDOVA

Shakhty

Don

CASPIAN DEPRESSION

Dnieper

Rostov na Donu

Taganrog

SEA OF AZOV

Astrakhan'

CASPIAN

Krasnodar

Stavropol'

Novorossiysk

Maykop

Pyatigorsk

El'brus 18,510 ft 5,642 m

CHECHNYA

SEA

BLACK SEA

Sochi

Groznyy

Makhachkala

CAUCASUS MOUNTAINS

Vladikavkaz

GEORGIA

TURKEY

ARMENIA

AZERBAIJAN

Map Key

✪ Country capital

••• City or town

⋯⋯ Boundary

0   200 miles
0   300 kilometers

Azimuthal Equidistant Projection

THE CONTINENT:
ASIA

PHYSICAL

Land area 17,208,000 sq mi (44,570,000 sq km)	**Lowest point** Dead Sea, Israel-Jordan -1,385 ft (-422 m)	**Largest lake entirely in Asia** Lake Baikal 12,200 sq mi (31,500 sq km)
Highest point Mount Everest, China-Nepal 29,035 ft (8,850 m)	**Longest river** Yangtze (Chang), China 3,964 mi (6,380 km)	

POLITICAL

Population 4,191,414,100	**Largest country entirely in Asia** China 3,705,405 sq mi (9,596,960 sq km)	**Economy** Farming: rice, wheat
Largest metropolitan area Tokyo, Japan Pop. 36,500,000	**Most densely populated country** Singapore 19,679 people per sq mi (7,565 per sq km)	Industry: petroleum, electronics Services

Asia

Asia

ATLANTIC OCEAN

PACIFIC OCEAN

NORTH AMERICA

Aleutian Islands

Bering Strait
Chukchi Peninsula
Commander Islands
Kamchatka Peninsula
Kuril Islands
Hokkaido
Sakhalin
BERING SEA
SEA OF OKHOTSK
Sikhote Alin Range
Amur
SEA OF JAPAN (EAST SEA)
Honshu
Shikoku
Kyushu
Ryukyu Islands
J A P A N
Nampō Shotō
Mariana Islands
TROPIC OF CANCER

CHUKCHI SEA
EAST SIBERIAN SEA
Wrangel Island
Kolyma Range
Kolyma
Chersky Range
Verkhoyansk Range
Aldan
Lena
S I B E R I A

ARCTIC OCEAN
ARCTIC CIRCLE
Taymyr Peninsula
Gulf of Ob
KARA SEA
North Land
Franz Josef Land
New Siberian Islands
LAPTEV SEA
BARENTS SEA
Greenland

CENTRAL SIBERIAN PLATEAU
Lake Baikal
Lena
Angara
Yenisey
Ob
Stanovoy Range
Amur
Greater Khingan Range
Northeast China Plain
NORTH KOREA
SOUTH KOREA
YELLOW SEA
EAST CHINA SEA
Yellow
North China Plain
Yangtze
Yangtze
Sichuan Basin
Three Gorges
Gongga Shan 24,790 ft 7,558 m
Yellow
Taiwan

PHILIPPINE SEA
CAROLINE ISLANDS
NEW GUINEA
EQUATOR
AUSTRALIA
ARAFURA SEA

WEST SIBERIAN PLAIN
Irtysh
Ob
GOBI
MONGOLIA
ALTAY MOUNTAINS
TIAN SHAN
TARIM BASIN
Taklimakan Desert
Qaidam Basin
KUNLUN MOUNTAINS
PLATEAU OF TIBET
C H I N A
H I M A L A Y A
Mt. Everest 29,035 ft 8,850 m World's highest point
BHUTAN
BANGLADESH
MYANMAR (BURMA)
Salween
Mekong
VIETNAM
LAOS
THAILAND
CAMBODIA
Gulf of Thailand
MALAY PENINSULA
SINGAPORE
Mekong
Brahmaputra
Ganges
NEPAL

R U S S I A
URAL MOUNTAINS
Ural
Volga
Europe–Asia Boundary
THE STEPPES
KAZAKHSTAN
Lake Balkhash
Syr Darya
UZBEKISTAN
Amu Darya
Aral Sea
TURKMENISTAN
Caspian Depression
Caspian Sea
KYRGYZSTAN
TAJIKISTAN
AFGHANISTAN
Hindu Kush
PAKISTAN
Indus
Thar Desert
Great Indian Desert
I N D I A
DECCAN PLATEAU
Eastern Ghats
Western Ghats
SRI LANKA
BAY OF BENGAL
Andaman Islands
Nicobar Islands
ANDAMAN SEA
Sumatra
BRUNEI
Borneo
MALAYSIA
INDONESIA
GREATER SUNDA ISLANDS
Java
Java Sea
LESSER SUNDA ISLANDS
Flores Sea
BANDA SEA
MOLUCCAS
CELEBES SEA
CELEBES
Mindanao
SULU SEA
Luzon
PHILIPPINES
PHILIPPINE ISLANDS
SOUTH CHINA SEA
Hainan
TIMOR SEA
EAST TIMOR (TIMOR-LESTE)
Timor

EUROPE
RUSSIA
Baltic Sea
BLACK SEA
Caucasus Mts.
GEORGIA
ARMENIA
AZERBAIJAN
Elburz Mountains
I R A N
Zagros Mountains
Tigris
Euphrates
Mesopotamia
Syrian Desert
SYRIA
LEBANON
ISRAEL
JORDAN
Dead Sea -1,385 ft -422 m World's lowest point
Suez Canal
Sinai
Mediterranean Sea
Aegean Sea
TURKEY
ANATOLIA
Persian Gulf
QATAR
BAHRAIN
KUWAIT
UNITED ARAB EMIRATES
Gulf of Oman
OMAN
SAUDI ARABIA
ARABIAN PENINSULA
Rub al Khali
YEMEN
Gulf of Aden
RED SEA
ARABIA
AFRICA

ARABIAN SEA
MALDIVES
LACCADIVE SEA
INDIAN OCEAN
EQUATOR

1,000 miles
1,500 kilometers

Map Key
— Country boundary

0
Two-Point Equidistant Projection

A commonly accepted division between Asia and Europe—here marked by an orange line—is formed by the Ural Mountains, Ural River, Caspian Sea, Caucasus Mountains, and the Black Sea, with its outlets to the Aegean Sea, the Bosporus, and the Dardanelles.

The People's Republic of China claims Taiwan as its 23rd province. Taiwan maintains that there are two political entities.

ATLANTIC OCEAN

ARCTIC OCEAN

PACIFIC OCEAN

Bering Strait
Chukchi Peninsula
Commander Islands
Kamchatka Peninsula
Gulf of Anadyr
Anadyr
BERING SEA
Kolyma Range
Magadan
Kuril Islands
SEA OF OKHOTSK
Sakhalin
Khabarovsk
Vladivostok
SEA OF JAPAN (EAST SEA)
Hokkaido
Sapporo
Sendai
Honshu
Tōkyō
JAPAN
Nagoya
Kyōto
Osaka
Hiroshima
Shikoku
Fukuoka
Kyushu
Marcus (JAPAN)
Bonin Is. (JAPAN)
Volcano Is. (JAPAN)
Parece Vela (JAPAN)
TROPIC OF CANCER
Ryukyu Islands
Okinawa

CHUKCHI SEA
Wrangel Island
ARCTIC CIRCLE
EAST SIBERIAN SEA
New Siberian Islands
North Land
LAPTEV SEA
Taymyr Peninsula
Cherskiy Range
Verkhoyansk Range
Aldan
Yakutsk
Kolyma Range
Magadan
Komsomol'sk na Amure
Khabarovsk

KARA SEA
Yamal Pen.
Gulf of Ob
Norilsk
Yenisey
Lena
Lake Baikal
Ulan Ude
Chita
Irkutsk
Bratsk
Krasnoyarsk
Tomsk
Novosibirsk
Barnaul
Semey
Öskemen

S I B E R I A
R U S S I A

Franz Josef Land
Novaya Zemlya
BARENTS SEA
Kola Peninsula
Murmansk
North Onega
Lake Ladoga
St. Petersburg
Moscow
Nizhny Novgorod
Kazan
Samara
Ufa
Perm
Yekaterinburg
Chelyabinsk
Tyumen'
URAL MOUNTAINS
Nizhny Tagil
Magnitogorsk
Orenburg
Orsk
Ob
Irtysh
Omsk

EUROPE
EUROPE-ASIA BOUNDARY
Volga
Rostov na Donu
Volgograd
BLACK SEA
Istanbul
Bursa
Izmir
Ankara
Konya
Adana
Kayseri
T U R K E Y
CYPRUS
LEBANON
Beirut
Damascus
SYRIA
ISRAEL
Jerusalem
JORDAN
Mediterranean Sea
Aegean Sea
Caucasus Mts.
Tbilisi
GEORGIA
ARMENIA
Yerevan
AZERBAIJAN
Baku
Caspian Sea
Tehrān
Mashhad
I R A N
Kermān
Zāhedān
Baghdad
Basra
IRAQ
KUWAIT
Al Kuwayt
Zagros Mts.
Persian Gulf
Manama
BAHRAIN
QATAR
Doha
Abu Dhabi
UNITED ARAB EMIRATES
Muscat
O M A N
Gulf of Oman
Strait of Hormuz
Gulf of Aden
Aden
YEMEN
Sanaa
Socotra (YEMEN)
ARABIAN SEA
Rub' al Khali
SAUDI ARABIA
Riyadh
Mecca
Jeddah
Medina
RED SEA
Gulf of Aqaba
Dead Sea -1,385 ft -422 m
Euphrates
Tigris
AFRICA

Caspian Depression
Aral Sea
Lake Balkhash
KAZAKHSTAN
Astana
Qaraghandy
Almaty
Bishkek
KYRGYZSTAN
Tashkent
UZBEKISTAN
Amu Darya
Syr Darya
Ashgabat
TURKMENISTAN
Dushanbe
TAJIKISTAN
Samarqand
Kabul
AFGHANISTAN
Hindu Kush
PAKISTAN
Islamabad
Faisalabad
Lahore
Karachi
Kashmir

MONGOLIA
Ulaanbaatar
GOBI
ALTAI MOUNTAINS
TIAN SHAN
Ürümqi
SINKIANG
Takliman Desert
KUNLUN SHAN
TIBET
Mt. Everest 29,035 ft 8,850 m
NEPAL
Kathmandu
BHUTAN
Thimphu
Boundary claimed by India
Boundary claimed by China

DONGBEI
Harbin
Qiqihar
Jilin
Changchun
Shenyang
Anshan
Fushun
Dalian
NORTH KOREA
Pyŏngyang
SOUTH KOREA
Seoul
Amur
Beijing
Tianjin
Shijiazhuang
Taiyuan
Zhengzhou
Luoyang
Xi'an
Lanzhou
Chengdu
Guiyang
Kunming
Wuwei
C H I N A
Huang (Yellow)
Yangtze
Qingdao
Xuzhou
Nanjing
Shanghai
Hangzhou
Wuhan
Nanchang
Changsha
Fuzhou
Shantou
Guangzhou
Shenzhen
Hong Kong
Nanning
Hainan
Haiphong
Hanoi
Da Nang
Vientiane
LAOS
VIETNAM
Ho Chi Minh City (Saigon)
CAMBODIA
Phnom Penh
THAILAND
Bangkok
Gulf of Thailand
MYANMAR (BURMA)
Nay Pyi Taw
Yangon (Rangoon)
Mandalay
Mawlamyine
Chiang Mai
Taipei
TAIWAN
Kaohsiung
Fuzhou

I N D I A
New Delhi
Delhi
Jaipur
Kanpur
Lucknow
Bhopal
Indore
Ahmadabad
Surat
Mumbai (Bombay)
Pune
Nagpur
Hyderabad
Bangalore
Mysore
Coimbatore
Chennai (Madras)
Vijayawada
Kolkata (Calcutta)
BANGLADESH
Dhaka
Chittagong
Ganges
Krishna
Godavari
Madurai
SRI LANKA
Colombo
Sri Jayewardenepura Kotte
MALDIVES
Male
Maldive Islands
Lakshadweep (INDIA)
Andaman Islands (INDIA)
Nicobar Is. (INDIA)
BAY OF BENGAL
Chagos Archipelago (BRITISH INDIAN OCEAN TERRITORY)
MALAY PENINSULA
Kuala Lumpur
MALAYSIA
SINGAPORE
Medan
Pekanbaru
Padang
Jambi
Palembang
Sumatra
Jakarta
Bandung
Semarang
Surabaya
GREATER SUNDA ISLANDS
JAVA SEA
Java
Borneo
SARAWAK
SABAH
Kuching
Pontianak
Banjarmasin
Balikpapan
Makassar
Celebes
Manado
BRUNEI
Bandar Seri Begawan
SOUTH CHINA SEA
PHILIPPINE SEA
PHILIPPINES
Manila
Quezon City
Cagayan de Oro
Zamboanga
Davao
Luzon
Mindoro
Panay
Negros
Leyte
Samar
Mindanao
Palawan
CAROLINE ISLANDS
MOLUCCAS
CERAM SEA
Halmahera
Morotai
Buru
Ceram
BANDA SEA
ARAFURA SEA
FLORES SEA
LESSER SUNDA ISLANDS
Flores
Kupang
Timor
TIMOR-LESTE (EAST TIMOR)
Dili
I N D O N E S I A
NEW GUINEA
Jayapura
Biak
Merauke
Dolak
Aru Is.
Tanimbar Islands
EQUATOR
AUSTRALIA
BANDA SEA

INDIAN OCEAN

0   1,000 miles
0   1,500 kilometers
Two-Point Equidistant Projection

Asia

WORLD CHAMPION

From Turkey to the eastern tip of Russia, Asia sprawls across nearly 180 degrees of longitude—almost half the globe! It boasts the highest (the Himalaya) and lowest (the Dead Sea) places on Earth's surface. Then there are Asia's people—more than four billion of them. That's more people than live on all the other continents put together. Asia has both the most farmers and the most million-plus cities. The world's first civilization arose in Sumer, in what is now southern Iraq. Rich cultures also emerged along rivers in present-day India and China, strongly influencing the world ever since.

🔵 **TASTY SNACK.** This black-and-white giant panda, native to China, munches on a stalk of bamboo, the mainstay of its diet.

🔴 **NEW VS. OLD.** An Afghan woman, completely covered by a traditional burka, sits among young girls dressed in Western clothes in Kabul.

◐ LUNAR NEW YEAR.
Young men carry a writhing
paper dragon on poles in this
Chinese New Year's parade in Singapore.

◐ NEON AVENUE.
Bright lights and
neon signs highlight
bustling Nanjing
Lu, Shanghai's main
shopping street.
With a population of
more than 23 million,
Shanghai is China's
largest city.

◐ WINGED HUNTER.
A Kazakh falconer sits
astride his pony as he
releases his golden eagle to
pursue prey on the dry Mongolian steppe.

more about
Asia

🔵 **EASTERN BELIEF.** From its origins in the foothills of the Himalaya, Buddhism has spread across much of eastern Asia. Statues of the Buddha, such as this one in Bangkok, Thailand, appear frequently in the landscape of the region.

🔵 **UP AND DOWN.** Traditional dress and a modern motorized walkway create a sharp contrast in a mall in Doha, Qatar.

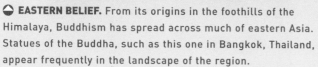

🔵 **A FINAL TOUCH.** Silk kimonos and perfectly applied makeup are part of the tradition of a *maiko*, or apprentice geisha, in Kyoto, Japan.

◐ **STONE BARRIER.** Construction on China's Great Wall began in 220 B.C. as a defense against invasion from the north and continued until the A.D. 1600s. Extending in sections for almost 4,000 miles (6,436 km), the wall attracts tourists from around the world.

WHERE THE PICTURES ARE

Kyrgyz goat herder p. 110
Samarkand market p. 111
Girls talking p. 116
Stone head p. 115
Galata Bridge p. 114
Swimmers p. 115
Petra p. 114
Ring p. 117
Horse and car pp. 116–117
Mall scene p. 106
Drummer p. 116
Afghan girls p. 104
Taj Mahal p. 118
Hindu god Shiva p. 119
Elephant at work p. 120
Tigers p. 107
Mountain climbers p. 118

Ger and yak p. 111
Falconer p. 105
Horse riders p. 110
Golden Buddha p. 106
Petronas Twin Towers p. 121
Lunar New Year pp. 104–105
Man and his cow p. 119

Nenet woman and child p. 108
Diamond mine p. 109
Lenin's head p. 109
Brown bears p. 108
Great Wall of China pp. 106–107
Woman in lab p. 112
Japanese snow monkeys p. 113
Tokyo city street pp. 112–113
Geisha p. 106
Shanghai city lights p. 105
Terra cotta soldiers p. 113
Panda p. 104
Jeepney p. 121
Buddhist monk p. 120
Container terminal p. 120
Rain forest p. 123
Boy with flag p. 122
Orangutan p. 123
Terraced rice fields p. 107
Ceremonial mask p. 123
Jakarta at night p. 122

◐ **MOUNTAIN STAIRWAY.** Terraces cut into a steep mountainside create fields for rice on the island of Bali, in Indonesia. Rice is the staple grain crop in much of eastern Asia. In the foreground, a man nimbly climbs a palm tree to harvest coconuts.

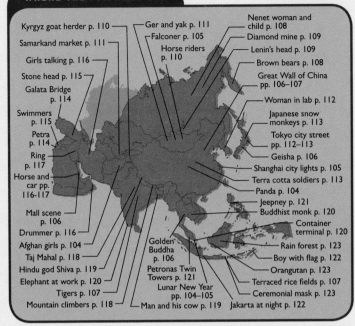

◐ **MOTHER KNOWS BEST.**
A Bengal tiger gently moves her cub to a safe hiding place before stalking her prey in India's Bandhavgarh National Park. Tigers are an endangered species.

THE BASICS

STATS*

Area
6,592,850 sq mi (17,075,400 sq km)

Population
143,165,000

Predominant languages
Russian, minority languages

Predominant religions
Christianity (Russian Orthodox), Islam

GDP per capita
$16,700

Life expectancy
66 years

Literacy rate
100%

*These figures are for all of Russia.
For European Russia, see pages 98–99.

GEO WHIZ

The name Siberia comes from the Turkic language and means "Sleeping Land."

Trophy hunting, oil and gas exploration, and gold mining have reduced the brown bear population on the Kamchatka Peninsula from 20,000 during the Soviet era, when the peninsula was restricted to military use, to about 12,500.

A region of northern coniferous forest called taiga stretches across northern Russia as far west as Norway. It covers an area that is more than 11 times the size of Texas.

It takes at least six days to travel 6,000 miles (9,656 km) on the Trans-Siberian Railroad from Moscow to the Pacific port of Vladivostok. The trip crosses eight time zones.

Russia produces more natural gas than the next six countries combined. More than a quarter of the world's proven reserves are in Russia, mainly in Siberia, the Urals, and the region around the Volga River.

Lake Baikal, nicknamed Siberia's "blue eye," is home to 1,500 unique species of plants and animals, including the nerpa, the world's only freshwater seal.

The Chukchi, the largest group of native people in Siberia, take their name from a word that means "rich in reindeer." They share their name with their homeland, a peninsula that borders the Arctic and Pacific Oceans.

Asian Russia

🔵 **NOMADIC HERDERS.** A Nenet woman and her grandson prepare to follow the family reindeer herd into northern Siberia for spring and summer grazing.

Forming more than half of gigantic Russia, this region stretches from the Ural Mountains east to the Pacific, and from the Arctic Ocean south to mountains and deserts along borders with Central Asia and China. Siberia, as this region is commonly known, has limited croplands but bountiful forests (the taiga) and rich mineral resources such as natural gas, oil, and gold. The Trans-Siberian Railroad, built between 1891 and 1905, opened up the region for settlement—but not too much. Only about one-sixth of Russia's population—fewer than 25 million people—lives in sprawling Siberia.

See page 99
European part of

NORWAY
SWEDEN
FINLAND
BALTIC SEA
RUSSIA
ESTONIA
POLAND LITHUANIA LATVIA
BELARUS
★ Moscow
UKRAINE
R
Nizhniy Ta
Yekaterinbu
Kamensk U
Chelyabins
Magnitogorsk
BLACK SEA
EUROPE-ASIA BOUNDARY
Volga
Ural
Orsk
CAUCASUS MTS.
GEORGIA
ARMENIA
AZERBAIJAN
TURKEY
Caspian Depression
CASPIAN SEA
KA

🔘 **FISHING FOR A MEAL.**
A brown bear and her cubs hunt for fish in a river below the snow-laced slopes of a volcano on Russia's Kamchatka Peninsula. Part of the Pacific Ring of Fire, this peninsula in far eastern Russia has 29 active volcanoes.

REVOLUTIONARY LEADER. Vladimir Ilyich Lenin, a founder of the Soviet Union, was honored with statues throughout the former Communist union and beyond. This one in Ulan Ude, in Siberia, is the largest still standing in Russia.

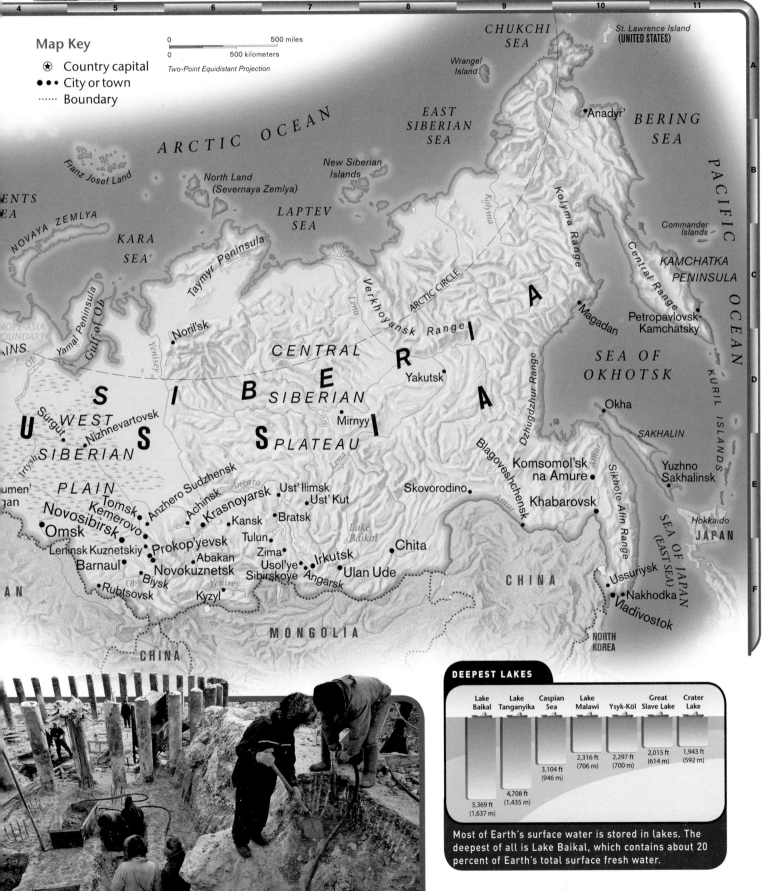

Map Key

⊛ Country capital
••• City or town
······ Boundary

0 ——————— 500 miles
0 ——————— 500 kilometers
Two-Point Equidistant Projection

ARCTIC OCEAN

CHUKCHI SEA

St. Lawrence Island (UNITED STATES)

Wrangel Island

EAST SIBERIAN SEA

BERING SEA

•Anadyr'

New Siberian Islands

LAPTEV SEA

Franz Josef Land

North Land (Severnaya Zemlya)

NOVAYA ZEMLYA

KARA SEA

Taymyr Peninsula

Commander Islands

Kolyma

Kolyma Range

Central Range

KAMCHATKA PENINSULA

PACIFIC OCEAN

ENTS EA

Yamal Peninsula

Gulf of Ob

•Noril'sk

Yenisey

CENTRAL

Verkhoyansk Range

ARCTIC CIRCLE

Lena

•Magadan

Petropavlovsk-Kamchatsky

SEA OF OKHOTSK

KURIL ISLANDS

EUROPE-ASIA BOUNDARY

AINS

Ob

U   S   S   I   A

SIBERIA

Yakutsk•

Dzhugdzhur Range

•Okha

SAKHALIN

WEST

•Surgut
Nizhnevartovsk•

SIBERIAN

SIBERIAN PLATEAU

Mirnyy•

Lena

Blagoveshchensk•

Komsomol'sk na Amure•

Amur

Yuzhno-Sakhalinsk

PLAIN

Irtysh

umen'
gan

Anzhero Sudzhensk•

Achinsk•

Angara

Ust'Ilimsk•
•Ust' Kut

Skovorodino•

Amur

Khabarovsk•

Sikhote Alin Range

Hokkaido

JAPAN

Tomsk•
Kemerovo•
•Krasnoyarsk
Kansk•
•Bratsk

Lake Baikal

Novosibirsk•
•Omsk
Leninsk Kuznetskiy•
•Prokop'yevsk
Barnaul•   •Abakan
•Novokuznetsk
•Biysk
•Rubtsovsk

Tulun•
Zima•
Usol'ye
Sibirskoye•

Irkutsk•
Angarsk•

Chita•

Ulan Ude

CHINA

Ob

Yenisey

Kyzyl•

MONGOLIA

CHINA

SEA OF JAPAN (EAST SEA)

Ussuriysk•
•Nakhodka
Vladivostok•

NORTH KOREA

AN

DEEPEST LAKES

Lake Baikal	Lake Tanganyika	Caspian Sea	Lake Malawi	Ysyk-Köl	Great Slave Lake	Crater Lake
			2,316 ft (706 m)	2,297 ft (700 m)	2,015 ft (614 m)	1,943 ft (592 m)
		3,104 ft (946 m)				
	4,708 ft (1,435 m)					
5,369 ft (1,637 m)						

Most of Earth's surface water is stored in lakes. The deepest of all is Lake Baikal, which contains about 20 percent of Earth's total surface fresh water.

GEMS IN THE ROUGH. Miners bundled in warm clothing cut through permafrost in the Mir diamond mine in northern Siberia. Although mined out and closed in 2004, it once produced two million carats a year.

THE BASICS

STATS

Largest country
Kazakhstan 1,049,155 sq mi
(2,717,300 sq km)

Smallest country
Tajikistan 55,251 sq mi (143,100 sq km)

Most populous country
Uzbekistan 29,780,000

Least populous country
Mongolia 2,873,000

Predominant languages
Russian, Kazakh, Uzbek, Kyrgyz, Tajik,
Mongol, Turkmen

Predominant religions
Islam, Christianity (Orthodox), Buddhism

Highest GDP per capita
Kazakhstan $13,000

Lowest GDP per capita
Tajikistan $2,100

Highest life expectancy
Uzbekistan 73 years

Highest literacy rate
Kazakhstan, Tajikistan
100%

GEO WHIZ

The main musical instrument of the steppes in Kazakhstan is the *dombra*, a long-necked lute with two strings.

Uzbekistan is among the world's top ten gold-producing countries, and the world's largest open-pit gold mine is at Muruntau in the Qizilqum Desert some 250 miles (400 km) from Tashkent.

The world's only surviving breed of wild horse, the *takh*, or Prezewalski, was "discovered" in southwestern Mongolia in the 1880s by Count Prezewalski. The largest number—some 300—now live in zoos around the world, but a select few that have been reintroduced into the wild graze on the steppe in Mongolia's Hustai National Park.

Kazakhstan's Baikonur Cosmodrome, site of most of the space flights launched by the Soviet Union from the late 1950s to the 1980s, is the world's oldest space-launch facility. It is still managed by the Russian Federal Space Agency.

The Pamir and the Tian Shan are among the mountain ranges that cover more than 90 percent of Tajikistan.

◗ SKILLED RIDERS.
Young people ride their horses across the steppe in the Darhad Valley, a region of nomadic herders in northern Mongolia. From the time of Genghis Khan's 13th-century armies, Mongolians have been known for their skill on horseback.

Central Asia

Mongolia and five *stans*—"homelands"—make up Central Asia. Kazakhs, Turkmen, Uzbeks, Tajiks, and Kyrgyz form the majority of the population in these largely Muslim countries. Russians are still present in each, a result of decades of Soviet efforts to control these lands. Sparsely settled, largely Buddhist Mongolia consists

BEST FRIENDS. A boy carries his goat in mountainous Kyrgyzstan, where almost half the land is used for pasture and hay to support herds of goats and sheep.

of valley grasslands and dry basins beneath towering peaks. Kazakhstan's short-grass steppes give way to deserts, arid plateaus, and rugged mountains to the south. Irrigation provides water for wheat, cotton, and fruit crops. Though far from any ocean, this region possesses several inland seas, including the salty Caspian. Beneath its floor lie huge oil deposits, both tapped and undeveloped, which will add to the region's future importance.

◖ **HOME ON THE STEPPE.** A *ger*, made of a wooden frame overlaid with felt, is the traditional Mongolian dwelling. The cowlike yak works as a pack animal and is a source of milk. Its waste is burned as fuel.

3   4   5   6   7   8   9   10

Map Key

⊛ Country capital
• • • City or town
······ Boundary

0   500 miles
0   500 kilometers
Two-Point Equidistant Projection

ROPE-ASIA
DARY

Qostanay
Rŭdnyy
Petropavlovsk
tŭ   Kökshetaü   Pavlodar
Ekibastuz
Astana ⊛   *Kasakh*
Temirtaū   Semey
EPPES   Qaraghandy
STAN   *Uplands*   Öskemen
NUR
ODROME
zylorda   Lake
Balkhash   Taldyqorghan
Shymkent
Chirchiq Angren Taraz
kent Namangan Bishkek
A.N ⊛   Almaty
KYRGYZSTAN
Andijon
Osh
khujand Farg'ona *Communism Peak*
TAJIKISTAN   24,590 ft 7,495 m
Dushanbe   *Pamirs*
gand
AN   PAKISTAN

R U S S I A

DARHAD
VALLEY
Yenisey
Hovd
Uliastay
Irtysch
Ertis
Ertix

A L T A Y   M O U N T A I N S

T I A N   S H A N
Victory Peak
24,406 ft
7,439 m

C H I N A

Lake Baikal

Choybalsan
Selenga Darhan
Ulaanbaatar ⊛   *Herlen*
HUSTAI   *Mongolian*
NATIONAL PARK Saynshand
MONGOLIA *Plateau*
HANGAYN
MOUNTAINS
Yellow

G O B I

A
B
C
D
E

◖ **WHERE BARGAINING IS AN ART.** Two men haggle over the price of cherries in a bazaar in Samarkand, Uzbekistan. Located on the fabled Silk Road, the country relies on agriculture, especially cotton production, to support its economy.

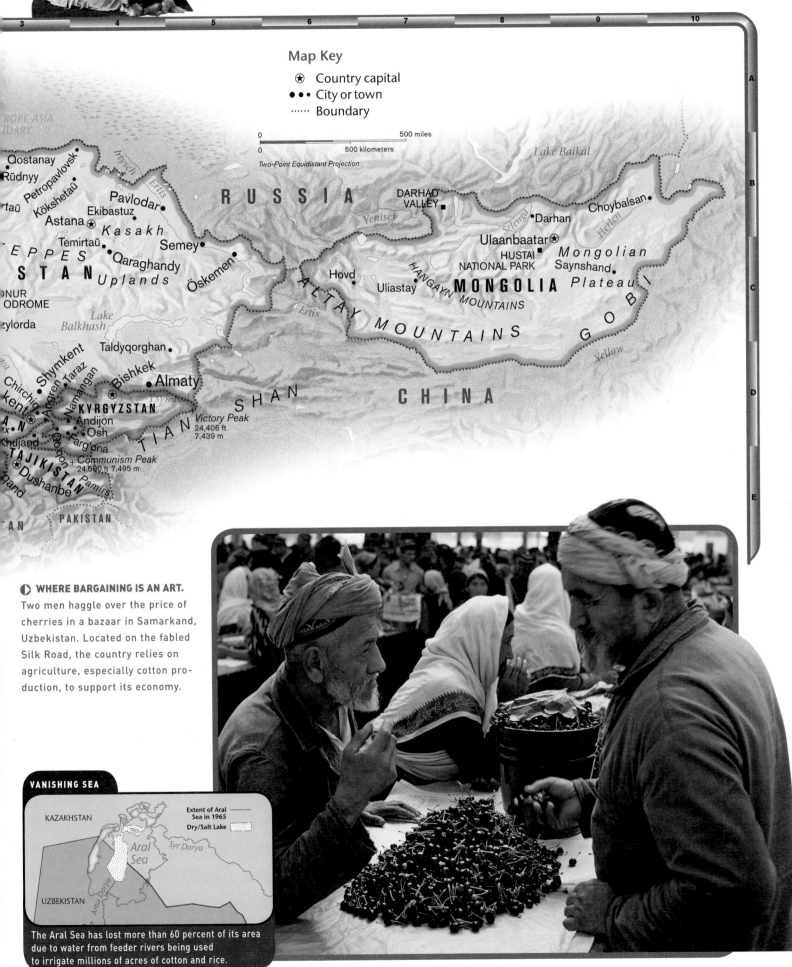

VANISHING SEA

KAZAKHSTAN

Extent of Aral
Sea in 1965 ———
Dry/Salt Lake ▨

Aral
Sea   *Syr Darya*

Amu Darya

UZBEKISTAN

The Aral Sea has lost more than 60 percent of its area due to water from feeder rivers being used to irrigate millions of acres of cotton and rice.

THE BASICS

STATS

Largest country
China 3,705,405 sq mi (9,596,960 sq km)

Smallest country
South Korea 38,321 sq mi (99,250 sq km)

Most populous country
China 1,350,378,000

Least populous country
North Korea 24,589,000

Predominant languages
Standard Chinese or Mandarin, Japanese, Korean, local dialects

Predominant religions
Daoism, Buddhism, Shintoism, Christianity, Confucianism

Highest GDP per capita
Japan $34,700

Lowest GDP per capita
North Korea $1,800

Highest life expectancy
Japan 83 years

Highest literacy rate
Japan, North Korea
99%

GEO WHIZ

The Seikan Tunnel, the world's longest railroad tunnel, links Japan's two largest islands: Honshu and Hokkaido.

Roughly 900 square miles (2,300 sq km) of farmland in northern China are blown away by the wind each year. Huge dust plumes travel hundreds of miles to Beijing and other cities. The clouds are often so thick that they hide the sun, slow traffic, and close airports.

Each year on October 9, people in South Korea celebrate their alphabet, which was created in 1446 to increase literacy.

Construction of the Three Gorges Dam across the Yangtze River created a reservoir that forced more than a million people to find new homes.

Kim Il-sung, who ruled North Korea from its founding in 1948 to his death in 1994, is referred to in the country's constitution as the Eternal President. Both his birthday and the anniversary of his death are public holidays.

Only about 18 percent of Japan's land is suitable for people to live on. Most people choose to live in cities along the narrow coastal plain.

East Asia

China takes up most of this region, with the Koreas and Japan lining the Pacific edge. With more than 1.3 billion people, China's population is unrivaled in size. Rich river valleys have nourished Chinese civilization for more than four millennia. The Tibetan Plateau, dry basins, and the hulking Himalaya border China's western regions. Rugged uplands limit living space in Japan and the Koreas. Japan's economic success—especially in technology and manufacturing—has made it a global powerhouse. South Korea has followed a similar economic path, whereas North Korea's dictator prefers to isolate his country. A gradual move to capitalism has led communist China near the top of the global marketplace.

◖ **HIGH TECH.** This young South Korean woman works in a laboratory that makes microcircuits in a semiconductor plant in Seoul.

◖ **NIGHTLIGHTS.** Tokyo's Shinjuku is both a shopping center and a theater district as well as the city's busiest train station. It serves more than two million passengers daily.

AUTO GIANTS

Country	Production
China	14.5 million*
Japan	7.2 million
Germany	5.9 million
South Korea	4.2 million
India	3.0 million
USA	3.0 million
Brazil	2.5 million
France	1.9 million
Spain	1.8 million
Russia	1.7 million

*Cars only, 2011 data

Once the leader in car production, the United States now ranks sixth. China's expanding production moved it from number two a few years ago to the top spot.

◀ **STANDING GUARD.** Lifelike terra cotta statues formed part of the "army" buried in 141 B.C. with Han Dynasty emperor Jing Di. The emperor believed the army, arranged in battle formation and facing enemy territory, would protect him after death.

THE CONTINENT:
ASIA

Map Key

⭐ Country capital
• • • City or town
· · · · · Boundary

0 ————————————— 500 miles
0 ————————————— 500 kilometers
Two-Point Equidistant Projection

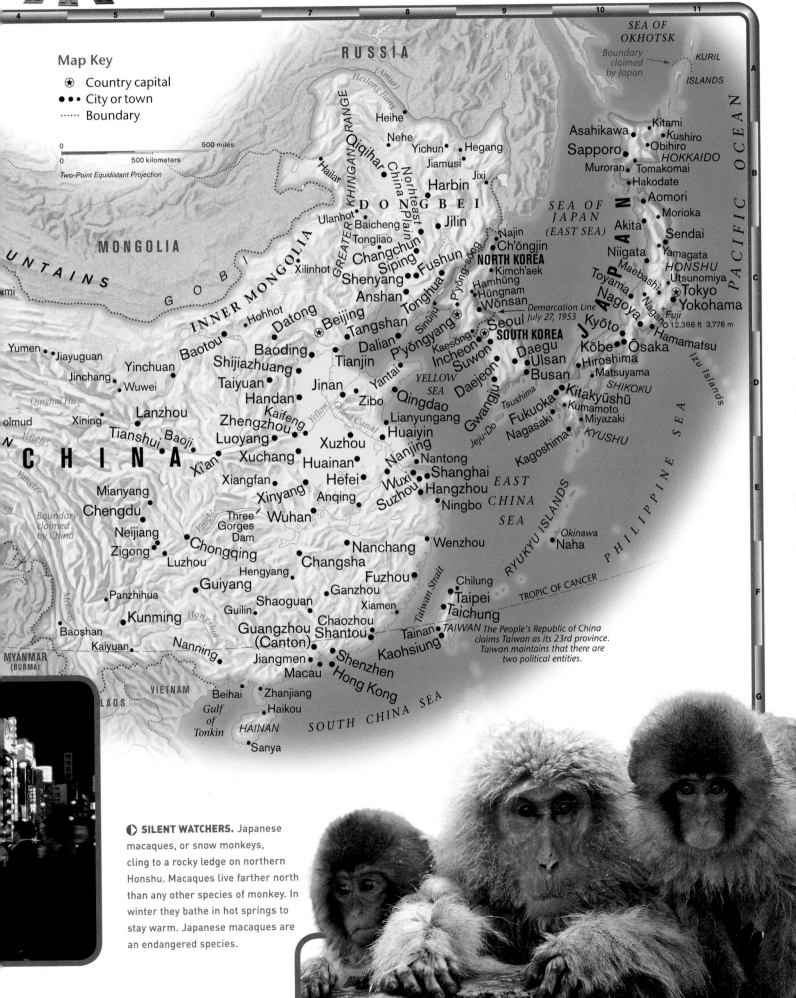

RUSSIA

SEA OF OKHOTSK

Boundary claimed by Japan

KURIL ISLANDS

Heilong Jiang (Amur)

Heihe
Nehe
Yichun
Hegang
Jiamusi
Jixi
Hailar
Harbin

GREATER KHINGAN RANGE
Qiqihar
Norhteast China Plain

DONGBEI

Ulanhot
Baicheng
Tongliao
Changchun
Jilin
Siping
Xilinhot
Shenyang
Fushun
Anshan
Tonghua

MONGOLIA

GOBI

INNER MONGOLIA

Hohhot
Datong
Baotou

Beijing
Tangshan

KITAMI
Asahikawa
Kushiro
Sapporo
Obihiro
HOKKAIDO
Muroran
Tomakomai
Hakodate
Aomori
Morioka
Akita
Sendai
Niigata
Yamagata
HONSHU
Maebashi
Utsunomiya
Toyama
Nagano
Tokyo
Nagoya
Yokohama
Fuji 12,388 ft 3,776 m
Kyōto
Hamamatsu
Izu Islands

SEA OF JAPAN (EAST SEA)

JAPAN

NORTH KOREA
Najin
Ch'ŏngjin
Kimch'aek
Hamhŭng
Hŭngnam
Wŏnsan
Pyŏng-song
Sinŭiju
P'yŏngyang
Seoul
Demarcation Line July 27, 1953
Kaesŏng
Incheon
SOUTH KOREA
Suwon
Daegu
Ulsan
Kōbe
Ōsaka
Hiroshima
Matsuyama
SHIKOKU
Gwangju
Daejeon
Busan
Fukuoka
Kitakyūshū
Kumamoto
Miyazaki
Nagasaki
Kagoshima
KYUSHU

Yumen
Jiayuguan
Yinchuan
Jinchang
Wuwei
Lanzhou
Xining
Qinghai Hu
olmud
Tianshui
Baoji
Yellow

CHINA

Boundary claimed by China

Yangtze

Mianyang
Chengdu
Neijiang
Zigong
Luzhou
Panzhihua
Guiyang
Kunming
Baoshan
Kaiyuan

MYANMAR (BURMA)

VIETNAM
LAOS

Mekong

Hong Shui

Nanning
Beihai
Zhanjiang
Haikou
Gulf of Tonkin
HAINAN
Sanya

Xi'an
Xuchang
Huainan
Xiangfan
Hefei
Xinyang
Anqing
Wuhan
Three Gorges Dam
Chongqing
Changsha
Hengyang
Ganzhou
Shaoguan
Guilin
Chaozhou
Guangzhou (Canton)
Shantou
Jiangmen
Macau
Shenzhen
Hong Kong

Baoding
Shijiazhuang
Taiyuan
Handan
Kaifeng
Zhengzhou
Luoyang
Tianjin
Jinan
Zibo
Yantai
Dalian
Qingdao
Lianyungang
Huaiyin
Xuzhou
Nanjing
Nantong
Wuxi
Suzhou
Shanghai
Hangzhou
Ningbo
Grand Canal

YELLOW SEA

EAST CHINA SEA

Wenzhou
Nanchang
Fuzhou
Xiamen
Taiwan Strait
Chilung
Taipei
Taichung
Tainan
Kaohsiung

Tsushima
Jeju-Do

RYUKYU ISLANDS
Okinawa
Naha

PHILIPPINE SEA

TROPIC OF CANCER

TAIWAN The People's Republic of China claims Taiwan as its 23rd province. Taiwan maintains that there are two political entities.

SOUTH CHINA SEA

PACIFIC OCEAN

◀ **SILENT WATCHERS.** Japanese macaques, or snow monkeys, cling to a rocky ledge on northern Honshu. Macaques live farther north than any other species of monkey. In winter they bathe in hot springs to stay warm. Japanese macaques are an endangered species.

THE CONTINENT:
ASIA

Eastern Mediterranean

This region forms a bridge between Europe and Asia, from the Caucasus Mountains to the desert lands of Jordan. Turkey, framed by the Black, Aegean, and Mediterranean Seas, leads the region in population and area. The historic and life-giving Tigris and Euphrates Rivers begin in Turkey and flow southeast through arid Syria and Iraq. Israel, Lebanon, and Syria share the Mediterranean shore. While Islam claims the majority of followers across these lands, Jewish, Christian, and other faiths are present. Indeed, the holiest places to Christians and Jews occupy Israeli soil in Jerusalem, adjacent to the third holiest site for Muslims, a situation that continues to cause tension and conflict.

ANCIENT MYSTERY. A camel walks before El-Khazneh in Petra, a World Heritage site in Jordan. Carved out of the mountainside more than 2,500 years ago, Petra was the capital of the Nabateans.

WEST BANK & GAZA STRIP
Captured by Israel in the 1967 Six Day War, areas of the West Bank and Gaza have limited Palestinian self-rule under a 1993 peace agreement. The future for these areas and four million Palestinians is subject to Israeli-Palestinian negotiations.

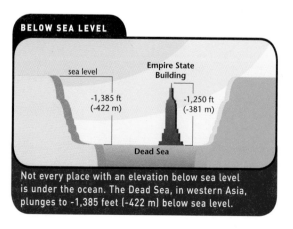

BELOW SEA LEVEL

sea level

Empire State Building

-1,385 ft (-422 m)   -1,250 ft (-381 m)

Dead Sea

Not every place with an elevation below sea level is under the ocean. The Dead Sea, in western Asia, plunges to -1,385 feet (-422 m) below sea level.

WATCHERS FROM THE PAST. Giant stone heads, representing Greek gods, guard the first-century B.C. burial site of King Antiochus I in remote southeastern Turkey. Many of the heads have been toppled in this earthquake-prone region.

THE CONTINENT:
ASIA

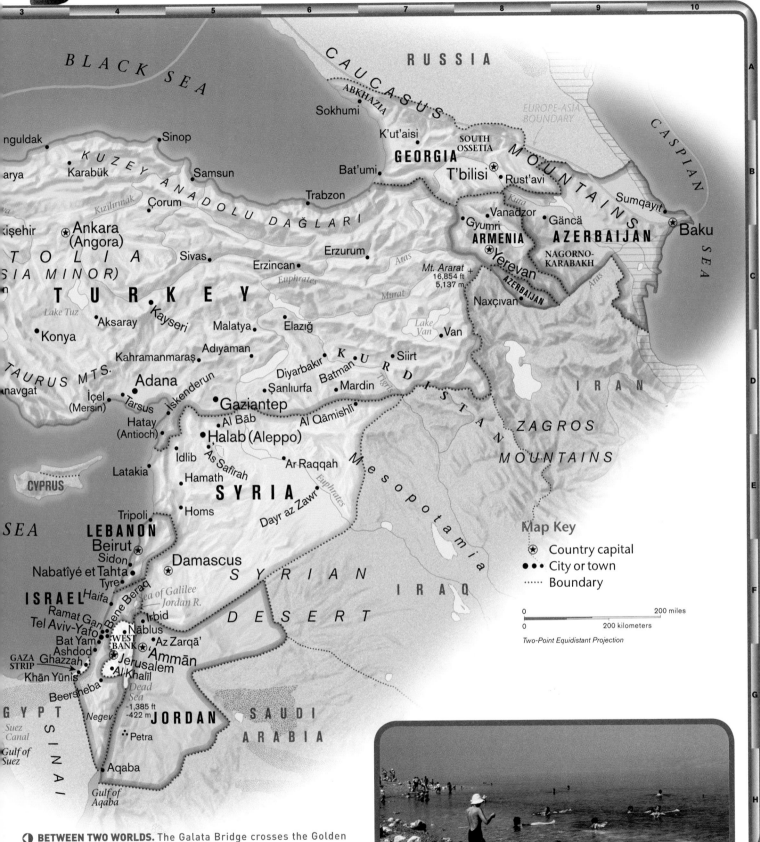

BLACK SEA

RUSSIA

CAUCASUS MOUNTAINS

nguldak
Sinop
arya
Karabük
Samsun
Çorum
KUZEY ANADOLU DAĞLARI
Trabzon
Sokhumi
ABKHAZIA
K'ut'aisi
Bat'umi
GEORGIA
SOUTH OSSETIA
T'bilisi
Rust'avi
EUROPE-ASIA BOUNDARY
CASPIAN SEA

kişehir
Ankara (Angora)
ATOLIA
SIA MINOR)
TURKEY
Sivas
Erzincan
Erzurum
Euphrates
Aras
Murat
Vanadzor
Gyumri
ARMENIA
Yerevan
Mt. Ararat 16,854 ft 5,137 m
Naxçıvan
AZERBAIJAN
NAGORNO-KARABAKH
AZERBAIJAN
Gäncä
Sumqayıt
Baku

Lake Tuz
Konya
Aksaray
Kayseri
Malatya
Elazığ
Lake Van
Van
IRAN

TAURUS MTS.
navgat
İçel (Mersin)
Adana
Tarsus
İskenderun
Hatay (Antioch)
Kahramanmaraş
Adıyaman
Gaziantep
Al Bāb
Diyarbakır
Şanlıurfa
Batman
Mardin
Siirt
KURDISTAN
Tigris
ZAGROS MOUNTAINS

Halab (Aleppo)
Al Qāmishli
Idlib
As Safirah
Ar Raqqah
Euphrates
Mesopotamia
Latakia
CYPRUS
Hamath
SYRIA
Homs
Dayr az Zawr
Tripoli
LEBANON
Beirut
Sidon
Nabatîyé et Tahta
Tyre
SEA
ISRAEL
Haifa
Sea of Galilee
Jordan R.
Ramat Gan
Tel Aviv-Yafo
Bene Beraq
Bat Yam
Ashdod
Nāblus
Az Zarqā'
WEST BANK
GAZA STRIP
Ghazzah
Jerusalem
Ammān
Khān Yūnis
Al Khalīl
Beersheba
Dead Sea -1,385 ft -422 m
SYRIAN DESERT
IRAQ

Map Key
⊛ Country capital
••• City or town
······ Boundary

0 ──────── 200 miles
0 ──────── 200 kilometers
Two-Point Equidistant Projection

GYPT
Suez Canal
Gulf of Suez
SINAI
Negev
JORDAN
Petra
SAUDI ARABIA
Aqaba
Gulf of Aqaba

BETWEEN TWO WORLDS. The Galata Bridge crosses the Golden Horn, connecting the Asian part of Istanbul, Turkey (foreground), to the Galata area in the city's European part.

SALTY EXTREME. The land between Israel and Jordan plunges down to the surface of the Dead Sea, which lies at -1,385 feet (-422 m) below sea level. The water of the sea is almost six times saltier than the ocean.

THE BASICS

STATS

Largest country
Saudi Arabia 756,985 sq mi
(1,960,582 sq km)

Smallest country
Bahrain 277 sq mi (717 sq km)

Most populous country
Iran 78,869,000

Least populous country
Bahrain 1,336,000

Predominant languages
Arabic, Farsi (modern-day Persian),
Kurdish

Predominant religion
Islam

Highest GDP per capita
Qatar $99,800

Lowest GDP per capita
Yemen $2,300

Highest life expectancy
Bahrain, Qatar 78 years

Highest literacy rate
Qatar
96%

GEO WHIZ

Rub' al Khali (Empty Quarter), the world's largest sand desert, covers 225,000 square miles (583,000 sq km), an area larger than France.

More than 4,000 years ago, the Sumerians built the first cities in the world on the plain between the Tigris and Euphrates Rivers in what is now Iraq.

The ancient Romans called Yemen "Arabia Felix," meaning "Happy Arabia."

Five times a day, every day, Muslims all over the world face the city of Mecca, in Saudi Arabia, to pray. Mecca is the birthplace of the Prophet Muhammad, the founder of Islam.

Iran drilled the first oil wells in the region in 1908.

Causeways connect Bahrain Island—the largest of the 35 islands that make up the country of Bahrain—to two others and to the mainland of Saudi Arabia.

Southwest Asia

This region, made up largely of deserts and mountains, includes the countries of the Arabian Peninsula and those that border the Persian Gulf. Islam is the dominant religion in each, and the two holiest places for Muslims—Mecca and Medina—are here. Arabic is the principal language everywhere but Iran, where most people speak Farsi. While water has been the most important natural resource here for millennia, global attention has focused in recent decades on the region's oil wealth. With the majority of the world's reserves found here, oil has brought outside influences and military conflict. Long a cradle of civilization, Southwest Asia continues to hold the world's attention.

⊙ **GIRL TALK.** Young Iranian girls get together at a film festival in Tehran. The scarves they are wearing are part of the Islamic dress code, hijab, which says that women and girls must cover their heads and dress modestly.

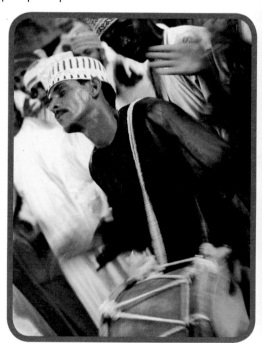

⊙ **HE'S GOT THE BEAT.** This Omani drummer plays at a dance in the Arabian Sea port of Qurayyat. Though modernizing in many ways, Oman works hard to preserve its traditional culture.

◗ **DIFFERENT WORLDS.** This roadside meeting in Qatar displays a contrast between horse and horsepower and that of traditional Arab and Western clothing styles. This Persian Gulf country preserves a rich history of Arabian horse breeding and continues to produce champions.

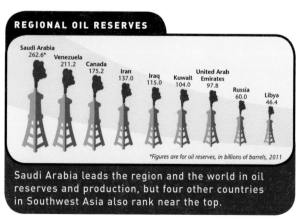

REGIONAL OIL RESERVES

Saudi Arabia
262.6*
Venezuela
211.2
Canada
175.2
Iran
137.0
Iraq
115.0
Kuwait
104.0
United Arab Emirates
97.8
Russia
60.0
Libya
46.4

*Figures are for oil reserves, in billions of barrels, 2011

Saudi Arabia leads the region and the world in oil reserves and production, but four other countries in Southwest Asia also rank near the top.

LOST AND FOUND. Thousands of treasures dating from ancient Mesopotamia were destroyed, lost, or stolen during the invasion of Iraq in April 2003. This ring is among the few items recovered.

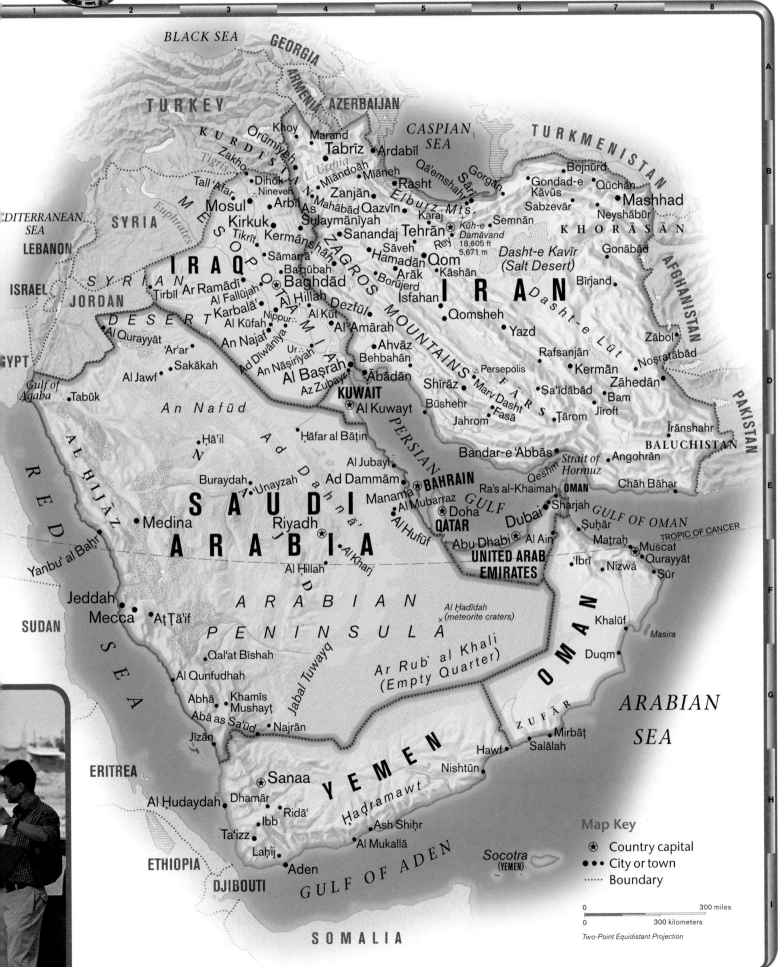

BLACK SEA

GEORGIA

ARMENIA

AZERBAIJAN

TURKEY

TURKMENISTAN

KURDISTAN

CASPIAN SEA

Khoy
Marand
Orūmīyeh
Tabrīz
Ardabīl
Qā'emshahr
Gorgān
Bojnūrd
Gondad-e Kāvūs
Qūchān
Mashhad

Zakho
Tall 'Afar
Dihōk
Nineveh
Miāndoāb
Miāneh
Rasht
Sārī
Sabzevār
Neyshābūr

Tigris
Mosul
Arbīl
As Mahābād
Zanjān
Qazvīn
Karaj
Tehrān
Semnān
Gonābād

KHORĀSĀN

MEDITERRANEAN SEA

SYRIA

Euphrates
Kirkuk
Kermānshāh
Sanandaj
Kūh-e Damāvand 18,605 ft 5,671 m

LEBANON

Tikrīt
Sulaymānīyah
Sāveh
Rey
Qom
Dasht-e Kavīr (Salt Desert)

ISRAEL

MESOPOTAMIA

Sāmarrā'
Baqūbah
Baghdad
Hamadān
Arāk
Borūjerd
Kāshān
Birjand

IRAQ

IRAN

JORDAN

Tirbīl
Ar Ramādī
Al Fallūjah
Al Hillah
Dezfūl
Al Kūt
Isfahan
Qomsheh
Zābol
Noṣratābād

SYRIAN DESERT

Karbalā'
Nippur
Al Kūfah
Al 'Amārah

Yazd
Rafsanjān
Kermān
Zāhedān

Dasht-e Lūt

An Najaf
Ad Dīwānīya
Ur
An Nāṣirīyah
Ahvāz
Behbahān
Persepolis
Sa'īdābād
Bam
Jīroft

EGYPT

'Ar'ar
Sakākah
Al Baṣrah
Āzbādān

Shīrāz
Marv Dasht
Jahrom
Fasā
Tārom
Īrānshahr

ZAGROS MOUNTAINS

FĀRS

Al Jawf
Az Zubayr
KUWAIT
Būshehr
Bandar-e 'Abbās
Strait of Hormuz
Angohrān
Chāh Bāhar

BALUCHISTAN

Gulf of Aqaba
Tabūk
Al Kuwayt
Qeshm

AFGHANISTAN

PAKISTAN

An Nafūd
Ḥafar al Bāṭin
PERSIAN GULF
Ra's al-Khaimah
OMAN

Ḥā'il
Al Jubayl
Ad Dammām
BAHRAIN
Sharjah
GULF OF OMAN

AL HIJĀZ

Buraydah
'Unayzah
Manama
Al Mubarraz
Dubai
Ṣuḥār

Ad Dahnā'
Doha
Al Ain
Matrah
Muscat

Medina
Riyadh
QATAR
Al Hufūf
Abu Dhabi
'Ibrī
Nizwá
Qurayyāt

SAUDI ARABIA

Al Khari
UNITED ARAB EMIRATES
Sūr

RED SEA

Al Hillah
Al Kharj

ARABIAN

TROPIC OF CANCER

Jeddah

Mecca
Aṭ Ṭā'if

PENINSULA

Al Ḥadīdah × (meteorite craters)

Khalūf
Masira

OMAN

SUDAN

Qal'at Bīshah

Jabal Tuwayq

Ar Rub' al Khali (Empty Quarter)

Duqm

Al Qunfudhah

ARABIAN SEA

Abhā
Khamīs Mushayt
Abā as Sa'ūd
Najrān

ZUFĀR

Mirbāṭ
Salālah

ERITREA

Jīzān

YEMEN

Hawf
Nishtūn

Sanaa
Hadramawt

Al Hudaydah
Dhamār
Ridā'
Ash Shiḥr

ETHIOPIA
Ibb
Ta'izz
Al Mukallā

DJIBOUTI
Lahij
Aden
GULF OF ADEN
Socotra (YEMEN)

SOMALIA

Map Key

⊛ Country capital
••• City or town
..... Boundary

0 _____ 300 miles
0 _____ 300 kilometers

Two-Point Equidistant Projection

THE CONTINENT:
ASIA

THE BASICS

STATS

Largest country
India 1,269,221 sq mi (3,287,270 sq km)

Smallest country
Maldives 115 sq mi (298 sq km)

Most populous country
India 1,259,721,000

Least populous country
Maldives 331,000

Predominant languages
Hindi, English, Punjabi, Bangla, Dari, Burmese, Pashtu, Urdu, Sinhala, Nepali, Dzongkha

Predominant religions
Hindu, Islam, Buddhism

Highest GDP per capita
Maldives $8,600

Lowest GDP per capita
Afghanistan $1,000

Highest life expectancy
Sri Lanka 76 years

Highest literacy rate
Maldives
94%

GEO WHIZ

India's rail system transports four billion passengers each year across nearly 38,000 miles (61,155 km) of track.

Bhutan, a Himalayan country known as Land of the Thunder Dragon, is the world's only Buddhist kingdom.

Nepal has the only national flag that is not a rectangle or a square. Its shape evokes the high Himalayan peaks that dominate its landscape (see page 172).

The mountains of the Hindu Kush in northeastern Afghanistan have been a source of rubies, silver, and other mineral wealth for thousands of years. The lapis lazuli that adorns the golden funeral mask of Egypt's King Tutankhamun was mined in this region.

Beaches along the southern and western coasts of Sri Lanka are nesting sites for five species of endangered sea turtle. The December 2004 tsunami wiped out several hatcheries, but the devastation has not kept the turtles from returning to their nesting areas.

South Asia

This region is home to the world's highest peaks, and three of the world's storied rivers—the Indus, Ganges, and Brahmaputra—support the hundreds of millions of people

⬤ **TAJ MAHAL.** In 1631 in Agra, India, the Mughal emperor Shah Jehan began construction of this magnificent marble memorial to his deceased wife.

who live here. India is at the center, with greater area than the other countries combined and three times their population. Born in India, Hinduism and Buddhism were spread to other places by traders, teachers, and priests. Muslims form the majority in Afghanistan, Pakistan, and Bangladesh, whereas there are large numbers of Buddhists in Bhutan, Nepal, Sri Lanka, and Myanmar. Poverty and prosperity live side by side across the region, with streams of migrants flowing from rural areas to mushrooming cities.

◗ **TOP OF THE WORLD.**
Climbers make their way through Nepal's treacherous Khumbu Icefall on their approach to Mount Everest.

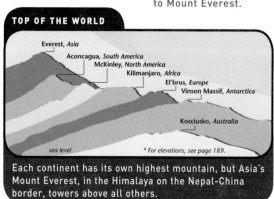

TOP OF THE WORLD

Everest, *Asia*
Aconcagua, *South America*
McKinley, *North America*
Kilimanjaro, *Africa*
El'brus, *Europe*
Vinson Massif, *Antarctica*

Kosciusko, *Australia*

sea level   * For elevations, see page 189.

Each continent has its own highest mountain, but Asia's Mount Everest, in the Himalaya on the Nepal-China border, towers above all others.

IRAN

AFG

BALUCHI
•Turk

TROPIC OF CAN

ARAB
SE

◆ **EASTERN BELIEF.** The god Shiva is part of the Hindu trinity, which also includes the gods Brahma and Vishnu. With more than 900 million followers, Hinduism is the world's third largest religion, after Christianity and Islam.

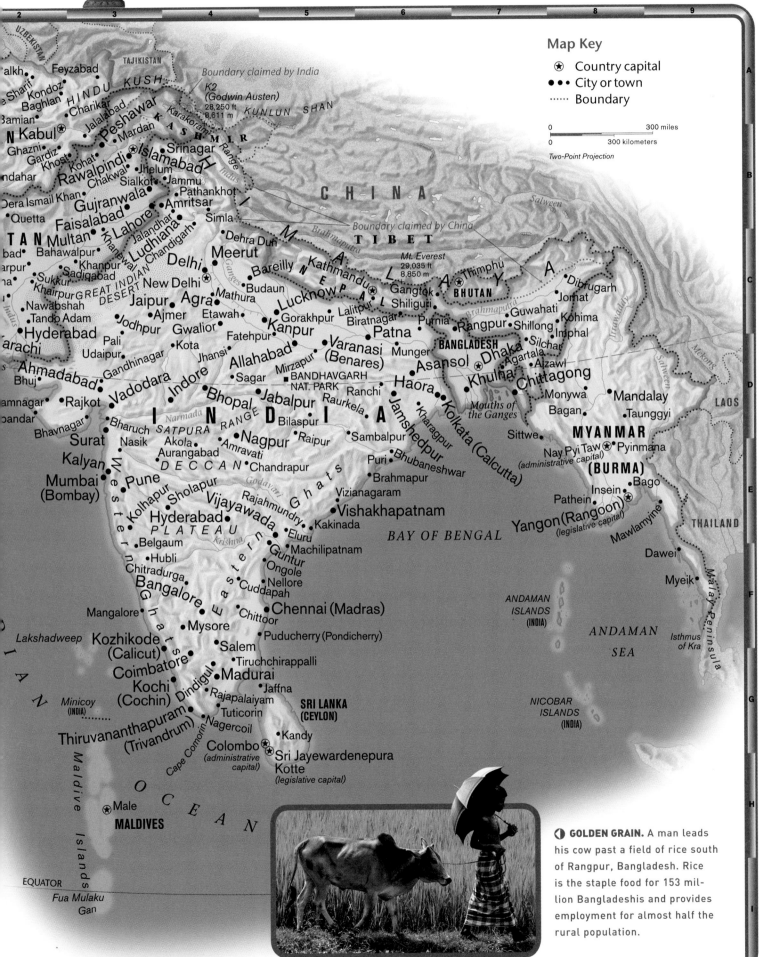

Map Key
⭐ Country capital
●●● City or town
⋯⋯ Boundary

0   300 miles
0   300 kilometers

Two-Point Projection

UZBEKISTAN
TAJIKISTAN

alkh
N Shari • Feyzabad
Kondoz
Baghlan • Charikar
Bamian
N Kabul ⭐ • Jalalabad
Ghazni • Khost
Gardiz
ndahar
•Quetta

HINDU KUSH
Boundary claimed by India
K2
(Godwin Austen)
28,250 ft
8,611 m

Karakoram Range
Peshawar
•Mardan
Srinagar
Islamabad ⭐
Rawalpindi
•Jhelum
Chakwal
Sialkot •Jammu
•Pathankot
Jalandhar
•Simla

KASHMIR
KUNLUN SHAN
Salween

Dera Ismail Khan
Gujranwala •Amritsar
T A N Multan •Khanewal Ludhiana •Chandigarh
bad •Bahawalpur
arpur •Sukkur •Sadiqabad
ha •Khairpur GREAT INDIAN •New Delhi
Nawabshah DESERT Jaipur •Agra
•Tando Adam •Ajmer Etawah •Mathura
Hyderabad •Pali Gwalior
arachi •Udaipur •Kota •Jhansi
Bhuj •Gandhinagar •Sagar
Ahmadabad• •Allahabad
amnagar• •Rajkot Vadodara Indore
andar •Bhavnagar •Bharuch SATPURA RANGE

C H I N A
T I B E T
Boundary claimed by China

Mt. Everest
29,035 ft
8,850 m

Lahore
Faisalabad
Delhi
Meerut
Dehra Dun
Bareilly
Budaun
Lucknow
Kathmandu
Gangtok Shiliguri
Thimphu ⭐
BHUTAN
Dibrugarh
Jorhat

NEPAL
Biratnagar
Gorakhpur Lalitpur
Purnia Rangpur
Kanpur Patna
Fatehpur Varanasi
Mirzapur (Benares) Munger Guwahati
BANGLADESH Shillong Kohima
Asansol Dhaka Imphal
Haora Silchar
BANDHAVGARH Khulna Agartala Aizawl
NAT. PARK Kolkata Chittagong

Jabalpur Raurkela Ranchi
Bhopal Bilaspur
INDIA Jamshedpur
Nagpur •Raipur Kharagpur Mouths of the Ganges
Surat Nasik Akola Amravati Sambalpur Monywa Mandalay
Aurangabad Chandrapur Bagan Taunggyi
Kalyan DECCAN Puri Bhubaneshwar Sittwe MYANMAR
Mumbai Pune Brahmapur (BURMA)
(Bombay) Kolhapur Vizianagaram Nay Pyi Taw ⭐ Pyinmana
Sholapur Vijayawada Vishakhapatnam (administrative capital) Bago
Hyderabad Rajahmundry Kakinada Insein ⭐
PLATEAU Eluru BAY OF BENGAL Yangon (Rangoon) Pathein
Belgaum Krishna Machilipatnam (legislative capital) Mawlamyine
Hubli Guntur
Chitradurga Ongole THAILAND
Bangalore Nellore
Cuddapah Dawei
Mangalore Chittoor ANDAMAN Myeik
Mysore Chennai (Madras) ISLANDS
Lakshadweep Puducherry (Pondicherry) (INDIA) ANDAMAN
Kozhikode Salem SEA Isthmus
(Calicut) Tiruchchirappalli of Kra
Coimbatore Madurai
Kochi Dindigul
(Cochin) Rajapalaiyam
Minicoy Jaffna NICOBAR
(INDIA) Tuticorin SRI LANKA ISLANDS
Thiruvananthapuram Nagercoil (CEYLON) (INDIA)
(Trivandrum) Kandy
Cape Comorin Colombo
(administrative Sri Jayewardenepura
capital) Kotte
(legislative capital)

Salween
Mekong
Irrawaddy
LAOS

OCEAN
Maldive Islands
Male ⭐
MALDIVES

EQUATOR
Fua Mulaku
Gan

INDIAN OCEAN

2   3   4   5   6   7   8   9
A   B   C   D   E   F   G   H   I

◆ **GOLDEN GRAIN.** A man leads his cow past a field of rice south of Rangpur, Bangladesh. Rice is the staple food for 153 million Bangladeshis and provides employment for almost half the rural population.

THE BASICS

STATS

Largest country
Thailand 198,115 sq mi (513,115 sq km)

Smallest country
Singapore 255 sq mi (660 sq km)

Most populous country
Philippines 96,218,000

Least populous country
Brunei 413,000

Predominant languages
Filipino (based on Tagalog),
English, Vietnamese, Thai,
Khmer, Lao, French, Malay,
Bahasa Melayu, Mandarin

Predominant religions
Christianity, Buddhism, Islam

Highest GDP per capita
Singapore $59,700

Lowest GDP per capita
Cambodia $2,200

Highest life expectancy
Singapore 84 years

Highest literacy rate
Vietnam
94%

GEO WHIZ

Cambodia's Mekong Fish Conservation Project pays fishermen more than the market price to release any giant fish they catch. This includes catfish as long as 10 feet (3 m) weighing up to 600 pounds (270 kg).

The Philippines has one of the highest rates of deforestation in the world. Based on the current rate of removal, studies estimate that the country's virgin forests are in danger of disappearing as soon as 2025.

The Cathedral of Notre Dame in Ho Chi Minh City, capital of predominantly Buddhist Vietnam, was built in the late 1800s during French colonial times, when the city was named Saigon.

The Plain of Jars, in northern Laos, takes its name from hundreds of huge stone urns spread across the ground. Archaeologists believe the jars were made by Bronze Age people who used them to hold the cremated remains of their dead.

Thailand means "Land of the Free." It is the only country in Southeast Asia that has never been ruled by a colonial power.

Singapore is a melting pot of cultures. Its name comes from the Sanskrit *Singha Pura* (Lion City), its national anthem is sung in Malay, and English is the lingua franca.

Southeast Asia

The countries of Southeast Asia have long been influenced by neighboring giants India and China. The result is a dazzling mix of cultures, rich histories, terrible conflicts, and future promise. Cambodia's spectacular 12th-century Angkor Wat provides a glimpse of former greatness. Colonial rule brought division and change, and struggles for independence took a heavy toll, as in Vietnam. Mainland countries are largely Buddhist, whereas peninsular Malaysia is mostly Muslim, and Christians dominate the Philippines. All but Laos have ocean access, with fisheries providing jobs and food for millions. Rivers like the Chao Phraya and the mighty Mekong provide transport and water-rich croplands dominated by rice growing. Tiny Singapore has gained global importance with its bustling port operations and high-tech focus.

◔ **SMILING BUDDHA.** A Buddhist monk admires a sculpture on a temple wall near Siem Reap, Cambodia. Built between A.D. 800 and 1200 by the Khmer, Angkor Wat includes Buddhist and Hindu temples.

◔ **WILLING WORKER.** Smaller and more easily tamed than the African variety, Asian elephants have been a part of the workforce for centuries. They are found from India to Indonesia.

◑ **SHIPPING HUB.** Huge container terminals, such as this one at Tanjong Pagar, make Singapore the world's busiest trans-shipment center, moving about one-seventh of the world's containers.

◀ **FLASHY RIDE.** Colorful Philippine taxis, called jeepneys, are a common sight on the streets of Manila. Originally rebuilt WWII jeeps, these wildly decorated vehicles offer inexpensive, but crowded, transportation.

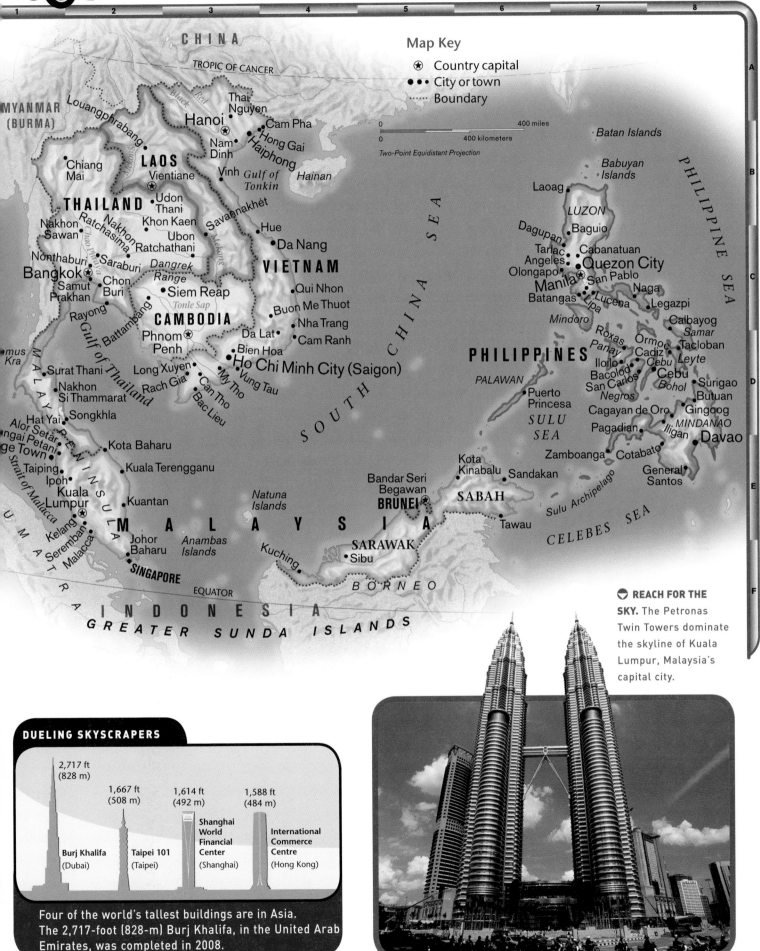

Map Key

★ Country capital
•• City or town
⋯⋯ Boundary

0 ——— 400 miles
0 ——— 400 kilometers
Two-Point Equidistant Projection

CHINA
TROPIC OF CANCER

MYANMAR (BURMA)

Louangphrabang
Black *Red*
Thai Nguyen
Hanoi ★
Cam Pha
Hong Gai
Nam Dinh
Haiphong
Chiang Mai
LAOS
Vientiane ★
Vinh
Gulf of Tonkin
Hainan

THAILAND
Udon Thani
Nakhon Sawan
Ratchasima
Nakhon Ratchasima
Khon Kaen
Savannakhét
Hue
Da Nang
Nonthaburi
Ubon Ratchathani
Saraburi
Chao Phraya
Dangrek Range
Mekong
VIETNAM
Bangkok ★
Chon Buri
Samut Prakhan
Siem Reap
Tonle Sap
Qui Nhon
Buon Me Thuot
Rayong
Battambang
CAMBODIA
Nha Trang
Da Lat
Cam Ranh
Phnom Penh ★
Bien Hoa
Isthmus of Kra
Surat Thani
Long Xuyen
Rach Gia
My Tho
Can Tho
Bac Lieu
Ho Chi Minh City (Saigon)
Vung Tau
Nakhon Si Thammarat
Hat Yai
Songkhla
Alor Setar
Sungai Petani
George Town
Taiping
Ipoh
Kota Baharu
Kuala Terengganu
MALAY PENINSULA
Gulf of Thailand
Kuala Lumpur
Kuantan
Kelang
Natuna Islands
M A L A Y S I A
Seremban
Johor Baharu
Malacca
Anambas Islands
Kuching
Strait of Malacca
SINGAPORE
SARAWAK
Sibu
EQUATOR
SUMATRA
B O R N E O
I N D O N E S I A
G R E A T E R   S U N D A   I S L A N D S

SOUTH CHINA SEA

Batan Islands

Babuyan Islands

Laoag
LUZON
Dagupan
Baguio
Tarlac
Cabanatuan
Angeles
Quezon City
Olongapo
Manila ★
San Pablo
Naga
Batangas
Lucena
Lipa
Legazpi
Mindoro
Calbayog
Roxas
Samar
Ormoc
Tacloban
Panay
Cadiz
Iloilo
Cebu
Leyte
PHILIPPINES
Bacolod
San Carlos
Cebu
Negros
Bohol
Surigao
PALAWAN
Cagayan de Oro
Gingoog
Puerto Princesa
SULU SEA
Pagadian
MINDANAO
Iligan
Butuan
Kota Kinabalu
Sandakan
Zamboanga
Cotabato
Davao
SABAH
Sulu Archipelago
General Santos
Tawau
CELEBES SEA

Bandar Seri Begawan ★
BRUNEI

PHILIPPINE SEA

⬢ **REACH FOR THE SKY.** The Petronas Twin Towers dominate the skyline of Kuala Lumpur, Malaysia's capital city.

DUELING SKYSCRAPERS

2,717 ft (828 m)
Burj Khalifa (Dubai)

1,667 ft (508 m)
Taipei 101 (Taipei)

1,614 ft (492 m)
Shanghai World Financial Center (Shanghai)

1,588 ft (484 m)
International Commerce Centre (Hong Kong)

Four of the world's tallest buildings are in Asia. The 2,717-foot (828-m) Burj Khalifa, in the United Arab Emirates, was completed in 2008.

THE BASICS

STATS

Largest country
Indonesia 742,308 sq mi (1,922,570 sq km)

Smallest country
Timor-Leste 5,640 sq mi (14,609 sq km)

Most populous country
Indonesia 240,990,000

Least populous country
Timor-Leste 1,126,000

Predominant languages
Indonesian, English, Dutch, Javanese, Tetum, Portuguese

Predominant religions
Islam, Christianity

Highest GDP per capita
Timor-Leste $8,700

Lowest GDP per capita
Indonesia $4,700

Highest life expectancy
Indonesia 72 years

Highest literacy rate
Indonesia
90%

GEO WHIZ

Two species of sharks that use their fins to "walk" on coral reefs were discovered off the northwestern coast of Indonesia's Papua province in 2006. Scientists believe they might be similar to the first vertebrates that moved from sea to land.

In an effort to reduce crowding on Java, the government adopted a program of relocating landless people to more remote islands, a policy that has created tensions and that led to Timor-Leste's independence in 2002.

With a length of 10 feet (3 m) and a weight of more than 300 pounds (135 kg), the Komodo dragon is Earth's heaviest lizard. This meat eater lives only on Indonesia's Lesser Sunda Islands, where it eats all types of prey—including people sometimes!

When seen from the air, Timor Island resembles a crocodile. According to local legend, a crocodile turned itself into the island as a way of saying thank you to a boy who saved its life.

In December 2004 an earthquake off the coast of Sumatra, measuring 9.1 on the Richter scale, triggered a massive tsunami that killed hundreds of thousands of people and left millions homeless in countries around the Indian Ocean, from Indonesia to Africa's east coast.

Indonesia & Timor-Leste

Stretching more than 2,200 miles (3,520 km) from Sumatra to New Guinea, Indonesia is the world's largest island nation and the fourth most populous country. Most of its 241 million people live on the volcanically active island of Java. Indonesia shares rainforested Borneo with Malaysia and Brunei. Most Indonesians are of Malay ethnicity, though there are large numbers of Melanesians, Chinese, and East Indians. Arab traders brought Islam to the islands in the 13th century, and today six of seven Indonesians are Muslim. Timor-Leste gained independence from Indonesia in 2002. It and the Philippines are Asia's only predominantly Catholic countries.

◉ **NEWLY INDEPENDENT.**
A young boy smiles broadly as he waves Timor-Leste's flag in Dili, the capital city. The country is also known as East Timor.

▶ **CITY ON THE MOVE.**
Skyscrapers and a busy freeway are just one face of Jakarta, Indonesia. In this city of almost 10 million people—national capital and center of trade and industry—the modern and traditional, the rich and poor, live side by side. Just like Indonesia as a whole, the city has a very diverse population.

◖ **SPIRIT WORLD.** Hand-carved masks, such as this one from Bali, Indonesia, were probably first created for traditional dance and storytelling rituals. Later, they incorporated Hindu and Islamic beliefs as well.

◖ **GIANT APE.** An adult male Borneo orangutan peers through the forest foliage. An endangered species, orangutans are found only on Sumatra and Borneo. They are the largest tree-living mammals in the world.

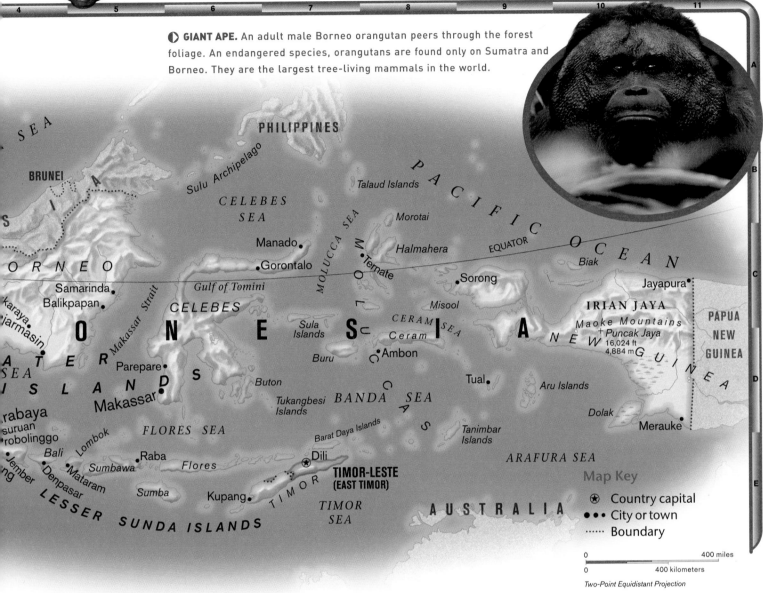

Map Key
⊛ Country capital
••• City or town
······ Boundary

0 ——— 400 miles
0 ——— 400 kilometers

Two-Point Equidistant Projection

FOLLOWERS OF ISLAM

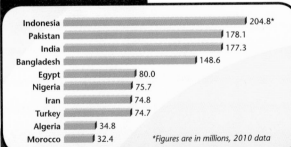

Country	Millions
Indonesia	204.8*
Pakistan	178.1
India	177.3
Bangladesh	148.6
Egypt	80.0
Nigeria	75.7
Iran	74.8
Turkey	74.7
Algeria	34.8
Morocco	32.4

Figures are in millions, 2010 data

Islam's origins trace to southwestern Asia, but the religion has spread around the world. The country with the largest Muslim population is Indonesia.

◖ **GENETIC STOREHOUSE.** About 75 percent of Indonesia's Kalimantan Province in eastern Borneo remains covered in rain forest that is home to 221 different types of mammals and 450 different species of birds. The forest and its inhabitants are at risk due to widespread logging and mining.

THE CONTINENT:
AFRICA

PHYSICAL

Land area	Lowest point	Largest lake
11,608,000 sq mi	Lake Assal, Djibouti	Victoria
(30,065,000 sq km)	-512 ft (-156 m)	26,800 sq mi (69,500 sq km)
Highest point	**Longest river**	
Kitimanjaro, Tanzania	Nile	
19,340 ft (5,895 m)	4,241 mi (6,825 km)	

POLITICAL

Population	Largest metropolitan area	Economy
1,061,224,000	Cairo, Egypt	**Farming: fruit, grains**
Largest country	Pop. 10,902,000	**Industry: chemicals,**
Algeria	**Most densely populated country**	**mining, cement**
919,595 sq mi	Mauritius	Services
(2,381,741 sq km)	1,638 people per sq mi (630 per sq km)	

Africa

Africa

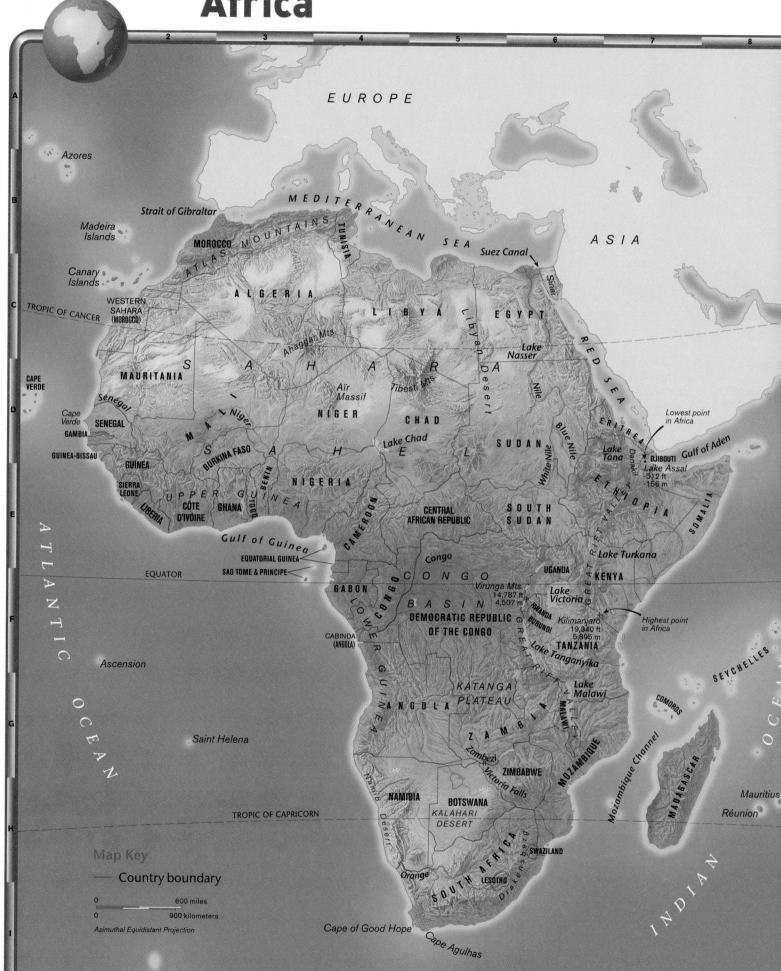

2   3   4   5   6   7   8

A

EUROPE

Azores

B   MEDITERRANEAN SEA   ASIA
Strait of Gibraltar
Madeira
Islands   Suez Canal
MOROCCO ATLAS MOUNTAINS TUNISIA   Sinai
Canary   RED SEA
Islands   ALGERIA   LIBYA   EGYPT
C TROPIC OF CANCER WESTERN
SAHARA
(MOROCCO)   Lake
Ahaggar Mts.   Nasser   Nile
S A H A R A
MAURITANIA   Aïr   Tibesti Mts.   Libyan Desert   ERITREA   Lowest point
Massif   in Africa
Sénégal   Niger   NIGER   CHAD   Lake   DJIBOUTI Gulf of Aden
D Cape   M   SUDAN   Blue Nile Tana   Lake Assal
Verde SENEGAL   A   Lake Chad   L   Danakil -512 ft
GAMBIA   L S A H E   White Nile   -156 m
GUINEA-BISSAU   I   ETHIOPIA SOMALIA
GUINEA   BURKINA FASO   NIGERIA   SOUTH
SIERRA   BENIN   CENTRAL   SUDAN
LEONE   U P P E R G U I N E A   AFRICAN
E LIBERIA CÔTE   GHANA   REPUBLIC
D'IVOIRE   CAMEROON   Lake Turkana
Gulf of Guinea   Congo   UGANDA
EQUATORIAL GUINEA   KENYA
EQUATOR SAO TOME & PRINCIPE   GABON C O N G O
Virunga Mts. Lake
F   14,787 ft Victoria
CONGO B A S I N 4,507 m RWANDA
DEMOCRATIC REPUBLIC   BURUNDI Kilimanjaro Highest point
CABINDA   OF THE CONGO   19,340 ft   in Africa
ATLANTIC (ANGOLA)   5,895 m
Ascension   L O W E R G U I N E A   TANZANIA
Lake Tanganyika
KATANGA
G OCEAN   Saint Helena   PLATEAU   Lake   SEYCHELLES
ANGOLA   Malawi
Z A M B I A   COMOROS
Zambezi   MOZAMBIQUE
H TROPIC OF CAPRICORN   ZIMBABWE
Victoria Falls
NAMIBIA   BOTSWANA   MADAGASCAR Mauritius
KALAHARI   Mozambique Channel   Réunion
DESERT
Map Key   Namib Desert
—— Country boundary   SOUTH AFRICA   Drakensberg INDIAN
SWAZILAND
0   600 miles   Orange   LESOTHO
0   900 kilometers   SOUTH AFRICA
I Azimuthal Equidistant Projection Cape of Good Hope   OCEAN
Cape Agulhas

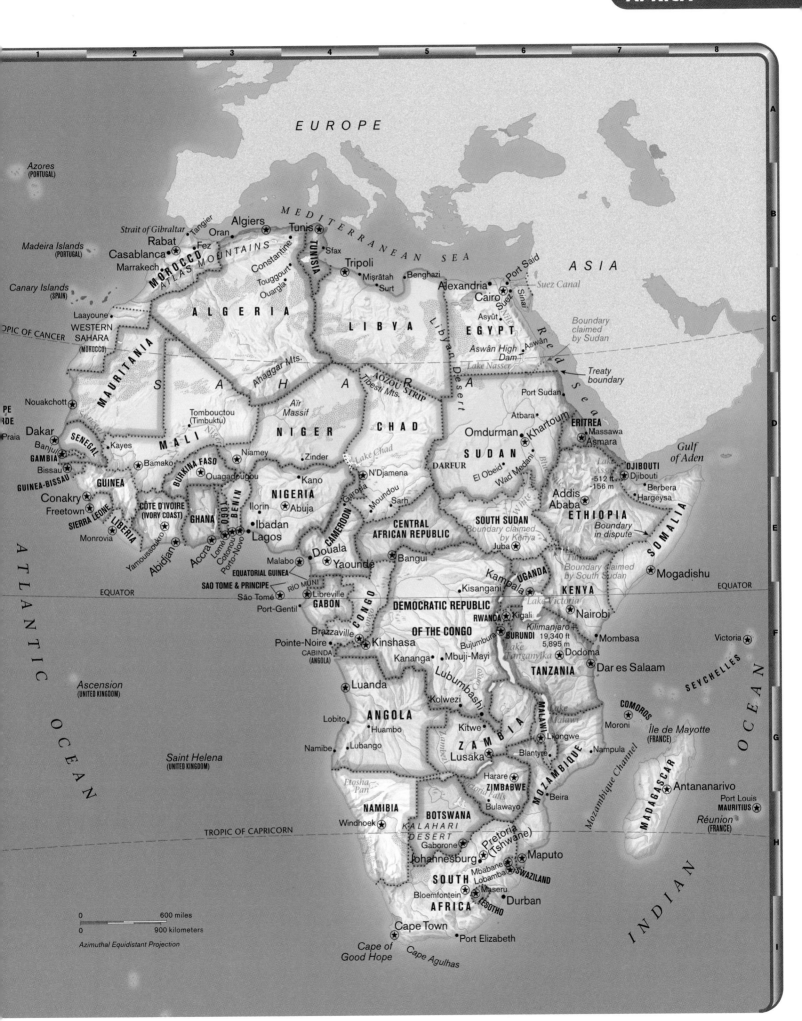

EUROPE

Azores (PORTUGAL)

MEDITERRANEAN SEA

ASIA

Madeira Islands (PORTUGAL)

Canary Islands (SPAIN)

Strait of Gibraltar
Tangier
Oran ◦ Algiers ☆
Rabat ☆ ◦ Fez
Casablanca ☆
Marrakech ◦
Tunis ☆
TUNISIA
◦ Sfax

ATLAS MOUNTAINS
MOROCCO
Constantine ◦
Touggourt ◦
Ouargla ◦

Tripoli ☆
◦ Misrātah ◦ Benghazi
◦ Surt

Port Said ◦
Alexandria ◦
Cairo ☆ ◦ Suez
Suez Canal
Sinai

TROPIC OF CANCER
Laayoune ◦
WESTERN SAHARA (MOROCCO)

ALGERIA

LIBYA

EGYPT

Boundary claimed by Sudan

MAURITANIA

Ahaggar Mts.
AOZOU STRIP
Tibesti Mts.

Asyût ◦
Aswân High Dam
Lake Nasser ◦ Aswân

Treaty boundary

PE RDE
Nouakchott ☆

S A H A R A

Libyan Desert

Red Sea

Port Sudan ◦

Gulf of Aden

Tombouctou (Timbuktu) ◦
Aïr Massif

Atbara ◦
Omdurman ◦ ☆ Khartoum

ERITREA
Massawa ◦
☆ Asmara

Praia
Dakar ☆
Banjul ☆
GAMBIA
Bissau ☆
GUINEA-BISSAU

SENEGAL
◦ Kayes
MALI
☆ Bamako
BURKINA FASO
☆ Ouagadougou

NIGER
Niamey ☆
◦ Zinder

CHAD
N'Djamena ☆

SUDAN
DARFUR
El Obeid ◦ Wad Medani ◦

Lake Assal
-512 ft
-156 m
DJIBOUTI
☆ Djibouti
◦ Berbera
◦ Hargeysa

GUINEA
Conakry ☆
Freetown ☆
SIERRA LEONE
Monrovia ☆
LIBERIA

CÔTE D'IVOIRE (IVORY COAST)
Yamoussoukro ☆
Abidjan ◦
GHANA
Accra ☆

Kano ◦
Garoua ◦
Sarh ◦
Moundou ◦

NIGERIA
Ilorin ◦
Abuja ☆
Ibadan ◦
Lagos ◦

TOGO
BENIN
Lomé ☆
Porto-Novo ☆
Cotonou ◦

CAMEROON
Douala ◦
Yaoundé ☆

CENTRAL AFRICAN REPUBLIC
Bangui ☆

SOUTH SUDAN
Boundary claimed by Kenya
Juba ☆

Addis Ababa ☆
ETHIOPIA

Boundary in dispute

SOMALIA
☆ Mogadishu

EQUATOR
Malabo ☆
EQUATORIAL GUINEA
SAO TOME & PRINCIPE
São Tomé ☆
RIO MUNI
Libreville ☆
Port-Gentil ◦
GABON

Kisangani ◦

UGANDA
Kampala ☆

Kigali ☆ RWANDA
Bujumbura ☆ BURUNDI
Boundary claimed by South Sudan

KENYA
☆ Nairobi

EQUATOR

Lake Victoria

ATLANTIC OCEAN

CONGO
Brazzaville ☆
Pointe-Noire ◦
CABINDA (ANGOLA)

DEMOCRATIC REPUBLIC OF THE CONGO
☆ Kinshasa
Kananga ◦
Mbuji-Mayi ◦

Kilimanjaro +
19,340 ft
5,895 m
Lake Tanganyika
Dodoma ☆
TANZANIA
◦ Mombasa
◦ Dar es Salaam

Victoria ☆
SEYCHELLES

Ascension (UNITED KINGDOM)

Luanda ☆
Lobito ◦
ANGOLA
Huambo ◦
Namibe ◦ Lubango ◦

Kolwezi ◦
Lubumbashi ◦
Kitwe ◦
ZAMBIA
Lusaka ☆

MALAWI
Lake Malawi
Lilongwe ☆
Blantyre ◦

COMOROS
Moroni ◦
Île de Mayotte (FRANCE)

Nampula ◦

Saint Helena (UNITED KINGDOM)

Zambezi

Victoria Falls

ZIMBABWE
Harare ☆
Bulawayo ◦
Beira ◦

MOZAMBIQUE

Mozambique Channel

MADAGASCAR
Antananarivo ☆
Port Louis
MAURITIUS ☆
Réunion (FRANCE)

TROPIC OF CAPRICORN
NAMIBIA
Windhoek ☆
KALAHARI DESERT
Etosha Pan

BOTSWANA
Gaborone ☆

Pretoria (Tshwane) ☆
Maputo ☆
Johannesburg ◦
Mbabane ☆ SWAZILAND
Lobamba ☆

Maseru ☆ LESOTHO
Durban ◦

SOUTH AFRICA
Bloemfontein ☆

Cape Town ☆
◦ Port Elizabeth
Cape of Good Hope
Cape Agulhas

INDIAN OCEAN

0 ————— 600 miles
0 ————— 900 kilometers

Azimuthal Equidistant Projection

Africa

A COMPLEX GIANT

A frica spans nearly as far west to east as it does north to south. The Sahara—the world's largest desert—covers Africa's northern third, while to the south lie bands of grassland, tropical rain forest, and more desert. The East African Rift system marks where shifting plates are splitting off the continent's edge. Africa has a wealth of cultures, speaking some 1,600 languages—more than on any other continent. Though the continent is still largely rural, Africans increasingly migrate to booming cities like Cairo, Lagos, and Johannesburg. While rich in natural resources, from oil and coal to gemstones and precious metals, Africa is the poorest continent, long plagued by outside interference, corruption, and disease.

FASHION STATEMENT. Maasai women in Kenya adorn themselves with distinctive, colorful bead jewelry.

CHARGE! Sensing danger, an African elephant charges. The world's largest land mammal, African elephants are at risk due to poaching and loss of habitat.

COLORFUL NEIGHBORHOOD. With houses dating to the 18th century, Bo-Kaap was once known as the Malay Quarter because of its early settlers. This multicultural suburb overlooks Cape Town's city center.

⬡ **AFRICAN SAVANNA.** Zebras graze on the tall grasses of the Serengeti Plain, in East Africa. Each year more than 200,000 zebras migrate through Serengeti, following the seasonal rains.

⬡ **CRYSTAL WATERS.** A snorkeler swims in the clear blue waters off the Seychelles, one of Africa's island countries. Made up of 116 granite and coral islands, it lies about 1,000 miles (1,600 km) east of Kenya.

◑ **FREE RIDE.**
A woman in Kumasi, Ghana, goes about her daily chores, with her infant wrapped snugly on her back in a colorful cloth.

more about Africa

◗ **WORSHIPPERS IN THE DESERT.** Muslim faithful gather before the Great Mosque in Mopti, Mali. An earthen structure typical of Muslim architecture in Africa's Sahel, the mosque was built between 1936 and 1943.

◗ **WINDOW ON THE PAST.** Traditional Egyptian sailing vessels called feluccas skim along the Nile River below the ruins at Qubbat al-Hawa. Tombs from ancient Egypt's 6th dynasty are carved into the hillside.

◗ **MODERN SKYLINE.** Established in 1899 as a railway supply depot, Nairobi, Kenya, is now one of Africa's most modern cities. In Maasai, the name means "place of cold water."

THE CONTINENT:
AFRICA

◀ TALL LOAD. A woman carries a stack of brightly dyed cotton cloth, called wax prints, through a market in Lomé, Togo.

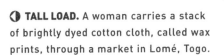

WHERE THE PICTURES ARE

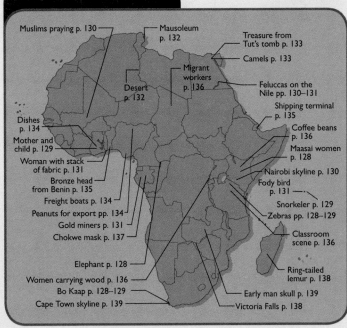

Muslims praying p. 130
Mausoleum p. 132
Treasure from Tut's tomb p. 133
Camels p. 133
Migrant workers p. 136
Desert p. 132
Feluccas on the Nile pp. 130–131
Shipping terminal p. 135
Dishes p. 134
Coffee beans p. 136
Mother and child p. 129
Maasai women p. 128
Woman with stack of fabric p. 131
Nairobi skyline p. 130
Fody bird p. 131
Bronze head from Benin p. 135
Snorkeler p. 129
Freight boats p. 134
Zebras pp. 128–129
Peanuts for export pp. 134
Gold miners p. 131
Classroom scene p. 136
Chokwe mask p. 137
Ring-tailed lemur p. 138
Elephant p. 128
Women carrying wood p. 136
Bo Kaap p. 128–129
Early man skull p. 139
Cape Town skyline p. 139
Victoria Falls p. 138

⬇ DIGGING FOR GOLD. Miners dig a pit mine near the edge of the rain forest in Gabon. Oil and mineral extraction is an important part of Gabon's economy. While searching for traces of gold, however, they expose the fragile soil to erosion.

⬆ TROPICAL JEWEL. A ruby red fody bird perches on a forest branch on Mahé Island in the Seychelles. Native to neighboring Madagascar, the fody eats seeds and insects.

THE CONTINENT:
AFRICA

North Africa

This region, which is made up of five countries, stretches from the Atlantic Ocean in the west to the Red Sea in the east. To the north the region is bounded by the Mediterranean Sea, while to the south lies the vast dry expanse of the Sahara. The world's longest river—the Nile—winds northward through Egypt, but most of the region is arid—meaning there is too little moisture to support trees or extensive vegetation. Most of the region's population lives in coastal areas or in the fertile valley of the Nile River. In recent years, the region has experienced widespread instability as a result of tensions between conservative Islamic groups and more liberal groups seeking modernization and democratic rule.

THE BASICS

STATS

Largest country
Algeria 919,595 sq mi (2,381,741 sq km)

Smallest country
Tunisia 63,170 sq mi (163,610 sq km)

Most populous country
Egypt 82,283,000

Least populous country
Libya 6,469,000

Predominant languages
Arabic, French, various indigenous languages

Predominant religions
Islam, indigenous beliefs

Highest GDP per capita
Libya $14,500

Lowest GDP capita
Morocco $3,100

Highest life expectancy
Libya 78 years

Highest literacy rate
Libya 89%

GEO WHIZ

Ibn Battuta, who was born in Tangier, Morocco, in 1304, set off on a pilgrimage to Mecca that turned into a 29-year, 75,000-mile (120,675-km) journey that took him from the Middle East to India, China, the East Indies, and back home.

Lake Nasser in southern Egypt, formed by the Aswan High Dam, is the world's third largest reservoir. Built to provide water for farms along the Nile in years of drought, it also produces more than 10 billion kilowatt hours of electricity every year.

The city of Kairouan in eastern Tunisia is considered by many to be the fourth holiest Islamic city after Mecca, Medina, and Jerusalem. A UNESCO World Heritage site, the city was founded in A.D. 670 and became a center for Islamic learning.

PORTUGAL (SPAIN)

Strait of Gibralt
Tang

Madeira Islands (PORTUGAL)

Rabat
Casablanca

ATLANTIC

Safi · Mekn

Marrakech · 13,665 ft MO P

OCEAN

Agadir · Jebel Toubkal 4,165 m ATL

Canary Islands (SPAIN)

Goulimine

Tarfaya

Laayoune

WESTERN SAHARA (MOROCCO)

Al Farciya

Tindouf

Erg

Ad Dakhla

Cap Barbas

Cap Blanc

Techla

MAURITANIA

S

0   400 miles
0   400 kilometers

Albers Equal-Area Projection

🔹 **SEA OF SAND.** Towering dunes, as well as barren, rocky expanses define Earth's largest desert—the Sahara, which separates North Africa from the rest of the continent.

🔹 **LEADER REMEMBERED.** Arab influence in North Africa is reflected in the dramatic mausoleum of Tunisia's first president, Habib Bourguiba, in the coastal town of Al Munastîr. Bourguiba led Tunisia's fight for independence from colonial rule by France.

◖ SPIRIT OF THE PAST. A gold hawk pendant adorned with semiprecious stones and colored glass may represent the god Horus, one of the oldest Egyptian gods. This treasure was found in the tomb of King Tut.

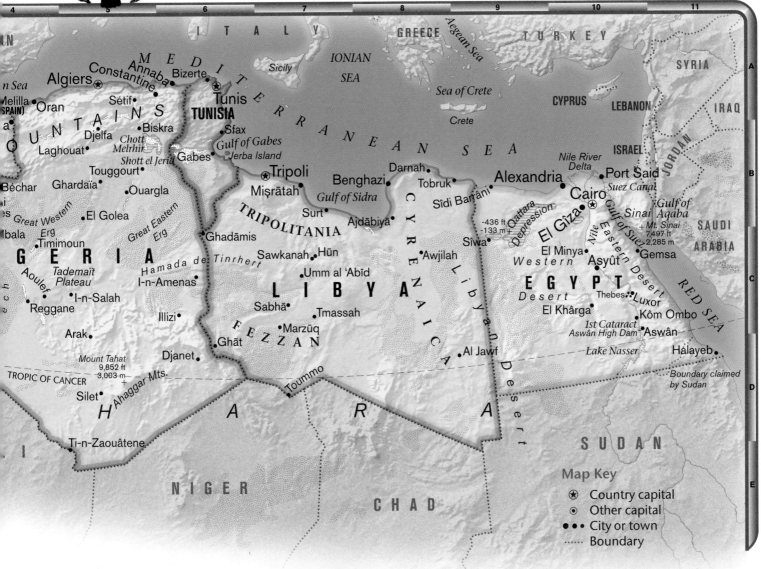

4 5 6 7 8 9 10 11

ITALY   GREECE   *Aegean Sea*   TURKEY

SYRIA

Sicily   IONIAN SEA

Sea of Crete   CYPRUS   LEBANON   IRAQ

n Sea   Algiers   Constantine   Annaba   Bizerte
Melilla (SPAIN)   Oran   Sétif   Tunis
a   Laghouat   Djelfa   Biskra   **TUNISIA**   Sfax   *Gulf of Gabes*   ISRAEL
Béchar   Ghardaïa   *Chott Melrhir*   Gabes   *Jerba Island*   JORDAN
Shott el Jerid

MEDITERRANEAN SEA

Béchar   Ghardaïa   Ouargla   Tripoli   Darnah   Alexandria   *Nile River Delta*   Port Said
es Great Western   El Golea   Mişrātah   Benghazi   Tobruk   *Suez Canal*
bala   Erg   Great Eastern   Surt   *Gulf of Sidra*   Sîdi Barrâni   Cairo   *Gulf of Aqaba*
Timimoun   *Erg*   TRIPOLITANIA   Ajdābiyā   -436 ft   *Qattara*   El Gîza   Sinai   *Mt. Sinai 7,497 ft 2,285 m*
GERIA   Ghadāmis   -133 m   *Depression*   SAUDI ARABIA
Tademaït Plateau   *Hamada de Tinrhert*   Sawkanah   Hūn   Awjilah   Sîwa   El Minya   Asyût   Gemsa
Aoulef   I-n-Amenas   Umm al 'Abīd   *Western*   RED SEA
I-n-Salah   **LIBYA**   *Desert*   El Khârga   Thebes   Luxor
Reggane   Sabhā   Tmassah   *1st Cataract*   Kôm Ombo
Arak   Illizi   *FEZZAN*   Marzūq   Aswān High Dam   Aswân
Ghāt   *Lake Nasser*   Halayeb
Mount Tahat   Djanet   Al Jawf   *Boundary claimed by Sudan*
9,852 ft   *CYRENAICA*   *Libyan*
TROPIC OF CANCER   3,003 m
Silet   *Ahaggar Mts.*   *H*   *Desert*
    Toummo   *A*   *R*   *A*   SUDAN
Ti-n-Zaouâtene   NIGER   CHAD

Map Key
★ Country capital
◉ Other capital
••• City or town
······ Boundary

◖ SYMBOLS OF ANCIENT EGYPT. Camels plod through the desert as the sun sets behind the ancient pyramids of Giza. Built 4,500 years ago, the pyramids were monumental tombs of pharaohs.

◖ BLACK GOLD. Silhouetted against the setting sun, oil wells draw this valuable resource from beneath desert sands. Libya holds the largest proven oil reserves in Africa.

CHANGING THE LAND

☐ true desert
☐ severe risk of desertification
☐ moderate to great risk

Source: UN Food and Agricultural Organization

Overgrazing, removal of vegetation by farmers, and unreliable rainfall are turning some land in Africa into desert—a process called desertification.

THE CONTINENT:
AFRICA

THE BASICS

STATS

Largest country
Niger 489,191 sq miles (1,267,000 sq km)

Smallest country
São Tomé and Principe 372 sq miles (964 sq km)

Most populous
Nigeria 170,124,000

Least populous
São Tomé and Principe 183,000

Predominant languages French, English, Portuguese, Arabic, Spanish, various indigenous languages and dialects

Predominant religions
Islam, Christianity, indigenous beliefs

Highest GDP per capita
Equatorial Guinea $15,500

Lowest GDP per capita
Niger $434

Highest life expectancy
Cape Verde 71 years

Highest literacy rate
Equatorial Guinea 93.9%

GEO WHIZ

Nigeria is Africa's largest producer and exporter of oil. Port Harcourt, in the Niger River delta, is the center of the country's oil industry.

For more than 300 years, the Slave House on Senegal's Gorée Island served as a holding pen for slaves before they were sent to the Americas and elsewhere. Today, it is a museum and a memorial to those slaves.

Measuring a foot (32 cm) long and weighing seven pounds (3 kg), the goliath frog has a hind foot bigger than a man's palm. The world's largest frog lives only in the rain forests of Cameroon and Equatorial Guinea.

Income from oil production gives Equatorial Guinea the highest GDP per capita in the region, but wealth is unevenly distributed. Most people still practice subsistence farming and enjoy few benefits from oil revenues.

West Africa

Stretching from Mauritania in the northwest to Gabon astride the equator in the southeast, 20 countries make up the region of West Africa. Three countries—Burkino Faso, Mali, and Niger—are landlocked. The remaining seventeen have coastlines along the Atlantic Ocean or the Gulf of Guinea. Early kingdoms thrived in Mali, Ghana, and Benin, but European conquest disrupted traditional societies and took away vast wealth, leaving a colonial legacy of disorder and conflict. Widespread use of French and English also reflect the colonial past. Palm oil, rubber, and cacao are produced in tropical areas. Drier lands grow peanuts and cotton. Nigeria, Equatorial Guinea, and Gabon are also major oil producers.

🌀 **RIVER TRANSPORT.** Traditional river boats are an important link in the movement of cargo and people along the Niger River.

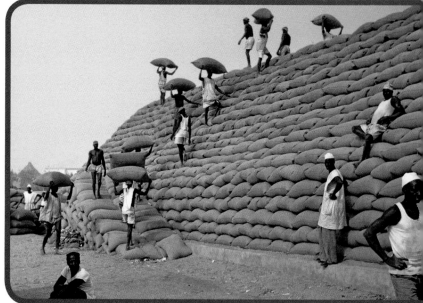

◐ **WAITING FOR SHIPMENT.** Sacks of peanuts create an artificial mountain in Kano, Nigeria, where they wait for transport to Lagos and then export to world markets. The Kano region produces about half of Nigeria's peanut crop.

◐ **FULL OF COLOR.** Artistic ceramic plates brighten an outdoor marketplace in Kumasi, Ghana. This country has a long and rich cultural tradition of creating pottery for cooking and for serving food and water.

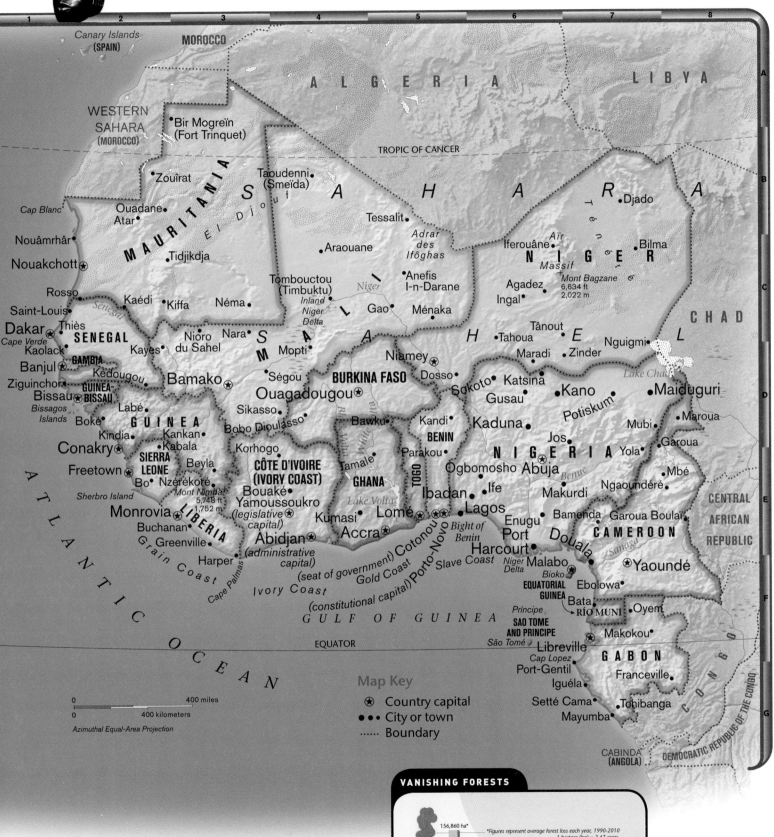

MASTER ARTISANS. The ancient African kingdom of Benin produced outstanding bronze work. Sculpted by hand and then cast in bronze by the lost-wax method, each piece was created to honor the king.

Map Key
⊛ Country capital
●●● City or town
····· Boundary

0   400 miles
0   400 kilometers
Azimuthal Equal-Area Projection

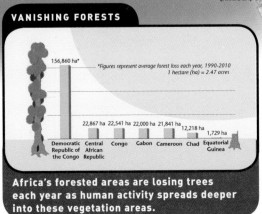

VANISHING FORESTS

156,860 ha*   *Figures represent average forest loss each year, 1990-2010
1 hectare (ha) = 2.47 acres

22,867 ha 22,541 ha 22,000 ha 21,841 ha 12,218 ha
1,729 ha

Democratic Republic of the Congo | Central African Republic | Congo | Gabon | Cameroon | Chad | Equatorial Guinea

Africa's forested areas are losing trees each year as human activity spreads deeper into these vegetation areas.

East Africa

THE BASICS

STATS

Largest country
Democratic Republic of the Congo
905,354 sq miles (2,344,858 sq km)

Smallest country
Djibouti 8,957 sq miles (23,200 sq km)

Most populous
Democratic Republic of the Congo
69,117,000

Least populous
Djibouti 923,000

Predominant languages
French, Arabic, English, various
indigenous languages and dialects

Predominant religions
Christianity, Islam, various indigenous
beliefs

Highest GDP per capita
Congo $3,300

Lowest GDP per capita
Democratic Republic of the Congo $251

Highest life expectancy
Kenya, Eritrea, Sudan 63 years

Highest literacy rate
Kenya 87%

GEO WHIZ

Lakes Malawi, Tanganyika, and Albert are
part of a chain of lakes that mark where
the Somali Plate (see page 17) is breaking
away from Africa. Millions of years from
now, much of the region from Djibouti to
Mozambique could be one big island.

As part of a coming-of-age ritual, each
Maasai boy must kill a lion. Read the true-
life story of Joseph Lemasolai Lekuton
in *Facing the Lion*, published by National
Geographic Children's Books.

In 2006 the 3.3-million-year-old fossilized
remains of a child were found in the Danakil
area of northern Ethiopia. The find was not
far from where the 2.3-million-year-old
remains of Lucy, an adult female of the
same primitive human species, were found
in 1974.

Only about 700 mountain gorillas remain
on Earth. About half of these magnificent
creatures live in forests on the slopes
of the volcanic Virunga Mountains in
Rwanda, Uganda, and the Democratic
Republic of the Congo. Mountain gorillas
are endangered due to poaching, loss of
habitat, and civil conflict that has disrupted the countries where they are found.

The Congo, the region's longest river and chief commercial highway, flows through rain forests that, despite efforts to save them, are being cut for timber and palm oil plantations. In Chad, many people make a living by raising livestock as well as cotton and other crops. Extended drought and diversion of water for agriculture have reduced Lake Chad to one-twentieth of its former size and threatened the animals that live there. Volcanic peaks such as Kilimanjaro—Africa's highest mountain—tower above fertile farmlands in Tanzania and Kenya. Tree-dotted grasslands, called savannas, are home to vast herds of wildlife that attract tourists from around the globe. For more than 50 years, religious and ethnic conflicts fueled warfare in the northeastern part of the region, resulting in political separation—Eritrea from Ethiopia and South Sudan from Sudan.

⬤ **EAGER LEARNERS.** Tanzania, a poor country with a literacy rate of only 69 percent, lags in education. Students in this crowded village school compete for the teacher's attention.

◐ **FROM FIELD TO CUP.** A worker on a coffee estate in Kenya holds freshly harvested coffee berries, which will soon be on their way to the world market. Coffee production was introduced to Kenya in 1900. Today, it employs more than six million workers.

⬤ **WOMEN'S WORK.** Villagers throughout Africa depend on wood as their main source of fuel to cook and heat their homes. This contributes to widespread deforestation. These women carry wood out of Virunga National Park in the Democratic Republic of the Congo.

GLITTERING WEALTH

25,000*	12,500	5,500	3,500	1,200	300	77
Botswana	Angola	Democratic Republic of the Congo	South Africa	Namibia	Ghana	Tanzania

Gem diamond mine production in thousands of carats, 2010 data

Diamonds are prized both for jewelry and for industrial uses. More than half of the world's diamond production comes from mines in Africa.

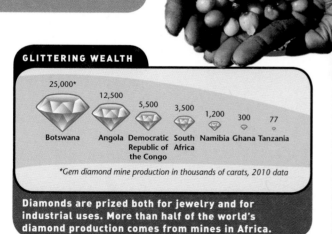

◖ **CELEBRATING A KING.** The Chokwe people of Central Africa used masks such as this to celebrate the inauguration of a new king. Considered sacred, the mask could only be worn by the current chief of a group.

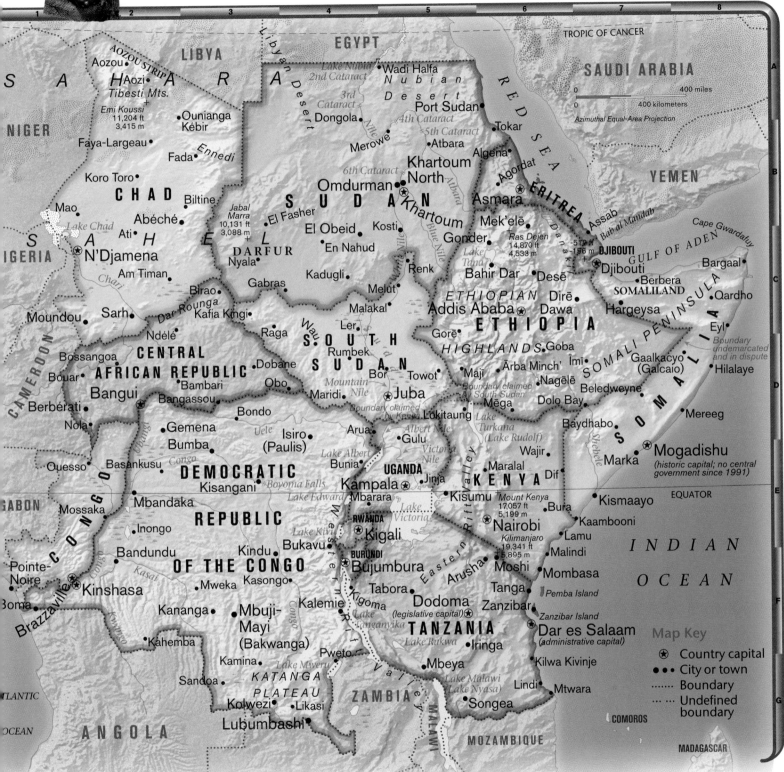

TROPIC OF CANCER

EGYPT

LIBYA

SAUDI ARABIA

0   400 miles
0   400 kilometers
Azimuthal Equal-Area Projection

NIGER

Aozou
AOZOU STRIP
Haozi
Tibesti Mts.
Emi Koussi
11,204 ft
3,415 m

Ounianga
Kébir

Faya-Largeau
Fada
Ennedi

Koro Toro

CHAD
Biltine

Mao

Abéché
Ati
Lake Chad

IGERIA
N'Djamena

Am Timan
Chari

Moundou

Sarh

Ndélé

CENTRAL
AFRICAN REPUBLIC
Bossangoa
Bouar
Bangui
Berbérati
Nola

Jabal
Marra
10,131 ft
3,088 m
DARFUR
Nyala

El Fasher

El Obeid
En Nahud

Kadugli

Gabras
Birao
Dar Rounga
Kafia Kingi
Raga
Dobane
Bambari
Bangassou
Obo
Maridi

SAHARA

SUDAN

Libyan Desert
Dongola
4th Cataract
5th Cataract
Merowe
Atbara

Lake Nubia
2nd Cataract
3rd Cataract
Wadi Halfa

Nubian Desert

Port Sudan
Tokar

Khartoum North
Omdurman
Khartoum
6th Cataract

Kosti

Renk

Melut

Malakal
Ler

Rumbek

SOUTH SUDAN
Bor

White Nile
Blue Nile
Atbara

RED SEA

Algena
Agordat
Asmara

ERITREA

Assab
Bab al Mandab
DJIBOUTI
Djibouti

YEMEN

Cape Gwardafuy

GULF OF ADEN

Berbera
SOMALILAND

Bargaal

Qardho

Mek'ele
Ras Dejen
14,870 ft
4,538 m
Gonder
Lake Tana
Bahir Dar
Desē
Dirē
Dawa

Addis Ababa
Gore
ETHIOPIA
HIGHLANDS
Goba

Maji
Arba Minch'
Ími
Nagēlē
Mēga
Dolo Bay

Boundary
undemarcated
and in dispute

Hargeysa
Eyl

SOMALI PENINSULA

S O M A L I A

Hilalaye

Beledweyne

Baydhabo

Mereeg

Marka

⊛ **Mogadishu**
(historic capital; no central
government since 1991)

-512 m
-156 m
Danakil

Maji
Wajir
Dif
Maralal

CAMEROON

Ubangi

Gemena
Bumba
Basankusu
Kisangani

DEMOCRATIC

REPUBLIC

Mbandaka
Inongo

Ouesso

Mossaka

GABON

Isiro
(Paulis)

Bondo

Uele
Congo
Boyoma Falls

OF THE CONGO

Bandundu

Pointe-
Noire
Brazzaville
Kinshasa
Boma

Arua
Gulu
Bunia
Lake Albert

UGANDA

Kampala

Mbarara

Lake Edward
RWANDA
Kigali
Bukavu
BURUNDI
Bujumbura

Kindu

Kasongo

Mweka

Kananga
Mbuji-
Mayi
(Bakwanga)

Kamina
Sandoa

Kasai
Kwango
Kwilu

Kahemba

Kalemie

Lake Tanganyika
Kigoma
Tabora

Juba
Boundary claimed
by South Sudan
Lokitaung
Lake Turkana
(Lake Rudolf)

Boundary claimed
by Kenya

Towot

Mountain Nile
Western Nile
Albert Nile
Victoria Nile
Lake Victoria

Kisumu

KENYA
Mount Kenya
17,057 ft
5,199 m
Nairobi
Kilimanjaro
19,341 ft
5,895 m
Moshi
Arusha

Bura

Kaambooni

Lamu
Malindi
Mombasa

Kismaayo

INDIAN

OCEAN

EQUATOR

Eastern Rift Valley

Dodoma
(legislative capital)

TANZANIA
Iringa
Mbeya
Lake Rukwa

KATANGA
PLATEAU
Kolwezi
Likasi
Lubumbashi

Kamina
Lake Mweru

Pweto

ZAMBIA

Western Rift Valley
Lake Malawi
(Lake Nyasa)

MALAWI

Tanga

Zanzibar
Zanzibar Island
Pemba Island

Dar es Salaam
(administrative capital)

Kilwa Kivinje

Lindi
Mtwara

Songea

COMOROS

MADAGASCAR

MOZAMBIQUE

ANGOLA

ATLANTIC
OCEAN

Map Key

⊛ Country capital
• City or town
...... Boundary
---- Undefined
boundary

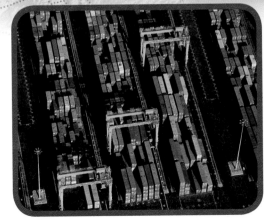

◖ **INTERNATIONAL PORT.** Shipping containers look like colorful ribbons at a port terminal in Djibouti. The recently modernized and expanded port facility, with its deep natural harbor, is the mainstay of this small East African country's economy.

THE BASICS

STATS

Largest country
Angola 481,354 sq mi (1,246,700 sq km)

Smallest country
Seychelles 176 sq mi (455 sq km)

Most populous country
South Africa 51,147,000

Least populous country
Seychelles 93,000

Predominant languages
English, French, Portuguese, various
indigenous languages and dialects

Predominant religions
Christianity, Islam, various indigenous
beliefs

Highest GDP per capita
Seychelles $11,200

Lowest GDP per capita
Malawi $262

Highest life expectancy
Mauritius 75 years

Highest literacy rate
Seychelles
92%

GEO WHIZ

South Africa's Kruger National Park,
the largest in Africa, covers more area
than the entire country of Israel. Within
its boundary are 14 different ecological
zones that provide habitat to a great variety of plants, birds, and other animals,
including the "big five": lions, elephants,
leopards, rhinos, and buffaloes.

Great Zimbabwe National Monument has
the largest ancient stone ruins south of the
Sahara. This massive fortress city was the
center of an empire that flourished from
the 11th to the 15th century.

The Makgadikgadi salt pans in the eastern
Kalahari of Botswana are what is left of
an immense lake. Each spring, rains flood
the area and attract herds of migrating
zebras and wildebeests.

Namibia is famed for sand dunes that
are reportedly the highest in the world.
The largest, Big Daddy, towers 1,200 feet
(366 m) above the surrounding land.
Along Namibia's northwestern coast,
treacherous crosscurrents have caused
countless shipwrecks, earning it the
nickname Skeleton Coast.

Southern Africa

Ringed by uplands, the region's central basin holds the seasonally lush
Okavango Delta and scorching Kalahari

Desert. The
mighty Zambezi
thunders over
Victoria Falls
on its way to
the Indian
Ocean, where
Madagascar is
home to plants
and animals
found nowhere
else in the world.

🔘 **NATURAL WONDER.**
Victoria Falls, third
largest waterfall in
the world, is 5,500 feet
(1,676 m) wide and
355 feet (108 m) high.

Bantu and San are among the indigenous people who saw their hold on
the land give way to Portuguese, Dutch,
and British traders and colonists. The
region offers a range of mineral resources
and a variety of climates and soils that in
some places yield bumper crops of grains,
grapes, and citrus. Rich deposits of coal,
gold, and diamonds have helped make South
Africa the continent's economic powerhouse.

◐ **STARING EYES.**
This ring-tailed
lemur sits on a forest
tree branch. The ring-
tail, found only in
Madagascar, spends
time both on the
ground and in the trees.
It eats fruits, leaves,
insects, small birds, and
even lizards.

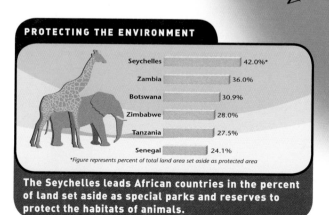

PROTECTING THE ENVIRONMENT

Country	Percent
Seychelles	42.0%*
Zambia	36.0%
Botswana	30.9%
Zimbabwe	28.0%
Tanzania	27.5%
Senegal	24.1%

*Figure represents percent of total land area set aside as protected area

**The Seychelles leads African countries in the percent
of land set aside as special parks and reserves to
protect the habitats of animals.**

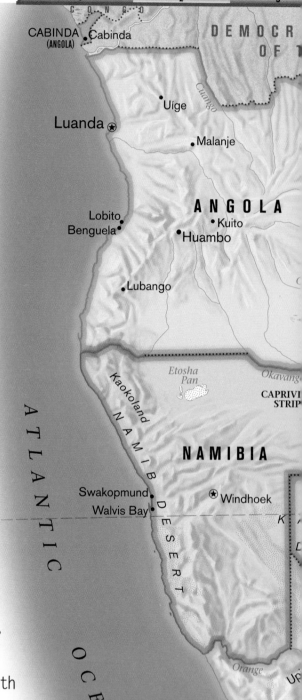

CONGO

CABINDA
(ANGOLA) • Cabinda

DEMOCR
OF T

• Uíge

Luanda ⊛

• Malanje

ANGOLA

Lobito • • Kuito
Benguela • • Huambo

• Lubango

Etosha
Pan

Okavang

**CAPRIVI
STRIP**

Kaokoland

N
A
M
I
B

NAMIBIA

A
T
L
A
N
T
I
C

Swakopmund •
Walvis Bay •

D
E
S
E
R
T

⊛ Windhoek

K

O
C
E
A
N

Orange

Worcester
•

Cape Town ⊛
(legislative capital)

Cape of Good Hope

Cape Agulhas

◖ **EARLY MAN.** Dating back perhaps 70,000 years, this skull of "Broken Hill Man," found in Zimbabwe, is thought to represent a transitional type between *Homo erectus* and *Homo sapiens*.

Map Key

⊛ Country capital
••• City or town
······ Boundary

0 ——————— 200 miles
0 ——————— 300 kilometers
Azimuthal Equidistant Projection

REPUBLIC
NGO

TANZANIA

Lake Tanganyika

Lake Malawi

Rovuma

Moroni ⊛

SEYCHELLES

Îles Glorieuses
(FRANCE)

Cap d'Ambre

COMOROS

Kasama

Mzuzu

Lugenda

Pemba

Île de Mayotte
(FRANCE)

Antsiranana

Mufulira

Muchinga Mountains

Lichinga

Nacala

+ Maromokotro
9,436 ft
2,876 m

Chingola
Kitwe
Luanshya
Ndola
Kabwe

M
A
L
A
W
I

Chipata

Nampula

Moçambique

Mahajanga

Zambezi

ZAMBIA

Lilongwe ⊛
Zomba
Blantyre

Mongu

Lusaka ⊛

M
O
Z
A
M
B
I
Q
U
E

Mozambique Channel

MADAGASCAR

Tete

Quelimane

Île Juan De Nova
(FRANCE)

Toamasina

Victoria Falls
Livingstone

Lake Kariba

Harare ⊛

Antananarivo ⊛

Okavango
Delta

Chitungwiza

Antsirabe

ZIMBABWE

Mutare

Chimoio

Makgadikgadi Pans

Gweru

Great
Zimbabwe

Beira

Bassas da India
(FRANCE)

Fianarantsoa

Bulawayo

Île Europa
(FRANCE)

TSWANA

Francistown

For Mauritius and Réunion, see maps on pages 126–127.

Serowe

TROPIC OF CAPRICORN

Toliara

A
R
I

Polokwane
(Pietersburg)

Inhambane

Gaborone ⊛

R
T

Pretoria (Tshwane)
(administrative capital)

Limpopo

Kanye

Xai-Xai

Johannesburg

Maputo ⊛

Soweto

Mbabane *(administrative capital)*

Cap Ste. Marie

Klerksdorp

Vereeniging

Vaal

SWAZILAND

OUTH

Lobamba *(legislative and royal capital)*

Welkom

Kroonstad

I
N
D
I
A
N

O
C
E
A
N

imberley

Richards Bay

Bloemfontein ⊛
(judicial capital)

Maseru ⊛

LESOTHO

Pietermaritzburg

RICA

Orange

Durban

ddelburg

Karroo

Queenstown

dtshoorn

East London
Grahamstown

Uitenhage

eorge

Port Elizabeth

◖ **SOUTHERN METROPOLIS.** Third most populous city in South Africa and seat of the national parliament, Cape Town began as a Dutch supply station in 1652. Table Mountain rises in the background.

PHYSICAL

Area and population totals are for the independent countries in the region only.

Land area
3,278,000 sq mi
(8,490,000 sq km)

Highest point
Mount Wilhelm, Papua New Guinea
14,793 ft (4,509 m)

Lowest point
Lake Eyre, Australia
-52 ft (-16 m)

Longest river
Murray-Darling, Australia
2,310 mi (3,718 km)

Largest lake
Lake Eyre, Australia
3,430 sq mi (8,884 sq km)

POLITICAL

Population
35,759,000

Largest metropolitan area
Sydney, Australia
Pop. 4,429,000

Largest country
Australia
2,969,906 sq mi (7,692,024 sq km)

Most densely populated country
Nauru
1,275 people per sq mi (485 per sq km)

Economy
Farming: livestock, wheat, fruit
Industry: mining, wool, oil
Services

Australia, New Zealand, & Oceania

Australia, New Zealand & Oceania

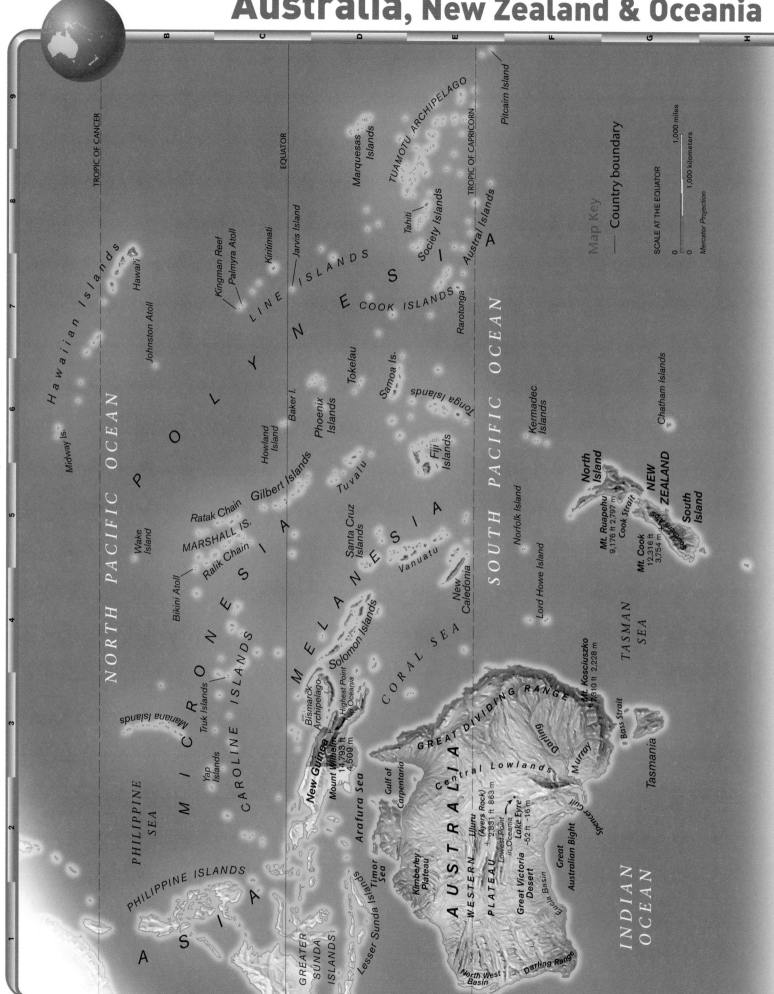

TROPIC OF CANCER

EQUATOR

TROPIC OF CAPRICORN

Map Key
— Country boundary

SCALE AT THE EQUATOR

1,000 miles

1,000 kilometers

Mercator Projection

NORTH PACIFIC OCEAN

SOUTH PACIFIC OCEAN

Hawaiian Islands

Midway Is.

Hawai'i

Johnston Atoll

Wake Island

Bikini Atoll

Ralik Chain

Ratak Chain

MARSHALL IS.

Gilbert Islands

Howland Island

Baker I.

Kingman Reef

Palmyra Atoll

Kiritimati

Jarvis Island

LINE ISLANDS

Marquesas Islands

TUAMOTU ARCHIPELAGO

Pitcairn Island

Tahiti

Society Islands

Austral Islands

P O L Y N E S I A

COOK ISLANDS

Rarotonga

Tokelau

Samoa Is.

Tonga Islands

Phoenix Islands

Tuvalu

Fiji Islands

Santa Cruz Islands

Vanuatu

New Caledonia

M E L A N E S I A

M I C R O N E S I A

Yap Islands

Truk Islands

Mariana Islands

CAROLINE ISLANDS

PHILIPPINE SEA

PHILIPPINE ISLANDS

A S I A

GREATER SUNDA ISLANDS

Lesser Sunda Islands

Timor Sea

Arafura Sea

New Guinea

Mount Wilhelm
14,793 ft
4,509 m

Highest Point in Oceania

Bismarck Archipelago

Solomon Islands

Gulf of Carpentaria

CORAL SEA

Norfolk Island

Lord Howe Island

Kermadec Islands

Chatham Islands

NEW ZEALAND

North Island

Mt. Ruapehu
9,176 ft 2,797 m

Cook Strait

Mt. Cook
12,316 ft
3,754 m

South Island

Southern Alps

TASMAN SEA

AUSTRALIA

WESTERN PLATEAU

Kimberley Plateau

North West Basin

Darling Range

Great Victoria Desert

Eucla Basin

Great Australian Bight

Spencer Gulf

Central Lowlands

Uluru
(Ayers Rock)
2,831 ft 863 m

Lake Eyre
-52 ft -16 m

Lowest Point in Oceania

GREAT DIVIDING RANGE

Mt. Kosciuszko
7,310 ft 2,228 m

Darling

Murray

Bass Strait

Tasmania

INDIAN OCEAN

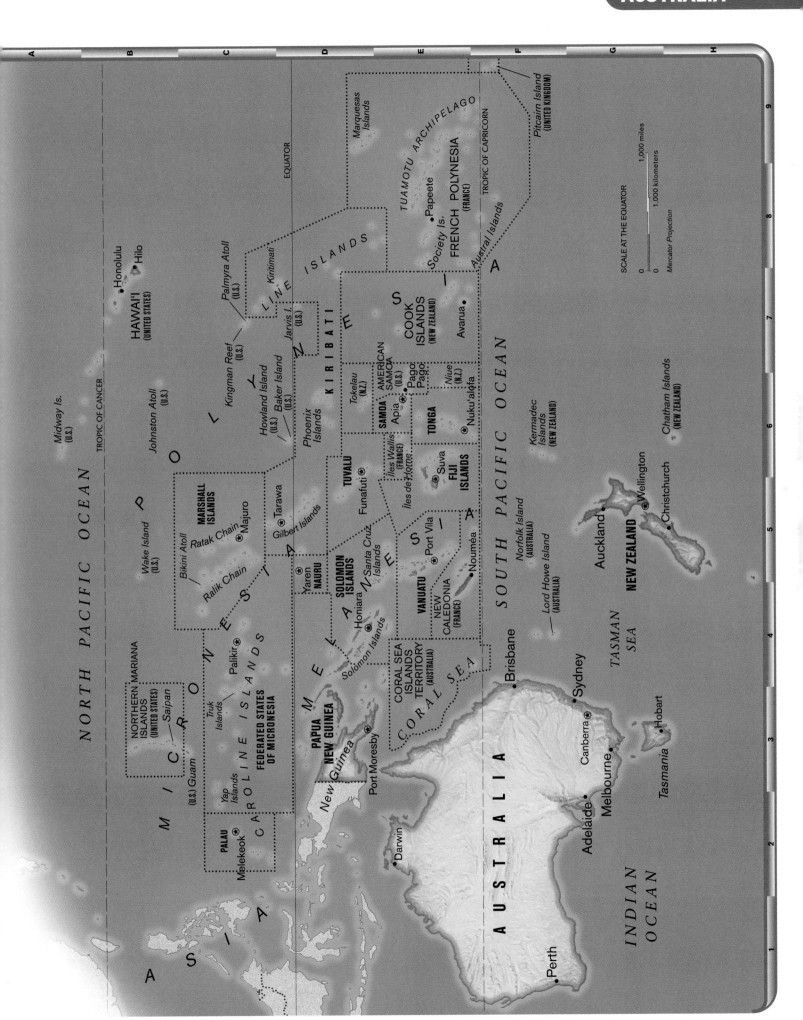

A B C D E F G H

9

8

7

6

5

4

3

2

1

SCALE AT THE EQUATOR

1,000 miles

1,000 kilometers

Mercator Projection

EQUATOR

TROPIC OF CANCER

TROPIC OF CAPRICORN

NORTH PACIFIC OCEAN

SOUTH PACIFIC OCEAN

INDIAN OCEAN

Midway Is.
(U.S.)

Honolulu
•Hilo
HAWAI'I
(UNITED STATES)

Johnston Atoll
(U.S.)

Wake Island
(U.S.)

Palmyra Atoll
(U.S.)

Kiritimati

Kingman Reef
(U.S.)

Howland Island
(U.S.)
Baker Island
(U.S.)

Jarvis I.
(U.S.)

LINE ISLANDS

Phoenix Islands

KIRIBATI

Marquesas Islands

TUAMOTU ARCHIPELAGO

•Papeete
Society Is. **FRENCH POLYNESIA**
(FRANCE)

Austral Islands

COOK ISLANDS
(NEW ZEALAND)
•Avarua

POLYNESIA

MICRONESIA

MELANESIA

NORTHERN MARIANA
ISLANDS
(UNITED STATES)
•Saipan

(U.S.) Guam

Yap Islands

Truk Islands

PALAU
Melekeok⊛

CAROLINE ISLANDS

FEDERATED STATES
OF MICRONESIA
Palikir⊛

MARSHALL ISLANDS

Bikini Atoll

Ratak Chain

Ralik Chain

⊛Majuro

•Tarawa

Gilbert Islands

TUVALU
Funafuti•

Yaren⊛
NAURU

SOLOMON ISLANDS
Honiara⊛
Solomon Islands

N.Santa Cruz Islands

VANUATU
•Port Vila

NEW CALEDONIA
(FRANCE)
Nouméa•

Tokelau
(N.Z.)

SAMOA
Apia•
AMERICAN SAMOA
(U.S.)
•Pago
Pago

Iles Wallis
(FRANCE)
Iles de Horne

TONGA
⊛Nuku'alofa

Niue
(N.Z.)

FIJI ISLANDS
Suva•

Kermadec Islands
(NEW ZEALAND)

Norfolk Island
(AUSTRALIA)

Lord Howe Island
(AUSTRALIA)

Chatham Islands
(NEW ZEALAND)

Pitcairn Island
(UNITED KINGDOM)

NEW ZEALAND
Auckland•
•Wellington
•Christchurch

TASMAN SEA

ASIA

PAPUA
NEW GUINEA
Port Moresby•

New Guinea

•Darwin

CORAL SEA ISLANDS
TERRITORY
(AUSTRALIA)

CORAL SEA

•Brisbane

•Sydney

AUSTRALIA

•Perth

•Adelaide
•Melbourne
Canberra⊛

•Hobart
Tasmania

Australia,
New Zealand, & Oceania

WORLDS APART

This vast region includes Australia—the world's smallest continent—New Zealand, and a fleet of mostly tiny island worlds scattered across the Pacific Ocean. Apart from Australia, New Zealand, and Papua New Guinea, Oceania's other 11 independent countries cover about 25,000 square miles (65,000 sq km), an area only slightly larger than half of New Zealand's North Island. Twenty-one other island groups are dependencies of the United States, France, Australia, New Zealand, or the United Kingdom. Long isolation has allowed the growth of diverse marine communities, such as Australia's Great Barrier Reef, and the evolution of platypuses, kangaroos, and other land animals that live nowhere else on the planet.

○ **AUSTRALIAN TEDDY BEAR.** Koalas, which are not bears at all, are native to the eucalyptus forests of eastern Australia.

◑ **ANCIENT VOYAGERS.** The Maoris are believed to have sailed to New Zealand from islands far to the northeast. Maori warriors traditionally adorned themselves with elaborate tattoos to frighten enemies.

PLACE OF LEGENDS. Sacred to native Aborigines, Uluru, also known as Ayers Rock, glows a deep red in the rays of the setting sun. Uluru is the tip of a massive sandstone block—part of an ancient seabed exposed by erosion.

TROPICAL HABITAT. Brilliantly colored fish swim among branching corals in the warm waters of the Vatu-i-Ra Channel in the Fiji Islands. The waters around Fiji have some of the richest and most diverse fish populations in the world.

NATIVE COWBOYS. Competition is fierce during a rodeo in Hope Vale, an Aboriginal community on Australia's Cape York Peninsula. Hope Vale is home to several Aboriginal clan groups.

THE CONTINENT:
AUSTRALIA

more about
Australia, New Zealand & Oceania

🔽 **BIG JUMPER.** The red kangaroo, the largest living marsupial—an animal that carries its young in a pouch—is at home on the dry inland plains of Australia. It can cover 30 feet (9 m) in a single hop.

◑ **WOOLY POPULATION.** Sheep outnumber people in Australia and New Zealand. Wool production is an important part of the economy of these two countries.

◑ **FLYING HIGH.**
Prevailing winds lift adventurous tourists in a tandem parasail high above the waters of New Zealand's Bay of Islands. Rising up to 1,200 feet (366 m) above the water, visitors get a bird's eye view of the islands.

⬥ **A WATER WORLD.** Located just 7 degrees north of the Equator in the western Pacific Ocean, the islands of the Republic of Palau were a United Nations Trust Territory until 1994, when they gained independence.

WHERE THE PICTURES ARE

Tropical islands of Palau pp. 146–147

New Guinea tribesman with painted face p. 151

Ambrym volcano p. 150

Aborigine cowboys p. 145

Catching octopus p. 151

Parasailing p. 146
Lagoon p. 150

Uluru (Ayers Rock) pp. 144–145

Easter Island statue p. 151

Red kangaroo p. 146

Coral reef with fish pp. 144–145

Auckland skyline pp. 146–147

Maori man p. 144

Great white shark p. 148

Sheep in pasture p. 146

Koala p. 144

Mount Cook p. 147

Dingo p. 149

Jet boat with tourists p. 147

Sydney Opera House p. 148

Fiordland National Park p. 149

◗ **A WET RIDE.** Tourists go for a wild ride in a jet boat on the roaring waters of New Zealand's Shotover River.

◗ **SNOWY PEAK.** New Zealand's Mount Cook rises above the clouds. Legend says the peak is a frozen Maori warrior.

SHOTOVER JET

⬥ **MODERN METROPOLIS.** Modern buildings rise against a twilight sky in Auckland, on New Zealand's North Island. It is home to almost one-third of the country's population.

THE CONTINENT:
AUSTRALIA

THE BASICS

STATS

Largest country
Australia 2,969,906 sq mi
(7,692,024 sq km)

Smallest country
New Zealand 104,454 sq mi
(270,534 sq km)

Most populous country
Australia 22,035,000

Least populous country
New Zealand 4,437,000

Predominant languages
English, Maori

Predominant religion
Christianity

Highest GDP per capita
Australia $40,800

Lowest GDP per capita
New Zealand $28,000

Highest life expectancy
Australia 82 years

Highest literacy rate
Australia, New Zealand
99%

GEO WHIZ

Australian Aborigines use a small tree trunk hollowed out by termites to make a musical instrument called a didgeridoo.

One-fourth of New Zealand's population lives in Auckland, on North Island, making it the largest city in Polynesia.

Lake Eyre is Australia's largest lake, but it is very shallow—not quite 20 feet (6 m) deep when full. Most of the rivers that flow into it dry up before reaching it. The lake has been filled to capacity only three times over the past 150 years.

Australia's location south of the Equator earned it the nickname Land Down Under.

The ceilings of grottoes in New Zealand's Waitomo Caves look like starry night skies thanks to the light given off by thousands of glowworms.

The Tasmanian devil is a meat-eating marsupial that lives only in Tasmania. Its high-pitched screeches can be heard at night when the animal is most active. This protected species is the symbol of the Tasmanian National Parks and Wildlife Service.

Australia & New Zealand

Most people in Australia live along the coast, far from the country's dry interior, known as the Outback. The most populous cities and the best croplands are in the southeast. This "Land Down Under" is increasingly linked by trade to Asian countries and to 4.4 million "neighbors" in New Zealand. Twelve hundred miles (1,930 km) across the Tasman Sea, New Zealand is cooler, wetter, and more mountainous than Australia. It is geologically active and has ecosystems ranging from subtropical forests on North Island to snowy peaks on South Island. Both countries enjoy high standards of living and strong agricultural and mining outputs, including wool, wines, gold, coal, and iron ore.

🌓 **KILLER OF THE DEEP.**
Great white sharks inhabit the warm waters off the coast of southern Australia. These warm-blooded marine predators can grow up to 20 feet (6 m) in length.

🌓 **SAILS AT SUNSET.** Reminiscent of a ship in full sail, the Sydney Opera House, in Sydney Harbor, has become a symbol of Australia that is recognized around the world.

DOG OF THE OUTBACK. The dingo is a wild dog found throughout Australia except for Tasmania. Unlike most domestic dogs, the dingo does not bark, although it howls. Aborigines sometimes use dingos as hunting companions or guard dogs.

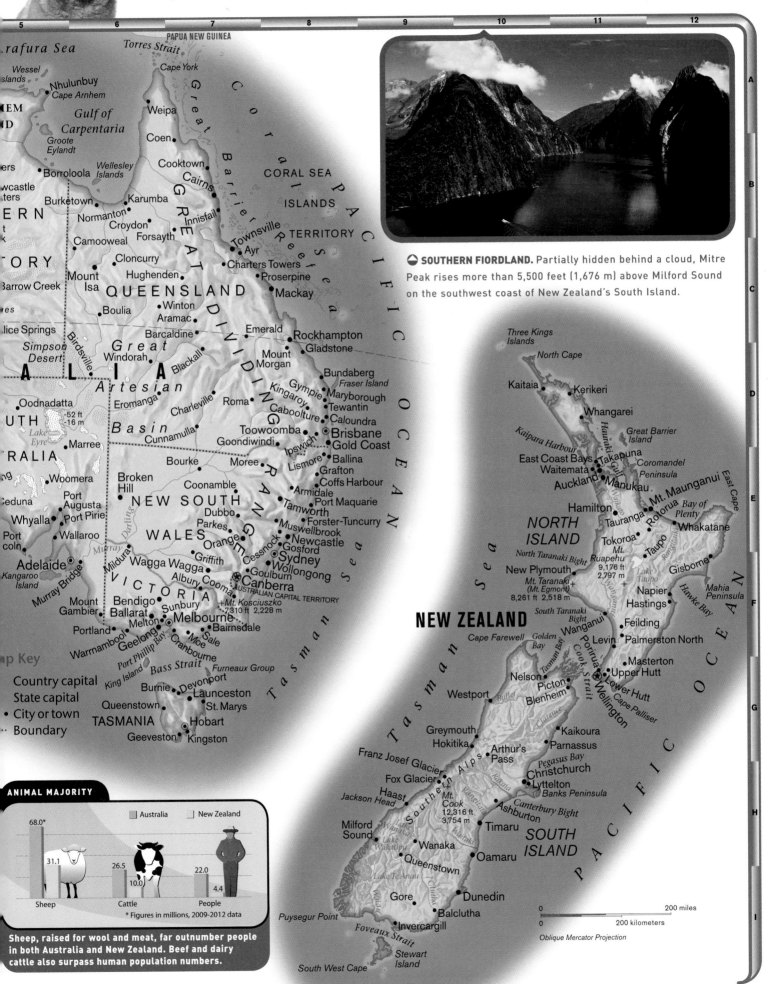

SOUTHERN FIORDLAND. Partially hidden behind a cloud, Mitre Peak rises more than 5,500 feet (1,676 m) above Milford Sound on the southwest coast of New Zealand's South Island.

Map Key
- ◉ Country capital
- ⊙ State capital
- • City or town
- -- Boundary

ANIMAL MAJORITY

	Australia	New Zealand
Sheep	68.0*	31.1
Cattle	26.5	10.0
People	22.0	4.4

*Figures in millions, 2009-2012 data

Sheep, raised for wool and meat, far outnumber people in both Australia and New Zealand. Beef and dairy cattle also surpass human population numbers.

PAPUA NEW GUINEA
Arafura Sea
Torres Strait
Wessel Islands
Nhulunbuy
Cape Arnhem
Gulf of Carpentaria
Cape York
Weipa
Groote Eylandt
Coen
Wellesley Islands
Borroloola
Cooktown
Cairns
Burketown
Karumba
Innisfail
Normanton
Croydon
Forsayth
Townsville
Camooweal
Ayr
CORAL SEA
Cloncurry
Charters Towers
ISLANDS
Mount Isa
Hughenden
Proserpine
TERRITORY
QUEENSLAND
Mackay
Barrow Creek
Boulia
Winton
Aramac
Alice Springs
Barcaldine
Emerald
Rockhampton
Simpson Desert
Great
Windorah
Mount Morgan
Gladstone
Oodnadatta
Artesian
Blackall
Bundaberg
-52 ft -16 m
Eromanga
Charleville
Gympie
Fraser Island
Lake Eyre
Basin
Roma
Kingaroy
Maryborough
Marree
Cunnamulla
Caboolture
Tewantin
Woomera
Bourke
Toowoomba
Caloundra
Port Augusta
Broken Hill
Goondiwindi
Ipswich
Brisbane
Whyalla
Coonamble
Moree
Lismore
Gold Coast
Port Pirie
NEW SOUTH
Coonabarabran
Ballina
Wallaroo
WALES
Dubbo
Armidale
Grafton
Port Lincoln
Parkes
Tamworth
Coffs Harbour
Adelaide
Orange
Muswellbrook
Port Maquarie
Kangaroo Island
Griffith
Cessnock
Forster-Tuncurry
Murray Bridge
Wagga Wagga
Gosford
Newcastle
Mildura
Goulburn
Sydney
VICTORIA
Albury
Cooma
Wollongong
Mount Gambier
Bendigo
Sunbury
Canberra
Ballarat
AUSTRALIAN CAPITAL TERRITORY
Portland
Melton
Melbourne
Mt. Kosciuszko 7310 ft 2,228 m
Warrnambool
Geelong
Bairnsdale
Cranbourne
Moe
Sale
Port Phillip Bay
King Island
Bass Strait
Furneaux Group
Burnie
Devonport
Launceston
Queenstown
St. Marys
TASMANIA
Hobart
Geeveston
Kingston

NEW ZEALAND

Three Kings Islands
North Cape
Kaitaia
Kerikeri
Whangarei
Kaipara Harbour
Great Barrier Island
East Coast Bays
Takapuna
Coromandel Peninsula
Waitemata
Auckland
Manukau
Hamilton
Tauranga
Mt. Maunganui
Rotorua
Bay of Plenty
NORTH ISLAND
Tokoroa
Taupo
Whakatane
North Taranaki Bight
Mt. Ruapehu 9,176 ft 2,797 m
New Plymouth
Lake Taupo
Gisborne
Mt. Taranaki (Mt. Egmont) 8,261 ft 2,518 m
Napier
Mahia Peninsula
South Taranaki Bight
Hastings
Hawke Bay
Cape Farewell
Wanganui
Feilding
Golden Bay
Levin
Palmerston North
Nelson
Masterton
Westport
Picton
Upper Hutt
Blenheim
Lower Hutt
Wellington
Cape Palliser
Greymouth
Kaikoura
Hokitika
Arthur's Pass
Parnassus
Franz Josef Glacier
Southern Alps
Pegasus Bay
Christchurch
Fox Glacier
Lyttelton
Banks Peninsula
Haast
Jackson Head
Mt. Cook 12,316 ft 3,754 m
Canterbury Bight
Milford Sound
Ashburton
Timaru
SOUTH ISLAND
Lake Wakatipu
Wanaka
Oamaru
Queenstown
Lake Te Anau
Gore
Dunedin
Puysegur Point
Balclutha
Invercargill
Foveaux Strait
Stewart Island
South West Cape

200 miles
200 kilometers
Oblique Mercator Projection

THE BASICS

STATS

Largest country
Papua New Guinea
178,703 sq mi (462,840 sq km)

Smallest country
Nauru 8 sq mi (21 sq km)

Most populous country
Papua New Guinea 7,034,000

Least populous country
Nauru 10,200

Predominant languages
English, various indigenous
languages and dialects

Predominant religion
Christianity, various
indigenous beliefs

Highest GDP per capita
Palau $8,100

Lowest GDP per capita
Micronesia $2,200

Highest life expectancy
Tonga 75 years

Highest literacy rate
Samoa
100%

GEO WHIZ

Tuvalu's highest point is roughly 16 feet
(5 m) above sea level. Predictions that
rising sea levels due to global warming
could drown the island within the next
50 years have caused some of its people
to emigrate to New Zealand and other
countries with higher elevations.

For centuries in Fiji, tribal officials would
bring out their best utensils for special
people—not to serve them, but to eat
them. Cannibalism in the islands ended
in the late 1800s, when Christianity was
adopted.

Only 36 of Tonga's 170 islands are inhab-
ited. It was in Tongan waters that the
infamous mutiny aboard the British ship
HMS *Bounty* took place in 1789.

The interior highland region of Papua New
Guinea is so mountainous and forested
that it wasn't explored by outsiders until
the 1930s. Europeans were surprised to
find people living there whose cultures
hadn't changed since the Stone Age.

Kennedy Island, in the Solomon Islands,
is named for U.S. President John F.
Kennedy. During World War II he and
some of his crew swam to this island—
known as Plum Pudding at the time—
after their PT boat was rammed by a
Japanese destroyer.

◗ LIVING EARTH.
Ambrym volcano, in
Vanuatu, is one of the most
active volcanoes in Oceania.
First observed by Captain
Cook in 1774, Ambrym
continues to erupt regularly,
adding to the island's black
sand beaches.

Oceania

Although in its broadest sense Oceania includes
Australia and New Zealand, more commonly it refers
to some 25,000 islands that make up three
large cultural regions in
the Pacific Ocean.
Melanesia, which
extends from
Papua New
Guinea to
Fiji, is closest
to Australia.
Micronesia lies
mostly north of
the Equator and
includes Palau
and the Federated States of Micronesia. New
Zealand, Hawai'i, and Rapa Nui (Easter Island)
mark the western, northern, and eastern limits
of Polynesia, with Tahiti, Samoa, and Tonga near its
heart. Oceania's people often face problems of limited
living space and fresh water. Plantation agriculture,
fishing, tourism, or mining form the economic base
for most of the islands in this region.

◒ TROPICAL PARADISE. A reef
separates an area of sea water
from the ocean, forming a quiet
lagoon around the island of
Bora Bora in the Society Islands
of French Polynesia.

◖ UNSOLVED MYSTERY. Carved from volcanic rock, the giant stone heads of Rapa Nui, also known as Easter Island, remain a mystery. Although culturally Polynesian, the island belongs to Chile, 2,400 miles (3,862 km) to the east (see page 32).

◑ LONG ARMS. Octopuses live on coral reefs in the warm tropical waters of the South Pacific Ocean. They use the suckers on their tentacles to move around and to catch crustaceans and small fish.

4   5   6   7   8   9   10   11

A

B

C

D

E

F

Midway Islands
(U.S.)

H A W A I I
(UNITED STATES)

TROPIC OF CANCER

Wake Island
(U.S.)

O'ahu
Honolulu ⊛ • Hilo
Hawai'i

Johnston Atoll
(U.S.)

P A C I F I C   O C E A N

P O L Y N E S I A

MARSHALL
ISLANDS

Ratak Chain

⊛ Majuro

Kingman Reef (U.S.)
Palmyra Atoll (U.S.)

Gilbert Islands

⊛ Tarawa

Howland Island (U.S.)
Baker Island (U.S.)

Kiritimati (Christmas I.)

EQUATOR

RU

K I R I B A T I

Jarvis Island (U.S.)

L I N E   I S L A N D S

Malden Island
Starbuck Island

ISLANDS

TUVALU
Funafuti ⊛

Phoenix Islands

Vostok Island
Caroline Island
Flint Island

MARQUESAS
ISLANDS
(FRANCE)

Santa Cruz
Is.

TOKELAU
(NEW ZEALAND)

Rotuma

Îles
(FRANCE) Wallis
Îles de
Horne

SAMOA
Apia ⊛ •
• Pago Pago
Samoa Islands

AMERICAN
SAMOA
(U.S.)

Cook Islands
(NEW ZEALAND)

T U A M O T U   A R C H I P E L A G O

UATU
t ⊛ •Éfaté
a

Vanua Levu

FIJI
Viti Levu ⊛ •Suva
ISLANDS

Society Islands

Tahiti
⊛ •Papeete
FRENCH POLYNESIA
(FRANCE)

Panié
1 ft 1,628 m
Nouméa

TONGA
⊛ Nuku'alofa

Austral Islands

TROPIC OF CAPRICORN

Henderson
Island
(UNITED KINGDOM)

aledonia

S O U T H   P A C I F I C   O C E A N

Pitcairn
Island
(U.K.)

Ducie
Island
(U.K.)

Sala-y-Gómez
(CHILE)

Norfolk Island

A) Phillip Island

Kermadec
Islands
(NEW ZEALAND)

Isla de Pascua
(Easter Island)
(CHILE)

NEW ZEALAND

Map Key

⊛ Country capital
⊙ State or province capital
••• City or town
..... Boundary

SCALE AT THE EQUATOR

0 ————————— 1,000 miles
0 ————————— 1,000 kilometers

Mercator Projection

◖ MELANESIAN CUSTOM.
In the Huli culture of Papua New Guinea's Eastern Highlands, men adorn themselves with colorful paints, feathers, and grasses in preparation for festivals.

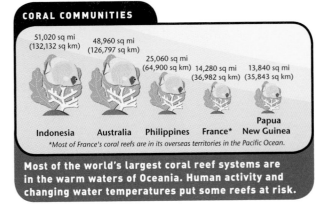

CORAL COMMUNITIES

Indonesia	Australia	Philippines	France*	Papua New Guinea
51,020 sq mi (132,132 sq km)	48,960 sq mi (126,797 sq km)	25,060 sq mi (64,900 sq km)	14,280 sq mi (36,982 sq km)	13,840 sq mi (35,843 sq km)

*Most of France's coral reefs are in its overseas territories in the Pacific Ocean.

Most of the world's largest coral reef systems are in the warm waters of Oceania. Human activity and changing water temperatures put some reefs at risk.

PHYSICAL

Land area
5,100,000 sq mi (13,209,000 sq km)

Highest point
Vinson Massif
16,067 ft (4,897 m)

Lowest point
Bentley Subglacial Trench
-8,383 ft (-2,555 m)

Coldest place
Plateau Station
Annual average temperature
-70°F (-56.7°C)

**Average precipitation
on the polar plateau**
Less than 2 in
(5 cm) per year

POLITICAL

Population
There are no indigenous
inhabitants, but there
are both permanent and
summer-only staffed
research stations.

**Number of independent
countries**
0

**Number of countries
claiming land**
7

**Number of countries
operating year-round
research stations**
20

**Number of year-round
research stations**
40

Antarctica

THE BASICS

Antarctica is the only continent that has no sovereign boundaries and no economy or permanent population. Seven countries claim portions of the landmass (see map below), but according to the Antarctic Treaty, which preserves the continent for peaceful use and scientific study, no country rules.

GEO WHIZ

In winter, sea ice averaging 6 feet (2 m) deep more than doubles the size of the continent as it forms a belt ranging from 300 miles (483 km) to more than 1,000 miles (1,620 km) wide.

The Antarctic Convergence, an area where the waters of the Pacific, Atlantic, and Indian Oceans meet the cold Antarctic Circumpolar Current, is one of Earth's richest marine ecosystems.

The largest iceberg ever spotted in Antarctic waters measured 208 miles (335 km) long by 60 miles (97 km) wide, making it slightly larger than Belgium.

Krill, a tiny shrimplike creature that thrives in the waters around the continent of Antarctica, is important in the Antarctic food chain. Whales, seals, and penguins are among the creatures that depend on it for survival.

A small insect known as the wingless midge is Antarctica's largest land animal.

Five species of penguins—considered aquatic animals—live on the continent and on nearby islands. The Emperor penguin is the only one that breeds during the winter.

Fierce, bitter cold winds batter the coast at speeds of as much as 180 miles per hour (300 kph).

Mount Erebus is the world's southernmost volcano. Polar explorer James Clark Ross named it after one of his ships.

The Antarctic Treaty was signed in 1959 by 12 countries. To date, 47 countries have signed the document, agreeing to cooperate in scientific research and forbidding military action, nuclear tests, and the dumping of radioactive waste on the continent and in its waters.

Antarctica

⬤ **SOUTHERN HEIGHTS.** Standing on the rocky summit of Mount Bearskin, named for a member of the team that established the 1956–57 IGY (International Geophysical Year) South Pole Station, a climber looks out across a vast snowfield.

Antarctica is the coldest, windiest, and even the driest continent. Though its immense ice cap holds 70 percent of the world's fresh water, its interior averages less than 2 inches (5 cm) of precipitation per year. Hidden beneath the ice is a continent of valleys, mountains, and lakes, but less than 2 percent of the land breaks through the ice cover. Reaching toward South America is the Antarctic Peninsula, the most visited of Antarctic regions. Though it is remote and mostly inhospitable, issues of human impact abound: fishing in rich but fragile waters that are sometimes called the Southern Ocean, future mining rights, and concern about the impact of global warming on the ice sheet.

South Orkney Islands

South Shetland Islands

Join

Alexander Island

Bellingshause

Ant

Th

PAC

In color are shown 7 nations' territorial claims recognized by the Antarctic Treaty.

0 — 2,000 mi
0 — 2,000 km
Azimuthal Equidistant Projection

0°
30°W — 30°S — 30°E
AFRICA
ATLANTIC OCEAN
60°W — 60°S — 60°E
SOUTH AMERICA
UNITED KINGDOM
ARGENTINA
CHILE
NORWAY
90°W — 90°E
AUSTRALIA
INDIAN OCEAN
UNCLAIMED
120°W — 120°E
AUSTRALIA
PACIFIC OCEAN
NEW ZEALAND
FRANCE
AUSTRALIA
150°W — 150°E
New Zealand
180°

◖ **STANDING GUARD.** Even while resting, this leopard seal is alert to danger. Although penguins are their main food, leopard seals also eat other species of seals and have even been known to attack humans.

ATLANTIC OCEAN

ANTARCTIC CIRCLE

Fimbul Ice Shelf

Cape Norvegia

Riiser-Larsen Ice Shelf

Riiser-Larsen Peninsula

Lützow-Holm Bay

Enderby Land

INDIAN OCEAN

Queen Maud Land

Weddell Sea

Coats Land

Mt. Jackson 10,446 ft 3,184 m

Filchner Ice Shelf

Berkner Island

Pensacola Mountains

■ Plateau Station (UNITED STATES)

Amery Ice Shelf

Cape Darnley

Prydz Bay

Peninsula

Ronne Ice Shelf

POLAR PLATEAU

EAST ANTARCTICA

American Highland

West Ice Shelf

Ellsworth Land

Vinson Massif 16,067 ft 4,897 m

Highest point in Antarctica

Transantarctic Mountains

★ South Pole
★ Amundsen-Scott Station (UNITED STATES)

Ellsworth Mts.

WEST

Bentley Subglacial Trench -8,383 ft -2,555 m

Lowest point in Antarctica

ANTARCTICA

Marie Byrd Land

■ Vostok Station (RUSSIA)

Shackleton Ice Shelf

Getz Ice Shelf

Ross Ice Shelf

Roosevelt Island

Mt. Erebus 12,448 ft 3,794 m

Ross I.

Cape Crozier

McMurdo Sound

Ross Sea

Victoria Land

Wilkes Land

Cape Poinsett

Porpoise Bay

Mt. Minto 13,665 ft 4,165 m

Cape Adare

ANTARCTIC CIRCLE

+ South Magnetic Pole

0   500 miles
0   500 kilometers
Azimuthal Equidistant Projection

WHERE THE PICTURES ARE

Leopard seal p. 155 — Climber p. 154

Gentoo penguins pp. 154–155

Scientists p. 155

◖ **FORMAL DRESS.** Black and white feathers make these Gentoo penguins appear to be wearing tuxedos on the rocky shore of Petermann Island. These flightless birds dive to more than 300 feet (90 m) to catch fish, an important part of their diet.

◖ **DIGGING FOR WORMS.** Scientists dig for microscopic worms called nematodes in a Victoria Land valley as they try to learn more about the effects of global warming on these creatures.

The Oceans

Investigating the Oceans

The map at right shows that more than 70 percent of Earth's surface is underwater, mainly covered by four great oceans. There is growing support for a fifth ocean, called the Southern Ocean, in the area from Antarctica to 60°S latitude. The oceans are really inter-connected bodies of water that together form one global ocean.

The ocean floor is as varied as the surface of the continents, but mapping the oceans is challenging. Past explorers cut their way through jungles of the Amazon and conquered icy heights of the Himalaya, but explorers could not march across the floor of the Pacific Ocean, which in places descends to more than 35,000 feet (10,668 m) below the surface of the water.

🔹 **UNDERWATER LANDSCAPE.** The landscape of the ocean floor is varied and constantly changing. A continental edge that slopes gently beneath the water is called a continental shelf. Mountain ranges, called mid-ocean ridges, rise where ocean plates are spreading and magma flows out to create new land. Other plates plunge into trenches more than six miles (10 km) deep. In addition, magma, rising through vents called hot spots, pushes through ocean plates, creating seamounts and volcanoes.

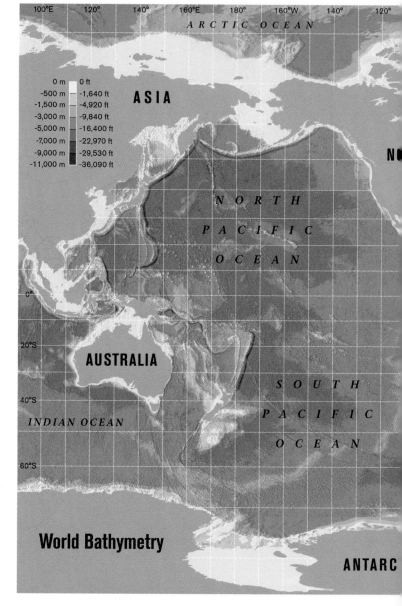

World Bathymetry

0 m	0 ft
-500 m	-1,640 ft
-1,500 m	-4,920 ft
-3,000 m	-9,840 ft
-5,000 m	-16,400 ft
-7,000 m	-22,970 ft
-9,000 m	-29,530 ft
-11,000 m	-36,090 ft

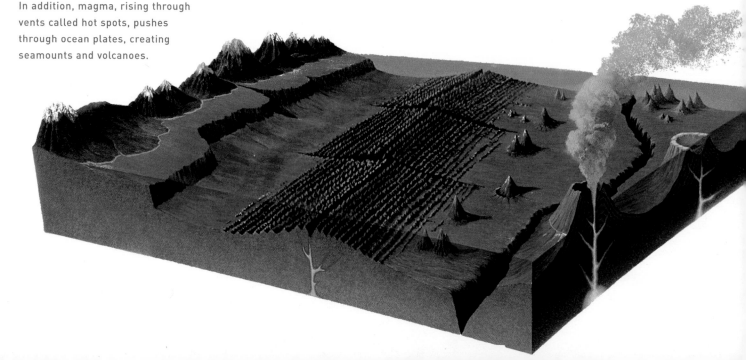

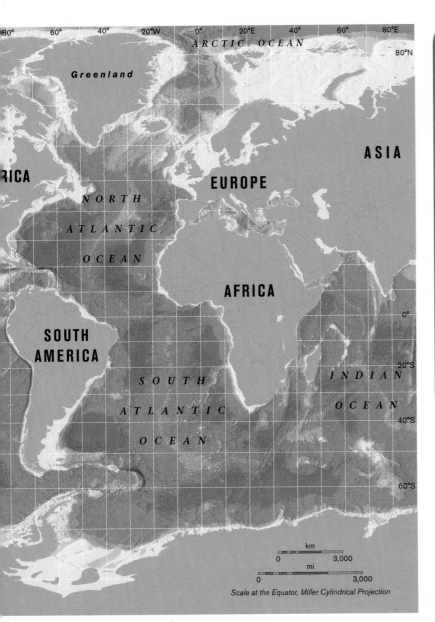

Scale at the Equator, Miller Cylindrical Projection

⬆ **FROM OCEAN TO SATELLITE.** In the 1990s, scientists developed the Argo Float to collect data from below the ocean surface. Argo Floats sink to a preset depth, often thousands of feet, where they gather data, such as temperature and salt content. At regular intervals, the floats rise to the surface (above) and transmit the data collected to a satellite. Then the cycle starts over again.

◗ **SEEING WITH YOUR EARS.** Special instruments, such as this acoustic buoy, use sound waves bounced off the ocean floor to record variations in water temperature. This technique, called Acoustic Thermometry of Ocean Climate (ATOC), may someday help monitor long-term climate changes.

◖ **EYE ON THE OCEAN.** The Sea-Viewing Wide Field-of-View Sensor (SeaWiFS) satellite records digital images of ocean colors that are used to identify and follow plant and animal activity in the oceans.

Pacific Ocean

The Pacific Ocean, largest of Earth's oceans, is about 15 times larger than the United States and covers more than 30 percent of Earth's surface. The edges of the Pacific are often called the Ring of Fire because many active volcanoes and earthquakes occur where the ocean plate is moving under the edges of continental plates. The southwestern Pacific is dotted with many islands. Also in the western Pacific, the Challenger Deep in the Mariana Trench plunges to 36,070 feet (10,994 m) below sea level. Most of the world's fish catch (see page 48) comes from the Pacific, and its oil and gas reserves are an important energy source.

(see page 48)

IN THE MIDST OF DANGER.
A false-clown anemonefish swims among the tentacles of a sea anemone off the coast of the Philippines, in the western Pacific. This colorful fish is immune to the anemone's paralyzing sting.

CIRCLE OF LIFE.
Atolls, such as this one near Okinawa, Japan, are ocean landforms created by tiny marine animals called corals. These creatures live in warm tropical waters. The circular shape of atolls often marks the coastline of sunken volcanic islands.

SCALE AT THE EQUATOR
0 | 1,000 miles
0 | 1,000 kilometers
Mercator Projection

Se
of
Okho

ASIA

Sakhalin

Amur

Kuril Is

Hokkaido

Sea of
Japan
(East Sea)

Japan
Trench

Korea

Honshu

Yellow

Yellow
Sea

Kyushu

Izu Trench

Yangtze

East
China
Sea

Ryukyu Is

Bonin
Trench

Taiwan

Ryukyu Trench

Philippine

Luzon

West
Mariana
Basin

Mariana Trough

Mariana Trench

South China Sea

Palau Ridge

Sea

PHILIPPINE
ISLANDS

Sulu
Basin

Mindanao

Palau
Trench

Palau

Yap
Trench

Kyushu

Challenger De
World's greate
ocean depth
-36,070 ft
-10,994 m

Borneo

Celebes
Basin

Caroline

West
Caroline
Basin

East
Caroline
Basin

INDONESIA

Celebes

Greater
Sunda
Islands

Banda Sea

Weber
Basin

New
Guinea

Bismarc
Archipela

Lesser Sunda Islands

Continental Shelf

North
Australian
Basin

Great Barrier R

Sea

TROPIC OF CAPRICORN

AUSTRALIA

South Australian Basin

Tasm

INDIAN
OCEAN

South
Tasman
Rise

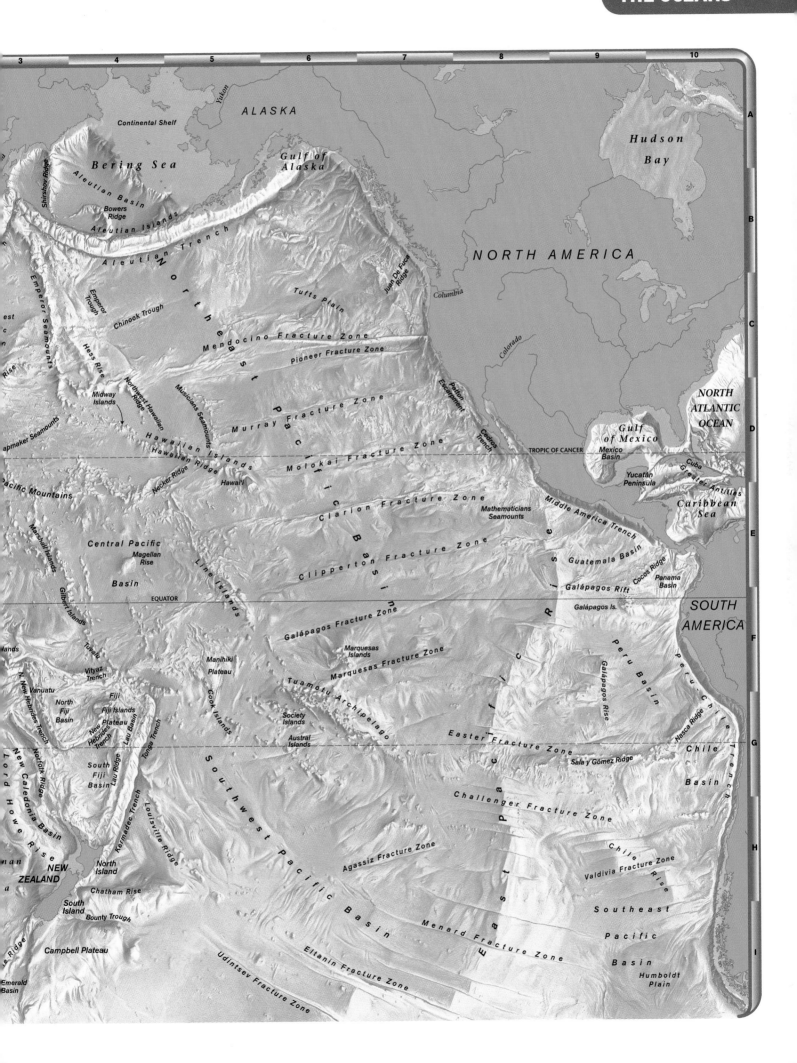

3   4   5   6   7   8   9   10

A

B

C

D

E

F

G

H

I

Shirshov Ridge

Bering Sea

Aleutian Basin

Bowers Ridge

Aleutian Islands

Emperor Seamounts

Emperor Trough

Hess Rise

Chinook Trough

Northwest Hawaiian Ridge

Midway Islands

Aleutian Trench

ALASKA

Continental Shelf

Yukon

Gulf of Alaska

Tufts Plain

Juan De Fuca Ridge

Columbia

NORTH AMERICA

Hudson Bay

*North*east

Mendocino Fracture Zone

Pioneer Fracture Zone

Pacific

Parton Escarpment

Colorado

West Rise

apmaker Seamounts

Pacific Mountains

Musicians Seamounts

Murray Fracture Zone

Hawaiian Islands

Hawaiian Ridge

Necker Ridge

Hawai'i

Molokai Fracture Zone

Cedros Trench

TROPIC OF CANCER

Mexico Basin

NORTH ATLANTIC OCEAN

Gulf of Mexico

Yucatán Peninsula

Cuba

Greater Antilles

Caribbean Sea

Marshall Islands

Central Pacific

Magellan Rise

Basin

Line Islands

Clarion Fracture Zone

Clipperton Fracture Zone

Mathematicians Seamounts

Middle America Trench

Guatemala Basin

Galápagos Rift

Cocos Ridge

Panama Basin

Gilbert Islands

EQUATOR

Galápagos Fracture Zone

Galápagos Is.

SOUTH AMERICA

ands

Tuvalu

Vityaz Trench

Manihiki Plateau

Marquesas Islands

Marquesas Fracture Zone

Tuamotu Archipelago

Peru Basin

Galápagos Rise

Nasca Ridge

N. New Hebrides Trench

Vanuatu

North Fiji Basin

Fiji

Fiji Islands

New Hebrides Trench

Plateau

Lau Basin

Cook Islands

Society Islands

Austral Islands

Easter Fracture Zone

Pacific

Sala y Gómez Ridge

Peru-Chile Trench

Chile Basin

Lord Howe Rise

New Caledonia Basin

Norfolk Ridge

South Fiji Basin

Lau Ridge

Tonga Trench

Southwest Pacific Basin

Challenger Fracture Zone

Chile Rise

Valdivia Fracture Zone

man

NEW ZEALAND

Kermadec Trench

Louisville Ridge

North Island

Agassiz Fracture Zone

East

Southeast

le Ridge

Emerald Basin

Chatham Rise

South Island

Bounty Trough

Campbell Plateau

Menard Fracture Zone

Eltanin Fracture Zone

Udintsev Fracture Zone

Pacific Rise

Basin

Humboldt Plain

Atlantic Ocean

THE BASICS

STATS

Surface area
35,338,500 sq mi
(91,526,400 sq km)

Percent of Earth's water area
25%

Greatest depth
Puerto Rico Trench
-28,232 ft (-8,605 m)

Surface temperatures
Summer high: 90°F (32°C)
Winter low: 28°F (-2°C)

Tides
Highest: 52 ft (16 m)
Bay of Fundy, Canada
Lowest: 1.5 ft (0.5 m)
Gulf of Mexico and Mediterranean Sea

GEO WHIZ

In 2005, the Atlantic Ocean produced a record-setting 15 hurricanes. For the first time in a single season, four hurricanes—Emily, Katrina, Rita, and Wilma—reached category 5 level, with sustained winds of at least 155 miles per hour (249 kph).

The Atlantic Ocean is about half the size of the Pacific, but it's growing. Spreading along the Mid-Atlantic Ridge allows molten rock from Earth's interior to escape and form new ocean floor.

Fishermen in the North Atlantic were eyewitnesses to the volcanic eruption that created the island of Surtsey, off the southeastern coast of Iceland, in November 1963.

Each year, the amount of water that flows into the Atlantic Ocean from the Amazon River is equal to 20 percent of Earth's available fresh water.

Among Earth's great oceans, the Atlantic is second only to the Pacific in size. The floor of the Atlantic is split by the Mid-Atlantic Ridge, which is part of the Mid-Ocean Ridge—the longest mountain chain on Earth. The Atlantic poses many hazards to human activity. Tropical storms called hurricanes form in the warm tropical waters off the west coast of Africa and move across the ocean to bombard the islands of the Caribbean and coastal areas of North America with damaging winds, waves, and rain in the late summer and fall. In the cold waters of the North Atlantic, sea ice and icebergs pose a danger to shipping, especially during winter and spring.

⬤ **CAMOUFLAGE ON ICE.** A young harp seal, called a pup, rests on the ice in Canada's Gulf of St. Lawrence. Pups are cared for by their mothers for only 12 days. After that, they must survive on their own.

The Atlantic has rich deposits of oil and natural gas, but drilling has resulted in pollution problems. In addition, the Atlantic has important marine fisheries, but overfishing has put some species at risk. Sea lanes between Europe and the Americas are among the most heavily trafficked in the world.

⬤ **HIDDEN DANGER.** Icebergs (above, right) are huge blocks of ice that break away, or calve, from the edges of glaciers. They pose a danger to ships because only about 10 percent of their bulk is visible above the waterline. A tragic disaster associated with an iceberg was the 1912 sinking of the RMS *Titanic,* whose ghostly ruins are shown above, left.

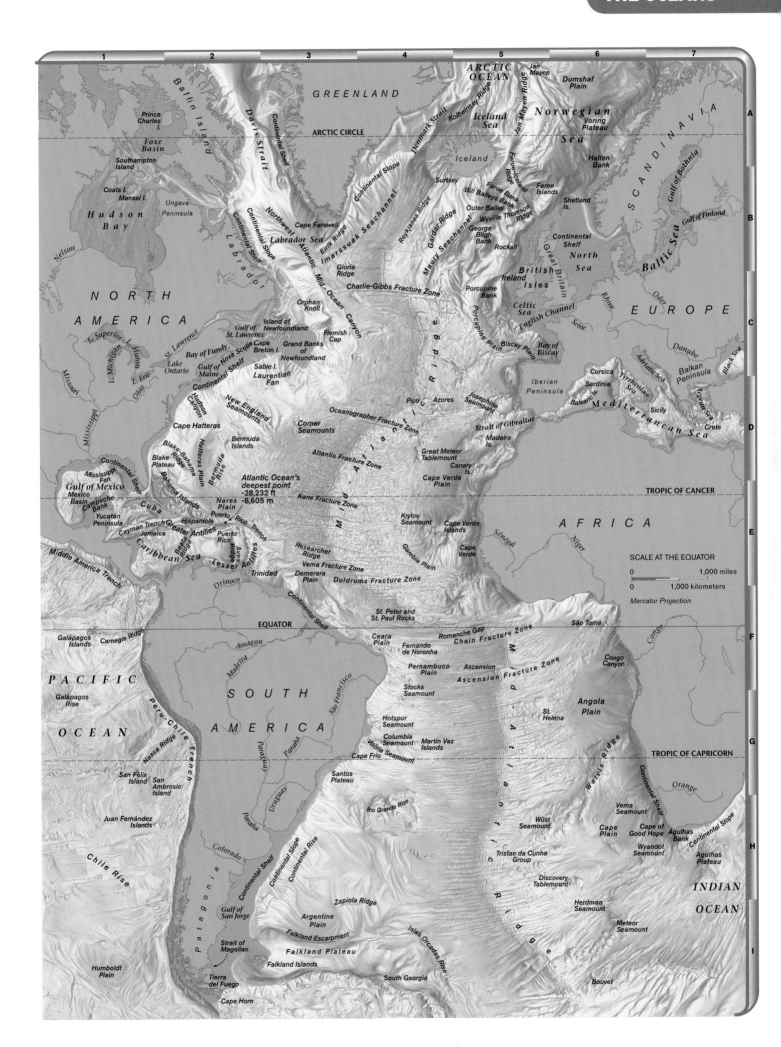

1 2 3 4 5 6 7

GREENLAND

ARCTIC OCEAN

ARCTIC CIRCLE

Jan Mayen

Dumshaf Plain

Kolbeinsey Ridge

Iceland Sea

Norwegian Sea

Voring Plateau

SCANDINAVIA

Prince Charles I.

Denmark Strait

Jan Mayen Ridge

Iceland

Surtsey

Halten Bank

Gulf of Bothnia

Foxe Basin

Davis Strait

Continental Shelf

Faroe-Iceland Ridge

Bill Bailey's Bank

Faroe Islands

Gulf of Finland

Southampton Island

Baffin Island

Continental Slope

Reykjanes Ridge

Gardar Ridge

Outer Bailey

Shetland Is.

Baltic Sea

Coats I.

Northwest Atlantic Mid-Ocean Canyon

Cape Farewell

Maury Seachannel

George Bligh Bank

Wyville Thomson Ridge

Continental Shelf

North Sea

Oder

Mansel I.

Labrador Sea

Eirik Ridge

Rockall

Ungava Peninsula

Labrador

Imarssuak Seachannel

Porcupine Bank

Great Britain

British Isles

EUROPE

HUDSON BAY

Gloria Ridge

Ireland

Rhine

Nelson

Charlie-Gibbs Fracture Zone

Porcupine Plain

Celtic Sea

English Channel

Seine

Danube

NORTH AMERICA

Orphan Knoll

Mid-Atlantic Ridge

Biscay Plain

Bay of Biscay

Balkan Peninsula

Black Sea

Island of Newfoundland

Iberian Peninsula

Corsica

Adriatic Sea

L. Superior

L. Huron

St. Lawrence

Gulf of St. Lawrence

Flemish Cap

Sardinia

Tyrrhenian Sea

L. Michigan

Bay of Fundy

Cape Breton I.

Grand Banks of Newfoundland

Pico

Azores

Josephine Seamount

Balearic Is.

Mediterranean Sea

Sicily

Lake Ontario

Gulf of Maine

Nova Scotia

Sable I.

Aegean Sea

L. Erie

Continental Shelf

Laurentian Fan

Strait of Gibraltar

Crete

Ohio

Hudson Canyon

New England Seamounts

Oceanographer Fracture Zone

Madeira Is.

Missouri

Cape Hatteras

Corner Seamounts

Great Meteor Tablemount

Mississippi

Bermuda Islands

Atlantis Fracture Zone

Canary Is.

Blake-Bahama Ridge

Hatteras Plain

Cape Verde Plain

Continental Shelf

Blake Plateau

Bermuda Rise

Atlantic Ocean's deepest point -28,232 ft -8,605 m

TROPIC OF CANCER

Mississippi Fan

Bahama Islands

Kane Fracture Zone

Gulf of Mexico

Mexico Basin

Nares Plain

Puerto Rico Trench

Krylov Seamount

Cape Verde Islands

AFRICA

Campeche Bank

Cuba

Puerto Rico

Gambia Plain

Cape Verde

Senegal

Niger

SCALE AT THE EQUATOR

Yucatán Peninsula

Cayman Trench

Greater Antilles

Hispaniola

Aves Ridge

0   1,000 miles

Jamaica

Beata Ridge

Researcher Ridge

0   1,000 kilometers

Middle America Trench

Caribbean Sea

Lesser Antilles

Vema Fracture Zone

Mercator Projection

Trinidad

Demerara Plain

Doldrums Fracture Zone

Orinoco

Continental Shelf

St. Peter and St. Paul Rocks

São Tomé

Congo

EQUATOR

Romanche Gap

Chain Fracture Zone

Galápagos Islands

Carnegie Ridge

Amazon

Ceara Plain

Fernando de Noronha

Mid-Atlantic Ridge

PACIFIC OCEAN

Madeira

Pernambuco Plain

Ascension

Ascension Fracture Zone

Congo Canyon

Galápagos Rise

São Francisco

Stocks Seamount

St. Helena

Angola Plain

SOUTH AMERICA

Peru-Chile Trench

Hotspur Seamount

TROPIC OF CAPRICORN

Nasca Ridge

Columbia Seamount

Martin Vaz Islands

Walvis Ridge

Orange

San Félix Island

Paraguay

Vitória Seamount

Cape Frio

Vema Seamount

Continental Shelf

San Ambrosio Island

Paraná

Santos Plateau

Cape Plain

Cape of Good Hope

Agulhas Bank

Continental Slope

Juan Fernández Islands

Uruguay

Rio Grande Rise

Wüst Seamount

Wyandot Seamount

Paraná

Colorado

Continental Slope

Continental Rise

Tristan da Cunha Group

Agulhas Plateau

Patagonia

Zapiola Ridge

Discovery Tablemount

INDIAN OCEAN

Humboldt Plain

Gulf of San Jorge

Argentine Plain

Herdman Seamount

Chile Rise

Falkland Escarpment

Islas Orcadas Rise

Meteor Seamount

Strait of Magellan

Falkland Plateau

Mid-Atlantic Ridge

Tierra del Fuego

Falkland Islands

South Georgia

Bouvet

Cape Horn

Indian Ocean

THE BASICS

STATS

Surface area
28,839,800 sq mi
(74,694,800 sq km)

Percent of Earth's water area
21%

Greatest depth
Java Trench
-23,376 ft (-7,125 m)

Surface temperatures
Summer high: 93°F (34°C)
Winter low: 28°F (-2°C)

Tides
Highest: 36 ft (11 m)
Lowest: 2 ft (0.6 m)
Both along Australia's west coast

GEO WHIZ

Each day tankers carrying 17 million barrels of crude oil from the Persian Gulf enter the waters of the Indian Ocean, transporting their cargo for distribution around the world.

Some of the world's largest breeding grounds for humpback whales are in the Indian Ocean, the Arabian Sea, and off the east coast of Africa.

The Bay of Bengal is sometimes called Cyclone Alley because of the large number of tropical storms that occur there each year between May and November.

Sailors from what is now Indonesia used seasonal winds called monsoons to reach Africa's east coast. They arrived on the continent long before Europeans did.

A December 2004 earthquake caused a tsunami that killed more than 225,000 people in countries bordering the Indian Ocean. Waves reached as high as 49 feet (15 m).

The Indian Ocean has several strategic chokepoints—narrow straits through which shipping must pass. They include Bab el Mandeb, between the Gulf of Aden and the Red Sea; the Strait of Hormuz, between the Persian Gulf and the Arabian Sea; the Gulf of Suez, between the Red Sea and the Suez Canal; and the Strait of Malacca, between Sumatra and the Malay Peninsula.

The Indian Ocean stretches from Africa's east coast to the southern coast of Asia and the western coast of Australia. It is the third largest of Earth's great oceans. Changing air pressure systems over the warm waters of the Indian Ocean trigger South Asia's famous monsoon climate—a weather pattern in which winds reverse directions seasonally. The Bay of Bengal, an arm of the Indian Ocean, experiences devastating tropical storms, similar to hurricanes, but called cyclones in this region. Islands along the eastern edge of the Indian Ocean plate experience earthquakes that sometimes cause destructive ocean waves, called tsunamis.

The Arabian Sea, Persian Gulf, and Red Sea, also extensions of the Indian Ocean, are important sources of oil and natural gas reserves and account for an estimated 40 percent of the world's offshore oil production. The sea routes of the Indian Ocean connect the Middle East to the rest of world, carrying much needed energy resources on huge tanker ships.

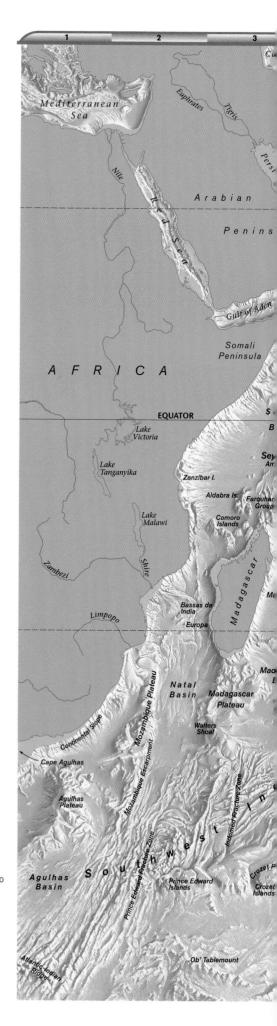

◖ **LIVING FOSSIL.**
A coelacanth swims in the warm waters of the western Indian Ocean off the Comoro Islands. Once thought to have become extinct 65 million years ago along with the dinosaurs, a living coelacanth was discovered in 1938.

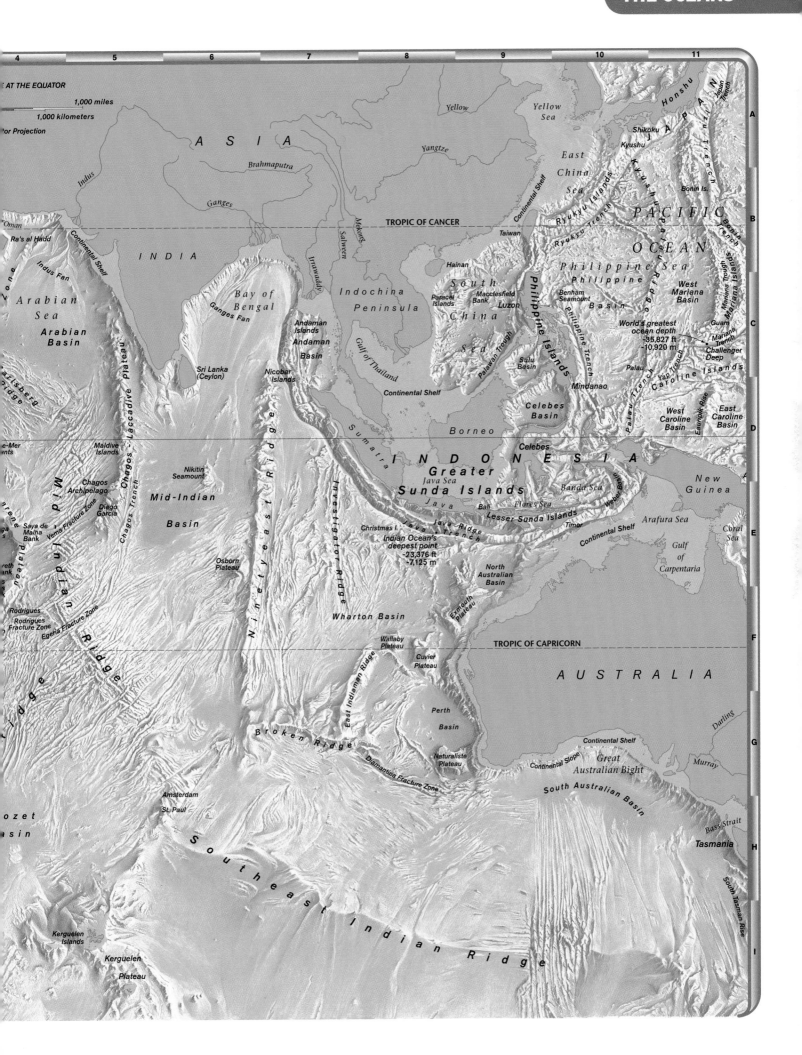

AT THE EQUATOR
1,000 miles
1,000 kilometers
or Projection

ASIA

Yellow

Yellow
Sea

Yangtze

East
China
Sea

Honshu

JAPAN

Japan Trench

Shikoku
Kyushu

Brahmaputra

Indus

Ganges

TROPIC OF CANCER

Taiwan

Ryukyu Islands

Izu Trench

Bonin Is.

Oman

Ra's al Hadd

Continental Shelf

INDIA

Indus Fan

PACIFIC

Ryukyu Trench

Kyushu–Palau Ridge

OCEAN

Arabian
Sea

Arabian
Basin

Bay of
Bengal

Ganges Fan

Irrawaddy

Salween

Mekong

Indochina

Peninsula

Hainan

South

China

Paracel
Islands

Macclesfield
Bank

Luzon

Philippine Sea

Philippine

Benham
Seamount

West
Mariana
Basin

Mariana Trough

Mariana Islands

Guam

C

lsberg

ge

Chagos–Laccadive Plateau

Sri Lanka
(Ceylon)

Andaman
Islands

Andaman

Basin

Nicobar
Islands

Gulf of Thailand

Continental Shelf

Sea

Palawan Trough

Sulu
Basin

Mindanao

World's greatest
ocean depth
−35,827 ft
−10,920 m

Palau

Yap Trench

Palau Trench

Caroline

Mariana
Trench
Challenger
Deep

Islands

Eauripik Rise

West
Caroline
Basin

East
Caroline
Basin

D

e-Mer
ounts

Maldive
Islands

Nikitin
Seamount

MID

Chagos
Archipelago

Diego
Garcia

Chagos Trench

Vema Fracture Zone

Mid-Indian

Basin

Ninetyeast Ridge

Investigator Ridge

Sumatra

INDONESIA

Greater

Java Sea

Sunda Islands

Celebes

Borneo

Banda Sea

Weber Basin

New

Guinea

Saya de
Malha
Bank

as

eth
ank

INDIAN

Rodrigues

Rodrigues
Fracture Zone

Egeria Fracture Zone

Osborn
Plateau

Christmas I.

Indian Ocean's
deepest point
−23,376 ft
−7,125 m

Java

Bali

Flores Sea

Java Ridge

Lesser Sunda Islands

Java Trench

Timor

North
Australian
Basin

Continental Shelf

Arafura Sea

Gulf
of
Carpentaria

Coral
Sea

E

dge

Ridge

Wharton Basin

East Indiaman Ridge

Wallaby
Plateau

Cuvier
Plateau

Exmouth Plateau

TROPIC OF CAPRICORN

AUSTRALIA

F

Broken Ridge

Diamantina Fracture Zone

Naturaliste
Plateau

Perth

Basin

Continental Slope

Continental Shelf

Great
Australian
Bight

Darling

Murray

G

Amsterdam
St. Paul

South Australian Basin

Bass Strait

South Tasman Rise

Tasmania

ozet
sin

Southeast Indian Ridge

H

Kerguelen
Islands

Kerguelen

Plateau

I

4   5   6   7   8   9   10   11

THE BASICS

STATS

Surface area
5,390,000 sq mi (13,960,100 sq km)

Percent of Earth's water area
4%

Greatest depth
Molloy Deep: -18,599 ft (-5,669 m)

Surface temperatures
Summer high: 41°F (5°C)
Winter low: 28°F (-2°C)

Tides
Less than a 1-ft (0.3-m) variation throughout the ocean

GEO WHIZ

Satellite monitoring of Arctic sea ice, which began in the late 1970s, shows that the extent of the sea ice is shrinking by approximately 8 percent every 10 years. Scientists think this may be caused by global warming.

The geographic North Pole lies roughly in the middle of the Arctic Ocean under 13,000 feet (3,962 m) of water.

Many of the features on the Arctic Ocean floor are named for early Arctic explorers and for bordering landmasses.

Mapping of the Arctic Ocean floor did not begin until 2001. The initial research was by a joint U.S.-German operation called AMORE (Arctic Mid-Ocean Ridge Expedition). Surprise findings included 12 volcanoes, hydrothermal vents, and a vast continental shelf off Siberia.

ARCTIC OCEAN

The Arctic Ocean lies mostly north of the Arctic Circle, bounded by North America, Europe, and Asia. Unlike the other oceans, the Arctic is subject to persistent cold throughout the year. Also, because of its very high latitude, the Arctic experiences winters of perpetual night and summers of continual daylight. Except for coastal margins, the Arctic Ocean is covered by permanent drifting pack ice that averages almost 10 feet (3 m) in thickness. Some scientists are concerned that the polar ice may be melting due to global warming, putting at risk the habitat of polar bears and other arctic animals.

◗ **ARCTIC RESEARCH.** Scientists wearing cold weather survival suits prepare to measure salt content, nutrients, and plant and animal life in ice and meltwater. They also monitor changes related to global warming, such as the shrinking of the polar ice cap.

◗ **FREE RIDE.** A baby polar bear catches a ride as its mother crosses Canada's Arctic. Polar bear populations are showing signs of stress as sea ice shrinks.

200 miles
200 kilometers
Azimuthal Equidistant Projection

4 5 6 7 8 9 10 11

A

A

EUROPE

Khatanga

Upper Taymyr

Taymyr Peninsula

Yenisey Gulf

Gulf of Ob

Yamal Peninsula

Baydaratta Bay

Pechora Bay

Chesha Bay

Northern Dvina

White Sea

ARCTIC CIRCLE

Continental Shelf

Kara Sea

East Novaya Zemlya Trough

Continental Shelf

Kola Peninsula

SCANDINAVIA

ntal Shelf

Cape Chelyuskin

Novaya Zemlya

Gusinaya Bank

Murmansk Rise

Gulf of Bothnia

ptev Sea

Bol'shevik I.

North Land

October Revolution I.

Barents Sea

North Cape

B

Komsomolets I.

Voronin Trough

Franz Josef Land

Graham Bell I.

Continental Shelf

C

Nansen Ridge

Svyataya Anna Trough

George Land

Spitsbergen Bank

Bjørnya

Røst Bank

Halten Bank

Continental Shelf

Nansen Basin

Svyataya Anna Fan

Alexandra Land

Olga Basin

North East Land

Svalbard

Continental Slope

Voring Plateau

D

Pole Plain

Wrangel Plain

Spitzbergen

Arctic Ocean's deepest point -18,599 ft -5,669 m

Norwegian Basin

Lomonosov Ridge

Fletcher Plain

Barents Plain

Yermak Plateau

Molloy Deep

Boreas Plain

Mohns Ridge

Dumshaf Plain

Norwegian Sea

karov Basin

Fram Basin

★ North Pole

Spitsbergen Fracture Zone

Greenland Fracture Zone

Greenland Plain

Aegir Ridge

E

v Ridge

eyev Plain

Morris Jesup Rise

Wandel Sea

Ob' Bank

Greenland Sea

Jan Mayen Fracture Zone

Jan Mayen

Jan Mayen Ridge

Oodaaq Island

Continental Shelf

Belgica Bank

Iceland Sea

Marvin Spur

Alpha Cordillera

Iceland Plateau

Kolbeinsey Ridge

F

asin

Lincoln Sea

Iceland

Reykjanes Ridge

Continental Slope

Continental Shelf

Ellesmere Island

Surtsey

Axel Heiberg Island

GREENLAND

Denmark Strait

G

Sverdrup Islands

Prince Patrick Island

Mackenzie King I.

Ellef Ringnes I.

Queen Elizabeth Islands

M'Clure Strait

Melville Island

Parry Islands

Bathurst Island

Devon Island

H

Island

P a r r y

Cornwallis I.

Channel

Baffin Bay

Viscount Melville Sound

M'Clintock Channel

Barrow Str.

Lancaster Sound

Bylot I.

Qeqertarsuaq (Disko)

ATLANTIC OCEAN

Somerset Island

Prince Regent Inlet

Victoria Island

Prince of Wales Island

Boothia Peninsula

Gulf of Boothia

Baffin Island

ARCTIC CIRCLE

A M E R I C A

King William Island

Melville Pen.

Davis Strait

Cape Farewell

I

FLAGS & STATS

These flags and fact boxes represent the world's 195 independent countries—those with national governments that are recognized as having the highest legal authority over the land and people within their boundaries. The flags shown are national flags recognized by the United Nations. Area figures include land, plus surface areas for inland bodies of water. Population figures are for mid-2012, as provided by the Population Reference Bureau. The languages listed are either the ones most commonly spoken within a country or official languages of a country.

NORTH AMERICA

Antigua and Barbuda
Area: 171 sq mi
(442 sq km)
Population: 87,000
Capital: St. John's
Languages: English (official), local dialects
Currency: East Caribbean dollar

Bahamas
Area: 5,382 sq mi
(13,939 sq km)
Population: 362,000
Capital: Nassau
Languages: English (official)
Currency: Bahamian dollar

Barbados
Area: 166 sq mi
(430 sq km)
Population: 277,000
Capital: Bridgetown
Language: English
Currency: Barbadian dollar

Belize
Area: 8,867 sq mi
(22,965 sq km)
Population: 326,000
Capital: Belmopan
Languages: Spanish, Creole, Mayan dialects, English, Garifuna (Carib), German
Currency: Belize dollar

Canada
Area: 3,855,101 sq mi
(9,984,670 sq km)
Population: 34,860,000
Capital: Ottawa
Languages: English, French (both official)
Currency: Canadian dollar

Costa Rica
Area: 19,730 sq mi
(51,100 sq km)
Population: 4,481,000
Capital: San José
Languages: Spanish (official), English
Currency: Costa Rican colón

Cuba
Area: 42,803 sq mi
(110,860 sq km)
Population: 11,219,000
Capital: Havana
Language: Spanish
Currency: Cuban peso

Dominica
Area: 290 sq mi
(751 sq km)
Population: 71,000
Capital: Roseau
Languages: English (official), French patois
Currency: East Caribbean dollar

Dominican Republic
Area: 18,704 sq mi
(48,442 sq km)
Population: 10,135,000
Capital: Santo Domingo
Language: Spanish
Currency: Dominican peso

El Salvador
Area: 8,124 sq mi
(21,041 sq km)
Population: 6,264,000
Capital: San Salvador
Languages: Spanish, Nahua
Currency: United States dollar

Grenada
Area: 133 sq mi
(344 sq km)
Population: 115,000
Capital: St. George's
Languages: English (official), French patois
Currency: East Caribbean dollar

Guatemala
Area: 42,042 sq mi
(108,889 sq km)
Population: 15,044,000
Capital: Guatemala City
Languages: Spanish, 23 Amerindian languages
Currency: Guatemalan quetzal

Haiti
Area: 10,714 sq mi
(27,750 sq km)
Population: 10,256,000
Capital: Port-au-Prince
Languages: French, Creole (both official)
Currency: Haitian gourde

Honduras
Area: 43,433 sq mi
(112,492 sq km)
Population: 8,385,000
Capital: Tegucigalpa
Languages: Spanish, Amerindian dialects
Currency: Honduran lempira

Jamaica
Area: 4,244 sq mi
(10,991 sq km)
Population: 2,716,000
Capital: Kingston
Languages: English, patois English
Currency: Jamaican dollar

Mexico
Area: 758,449 sq mi
(1,964,375 sq km)
Population: 116,147,000
Capital: Mexico City
Languages: Spanish, Maya, Nahuatl, other indigenous languages
Currency: Mexican peso

Nicaragua
Area: 50,193 sq mi
(130,000 sq km)
Population: 5,955,000
Capital: Managua
Languages: Spanish (official), English, indigenous languages
Currency: Nicaraguan córdoba

Panama
Area: 29,157 sq mi
(75,517 sq km)
Population: 3,610,000
Capital: Panama City
Languages: Spanish (official), English
Currency: Panamanian balboa/United States dollar

St. Kitts and Nevis
Area: 104 sq mi
(269 sq km)
Population: 54,000
Capital: Basseterre
Language: English
Currency: East Caribbean dollar

St. Lucia
Area: 238 sq mi
(616 sq km)
Population: 169,000
Capital: Castries
Languages: English (official), French patois
Currency: East Caribbean dollar

St. Vincent and the Grenadines
Area: 150 sq mi
(389 sq km)
Population: 108,000
Capital: Kingstown
Languages: English, French patois
Currency: East Caribbean dollar

Trinidad and Tobago
Area: 1,980 sq mi
(5,128 sq km)
Population: 1,315,000
Capital: Port of Spain
Languages: English (official), Caribbean Hindustani, French, Spanish, Chinese
Currency: Trinidad and Tobago dollar

United States
Area: 3,794,083 sq mi
(9,826,630 sq km)
Population: 313,858,000
Capital: Washington, D.C.
Languages: English, Spanish
Currency: United States dollar

SOUTH AMERICA

Argentina
Area: 1,073,518 sq mi
(2,780,400 sq km)
Population: 40,829,000
Capital: Buenos Aires
Languages: Spanish (official),
English, Italian, German,
French
Currency: Argentine peso

Bolivia
Area: 424,164 sq mi
(1,098,581 sq km)
Population: 10,836,000
Capitals: La Paz, Sucre
Languages: Spanish,
Quechua, Aymara (all official)
Currency: Bolivian boliviano

Brazil
Area: 3,300,171 sq mi
(8,547,403 sq km)
Population: 194,334,000
Capital: Brasília
Language: Portuguese (official)
Currency: Brazilian real

Chile
Area: 291,930 sq mi
(756,096 sq km)
Population: 17,403,000
Capital: Santiago
Language: Spanish
Currency: Chilean peso

Colombia
Area: 440,831 sq mi
(1,141,748 sq km)
Population: 47,415,000
Capital: Bogotá
Language: Spanish
Currency: Colombian peso

Ecuador
Area: 109,483 sq mi
(283,560 sq km)
Population: 14,865,000
Capital: Quito
Languages: Spanish (official),
Quechua, other Amerindian
languages
Currency: United States dollar

Guyana
Area: 83,000 sq mi
(214,969 sq km)
Population: 796,000
Capital: Georgetown
Languages: English,
Amerindian dialects, Creole,
Hindi, Urdu
Currency: Guyanese dollar

Paraguay
Area: 157,048 sq mi
(406,752 sq km)
Population: 6,683,000
Capital: Asunción
Languages: Spanish, Guaraní
(both official)
Currency: Paraguayan guarani

Peru
Area: 496,224 sq mi
(1,285,216 sq km)
Population: 30,136,000
Capital: Lima
Languages: Spanish, Quechua
(both official), Aymara, minor
Amazonian languages
Currency: Peruvian nuevo sol

Suriname
Area: 63,037 sq mi
(163,265 sq km)
Population: 542,000
Capital: Paramaribo
Languages: Dutch (official),
English, Sranang Tongo (Taki-
Taki), Hindustani, Javanese
Currency: Surinamese dollar

Uruguay
Area: 68,037 sq mi
(176,215 sq km)
Population: 3,381,000
Capital: Montevideo
Languages: Spanish,
Portunol, Brazilero
Currency: Uruguayan peso

Venezuela
Area: 352,144 sq mi
(912,050 sq km)
Population: 29,718,000
Capital: Caracas
Languages: Spanish (official),
many indigenous languages
Currency: Venezuelan bolívar

EUROPE

Albania
Area: 11,100 sq mi
(28,748 sq km)
Population: 2,833,000
Capital: Tirana
Languages: Albanian
(official), Greek, Vlach,
Romani, Slavic dialects
Currency: Albanian lek

Andorra
Area: 181 sq mi
(468 sq km)
Population: 72,000
Capital: Andorra la Vella
Languages: Catalan (official),
French, Castilian, Portuguese
Currency: Euro

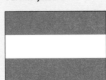

Austria
Area: 32,378 sq mi
(83,858 sq km)
Population: 8,845,000
Capital: Vienna
Languages: German (official),
Slovene, Croatian, Hungarian
Currency: Euro

Belarus
Area: 80,153 sq mi
(207,595 sq km)
Population: 9,457,000
Capital: Minsk
Languages: Belarusian,
Russian
Currency: Belarusian ruble

Belgium
Area: 11,787 sq mi
(30,528 sq km)
Population: 11,121,000
Capital: Brussels
Languages: Flemish (Dutch),
French, German (all official)
Currency: Euro

Bosnia and Herzegovina
Area: 19,741 sq mi
(51,129 sq km)
Population: 3,843,000
Capital: Sarajevo
Languages: Croatian,
Serbian, Bosnian
Currency: Bosnia and
Herzegovina convertible mark

Bulgaria
Area: 42,855 sq mi
(110,994 sq km)
Population: 7,240,000
Capital: Sofia
Languages: Bulgarian,
Turkish, Roma
Currency: Bulgarian lev

Croatia
Area: 21,831 sq mi
(56,542 sq km)
Population: 4,274,000
Capital: Zagreb
Language: Croatian
Currency: Croatian kuna

Cyprus
Area: 3,572 sq mi
(9,251 sq km)
Population: 1,172,000
Capital: Nicosia
Languages: Greek, Turkish,
English
Currency: Euro

Czech Republic
Area: 30,450 sq mi
(78,866 sq km)
Population: 10,490,000
Capital: Prague
Language: Czech
Currency: Czech koruna

Denmark
Area: 16,640 sq mi
(43,098 sq km)
Population: 5,591,000
Capital: Copenhagen
Languages: Danish, Faroese,
Greenlandic, German
Currency: Danish krone

Estonia
Area: 17,462 sq mi
(45,227 sq km)
Population: 1,339,000
Capital: Tallinn
Languages: Estonian
(official), Russian
Currency: Euro

Finland
Area: 130,558 sq mi
(338,145 sq km)
Population: 5,414,000
Capital: Helsinki
Languages: Finnish, Swedish
(both official)
Currency: Euro

FLAGS & STATS

France
Area: 210,026 sq mi
(543,965 sq km)
Population: 63,605,000
Capital: Paris
Language: French
Currency: Euro

Germany
Area: 137,847 sq mi
(357,022 sq km)
Population: 81,825,000
Capital: Berlin
Language: German
Currency: Euro

Greece
Area: 50,949 sq mi
(131,957 sq km)
Population: 10,833,000
Capital: Athens
Languages: Greek, English,
French
Currency: Euro

Hungary
Area: 35,919 sq mi
(93,030 sq km)
Population: 9,947,000
Capital: Budapest
Language: Hungarian
Currency: Hungarian forint

Iceland
Area: 39,769 sq mi
(103,000 sq km)
Population: 320,000
Capital: Reykjavík
Languages: Icelandic,
English, Nordic languages,
German
Currency: Icelandic króna

Ireland
Area: 27,133 sq mi
(70,273 sq km)
Population: 4,683,000
Capital: Dublin
Languages: Irish (Gaelic),
English
Currency: Euro

Italy
Area: 116,345 sq mi
(301,333 sq km)
Population: 60,950,000
Capital: Rome
Languages: Italian (official),
German, French, Slovene
Currency: Euro

Kosovo
Area: 4,203 sq mi
(10,887 sq km)
Population: 2,290,000
Capital: Pristina
Languages: Albanian, Serbian,
Bosnian, Turkish, Roma
Currency: Euro

Latvia
Area: 24,938 sq mi
(64,589 sq km)
Population: 2,049,000
Capital: Riga
Languages: Latvian (official),
Russian, Lithuanian
Currency: Latvian lats

Liechtenstein
Area: 62 sq mi
(160 sq km)
Population: 37,000
Capital: Vaduz
Languages: German (official),
Alemannic dialect
Currency: Swiss franc

Lithuania
Area: 25,212 sq mi
(65,300 sq km)
Population: 3,179,000
Capital: Vilnius
Languages: Lithuanian
(official), Polish, Russian
Currency: Lithuanian litas

Luxembourg
Area: 998 sq mi
(2,586 sq km)
Population: 527,000
Capital: Luxembourg
Languages: Luxembourgish
(official), German, French
Currency: Euro

Macedonia
Area: 9,928 sq mi
(25,713 sq km)
Population: 2,064,000
Capital: Skopje
Languages: Macedonian,
Albanian, Turkish
Currency: Macedonian denar

Malta
Area: 122 sq mi
(316 sq km)
Population: 399,000
Capital: Valletta
Languages: Maltese, English
(both official)
Currency: Euro

Moldova
Area: 13,050 sq mi
(33,800 sq km)
Population: 4,114,000
Capital: Chișinău
Languages: Moldovan
(official), Russian, Gagauz
Currency: Moldovan leu

Monaco
Area: 0.8 sq mi
(2 sq km)
Population: 36,000
Capital: Monaco
Languages: French (official),
English, Italian, Monegasque
Currency: Euro

Montenegro
Area: 5,415 sq mi
(14,026 sq km)
Population: 622,000
Capital: Podgorica
Languages: Serbian (official),
Bosnian, Albanian, Croatian
Currency: Euro

Netherlands
Area: 16,034 sq mi
(41,528 sq km)
Population: 16,749,000
Capital: Amsterdam
Languages: Dutch, Frisian
(both official)
Currency: Euro

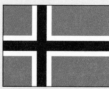

Norway
Area: 125,004 sq mi
(323,758 sq km)
Population: 5,019,000
Capital: Oslo
Language: Norwegian (official)
Currency: Norwegian krone

Poland
Area: 120,728 sq mi
(312,685 sq km)
Population: 38,195,000
Capital: Warsaw
Language: Polish
Currency: Euro

Portugal
Area: 35,655 sq mi
(92,345 sq km)
Population: 10,561,000
Capital: Lisbon
Languages: Portuguese,
Mirandese (both official)
Currency: Euro

Romania
Area: 92,043 sq mi
(238,391 sq km)
Population: 21,408,000
Capital: Bucharest
Languages: Romanian
(official), Hungarian, German
Currency: Romanian leu

Russia
Area: 6,592,850 sq mi
(17,075,400 sq km)
Population: 143,165,000
Capital: Moscow
Languages: Russian, many
minority languages
Currency: Russian ruble

San Marino
Area: 24 sq mi
(61 sq km)
Population: 32,000
Capital: San Marino
Language: Italian
Currency: Euro

Serbia
Area: 29,913 sq mi
(77,474 sq km)
Population: 7,102,000
Capital: Belgrade
Languages: Serbian (official),
Romanian, Hungarian, Slovak,
Croatian
Currency: Serbian dinar

Slovakia
Area: 18,932 sq mi
(49,035 km)
Population: 5,394,000
Capital: Bratislava
Languages: Slovak (official),
Hungarian
Currency: Euro

Slovenia
Area: 7,827 sq mi
(20,273 sq km)
Population: 2,058,000
Capital: Ljubljana
Languages: Slovene,
Serbo-Croatian
Currency: Euro

Spain
Area: 195,363 sq mi
(505,988 sq km)
Population: 46,195,000
Capital: Madrid
Languages: Castilian Spanish
(official), Catalan, Galician,
Basque
Currency: Euro

Sweden
Area: 173,732 sq mi
(449,964 sq km)
Population: 9,514,000
Capital: Stockholm
Languages: Swedish, Sami,
Finnish
Currency: Swedish krona

Switzerland
Area: 15,940 sq mi
(41,284 sq km)
Population: 7,994,000
Capital: Bern
Languages: German, French,
Italian (all official), Romansch
Currency: Swiss franc

Ukraine
Area: 233,090 sq mi
(603,700 sq km)
Population: 45,556,000
Capital: Kiev
Languages: Ukrainian
(official), Russian
Currency: Ukrainian hryvnia

United Kingdom
Area: 93,788 sq mi
(242,910 sq km)
Population: 63,213,000
Capital: London
Languages: English, Welsh,
Scottish form of Gaelic
Currency: British pound

Vatican City
Area: 0.2 sq mi
(0.4 sq km)
Population: 836
Languages: Italian,
Latin, French
Currency: Euro

ASIA

Afghanistan
Area: 251,773 sq mi
(652,090 sq km)
Population: 33,397,000
Capital: Kabul
Languages: Afghan Persian
(Dari), Pashtu (both official),
Turkic languages
Currency: Afghan Afghani

Armenia
Area: 11,484 sq mi
(29,743 sq km)
Population: 3,282,000
Capital: Yerevan
Language: Armenian
Currency: Armenian dram

Azerbaijan
Area: 33,436 sq mi
(86,600 sq km)
Population: 9,284,000
Capital: Baku
Language: Azerbaijani (Azeri)
Currency: Azerbaijan manat

Bahrain
Area: 277 sq mi
(717 sq km)
Population: 1,336,000
Capital: Manama
Languages: Arabic, English,
Farsi, Urdu
Currency: Bahraini dinar

Bangladesh
Area: 56,977 sq mi
(147,570 sq km)
Population: 152,875,000
Capital: Dhaka
Languages: Bangla (Bengali)
(official), English
Currency: Bangladeshi taka

Bhutan
Area: 17,954 sq mi
(46,500 sq km)
Population:708,000
Capital: Thimphu
Languages: Dzongkha
(official), Tibetan dialects,
Nepali dialects
Currency: Bhutanese
ngultrum/Indian rupee

Brunei
Area: 2,226 sq mi
(5,765 sq km)
Population: 413,000
Capital: Bandar Seri Begawan
Languages: Malay (official),
English, Chinese
Currency: Brunei dollar

Cambodia
Area: 69,898 sq mi
(181,035 sq km)
Population: 14,953,000
Capital: Phnom Penh
Language: Khmer (official)
Currency: Cambodian riel

China
Area: 3,705,405 sq mi
(9,596,960 sq km)
Population: 1,350,378,000
Capital: Beijing
Languages: Standard Chinese
(Mandarin), Yue, Wu, Minbei,
other dialects and minority
languages
Currency: Chinese yuan

Timor-Leste
(East Timor)
Area: 5,640 sq mi
(14,609 sq km)
Population: 1,126,000
Capital: Dili
Languages: Tetum, Portuguese
(official), Indonesian, English
Currency: United States dollar

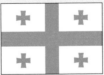

Georgia
Area: 26,911 sq mi
(69,700 sq km)
Population: 4,519,000
Capital: T'bilisi
Languages: Georgian
(official), Russian, Armenian,
Azeri, Abkhaz
Currency: Georgian lari

India
Area: 1,269,222 sq mi
(3,287,270 sq km)
Population: 1,259,721,000
Capital: New Delhi
Languages: Hindi, English
(both official), 21 other
official languages
Currency: Indian rupee

Indonesia
Area: 742,308 sq mi
(1,922,570 sq km)
Population: 240,990,000
Capital: Jakarta
Languages: Bahasa
Indonesian (official), English,
Dutch, Javanese
Currency: Indonesian rupiah

Iran
Area: 636,296 sq mi
(1,648,000 sq km)
Population: 78,869,000
Capital: Tehran
Languages: Farsi (modern-
day Persian), Turkic, Kurdish
Currency: Iranian rial

Iraq
Area: 168,754 sq mi
(437,072 sq km)
Population: 33,703,000
Capital: Baghdad
Languages: Arabic, Kurdish,
Assyrian, Armenian
Currency: Iraqi dinar

Israel
Area: 8,550 sq mi
(22,145 sq km)
Population: 7,906,000
Capital: Jerusalem
Languages: Hebrew (official),
Arabic, English
Currency: Israeli new shekel

Japan
Area: 145,902 sq mi
(377,887 sq km)
Population: 127,588,000
Capital: Tokyo
Language: Japanese
Currency: Japanese yen

FLAGS & STATS

Jordan
Area: 34,495 sq mi
(89,342 sq km)
Population: 6,318,000
Capital: Amman
Languages: Arabic (official),
English
Currency: Jordanian dinar

Kazakhstan
Area: 1,049,155 sq mi
(2,717,300 sq km)
Population: 16,793,000
Capital: Astana
Languages: Kazakh (Qazaq),
Russian (official)
Currency: Kazakhstani tenge

Korea, North
Area: 46,540 sq mi
(120,538 sq km)
Population: 24,589,000
Capital: Pyongyang
Language: Korean
Currency: North Korean won

Korea, South
Area: 38,321 sq mi
(99,250 sq km)
Population: 48,906,000
Capital: Seoul
Languages: Korean,
English widely taught
Currency: South Korean won

Kuwait
Area: 6,880 sq mi
(17,818 sq km)
Population: 2,892,000
Capital: Kuwait
Languages: Arabic (official),
English
Currency: Kuwaiti dinar

Kyrgyzstan
Area: 77,182 sq mi
(199,900 sq km)
Population: 5,668,000
Capital: Bishkek
Languages: Kyrgyz, Russian
(both official)
Currency: Kyrgyzstani som

Laos
Area: 91,429 sq mi
(236,800 sq km)
Population: 6,521,000
Capital: Vientiane
Languages: Lao (official),
French, English, other ethnic
Currency: Lao kip

Lebanon
Area: 4,036 sq mi
(10,452 sq km)
Population: 4,304,000
Capital: Beirut
Languages: Arabic (official),
French, English, Armenian
Currency: Lebanese pound

Malaysia
Area: 127,355 sq mi
(329,847 sq km)
Population: 28,975,000
Capital: Kuala Lumpur
Languages: Bahasa Melayu
(official), English, Chinese
dialects, Tamil, Telugu,
indigenous languages
Currency: Malaysian ringgit

Maldives
Area: 115 sq mi
(298 sq km)
Population: 331,000
Capital: Male
Languages: Maldivian
Dhivehi, English
Currency: Maldivian rufiyaa

Mongolia
Area: 603,909 sq mi
(1,564,116 sq km)
Population: 2,873,000
Capital: Ulaanbaatar
Languages: Khalkha Mongol,
Turkic, Russian
Currency: Mongolian tögrög

Myanmar (Burma)
Area: 261,218 sq mi
(676,552 sq km)
Population: 54,585,000
Capitals: Nay Pyi Taw,
Yangon (Rangoon)
Languages: Burmese,
minority ethnic languages
Currency: Burmese kyat

Nepal
Area: 56,827 sq mi
(147,181 sq km)
Population: 30,918,000
Capital: Kathmandu
Languages: Nepali, Maithali,
Bhojpuri, Tharu, Tamang,
English
Currency: Nepalese rupee

Oman
Area: 119,500 sq mi
(309,500 sq km)
Population: 3,090,000
Capital: Muscat
Languages: Arabic (official),
English, Baluchi, Urdu,
Indian dialects
Currency: Omani rial

Pakistan
Area: 307,374 sq mi
(796,095 sq km)
Population: 180,428,000
Capital: Islamabad
Languages: Urdu, English
(both official), Punjabi, Sindhi,
Siraiki, Pashtu
Currency: Pakistani rupee

Philippines
Area: 115,831 sq mi
(300,000 sq km)
Population: 96,218,000
Capital: Manila
Languages: Filipino (based
on Tagalog), English (both
official), 8 major dialects
Currency: Philippine peso

Qatar
Area: 4,448 sq mi
(11,521 sq km)
Population: 1,882,000
Capital: Doha
Languages: Arabic (official),
English
Currency: Qatari riyal

Saudi Arabia
Area: 756,985 sq mi
(1,960,582 sq km)
Population: 28,705,000
Capital: Riyadh
Language: Arabic
Currency: Saudi riyal

Singapore
Area: 255 sq mi
(660 sq km)
Population: 5,294,000
Capital: Singapore
Languages: Mandarin,
English, Malay, Hokkien
Currency: Singapore dollar

Sri Lanka
Area: 25,299 sq mi
(65,525 sq km)
Population: 21,166,000
Capital: Colombo,
Sri Jayewardenepura
Languages: Sinhala
(official), Tamil, English
Currency: Sri Lankan rupee

Syria
Area: 71,498 sq mi
(185,180 sq km)
Population: 22,531,000
Capital: Damascus
Languages: Arabic (official),
Kurdish, Armenian, Aramaic,
Circassian
Currency: Syrian pound

Tajikistan
Area: 55,251 sq mi
(143,100 sq km)
Population: 7,079,000
Capital: Dushanbe
Languages: Tajik (official),
Russian
Currency: Tajikistani somoni

Thailand
Area: 198,115 sq mi
(513,115 sq km)
Population: 69,892,000
Capital: Bangkok (Krung Thep)
Languages: Thai, English,
ethnic and regional dialects
Currency: Thai baht

Turkey
Area: 300,948 sq mi
(779,452 sq km)
Population: 74,885,000
Capital: Ankara
Languages: Turkish (official),
Kurdish, Arabic, Armenian,
Greek
Currency: Turkish lira

Turkmenistan
Area: 188,300 sq mi
(488,100 sq km)
Population: 5,170,000
Capital: Ashgabat
Languages: Turkmen,
Russian, Uzbek
Currency: Turkmenistan manat

United Arab Emirates
Area: 30,000 sq mi
(77,700 sq km)
Population: 8,106,000
Capital: Abu Dhabi
Languages: Arabic (official),
Persian, English, Hindi, Urdu
Currency: United Arab
Emirates dirham

Uzbekistan
Area: 172,742 sq mi
(447,400 sq km)
Population: 29,780,000
Capital: Tashkent
Languages: Uzbek, Russian
Currency: Uzbekistani som

Vietnam
Area: 127,844 sq mi
(331,114 sq km)
Population: 88,984,000
Capital: Hanoi
Languages: Vietnamese
(official), English, French,
Chinese, Khmer
Currency: Vietnamese dong

Yemen
Area: 207,286 sq mi
(536,869 sq km)
Population: 25,569,000
Capital: Sanaa
Language: Arabic
Currency: Yemeni rial

AFRICA

Algeria
Area: 919,595 sq mi
(2,381,741 sq km)
Population: 37,402,000
Capital: Algiers
Languages: Arabic (official),
French, Berber dialects
Currency: Algerian dinar

Angola
Area: 481,354 sq mi
(1,246,700 sq km)
Population: 20,945,000
Capital: Luanda
Languages: Portuguese
(official), Bantu, other African
languages
Currency: Angolan kwanza

Benin
Area: 43,484 sq mi
(112,622 sq km)
Population: 9,374,000
Capitals: Porto-Novo, Cotonou
Languages: French (official),
Fon, Yoruba, tribal languages
Currency: West African
CFA franc

Botswana
Area: 224,607 sq mi
(581,730 sq km)
Population: 1,850,000
Capital: Gaborone
Languages: English (official),
Setswana, Kalanga, Sekgalgadi
Currency: Botswana pula

Burkina Faso
Area: 105,869 sq mi
(274,200 sq km)
Population: 17,482,000
Capital: Ouagadougou
Languages: French (official),
indigenous languages
Currency: West African
CFA franc

Burundi
Area: 10,747 sq mi
(27,834 sq km)
Population: 10,557,000
Capital: Bujumbura
Languages: Kirundi, French
(both official), Swahili
Currency: Burundian franc

Cameroon
Area: 183,569 sq mi
(475,442 sq km)
Population: 20,919,000
Capital: Yaoundé
Languages: French, English
(both official), 24 major
African language groups
Currency: Central African
CFA franc

Cape Verde
Area: 1,558 sq mi
(4,036 sq km)
Population: 510,000
Capital: Praia
Languages: Portuguese,
Crioulo
Currency: Cape Verdean
escudo

**Central African
Republic**
Area: 240,535 sq mi
(622,984 sq km)
Population: 4,576,000
Capital: Bangui
Languages: French (official),
Sangho, tribal languages
Currency: Central African
CFA franc

Chad
Area: 495,755 sq mi
(1,284,000 sq km)
Population: 11,831,000
Capital: N'Djamena
Languages: French, Arabic
(both official), Sara, more
than 120 other languages
and dialects
Currency: Central African
CFA franc

Comoros
Area: 719 sq mi
(1,862 sq km)
Population: 773,000
Capital: Moroni
Languages: Arabic, French
(both official), Shikomoro
Currency: Comorian franc

Congo
Area: 132,047 sq mi
(342,000 sq km)
Population: 4,247,000
Capital: Brazzaville
Languages: French (official),
Lingala, Monokutuba, many
local languages and dialects
Currency: Central African
CFA franc

**Congo, Democratic
Republic of the**
Area: 905,365 sq mi
(2,344,885 sq km)
Population: 69,117,000
Capital: Kinshasa
Languages: French (official),
Lingala, Kingwana, Kikongo,
Tshiluba
Currency: Congolese franc

**Côte d'Ivoire (Ivory
Coast)**
Area: 124,503 sq mi
(322,462 sq km)
Population: 20,646,000
Capitals: Abidjan,
Yamoussoukro
Languages: French (official),
Dioula, 60 native dialects
Currency: West African
CFA franc

Djibouti
Area: 8,958 sq mi
(23,200 sq km)
Population: 923,000
Capital: Djibouti
Languages: French, Arabic
(both official), Somali, Afar
Currency: Djiboutian franc

Egypt
Area: 386,874 sq mi
(1,002,000 sq km)
Population: 82,283,000
Capital: Cairo
Languages: Arabic (official),
English, French
Currency: Egyptian pound

Equatorial Guinea
Area: 10,831 sq mi
(28,051 sq km)
Population: 740,000
Capital: Malabo
Languages: Spanish, French
(both official), pidgin English,
Fang, Bubi, Ibo
Currency: Central African
CFA franc

Eritrea
Area: 46,774 sq mi
(121,144 sq km)
Population: 5,581,000
Capital: Asmara
Languages: Afar, Arabic,
Tigre, Kunama, Tigrinya,
other Cushitic languages
Currency: Eritrean nakfa

Ethiopia
Area: 437,600 sq mi
(1,133,380 sq km)
Population: 86,960,000
Capital: Addis Ababa
Languages: Amharic,
Tigrinya, Oromigna,
Guaragigna, Somali
Currency: Ethiopian birr

FLAGS & STATS

Gabon
Area: 103,347 sq mi
(267,667 sq km)
Population: 1,564,000
Capital: Libreville
Languages: French (official),
Fang, Myene, Nzebi,
Bapounou/Eschira
Currency: Central African
CFA franc

Gambia
Area: 4,361 sq mi
(11,295 sq km)
Population: 1,825,000
Capital: Banjul
Languages: English (official),
Mandinka, Wolof, Fula
Currency: Gambian dalasi

Ghana
Area: 92,100 sq mi
(238,537 sq km)
Population: 25,546,000
Capital: Accra
Languages: English (official),
Akan, Moshi-Dagomba, Ewe, Ga
Currency: Ghana cedi

Guinea
Area: 94,926 sq mi
(245,857 sq km)
Population: 11,498,000
Capital: Conakry
Languages: French (official),
indigenous languages
Currency: Guinean franc

Guinea-Bissau
Area: 13,948 sq mi
(36,125 sq km)
Population: 1,637,000
Capital: Bissau
Languages: Portuguese
(official), Crioulo, indigenous
languages
Currency: West African
CFA franc

Kenya
Area: 224,081 sq mi
(580,367 sq km)
Population: 43,013,000
Capital: Nairobi
Languages: English,
Kiswahili (both official),
indigenous languages
Currency: Kenyan shilling

Lesotho
Area: 11,720 sq mi
(30,355 sq km)
Population: 2,217,000
Capital: Maseru
Languages: Sesotho, English
(official), Zulu, Xhosa
Currency: Lesotho loti

Liberia
Area: 43,000 sq mi
(111,370 sq km)
Population: 4,245,000
Capital: Monrovia
Languages: English (official),
20 ethnic group languages
Currency: Liberian dollar

Libya
Area: 679,362 sq mi
(1,759,540 sq km)
Population: 6,469,000
Capital: Tripoli
Languages: Arabic, Italian,
English
Currency: Libyan dinar

Madagascar
Area: 226,658 sq mi
(587,041 sq km)
Population: 21,929,000
Capital: Antananarivo
Languages: French, Malagasy
(both official), English
Currency: Malagasy ariary

Malawi
Area: 45,747 sq mi
(118,484 sq km)
Population: 15,883,000
Capital: Lilongwe
Languages: Chichewa (official),
Chinyanja, Chiyao, Chitumbuka
Currency: Malawian kwacha

Mali
Area: 478,841 sq mi
(1,240,192 sq km)
Population: 16,014,000
Capital: Bamako
Languages: French, Bambara
(both official), numerous
African languages
Currency: West African
CFA franc

Mauritania
Area: 397,955 sq mi
(1,030,700 sq km)
Population: 3,623,000
Capital: Nouakchott
Languages: Arabic (official),
Pulaar, Soninke, French,
Hassaniya, Wolof
Currency: Mauritanian ouguiya

Mauritius
Area: 788 sq mi
(2,040 sq km)
Population: 1,291,000
Capital: Port Louis
Languages: Creole, Bhojpuri,
French (official)
Currency: Mauritian rupee

Morocco
Area: 274,461 sq mi
(710,850 sq km)
Population: 32,597,000
Capital: Rabat
Languages: Arabic (official),
Berber dialects, French
Currency: Moroccan dirham

Mozambique
Area: 308,642 sq mi
(799,380 sq km)
Population: 23,702,000
Capital: Maputo
Languages: Emakhuwa,
Xichangana, Portuguese
(official), Elomwe, Cisena,
Echuwabo
Currency: Mozambican metical

Namibia
Area: 318,261 sq mi
(824,292 sq km)
Population: 2,364,000
Capital: Windhoek
Languages: English
(official), Afrikaans, German,
indigenous languages
Currency: Namibian dollar

Niger
Area: 489,191 sq mi
(1,267,000 sq km)
Population: 16,276,000
Capital: Niamey
Languages: French (official),
Hausa, Djerma
Currency: West African
CFA franc

Nigeria
Area: 356,669 sq mi
(923,768 sq km)
Population: 170,124,000
Capital: Abuja
Languages: English (official),
Hausa, Yoruba, Igbo (Ibo), Fulani
Currency: Nigerian naira

Rwanda
Area: 10,169 sq mi
(26,338 sq km)
Population: 10,815,000
Capital: Kigali
Languages: Kinyarwanda,
French, English (all official),
Kiswahili
Currency: Rwandan franc

São Tomé and Principe
Area: 386 sq mi
(1,001 sq km)
Population: 183,000
Capital: São Tomé
Language: Portuguese (official)
Currency: São Tomé and
Principe dobra

Senegal
Area: 75,955 sq mi
(196,722 sq km)
Population: 13,108,000
Capital: Dakar
Languages: French (official),
Wolof, Pulaar, Jola, Mandinka
Currency: West African
CFA franc

Seychelles
Area: 176 sq mi
(455 sq km)
Population: 93,000
Capital: Victoria
Languages: English (official),
Creole
Currency: Seychellois rupee

Sierra Leone
Area: 27,699 sq mi
(71,740 sq km)
Population: 6,126,000
Capital: Freetown
Languages: English (official),
Mende, Temne, Krio
Currency: Sierra Leone leone

Somalia
Area: 246,201 sq mi
(637,657 sq km)
Population: 10,086,000
Capital: Mogadishu
Languages: Somali (official),
Arabic, Italian, English
Currency: Somali shilling

South Africa
Area: 470,693 sq mi
(1,219,090 sq km)
Population: 51,147,000
Capitals: Pretoria (Tshwane),
Cape Town, Bloemfontein
Languages: IsiZulu, IsiXhosa,
Afrikaans, Sepedi, English,
Setswana
Currency: South African rand

South Sudan
Area: 248,777 sq mi
(644,329 sq km)
Population: 9,385,000
Capital: Juba
Languages: English (official),
Arabic, regional languages
Currency: South Sudanese
pound

Sudan
Area: 967,500 sq mi
(2,505,813 sq km)
Population: 33,494,000
Capital: Khartoum
Languages: Arabic (official),
Nubian, Ta Bedawie, many
local dialects
Currency: Sudanese pound

Swaziland
Area: 6,704 sq mi
(17,363 sq km)
Population: 1,220,000
Capitals: Mbabane, Lobamba
Languages: English, siSwati
(both official)
Currency: Swazi lilangeni

Tanzania
Area: 364,900 sq mi
(945,087 sq km)
Population: 47,656,000
Capitals: Dar es Salaam, Dodoma
Languages: Swahili, English
(both official), Arabic, many
local languages
Currency: Tanzanian shilling

Togo
Area: 21,925 sq mi
(56,785 sq km)
Population: 6,011,000
Capital: Lomé
Languages: French (official),
Ewe, Mina, Kabye, Dagomba
Currency: West African
CFA franc

Tunisia
Area: 63,170 sq mi
(163,610 sq km)
Population: 10,800,000
Capital: Tunis
Languages: Arabic (official),
French
Currency: Tunisian dinar

Uganda
Area: 93,104 sq mi
(241,139 sq km)
Population: 35,621,000
Capital: Kampala
Languages: English (official),
Ganda or Luganda, many
local languages
Currency: Ugandan shilling

Zambia
Area: 290,586 sq mi
(752,614 sq km)
Population: 13,711,000
Capital: Lusaka
Languages: English (official),
75 indigenous languages
Currency: Zambian kwacha

Zimbabwe
Area: 150,872 sq mi
(390,757 sq km)
Population: 12,620,000
Capital: Harare
Languages: English (official),
Shona, Sindebele, tribal dialects
Currency: United States
dollar/South African
rand/Euro/British pound/
Botswana pula

AUSTRALIA
NEW ZEALAND, & OCEANIA

Australia
Area: 2,969,906 sq mi
(7,692,024 sq km)
Population: 22,035,000
Capital: Canberra
Language: English
Currency: Australian dollar

Fiji Islands
Area: 7,095 sq mi
(18,376 sq km)
Population: 844,000
Capital: Suva
Languages: English (official),
Fijian, Hindustani
Currency: Fijian dollar

Kiribati
Area: 313 sq mi
(811 sq km)
Population: 105,000
Capital: Tarawa
Languages: English (official),
I-Kiribati
Currency: Kiribati dollar/
Australian dollar

Marshall Islands
Area: 70 sq mi
(181 sq km)
Population: 55,000
Capital: Majuro
Languages: Marshallese
(official), English
Currency: United States dollar

Micronesia
Area: 271 sq mi
(702 sq km)
Population: 107,000
Capital: Palikir
Languages: English (official),
Trukese, Pohnpeian, Yapese,
Kosrean
Currency: United States dollar

Nauru
Area: 8 sq mi
(21 sq km)
Population: 10,200
Capital: Yaren
Languages: Nauruan
(official), English
Currency: Australian dollar

New Zealand
Area: 104,454 sq mi
(270,534 sq km)
Population: 4,437,000
Capital: Wellington
Languages: English, Maori
(both official)
Currency: New Zealand dollar

Palau
Area: 189 sq mi
(489 sq km)
Population: 20,800
Capital: Melekeok
Languages: Palauan, Filipino,
English, Chinese
Currency: United States dollar

Papua New Guinea
Area: 178,703 sq mi
(462,840 sq km)
Population: 7,034,000
Capital: Port Moresby
Languages: Melanesian pidgin,
715 indigenous languages
Currency: Papua New
Guinea kina

Samoa
Area: 1,093 sq mi
(2,831 sq km)
Population: 187,000
Capital: Apia
Languages: Samoan
(Polynesian), English
Currency: Samoan tala

Solomon Islands
Area: 10,954 sq mi
(28,370 sq km)
Population: 552,000
Capital: Honiara
Languages: Melanesian pidgin,
120 indigenous languages
Currency: Solomon Islands
dollar

Tonga
Area: 289 sq mi
(748 sq km)
Population: 103,000
Capital: Nuku'alofa
Languages: Tongan, English
Currency: Tongan pa'anga

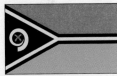

Tuvalu
Area: 10 sq mi
(26 sq km)
Population: 11,300
Capital: Funafuti
Languages: Tuvaluan,
English, Samoan, Kiribati
Currency: Tuvaluan dollar/
Australian dollar

Vanuatu
Area: 4,707 sq mi
(12,190 sq km)
Population: 258,000
Capital: Port Vila
Languages: more than 100
local languages, pidgin
(Bislama or Bichelama)
Currency: Vanuatu vatu

SPOT THE
Difference

Can you spot the ten differences between these two pictures? (Answers on page 184)

A shop in Marrakech, Morocco, sells hundreds of colorful pots, jugs, plates, and other ceramics.

GIVE IT
A Swirl

Use the clues below to figure out which animals appear in these swirled pictures. (Answers on page 184)

1 You don't want to touch the skin of this colorful little creature that lives in the rain forests of central and South America.

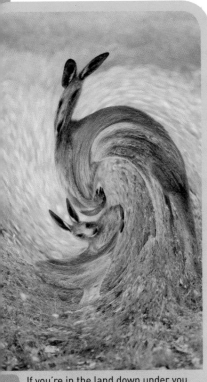

2 If you're in the land down under you might see these creatures hopping by with their joeys in tow.

3 These animals live in and around the icy waters of the Antarctic. They may look funny walking on land, but underwater, they are graceful swimmers.

4 Coral reefs are where you'll find these bright and colorful creatures.

5 These funny African animals live in groups called mobs, clans, or gangs.

6 This large North American mammal is great at catching a meal.

7 Cute and cuddly, this furry mammal lives in the land of the Great Wall and is always eating its favorite food.

8 You don't want to get too close to this marine stinger!

9 If you see this insect fluttering around the mountainous meadows of Europe, you might mistake its red spots for eyes.

FIND THE
Hidden Animals

C Vietnam and China

Many animals blend into their environment in order to protect themselves. See if you can identify the camouflaged animals in these pictures. (Answers on page 184)

D Argentina and Chile

A Eastern Atlantic Ocean and Mediterranean Sea

E Gabon

B The Amazon

India F

J Nepal

G North America

K Australia

H Costa Rica

L Mexico

I United States

Wild Guess

Compare these pairs, if you dare.
(Answers on page 185)

Which sound travels farther?
The howl of a howler monkey or the vocals of a blue whale?

Argentina ↔ **India**

Which is bigger?
Countries are not to scale.

Which takes longer?
Travel by car from Rome, Italy, to Istanbul, Turkey, or travel by foot from New York, New York, to Philadelphia, Pennsylvania, U.S.A.?

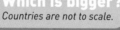

Which is taller?
Washington Monument in Washington, D.C., U.S.A., or Eiffel Tower in Paris, France?

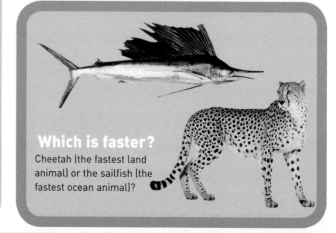

Which is faster?
Cheetah (the fastest land animal) or the sailfish (the fastest ocean animal)?

SPOT THE
Difference

Can you spot the ten differences between these two pictures? (Answers on page 185)

Colorful buoys hang outside a lobster shack in Bar Harbor, Maine, United States.

BACK
OF THE BOOK

Name That Place

Name the landmark or feature in these images and the place each is located. (Answers on page 185)

3

5

4

1

6

7

2

8

9

**BACK
OF THE BOOK**

10

11

12

13

14

15

16

Answers

Spot the difference, page 176:

Give it a swirl, page 177:
1. Red poison dart frog in the Amazon rain forest of Peru
2. A mother and baby kangaroo in the Australian wilderness
3. A Gentoo penguin walking on ice in Antarctica
4. Two butterfly fish in the Red Sea off the coast of Egypt
5. Five meerkats looking around outside their burrow in Africa
6. A grizzly bear catching salmon in Alaska, United States
7. A giant panda climbing a tree in China
8. A compass jellyfish swimming in the Cerbère-Banyuls Marine Reserve in France
9. A nomion butterfly sitting on a leaf. This butterfly is found mostly in Europe.

Hidden Animals, page 178–179:
A. A red scorpionfish, found in the Eastern Atlantic Ocean and the Mediterranean Sea
B. A Black caiman in the Amazon
C. A Vietnamese mossy frog, found in northern Vietnam and southern China
D. Sea lions and penguins on the islands of Tierra del Fuego on the southern tip of South America
E. A Gaboon viper snake in the country of Gabon in Africa
F. A tiger in the national park in India
G. A species of green butterfly found in North America
H. A ghost crab on a beach in Costa Rica
I. A snowshoe hare in Maine, United States
J. A crocodile in a national park in Nepal
K. A koala high in a gum tree in Australia
L. A jaguar cub in a jungle in Mexico

Spot the Difference, page 181:

Wild Guess, page 180:

Which sound travels farther?
A blue whale's vocals travel farther than a howler monkey's. A blue whale can be louder than a jet plane and detected from more than 500 miles (805 km) away. On land, the howler monkey's howl can be heard 3 miles (5 km) away.

Which is bigger?
India with a land area of 1,269,219 sq mi (3,287,263 sq km) is larger than Argentina, which has a land area of 1,073,518 sq mi (2,780,400 sq km).

Which is taller?
The Eiffel Tower at 1,063 ft (324 m) is taller than the Washington Monument, which is 555 feet (169 m).

Which takes longer?
It takes longer to travel by foot from New York, New York, to Philadelphia, Pennsylvania (about 29 hours) than to drive from Rome, Italy, to Istanbul, Turkey (about 24 hours).

Which is faster?
The sailfish can travel 68 miles per hour (110 kph), making it faster than the cheetah, which can reach speeds of 60 to 65 mph (96.5 to 104 kph).

Name That Place, pages 182–183:
1. Taj Mahal in Agra, India
2. The Incan ruins of Machu Picchu in Peru
3. Uluru (Ayers Rock) in Australia
4. Mayan Pyramid Chichen Itza in Mexico
5. Leaning Tower of Pisa in Italy
6. The Himalaya in Nepal
7. Sydney Opera House in Australia
8. Great Wall of China
9. Mount Kilimanjaro in Kenya
10. Grand Canyon in Arizona, U.S.A.
11. Colosseum of Rome in Italy
12. The CN Tower in Toronto, Canada
13. Big Ben in London, United Kingdom
14. Christ the Redeemer Monument in Rio de Janeiro, Brazil
15. Golden Gate Bridge in San Francisco, California, U.S.A.
16. The Great Sphinx of Giza guarding a Pyramid in Egypt

GLOSSARY

acid rain precipitation containing acid droplets resulting from the mixture of moisture in the air with carbon dioxide, nitrogen oxide, sulfur dioxide, and hydrocarbons released by factories and motor vehicles

archipelago a group or chain of islands

bathymetry measurement of depth at various places in the ocean or other body of water

bay a body of water, usually smaller than a gulf, that is partially surrounded by land

biomass the total volume of organic material in a certain area or ecosystem that can be used as a renewable energy source

border the area close to a boundary

boundary most commonly, a line that has been established by people to mark the limit of one political unit, such as a country or state, and the beginning of another; geographical features such as mountains sometimes act as boundaries

breakwater a structure, such as a wall, that protects a harbor or beach from pounding waves

caloric supply a measure of the amount of food available to a particular person, household, or community

canal a human-made waterway that is used by ships or to carry water for irrigation

canyon a deep, narrow valley that has steep sides

cape a point of land that extends into an ocean, a lake, or a river

carat a unit of weight for precious stones equal to 200 milligrams

cataract a steplike series of waterfalls or rapids such as occur on the Nile River

cliff a very steep rock face, usually along a coast but also on the side of a mountain

continent one of the seven main landmasses on Earth's surface

country a territory whose government is the highest legal authority over the land and people within its boundaries

delta lowland formed by silt, sand, and gravel deposited by a river at its mouth

desert a hot or cold region that receives 10 inches (25 cm) or less of rain or other kinds of precipitation a year

desertification the spread of desertlike conditions in semiarid regions that is the result of climatic changes and increasing human pressures, such as overgrazing, removal of natural vegetation, and cultivation of land

dialect a regional variation of a language

divide an elevated area drained by different river systems flowing in different directions

elevation distance above sea level, usually measured in feet or meters

escarpment a cliff that separates two nearly flat land areas that lie at different elevations

fault a break in Earth's crust along which movement up, down, or sideways occurs

fork the place in a river where two streams come together

geographic pole 90°N, 90°S latitude; location of the ends of Earth's axis

geomagnetic pole point at which the axis of Earth's magnetic field intersects Earth's surface; compass needles align with Earth's magnetic field so that one end points to the magnetic north pole, the other to the magnetic south pole

glacier a large, slow-moving mass of ice

global warming a theory explaining that the recent increase in Earth's average global temperature is due to a buildup of greenhouse gases, such as carbon dioxide and methane, in excess of natural levels due mainly to human activities

greenhouse gases atmospheric gases, such as carbon dioxide and methane, in excess of natural levels due mainly to human activities

gross domestic product (GDP) the total market value of goods and services produced by a country's economy in a year

gulf a portion of the ocean that cuts into the land; usually larger than a bay

harbor a body of water, sheltered by natural or artificial barriers, that is deep enough for ships

hemisphere literally half a sphere; Earth has four hemispheres: Northern, Southern, Eastern, and Western

highlands an elevated area or the more mountainous region of a country

hybrid car a car that is powered by gasoline and electricity

hydrothermal vent a crack in the ocean floor that releases mineral-rich, superheated water

inlet a narrow opening in the land that is filled with water flowing from an ocean, a lake, or a river

island a landmass, smaller than a continent, that is completely surrounded by water

isthmus a narrow strip of land that connects two larger landmasses and has water on two sides

lagoon a shallow body of water that is open to the sea but also protected from it by a reef or sandbar

lake a body of water that is surrounded by land; large lakes are sometimes called seas

landform a physical feature shaped by tectonic activity, weathering, and erosion; the four major kinds on Earth are plains, mountains, plateaus, and hills

landmass a large area of Earth's crust that lies above sea level, such as a continent

large-scale map a map, such as a street map, that shows a small area in great detail

Latin America cultural region generally considered to include Mexico, Central America, South America, and the West Indies; Portuguese and Spanish are the prinicipal languages

latitude distance north and south of the Equator, which is 0° latitude

leeward the side away from or sheltered from the wind

lingua franca a language not native to the local population that is used as a common or commercial language

longitude distance east and west of the prime meridian, which is 0° longitude

magma molten rock in Earth's mantle

mesa an eroded plateau, broader than it is high, that is found in arid or semiarid regions

metropolitan area a city and its surrounding suburbs or communities

Middle East term commonly used for the countries of Southwest Asia, but which can also include northern Africa from Morocco to Somalia

molten liquefied by heat; melted

mountain a landform, higher than a hill, that rises at least 1,000 feet (300 m) above the surrounding land and is wider at its base than at its top, or peak; a series of mountains is called a range

nation people who share a common culture; often used as another word for "country," although people within a country may be of many cultures

ocean the large body of saltwater that surrounds the continents and covers more than two-thirds of Earth's surface

peninsula a piece of land that is almost completely surrounded by water

permafrost a permanently frozen subsurface soil in frigid regions

plain a large area of relatively flat land that is often covered with grasses

plateau a relatively flat area, larger than a mesa, that rises above the surrounding landscape

poaching the illegal killing or taking of animals from their natural habitats

point a narrow piece of land smaller than a cape that extends into a body of water

population density in a country, the number of people living on each square mile or square kilometer of land (calculated by dividing population by land area)

Prairie Provinces popular name for the Canadian provinces of Manitoba, Saskatchewan, and Alberta

prime meridian an imaginary line that runs through Greenwich, England, and is accepted as the line of 0° longitude

projection the process of representing the round Earth on a flat surface, such as a map

rain shadow the dry region on the leeward side of a mountain range

reef an offshore ridge made of coral, rocks, or sand

renewable resources resources that are replenished naturally, but the supply of which can be endangered by overuse and pollution

Sahel a semiarid grassland in Africa along the Sahara's southern border

savanna a tropical grassland with scattered trees

scale on a map, a means of explaining the relationship between distances on the map and actual distances on Earth's surface

sea the ocean or a partially enclosed body of saltwater that is connected to the ocean; completely enclosed bodies of saltwater, such as the Dead Sea, are really lakes

slot canyon a very narrow, deep canyon formed by water and wind erosion

small-scale map a map, such as a country map, that shows a large area without much detail

sound a long, broad inlet of the ocean that lies parallel to the coast and often separates an island and the mainland

Soviet Union shortened name for the Union of Soviet Socialist Republics (U.S.S.R.), a former Communist republic (1920–1991) in eastern Europe and northern and Central Asia. It was made up of 15 republics, of which Russia was the largest.

spit a long, narrow strip of land, often of sand or silt, that extends into a body of water from the land

staple a chief ingredient of a people's diet

steppe a Slavic word referring to relatively flat, mostly treeless temperate grasslands that stretch across much of central Europe and Central Asia

strait a narrow passage of water that connects two larger bodies of water

territory land that is under the jurisdiction of a country but is not a state or a province

tributary a stream that flows into a larger river

tropics region lying within $23\frac{1}{2}°$ north and south of the Equator that experiences warm temperatures year-round

topography the relief features that are evident on a planet's surface

upwelling process by which nutrient-rich water rises from ocean depths to the surface

valley a long depression, usually created by a river, that is bordered by higher land

virgin forest a forest made up of trees that have never been cut down by humans

volcano an opening in Earth's crust through which molten rock erupts

windward the unsheltered side toward which the wind blows

GEO FACTS & FIGURES

PLANET EARTH

Mass:
6,583,348,000,000,000,000,000
tons
(5,974,000,000,000,000,000,000
metric tons)
Distance around the Equator:
24,901 mi
(40,073 km)
Area: 196,938,000 sq mi
(510,066,000 sq km)
Land area: 57,393,000 sq mi
(148,647,000 sq km)
Water area: 139,545,000 sq mi
(361,419,000 sq km)

The Continents

Asia: 17,208,000 sq mi
(44,570,000 sq km)
Africa: 11,608,000 sq mi
(30,065,000 sq km)
North America: 9,449,000 sq mi
(24,474,000 sq km)
South America: 6,880,000 sq mi
(17,819,000 sq km)
Antarctica: 5,100,000 sq mi
(13,209,000 sq km)
Europe: 3,841,000 sq mi
(9,947,000 sq km)
Australia: 2,968,000 sq mi
(7,687,000 sq km)

Highest Mountain on Each Continent

Everest, Asia: 29,035 ft (8,850 m)
Aconcagua, South America:
22,834 ft (6,960 m)
McKinley (Denali), North America:
20,320 ft (6,194 m)
Kilimanjaro, Africa: 19,340 ft
(5,895 m)
El'brus, Europe: 18,510 ft
(5,642 m)
Vinson Massif, Antarctica:
16,067 ft (4,897 m)

Kosciuszko, Australia: 7,310 ft
(2,228 m)

Lowest Point on Each Continent

Bentley Subglacial Trench, Antarctica: –8,383 ft (–2,555 m)
Dead Sea, Asia: –1,385 ft (–422 m)
Lake Assal, Africa: –512 ft
(–156 m)
Death Valley, North America:
–282 ft (–86 m)
Laguna del Carbón, South America: –344 ft
(–105 m)
Caspian Sea, Europe: –92 ft
(–28 m)
Lake Eyre, Australia: –52 ft
(–16 m)

Longest Rivers

Nile, Africa: 4,241 mi (6,825 km)
Amazon, South America: 4,000 mi
(6,437 km)
Yangtze (Chang), Asia: 3,964 mi
(6,380 km)
Mississippi-Missouri, North America: 3,710 mi (5,971 km)
Yenisey-Angara, Asia: 3,440 mi
(5,536 km)
Yellow (Huang), Asia: 3,395 mi
(5,464 km)
Ob-Irtysh, Asia: 3,362 mi
(5,410 km)
Congo (Zaire), Africa: 2,715 mi
(4,370 km)
Amur, Asia: 2,744 mi (4,416 km)
Lena, Asia: 2,734 mi (4,400 km)

Largest Islands

Greenland: 836,000 sq mi
(2,166,000 sq km)
New Guinea: 306,000 sq mi
(792,500 sq km)
Borneo: 280,100 sq mi
(725,500 sq km)
Madagascar: 226,600 sq mi
(587,000 sq km)

Baffin: 196,000 sq mi
(507,500 sq km)
Sumatra: 165,000 sq mi
(427,300 sq km)
Honshu: 87,800 sq mi
(227,400 sq km)
Great Britain: 84,200 sq mi
(218,100 sq km)
Victoria: 83,900 sq mi
(217,300 sq km)
Ellesmere: 75,800 sq mi
(196,200 sq km)

Largest Lakes (by area)

Caspian Sea, Europe-Asia:
143,200 sq mi
(371,000 sq km)
Superior, North America: 31,700
sq mi (82,100 sq km)
Victoria, Africa: 26,800 sq mi
(69,500 sq km)
Huron, North America: 23,000 sq
mi (59,600 sq km)
Michigan, North America: 22,300
sq mi (57,800 sq km)
Tanganyika, Africa: 12,600 sq mi
(32,600 sq km)
Baikal, Asia: 12,200 sq mi
(31,500 sq km)
Great Bear, North America:
12,100 sq mi (31,300 sq km)
Malawi, Africa: 11,200 sq mi
(28,900 sq km)
Great Slave Lake, Canada, North America: 11,000 sq mi
(28,600 sq km)

Oceans

Pacific: 65,436,200 sq mi
(169,479,000 sq km)
Atlantic: 35,338,500 sq mi
(91,526,400 sq km)
Indian: 28,839,800 sq mi
(74,694,800 sq km)
Arctic: 5,390,000 sq mi
(13,960,100 sq km)

Largest Seas (by area)
Coral: 1,615,260 sq mi (4,183,510 sq km)
South China: 1,388,570 sq mi (3,596,390 sq km)
Caribbean: 1,094,330 sq mi (2,834,290 sq km)
Bering: 972,810 sq mi (2,519,580 sq km)
Mediterranean: 953,320 sq mi (2,469,100 sq km)
Sea of Okhotsk: 627,490 sq mi (1,625,190 sq km)
Gulf of Mexico: 591,430 sq mi (1,531,810 sq km)
Norwegian: 550,300 sq mi (1,425,280 sq km)
Greenland: 447,050 sq mi (1,157,850 sq km)
Sea of Japan: 389,290 sq mi (1,008,260 sq km)

GEOGRAPHIC EXTREMES

Highest Mountain
Everest, China/Nepal: 29,035 ft (8,850 m)

Deepest Point in the Ocean
Challenger Deep, Mariana Trench, Pacific: -36,070 ft (-10,994 m)

Hottest Place
Dalol, Danakil Depression, Ethiopia: annual average temperature 93°F (34°C)

Coldest Place
Plateau Station, Antarctica: annual average temperature -70°F (-56.7°C)

Wettest Place
Mawsynram, Assam, India: annual average rainfall 467 in (1,187 cm)

Driest Place
Arica, Atacama Desert, Chile: barely measurable rainfall

Largest Hot Desert
Sahara, Africa: 3,475,000 sq mi (9,000,000 sq km)

Largest Cold Desert
Antarctica: 5,100,000 sq mi (13,209,000 sq km)

PEOPLE

Most People by Continent
Asia: 4,191,414,100

Least People by Continent
Antarctica: 4,400 (transient)
Australia: 22,035,000

Most Densely Populated Country
Monaco: 45,000 people per sq mi/18,000 per sq km
Least Densely Populated Country
Mongolia: 5 people per sq mi/2 per sq km

Most Populated Metropolitan Areas
Tokyo, Japan: 36,669,000
Delhi, India: 22,157,000
São Paulo, Brazil: 20,262,000
Mumbai, India: 20,041,000
Mexico City, Mexico: 19,460,000
New York, United States: 19,425,000
Shanghai, China: 16,575,000
Kolkata (Calcutta), India: 15,552,000
Dhaka, Bangladesh: 14,648,000
Karachi, Pakistan: 13,125,000

Countries With the Highest Life Expectancy
Japan: 83 years
San Marino: 83 years
Australia: 82 years
Spain: 82 years
Israel: 82 years
France: 82 years
Switzerland: 82 years
Sweden: 82 years

Countries With the Lowest Life Expectancy
Afghanistan: 44 years
Zimbabwe: 46 years
Guinea-Bissau: 48 years
Swaziland: 49 years
Zambia: 49 years
Dem. Rep. of the Congo: 49 years
Lesotho: 49 years
Central Africa Republic: 50 years

Countries With the Highest Gross Domestic Product per Person
Luxembourg: $104,196
Norway: $102,249
Qatar: $99,839
Switzerland: $76,598
Australia: $69,582

Countries With the Lowest Gross Domestic Product per Person
Dem. Rep. of the Congo: $251
Malawi: $262
Burundi: $317
Niger: $434
Central African Republic: $451

OUTSIDE WEBSITES

The following websites will provide you with additional valuable information about various topics discussed in this atlas.

Antarctic wildlife:
www.antarcticconnection.com/antarctic/wildlife/index.shtml

Biomes:
www.blueplanetbiomes.org

Currency converter:
www.xe.com/ucc

Earth's climates:
www.worldclimate.com

Earth's geologic history:
Earthquakes: earthquake.usgs.gov
Tsunamis: www.tsunami.noaa.gov
Volcanoes: www.geo.mtu.edu/volcanoe/

Extreme facts about the world:
www.extremescience.com

Flags of the world:
www.fotw.us/flags/index.html

Languages of the world:
www.ipl.org/div/hello/

Mapping sites:
earth.google.com
www.skylineglobe.com

National anthems:
www.nationalanthems.info

Political world (lots of statistics):
https://www.cia.gov/library/publications/the-world-factbook/index.html

Religions of the world:
www.adherents.com/Religions_By_Adherents.html

Solar system:
solarsystem.nasa.gov/planets

Time differences between places:
www.worldtimeserver.com

Time zone map:
www.worldtimezone.com

Tracking Quakes (page 33)
www.iris.edu/seismon

Weather around the world right now:
www.weather.com

World heritage sites (important historic places around the world):
whc.unesco.org/en/list

Index

Map references are in boldface (**50**) type. Letters and numbers following in lightface (D12) locate the place-names using the map grid. (Refer to page 7 for more details.)

PLACE-NAMES

A

1st Cataract (falls), Egypt **133** C10
2nd Cataract (falls), Sudan **137** A4
3rd Cataract (falls), Sudan **137** A4
4th Cataract (falls), Sudan **137** A5
5th Cataract (falls), Sudan **137** B5
6th Cataract (falls), Sudan **137** B4
Aba as Saud, Saudi Arabia **117** G3
Abaco Island, Bahamas **67** A3
Abadan, Iran **117** D4
Abéché, Chad **137** B2
Aberdeen, United Kingdom **93** B3
Abha, Saudi Arabia **117** G3
Abidjan, Côte d'Ivoire **135** E3
Abilene, Texas (U.S.) **63** E5
Abkhazia (region), Georgia **115** A7
Abu Dhabi, United Arab Emirates **117** E6
Abuja, Nigeria **135** E6
Acapulco, Mexico **65** E3

Accra, Ghana **135** E4
Acklins Island, Bahamas **67** B3
Aconcagua, Cerro, Argentina **81** D1
A Coruña, Spain **93** G1
Adana, Turkey **115** D4
Adare, Cape, Antarctica **155** G5
Ad Dahna (region), Saudi Arabia **117** E4
Ad Dakhla, Western Sahara (Morocco) **132** C1
Ad Dammam, Saudi Arabia **117** E5
Addis Ababa, Ethiopia **137** C5
Adelaide, Australia **149** F5
Aden, Yemen **117** I4
Admiralty Gulf, Australia **148** A3
Admiralty Islands, Papua New Guinea **150** D2
Adrar des Ifôghas (range), Mali **135** C5
Adriatic Sea, Europe **84** F4
Aegean Sea, Europe **84** G6
Afghanistan (country), Asia **103** E3
Agadez, Niger **135** C6
Agadir, Morocco **132** B2
Agordat, Eritrea **137** B6
Agra, India **119** C4

Agulhas, Cape, South Africa **138** H3
Ahaggar Mountains, Algeria **133** D5
Ahmadabad, India **119** D3
Ahvaz, Iran **117** D4
Aïr Massif (range), Niger **135** C6
Ajaccio, France **93** G6
Ajdābiyā, Libya **133** B7
Ajmer, India **119** C3
Akimiski Island, Nunavut, Canada **61** F6
Akita, Japan **113** B10
Akola, India **119** E4
Akureyri, Iceland **91** A2
Alabama (state), U.S. **63** E8
Alajuela, Costa Rica **65** G7
Al Amarah, Iraq **117** C4
Aland Islands, Finland **91** F5
Alaska (state), U.S. **62** G2
Alaska, Gulf of, U.S. **54** C1
Alaska Peninsula, Alaska (U.S.) **62** GS
Alaska Range, Alaska (U.S.) **62** G2
Albania (country), Europe **85** G5
Albany, Australia **148** F2
Albany, New York (U.S.) **63** B10
Albert, Lake, Africa **137** E4
Alberta (province), Canada **61** E3

Albert Nile (river), Uganda **137** D5
Alboran Sea, Europe **93** I2
Albuquerque, New Mexico (U.S.) **63** E4
Aldan (river), Russia **102** C6
Aleppo, see Halab, Syria **115** D5
Ålesund, Norway **91** E2
Aleutian Islands, Alaska (U.S.) **62** G1
Aleutian Range, Alaska (U.S.) **54** B1
Alexander Archipelago, Alaska (U.S.) **54** C2
Alexander Island, Antarctica **154** C1
Alexandria, Egypt **133** B9
Al Farciya, Western Sahara (Morocco) **132** C2
Algena, Eritrea **137** B5
Algeria (country), Africa **133** C3
Algiers, Algeria **133** A4
Al Hadidah (crater), Saudi Arabia **117** F5
Al Hijaz (region), Saudi Arabia **117** E2
Al Hillah, Iraq **117** C3
Al Hillah, Saudi Arabia **117** F4
Al Hudaydah, Yemen **117** H3
Alice Springs, Australia **149** C5

Al Jawf, Libya **125** D9
Al Jawf, Saudi Arabia **133** D9
Al Kharj, Saudi Arabia **117** F4
Allahabad, India **119** D5
Almaty, Kazakhstan **111** D4
Al Mukalla, Yemen **117** H4
Alps (range), Europe **84** F3
Al Qamishli, Syria **115** D6
Al Qunfudhah, Saudi Arabia **117** G2
Altay Mountains, Asia **102** D5
Altiplano (region), South America **77** H4
Altun Ha (ruins), Belize **65** E6
Altun Shan (range), China **112** D3
Amarillo, Texas (U.S.) **63** E5
Amazon (Solimões) (river), South America **70** B6
Amazon Basin, South America **70** B4
Ambon, Indonesia **123** D8
Ambre, Cap d', Madagascar **139** B11
American Highland, Antarctica **155** C8
American Samoa (islands), U.S. **151** E6
Amery Ice Shelf, Antarctica **155** C8

Amman — Beni Abbes

Amman, Jordan **115** G4
Amritsar, India **119** B3
Amsterdam, Netherlands **93** D5
Am Timan, Chad **137** C2
Amu Darya (river), Asia **110** D2
Amundsen Gulf, Northwest Territories (Canada) **61** C3
Amundsen-Scott Station, Antarctica **155** D5
Amundsen Sea, Antarctica **155** E2
Amur (river), Asia **102** C7
Anadyr, Russia **103** A7
Anadyr, Gulf of, Russia **103** A7
Anambas Islands, Indonesia **122** B2
Anatolia (Asia Minor) (region), Turkey **115** C3
Anchorage, Alaska (U.S.) **62** G3
Andaman Islands, India **119** F8
Andaman Sea, Asia **102** G5
Andes (range), South America **70** C2
Andorra, Andorra **93** G4
Andorra (country), Europe **85** G2
Andros Island, Bahamas **67** B2
Anefis I-n-Darane, Mali **135** C5
Angara (river), Russia **109** E6
Angarsk, Russia **103** D5
Angel Falls, Venezuela **77** B6
Ångermanälven (river), Sweden **91** D4
Angohran, Iran **117** E7
Angola (country), Africa **127** G5
Angora, see Ankara, Turkey **115** C3
Anguilla (island), United Kingdom **67** C6
Ankara (Angora), Turkey **115** C3
Annaba, Algeria **133** A5
An Nafud (region), Saudi Arabia **117** D3
An Najaf, Iraq **117** C3
Annapolis, Maryland (U.S.) **63** C10
Anshan, China **113** C8
Antalya, Turkey **114** D2
Antananarivo, Madagascar **139** D10
Antarctic Peninsula, Antarctica **155** C2
Anticosti, Île de, Quebec (Canada) **61** F9
Anticosti Island, see Anticosti, Île de, Quebec (Canada) **61** F9
Antigua and Barbuda (country), North America **55** H8
Antioch, see Hatay, Turkey **115** D4
Antofagasta, Chile **81** B1
Antsirabe, Madagascar **139** D10
Antsiranana, Madagascar **139** B11
Antwerp, Belgium **93** D4

Aomori, Japan **113** B10
Aoulef, Algeria **133** C4
Aozi, Chad **137** A2
Aozou, Chad **137** A2
Aozou Strip (region), Chad **137** A2
Apennines (range), Italy **93** G7
Apia, Samoa **151** E6
Appalachian Mountains, U.S. **63** D9
Apurímac (river), Peru **77** G3
Aqaba, Gulf of, Asia **133** B11
Aqaba, Jordan **115** H4
Aqtöbe, Kazakhstan **110** B2
Arabian Peninsula, Asia **102** E1
Arabian Sea, Asia **102** F2
Aracaju, Brazil **79** D7
Arad, Romania **97** B5
Arafura Sea, Asia **123** E9
Araguaia (river), Brazil **79** E5
Arak, Algeria **133** D5
Arak, Iran **117** C5
Aral Sea, Asia **110** C2
Aramac, Australia **149** C7
Araouane, Mali **135** C4
Ararat, Mount, Turkey **115** C8
Aras (river), Asia **115** C9
Ārba Minch', Ethiopia **137** D6
Arbil, Iraq **117** B3
Ardabil, Iran **117** B4
Åre, Sweden **85** C4
Arequipa, Peru **77** H3
Argentina (country), South America **71** G4
Århus, Denmark **91** H3
Arica, Chile **81** A1
Arizona (state), U.S. **62** E3
Arkansas (river), U.S. **63** D5
Arkansas (state), U.S. **63** E7
Arkhangel'sk, Russia **99** C4
Armenia (country), Asia **103** D2
Armidale, Australia **149** E8
Arnhem, Cape, Australia **149** A5
Arnhem Land, Australia **149** A5
Ar Ramadi, Iraq **117** C3
Ar Raqqah, Syria **115** E6
Ar Rub' al Khali (Empty Quarter) (desert), Saudi Arabia **117** G5
Arthur's Pass, New Zealand **149** G10
Arua, Uganda **137** D4
Aruba (island), Netherlands **67** E5
Aru Islands, Indonesia **123** D9
Arusha, Tanzania **137** F5
Asansol, India **119** D6
Ascension (island), United Kingdom **126** F1
Ashburton, New Zealand **149** H10
Ashgabat, Turkmenistan **110** D1
Ashmore Islands, Australia **148** A3
Ash Shihr, Yemen **117** H4
Asia Minor (region), see Anatolia, Turkey **115** C3
Asmara, Eritrea **137** B5
Assab, Eritrea **137** B7
As Sulaymaniyah, Iraq **117** B4
Astana, Kazakhstan **111** B4

Astrakhan', Russia **99** H6
Asunción, Paraguay **81** B4
Aswân, Egypt **133** D10
Aswân High Dam, Egypt **133** D10
Asyût, Egypt **133** C10
Atacama Desert, Chile **81** A1
Atar, Mauritania **135** B2
Atbara, Sudan **137** B5
Atbara (river), Sudan **137** B5
Athabasca (river), Alberta (Canada) **54** D3
Athabasca, Lake, Canada **61** E3
Athens, Greece **97** G6
Ati, Chad **137** C2
Atlanta, Georgia (U.S.) **63** E9
Atlas Mountains, Africa **126** C2
At Ta'if, Saudi Arabia **117** F2
Atyrau, Kazakhstan **110** B1
Auckland, New Zealand **149** E11
Augusta, Australia **148** F2
Augusta, Maine (U.S.) **63** B11
Austin, Texas (U.S.) **63** F6
Australia (country), Oceania **143** F2
Australian Capital Territory, Australia **149** F7
Austral Islands, French Polynesia, France **151** F7
Austria (country), Europe **85** F4
Avalon Peninsula, Newfoundland & Labrador (Canada) **54** D7
Avarua, Cook Islands, N.Z. **143** E7
Avignon, France **93** G5
Awjilah, Libya **133** C8
Axel Heiberg Island, Nunavut (Canada) **54** A4
Ayers Rock (peak), see Uluru, Australia **148** D4
Ayr, Australia **149** C7
Azerbaijan (country), Asia **103** D2
Azores (islands), Portugal **126** B1
Azov, Sea of, Europe **84** F7
Az Zarqa', Jordan **115** F4

B
Bab el Mandab (strait), Djibouti **137** C7
Babruysk, Belarus **95** C7
Babuyan Islands, Philippines **121** B7
Bacolod, Philippines **121** D7
Baetic Mountains, Spain **84** G1
Baffin Bay, North America **61** B7
Baffin Island, Nunavut (Canada) **61** C6
Bagan, Myanmar **119** D8
Baghdad, Iraq **117** C4
Baguio, Philippines **121** C7
Bagzane, Mont, Niger **135** C7
Bahamas (country), North America **55** G6
Bahia, see Salvador, Brazil **79** E7
Bahía Blanca, Argentina **81** F3
Bahir Dar, Ethiopia **137** C5

Bahrain (country), Asia **103** E2
Baia Mare, Romania **97** A6
Baikal, Lake, Russia **109** E7
Baja California (peninsula), Mexico **64** B1
Baker Island, U.S. **151** D5
Bakersfield, California (U.S.) **62** D2
Baku, Azerbaijan **115** B10
Balclutha, New Zealand **149** I9
Balearic Islands, Spain **93** H4
Balearic Sea, Spain **93** H4
Bali (island), Indonesia **123** E4
Balıkesir, Turkey **114** B2
Balikpapan, Indonesia **123** C5
Balkan Mountains, Bulgaria **97** D5
Balkan Peninsula, Europe **97** D5
Balkhash, Lake, Kazakhstan **111** C4
Ballarat, Australia **149** F6
Balsas (river), Mexico **65** E3
Balti, Moldova **95** F6
Baltic Sea, Europe **84** D5
Baltimore, Maryland (U.S.) **63** C10
Baluchistan (region), Iran **117** E8
Bam, Iran **117** D7
Bamako, Mali **135** D2
Bambari, Central African Rep. **137** D3
Bamenda, Cameroon **135** E7
Banaras, see Varanasi, India **119** D5
Banda Aceh, Indonesia **122** A1
Bandar-e Abbas, Iran **117** E6
Bandar-e Bushehr, Iran **117** D5
Bandar Seri Begawan, Brunei **121** E5
Banda Sea, Indonesia **123** D8
Bandhavgarh National Park, India **119** D5
Bandundu, Dem. Rep. of the Congo **137** F2
Bandung, Indonesia **122** D2
Banff National Park, Alberta (Canada) **60** F2
Bangalore, India **119** F4
Bangassou, Central African Rep. **137** D3
Bangkok, Thailand **121** C2
Bangladesh (country), Asia **103** F4
Bangui, Central African Rep. **137** D2
Banja Luka, Bosnia & Herzegovina **97** C3
Banjarmasin, Indonesia **123** D4
Banjul, Gambia **135** D1
Banks Island, Northwest Territories (Canada) **61** B3
Banks Peninsula, New Zealand **149** H10
Baotou, China **113** C6
Baranavichy, Belarus **95** C6
Barat Daya Islands, Indonesia **123** E7
Barbados (country), North America **55** H8

Barcaldine, Australia **149** C7
Barcelona, Spain **93** G4
Bareilly, India **119** C4
Barents Sea, Europe **84** A6
Bargaal, Somalia **137** C8
Bari, Italy **93** G8
Barisan Mountains, Indonesia **122** C1
Barnaul, Russia **109** F5
Barquisimeto, Venezuela **77** A4
Barranquilla, Colombia **77** A2
Barrow, Point, Alaska (U.S.) **54** B2
Barrow Creek, Australia **149** C5
Barrow Island, Australia **148** C1
Barú, Volcán, Panama **65** G7
Basankusu, Dem. Rep. of the Congo **137** E2
Basel, Switzerland **93** E5
Basra, Iraq **117** D4
Bassas da India (islands), France **139** E8
Basseterre, St. Kitts & Nevis **67** C7
Bass Strait, Australia **149** G7
Bata, Equatorial Guinea **135** F7
Batan Islands, Philippines **121** B7
Bathurst Island, Nunavut (Canada) **61** B5
Baton Rouge, Louisiana (U.S.) **63** F7
Battambang, Cambodia **121** C2
Bat'umi, Georgia **115** B7
Bawku, Ghana **135** D4
Baydhabo, Somalia **137** D6
Baykonur Cosmodrome, Kazakhstan **110** C2
Beaufort Sea, North America **54** B3
Beaumont, Texas, (U.S.) **63** F7
Béchar, Algeria **133** B4
Beersheba, Israel **115** G4
Beijing, China **113** C7
Beira, Mozambique **139** D7
Beirut, Lebanon **115** F4
Belarus (country), Europe **85** E6
Belaya (river), Russia **99** F7
Belcher Islands, Nunavut (Canada) **61** F7
Beledweyne, Somalia **137** D7
Belém, Brazil **79** C5
Belfast, United Kingdom **93** C2
Belgaum, India **119** E3
Belgium (country), Europe **85** E3
Belgorod, Russia **99** G3
Belgrade, Serbia **97** C4
Belize (country), North America **55** H5
Belize City, Belize **65** E6
Bellingshausen Sea, Antarctica **154** D1
Belmopan, Belize **65** E6
Belo Horizonte, Brazil **79** F6
Bendigo, Australia **149** F6
Bengal, Bay of, Asia **102** F4
Benghazi, Libya **133** B7
Benguela, Angola **138** C1
Beni Abbes, Algeria **133** B4

Benin (country), Africa
135 D5
Benin, Bight of, Africa
135 E5
Bentley Subglacial Trench,
Antarctica 155 E3
Benue (river), Africa 135 E6
Berbera, Somalia 137 C7
Berbérati, Central African
Rep. 137 D1
Berdyans'k, Ukraine 95 F10
Berezniki, Russia 99 D7
Bergen, Norway 91 F2
Bering Sea, Asia/North
America 102 A7
Bering Strait, Asia/North
America 102 A7
Berkner Island, Antarctica
155 C3
Berlin, Germany 93 D6
Bermuda Islands, United
Kingdom 54 F7
Bern, Switzerland 93 F5
Beyla, Guinea 135 E3
Bhopal, India 119 D4
Bhutan (country), Asia
103 F5
Biak (island), Indonesia
123 C10
Bialystok, Poland 95 C5
Bikini Atoll, Marshall Islands
151 C4
Bila Tserkva, Ukraine 95 D7
Bilbao, Spain 93 G3
Billings, Montana (U.S.)
63 B4
Bilma, Niger 135 C7
Biloxi, Mississippi (U.S.)
63 F8
Biltine, Chad 137 B3
Bioko (island), Equatorial
Guinea 135 F6
Birao, Central African Rep.
137 C3
Birjand, Iran 117 C7
Birmingham, Alabama (U.S.)
63 E8
Birmingham, United
Kingdom 93 D3
Bir Mogreïn (Fort Trinquet),
Mauritania 135 A3
Biscay, Bay of, Europe 93 F2
Bishkek, Kyrgyzstan 111 D4
Biskra, Algeria 133 B5
Bismarck, North Dakota
(U.S.) 63 B5
Bismarck Archipelago,
Papua New Guinea 150 D2
Bissagos Islands, Guinea-
Bissau 135 D1
Bissau, Guinea-Bissau
135 D1
Bitola, Macedonia 97 E4
Bizerte, Tunisia 133 A6
Black (river), Vietnam
121 A3
Blackall, Australia 149 D7
Black Sea, Europe/Asia
84 F7
Black Volta (river), Africa
135 D4
Blagoveshchensk, Russia
109 E9
Blanc, Mont, Europe 93 F5
Blantyre, Malawi 139 C7
Blenheim, New Zealand
149 G11
Bloemfontein, South Africa
139 G5
Bluefields, Nicaragua 65 F8

Blue Nile (river), Africa
137 B5
Bo, Sierra Leone 135 E2
Boa Vista, Brazil 79 B3
Bobo Dioulasso, Burkina
Faso 135 D3
Bodø, Norway 91 C4
Bogor, Indonesia 122 D2
Bogotá, Colombia 77 C3
Bohol (island), Philippines
121 D8
Boise, Idaho (U.S.) 62 B3
Boké, Guinea 135 D2
Bolívar, Pico, Venezuela
77 B4
Bolivia (country), South
America 71 D4
Bologna, Italy 93 F6
Boma, Dem. Rep. of the
Congo 137 F1
Bombay, see Mumbai, India
119 E3
Bonaire (island),
Netherlands Antilles
(Netherlands) 67 E5
Bondo, Dem. Rep. of the
Congo 137 D3
Bonin Islands, Japan 150 A2
Bonn, Germany 93 D5
Boothia, Gulf of, Nunavut
(Canada) 61 C5
Boothia Peninsula, Nunavut
(Canada) 61 C5
Bor, South Sudan 137 D4
Borås, Sweden 91 H4
Bordeaux, France 93 F3
Borden Island, Canada
54 B4
Borneo (island), Asia 102 G7
Bornholm (island), Denmark
91 I4
Borroloola, Australia 149 B5
Bosnia and Herzegovina
(country), Europe 85 F4
Bosporus (strait), Turkey
114 B2
Bossangoa, Central African
Rep. 137 D1
Boston, Massachusetts
(U.S.) 63 B11
Bothnia, Gulf of, Europe
91 E6
Botosani, Romania 97 A7
Botswana (country), Africa
127 H5
Bouaké, Côte d'Ivoire 135 E3
Bouar, Central African Rep.
137 D1
Bougainville (island), Papua
New Guinea 150 D3
Boulder, Colorado (U.S.)
63 C4
Boulia, Australia 149 C6
Bourke, Australia 149 E7
Boyoma Falls, Dem. Rep. of
the Congo 137 E3
Brahmaputra (river), Asia
119 C7
Braila, Romania 97 B7
Brasília, Brazil 79 E5
Brasov, Romania 97 B6
Bratislava, Slovakia 94 E2
Bratsk, Russia 109 E7
Brazil (country), South
America 71 D6
Brazilian Highlands, Brazil
79 E5
Brazos (river), Texas (U.S.)
63 E6
Brazzaville, Congo 137 F1

Bremen, Germany 93 C5
Brest, Belarus 95 C5
Brest, France 93 E2
Bridgetown, Barbados 67 D8
Brisbane, Australia 149 D8
Bristol, United Kingdom
93 D3
Bristol Bay, Alaska (U.S.)
54 B1
British Columbia (province),
Canada 60 F2
British Isles, Europe 84 C2
Brittany (region), France
84 E2
Brno, Czech Republic 94 D2
Broken Hill, Australia
149 E6
Brooks Range, Alaska (U.S.)
62 F2
Broome, Australia 148 B3
Brownsville, Texas (U.S.)
63 G6
Brussels, Belgium 93 D4
Bryansk, Russia 99 F3
Bucaramanga, Colombia
77 B3
Buchanan, Liberia 135 E2
Bucharest, Romania 97 C7
Budapest, Hungary 94 F3
Buenos Aires, Argentina
81 E4
Buffalo, New York (U.S.)
63 B9
Bujumbura, Burundi 137 F4
Bukavu, Dem. Rep. of the
Congo 137 E4
Bukhara, Uzbekistan 110 D2
Bulawayo, Zimbabwe 139 E5
Bulgaria (country), Europe
85 G5
Buller (river), New Zealand
149 G10
Bumba, Dem. Rep. of the
Congo 137 E2
Bunbury, Australia 148 E2
Bundaberg, Australia 149 D8
Bunia, Dem. Rep. of the
Congo 137 E4
Bura, Kenya 137 E6
Buraydah, Saudi Arabia
117 E3
Burgas, Bulgaria 97 D7
Burketown, Australia 149 B6
Burkina Faso (country),
Africa 135 D4
Burlington, Vermont (U.S.)
63 B10
Burma (country), see
Myanmar, Asia 103 F5
Burnie, Australia 149 G7
Bursa, Turkey 114 B2
Buru (island), Indonesia
123 D7
Burundi (country), Africa
137 F4
Busan, South Korea 113 D9
Butte, Montana (U.S.) 62 B3
Bydgoszcz, Poland 94 B3
Bytom, Poland 94 D3

C

Cabot Strait, Canada 61 G10
Cádiz, Spain 93 I1
Cagayan de Oro, Philippines
121 D8
Cagliari, Italy 93 H6
Caicos Islands, Turks &
Caicos Islands (U.K.)
67 B4
Cairns, Australia 149 B7

Cairo, Egypt 133 B10
Cajamarca, Peru 77 F2
Calcutta, see Kolkata, India
119 D6
Cali, Colombia 77 C2
Calicut, see Kozhikode, India
119 F3
California (state), U.S. 62 D2
California, Gulf of, Mexico
64 B1
Callao, Peru 77 G2
Camagüey, Cuba 67 C2
Cambodia (country), Asia
103 G6
Cambridge Bay, Nunavut
(Canada) 61 C4
Cameroon (country), Africa
135 E7
Camooweal, Australia
149 C6
Campeche, Mexico 65 E5
Campo Grande, Brazil 79 F4
Canada (country), North
America 55 C3
Canadian Shield, Canada
54 D4
Canary Islands, Spain
132 B1
Canaveral, Cape, Florida
(U.S.) 63 F10
Canberra, Australia 149 F7
Cancún Island, Mexico 65 D6
Cantabrian Mountains, Spain
84 F1
Canterbury Bight, New
Zealand 149 H10
Can Tho, Vietnam 121 D3
Canton, see Guangzhou,
China 113 F7
Cap Barbas (cape), Western
Sahara (Morocco) 132 D1
Cape Breton Island, Nova
Scotia (Canada) 61 G9
Cape Dorset, Nunavut
(Canada) 61 D6
Cape Palmas, Côte d'Ivoire
135 F3
Cape Town, South Africa
138 H3
Caprivi Strip, Namibia
138 D3
Caracas, Venezuela 77 A5
Carbón, Laguna del,
Argentina 81 H2
Cardiff, United Kingdom
93 D3
Caribbean Sea, North
America 54 H6
Carnarvon, Australia 148 D1
Carolina Island, French
Polynesia (France) 151 E8
Caroline Islands, Federated
States of Micronesia
150 D2
Carpathian Mountains,
Europe 84 E5
Carpentaria, Gulf of,
Australia 149 A6
Carson City, Nevada (U.S.)
62 C2
Cartagena, Colombia 77 A2
Cartagena, Spain 93 I3
Cartier Island, Australia
148 A3
Casablanca, Morocco 132 B2
Cascade Range, U.S. 62 B1
Casper, Wyoming (U.S.)
63 C4
Caspian Depression, Europe/
Asia 110 B1

Caspian Sea, Europe/Asia
102 D2
Cassai (river), Africa 138 B3
Castries, St. Lucia 67 D7
Catania, Italy 93 I8
Cat Island, Bahamas 67 B3
Cauca (river), Colombia
77 B2
Caucasus Mountains,
Europe/Asia 115 A7
Cayambe, Ecuador 77 D2
Cayman Islands, United
Kingdom 54 H6
Cebu (island), Philippines
121 D8
Cebu, Philippines 121 D8
Cedar Rapids, Iowa (U.S.)
63 C7
Ceduna, Australia 149 E5
Celebes (island), Indonesia
123 C6
Celebes Sea, Asia 123 B6
Celtic Sea, Europe 93 D2
Central African Republic
(country), Africa 137 D2
Central America, North
America 54 I5
Central Lowland, U.S. 54 F5
Central Lowlands, Australia
142 E3
Central Range, Russia
109 C11
Central Russian Upland,
Russia 99 F3
Central Siberian Plateau,
Russia 109 D7
Ceram (island), Indonesia
123 D8
Ceram Sea, Indonesia
123 C8
Ceuta, Spain 132 A3
Ceylon (country), see Sri
Lanka, Asia 103 G4
Chabahar, Iran 117 E8
Chad (country), Africa
137 B2
Chad, Lake, Africa 135 D7
Chagos Archipelago, British
Indian Ocean Territory,
U.K. 103 H3
Champlain, Lake, U.S.
63 B10
Changchun, China 113 C8
Changsha, China 113 F7
Channel Islands, California
(U.S.) 62 D1
Channel Islands, United
Kingdom 93 E3
Chao Phraya (river),
Thailand 121 C2
Chaozhou, China 113 F8
Chapala, Lake, Mexico 65 D2
Chari (river), Africa 137 C2
Charleston, South Carolina
(U.S.) 63 E10
Charleston, West Virginia
(U.S.) 63 D9
Charleville, Australia 149 D7
Charlotte, North Carolina
(U.S.) 63 D9
Charlottetown, Prince
Edward Island (Canada)
61 G9
Charters Towers, Australia
149 C7
Chatham Island, New
Zealand 142 G6
Chattanooga, Tennessee
(U.S.) 63 E8

Chechnya — Dzhugdzhur Range

Chechnya (region), Russia **99** I5
Chelyabinsk, Russia **108** E3
Chengdu, China **113** E5
Chennai (Madras), India **119** F5
Cherepovets, Russia **99** D4
Cherkasy, Ukraine **95** E8
Chernihiv, Ukraine **95** C8
Chernivtsi, Ukraine **95** E6
Cherskiy Range, Russia **102** B6
Chesapeake Bay, U.S. **63** D11
Cheyenne, Wyoming (U.S.) **63** C4
Chiang Mai, Thailand **121** B2
Chicago, Illinois (U.S.) **63** C8
Chichén Itza (ruins), Mexico **65** D6
Chiclayo, Peru **77** F1
Chicoutimi, Quebec (Canada) **61** G8
Chihuahua, Mexico **65** B2
Chile (country), South America **71** G4
Chiloé Island, Chile **81** G1
Chimborazo (peak), Ecuador **77** D1
Chimbote, Peru **77** F1
China (country), Asia **103** E5
Chinandega, Nicaragua **65** F6
Chingola, Zambia **139** C5
Chios (island), Greece **97** G7
Chirripó, Cerro, Costa Rica **65** G7
Chisasibi, Quebec (Canada) **61** F7
Chisinau, Moldova **95** F7
Chita, Russia **109** F8
Chittagong, Bangladesh **119** F5
Choluteca, Honduras **65** F6
Ch'ongjin, North Korea **113** C9
Chongqing, China **113** E6
Chornobyl', Ukraine **95** D7
Chott Melrhir (dry salt lake), Algeria **133** B5
Choybalsan, Mongolia **111** B9
Christchurch, New Zealand **149** H10
Christmas Island, see Kirimati, Kiribati **151** D7
Chukchi Peninsula, Russia **102** A7
Chukchi Sea, Asia/North America **102** A6
Chuquicamata, Chile **81** B2
Churchill (river), Manitoba (Canada) **61** F5
Churchill, Manitoba (Canada) **61** F5
Cincinnati, Ohio (U.S.) **63** D9
Cirebon, Indonesia **122** D3
Ciudad Bolívar, Venezuela **77** B6
Ciudad del Este, Paraguay **81** B5
Ciudad Guayana, Venezuela **77** B6
Ciudad Juárez, Mexico **65** A2
Ciudad Obregón, Mexico **64** B1
Ciudad Victoria, Mexico **65** D4
Clarence (river), New Zealand **149** G10

Cleveland, Ohio (U.S.) **63** C9
Clipperton (island), France **54** I2
Cloncurry, Australia **149** C6
Cluj-Napoca, Romania **97** B5
Clutha (river), New Zealand **149** I9
Coastal Plain, U.S. **54** G4
Coast Mountains, North America **54** D2
Coast Ranges, U.S. **62** B1
Coats Island, Nunavut (Canada) **61** E6
Coats Land, Antarctica **155** B4
Cobourg Peninsula, Australia **148** A4
Cochabamba, Bolivia **77** H5
Cochin, see Kochi, India **119** G4
Coco (river), North River **65** F7
Cocos Island, Costa Rica **54** I5
Cod, Cape, Massachusetts (U.S.) **54** E6
Coen, Australia **149** B7
Coiba Island, Panama **65** H8
Coimbatore, India **119** G4
Coimbra, Portugal **93** H1
Collier Bay, Australia **148** B3
Colombia (country), South America **71** B3
Colombo, Sri Lanka **119** G4
Colón, Panama **65** G8
Colorado (river), Argentina **81** F3
Colorado (river), U.S. **62** E2
Colorado (state), U.S. **63** D4
Colorado Plateau, U.S. **54** F3
Colorado Springs, Colorado (U.S.) **63** D4
Columbia (river), North America **54** E2
Columbia, South Carolina (U.S.) **63** E9
Columbia Mountains, Canada **54** D2
Columbia Plateau, U.S. **54** E2
Columbus, Georgia (U.S.) **63** E9
Columbus, Ohio (U.S.) **63** C9
Commander Islands, Russia **109** C11
Communism Peak, Tajikistan **111** E4
Comodoro Rivadavia, Argentina **81** G2
Comoros (country), Africa **127** G7
Conakry, Guinea **135** E1
Concepción, Chile **81** E1
Concepción, Paraguay **81** B4
Conception, Point, California (U.S.) **62** D1
Conchos (river), Mexico **65** B2
Concord, New Hampshire (U.S.) **63** B11
Congo (country), Africa **126** E1
Congo (river), Africa **137** F2
Congo Basin, Africa **126** F5
Connecticut (river), U.S. **63** B11
Connecticut (state), U.S. **63** C11
Constanta, Romania **97** C8
Constantine, Algeria **133** A5

Cook, Mount, New Zealand **149** H9
Cook Islands, New Zealand **151** E7
Cook Strait, New Zealand **149** G11
Cooktown, Australia **149** B7
Cooma, Australia **149** F7
Coonamble, Australia **149** E7
Copán (ruins), Honduras **65** F6
Copenhagen, Denmark **91** I3
Coral Sea, Oceania **142** E4
Coral Sea Islands Territory, Australia **149** B8
Córdoba, Argentina **81** D3
Córdoba, Spain **93** I2
Corfu (island), Greece **97** F4
Corinth, Greece **97** G5
Cork, Ireland **93** D2
Coromandel Peninsula, New Zealand **149** E11
Corpus Christi, Texas (U.S.) **63** F6
Corrientes, Argentina **81** C4
Corsica (island), France **93** G6
Costa Rica (country), North America **55** I5
Cotabato, Philippines **121** E8
Côte d'Ivoire (Ivory Coast) (country), Africa **135** E3
Cotonou, Benin **135** E5
Cozumel Island, Mexico **65** D6
Craiova, Romania **97** C6
Crater Lake, Oregon (U.S.) **62** B1
Crete (island), Greece **97** I6
Crete, Sea of, Greece **97** H6
Crimea (region), Ukraine **95** G9
Croatia (country), Europe **85** F4
Croydon, Australia **149** B6
Crozier, Cape, Antarctica **155** F5
Cuando (river), Africa **138** C3
Cuango (river), Africa **138** A2
Cuba (country), North America **55** H6
Cúcuta, Colombia **77** B3
Cuenca, Ecuador **77** E1
Cuiabá, Brazil **79** E4
Culiacán, Mexico **65** C2
Cumaná, Venezuela **77** A5
Cunnamulla, Australia **149** D7
Curaçao (island), Netherlands Antilles (Netherlands) **67** E5
Curitiba, Brazil **79** G5
Cusco, Peru **77** G3
Cyclades (islands), Greece **97** G6
Cyrenaica (region), Libya **133** B8
Czech Republic (country), Europe **85** E4

D

Daegu, South Korea **113** D9
Dakar, Senegal **135** C1
Dalian, China **113** D8
Dallas, Texas (U.S.) **63** E6
Dalmatia (region), Europe **97** C2

Daly Waters, Australia **149** B5
Damascus, Syria **115** F5
Damavand, Mount, Iran **117** B5
Dampier, Australia **148** C2
Dampier Land, Australia **148** B3
Danakil (region), Ethiopia **137** C6
Da Nang, Vietnam **121** C4
Dangrek Range, Thailand **121** C2
Danube (river), Europe **84** F6
Dardanelles (strait), Turkey **114** B1
Dar es Salaam, Tanzania **137** F6
Darfur (region), Sudan **137** C3
Darhad Valley, Mongolia **111** B7
Darhan, Mongolia **111** B8
Darling (river), Australia **149** E6
Darling Range, Australia **142** F1
Darnah, Libya **133** B8
Darnley, Cape, Antarctica **155** C8
Dar Rounga, Central African Rep. **137** C2
Darwin, Australia **148** A4
Dasht-e Kavir (region), Iran **117** C6
Dasht-e Lut (region), Iran **117** C7
Datong, China **113** C7
Daugavpils, Latvia **91** H7
Davao, Philippines **121** E8
David, Panama **65** G7
Davis Strait, Canada **61** C8
Dawei, Myanmar **119** F9
Dawson Creek, British Columbia (Canada) **60** E2
Dayr az Zawr, Syria **115** E6
Dayton, Ohio (U.S.) **63** C9
Dead Sea, Asia **115** G4
Death Valley, California (U.S.) **62** D2
Deccan Plateau, India **119** E4
Dehra Dun, India **119** C4
Delaware (state), U.S. **63** C10
Delhi, India **119** C4
Democratic Republic of the Congo (country), Africa **137** E2
Denizli, Turkey **114** C2
Denmark (country), Europe **85** D4
Denpasar, Indonesia **123** E4
Denver, Colorado (U.S.) **63** C4
Derby, Australia **148** B3
Desē, Ethiopia **137** C6
Des Moines, Iowa (U.S.) **63** C7
Detroit, Michigan (U.S.) **63** C9
Devon Island, Nunavut (Canada) **61** B5
Devonport, Australia **149** G7
Dezful, Iran **117** C4
Dhaka, Bangladesh **119** D7
Dibrugarh, India **119** C8
Dif, Kenya **137** E6
Dijon, France **93** E5
Dili, East Timor **123** E7

Dinaric Alps (range), Europe **97** C3
Dindigul, India **119** G4
Dirē Dawa, Ethiopia **137** C6
District of Columbia, U.S. **63** D11
Diyarbakır, Turkey **115** D6
Djado, Niger **135** B7
Djanet, Algeria **133** D6
Djelfa, Algeria **133** B5
Djibouti (country), Africa **137** C7
Djibouti (city), Djibouti **137** C7
Dnieper (river), Europe **95** F9
Dniester (river), Europe **95** E6
Dniprodzerzhyns'k, Ukraine **95** E9
Dnipropetrovs'k, Ukraine **95** E9
Dobane, Central African Rep. **137** D3
Dodecanese (islands), Greece **97** H7
Dodge City, Kansas (U.S.) **63** D5
Dodoma, Tanzania **135** H3
Doha, Qatar **117** E5
Dolak (island), Indonesia **123** D10
Dolo Bay, Ethiopia **137** D6
Dominica (country), North America **55** H8
Dominican Republic (country), North America **55** H7
Don (river), Russia **99** G4
Donets'k, Ukraine **95** E10
Dongara, Australia **148** E1
Dongbei (region), China **113** B8
Dongola, Sudan **137** A4
Donostia-San Sebastián, Spain **93** G3
Dosso, Niger **135** D5
Douala, Cameroon **135** E6
Douro (river), Portugal **93** G1
Dover, Delaware (U.S.) **63** C10
Dover, Strait of, Europe **93** D4
Drakensberg (range), South Africa **139** G5
Drammen, Norway **91** F3
Drava (river), Europe **84** F5
Dresden, Germany **93** D7
Dubai, United Arab Emirates **117** E6
Dubbo, Australia **149** E7
Dublin, Ireland **93** C2
Dubrovnik, Croatia **97** D3
Ducie Island, United Kingdom **151** F10
Duero (river), Spain **93** G3
Duluth, Minnesota (U.S.) **63** B7
Dunedin, New Zealand **149** I10
Duqm, Oman **117** G7
Durango, Mexico **65** C2
Durban, South Africa **139** G6
Durrës, Albania **97** E4
Dushanbe, Tajikistan **111** E3
Dzhugdzhur Range, Russia **109** D9

E

East Antarctica, Antarctica **155** D7
East Cape, New Zealand **149** E12
East China Sea, Asia **102** E7
Easter Island, *see* Rapa Nui, Chile **151** F11
Eastern Desert, Egypt **133** B10
Eastern Ghats (range), India **119** F4
Eastern Rift Valley, Africa **137** F5
East London, South Africa **139** H5
East Sea, *see* Japan, Sea of, Asia **102** D7
East Siberian Sea, Russia **102** A6
East Timor (country), *see* Timor-Leste, Asia **123** E7
Ebolowa, Cameroon **135** F7
Ebro (river), Spain **93** G3
Ecuador (country), South America **71** C2
Edge Island, Norway **91** A3
Edinburgh, United Kingdom **93** B3
Edmonton, Alberta (Canada) **61** F3
Edward, Lake, Africa **137** E4
Éfaté (island), Vanuatu **151** E4
Egmont, Mount, *see* Taranaki, Mount, N.Z. **149** F11
Egypt (country), Africa **133** C9
Elazığ, Turkey **115** C6
Elbasan, Albania **97** E4
Elbe (river), Europe **93** C6
Elbert, Mount, Colorado (U.S.) **63** D4
El'brus (peak), Russia **99** I4
Elburz Mountains, Iran **117** B5
El Djouf, Mauritania **135** B3
Eleuthera Island, Bahamas **67** B3
El Fasher, Sudan **137** B3
El Gîza, Egypt **133** C9
El Golea, Libya **133** B5
El Khârga, Egypt **133** C9
Ellesmere Island, Nunavut (Canada) **61** A6
Ellsworth Land, Antarctica **155** D2
Ellsworth Mountains, Antarctica **155** D3
El Minya, Egypt **133** C9
El Obeid, Sudan **137** C4
El Paso, Texas (U.S.) **63** E4
El Salvador (country), North America **55** I5
Emerald, Australia **149** C7
Emi Koussi (peak), Chad **137** A2
Empty Quarter, *see* Ar Rub' al Khali, Saudi Arabia **117** G5
Enderby Land, Antarctica **155** B8
Enewetak Atoll, Marshall Islands **150** C3
England (country), United Kingdom **93** D4
English Channel, Europe **93** E3

En Nahud, Sudan **137** C4
Ennedi (range), Chad **137** B3
Enugu, Nigeria **135** E6
Equatorial Guinea (country), Africa **135** F6
Erebus, Mount, Antarctica **155** F5
Eritrea (country), Africa **137** B6
Erg Chech (desert), Algeria **132** D3
Erg Iguidi (desert), Algeria **132** C3
Erie, Pennsylvania (U.S.) **63** C9
Erie, Lake, North America **54** F5
Eromanga, Australia **149** D6
Ertis (river), Kazakhstan **111** B4
Ertix (river), China **111** C6
Erzurum, Turkey **115** C7
Esbjerg, Denmark **91** I2
Eskisehir, Turkey **115** B3
Esperance, Australia **148** E3
Essen, Germany **93** D5
Estonia (country), Europe **85** D5
Ethiopia (country), Africa **137** C6
Ethiopian Highlands (region), Africa **137** C5
Etna (peak), Italy **84** H4
Etosha Pan, Namibia **138** D2
Eucla Basin, Australia **142** F1
Eucla Motel, Australia **148** E4
Eugene, Oregon (U.S.) **62** B1
Eugenia Point, Mexico **54** G2
Euphrates (river), Asia **102** D2
Eureka, California (U.S.) **62** C1
Europa, Île, France **139** E8
Evansville, Indiana (U.S.) **63** D8
Everest, Mount, Asia **102** E4
Everglades, The, Florida (U.S.) **63** G10
Exmouth, Australia **148** C1
Eyl, Somalia **137** C8
Eyre, Lake, Australia **149** D5

F

Fada, Chad **137** B2
Fairbanks, Alaska (U.S.) **62** F3
Faisalabad, Pakistan **119** B3
Falkland Islands (Islas Malvinas), United Kingdom **81** H4
Falun, Sweden **91** F4
Farewell, Cape, Greenland (Denmark) **54** C7
Farewell, Cape, N.Z. **149** F10
Fargo, North Dakota (U.S.) **63** B6
Faroe Islands, Denmark **84** B2
Fars (region), Iran **117** D6
Faya, Chad **137** B1
Federated States of Micronesia (country), Oceania **143** C3
Feilding, New Zealand **149** F11
Feira de Santana, Brazil **79** E7
Fez, Morocco **132** B3

Fezzan (region), Libya **133** C6
Fianarantsoa, Madagascar **139** E10
Fiji Islands (country), Oceania **143** E6
Filchner Ice Shelf, Antarctica **155** C4
Fimbul Ice Shelf, Antarctica **155** A5
Finland (country), Europe **85** C5
Finland, Gulf of, Europe **84** C5
Fitzroy (river), Australia **148** B3
Fitzroy Crossing, Australia **148** B3
Flagstaff, Arizona (U.S.) **62** D3
Flattery, Cape, Washington (U.S.) **62** A1
Flint Island, French Polynesia (France) **151** E7
Florence, Italy **93** G6
Florencia, Colombia **77** C2
Flores (island), Indonesia **123** E6
Flores Sea, Indonesia **123** D6
Florida (state), U.S. **63** F9
Florida, Straits of, North America **54** G6
Florida Keys, Florida (U.S.) **63** G10
Fly (river), Papua New Guinea **150** D2
Formosa, Argentina **81** C4
Forsayth, Australia **149** B7
Fort Albany, Ontario (Canada) **61** F6
Fortaleza, Brazil **79** C7
Fort Collins, Colorado (U.S.) **63** C4
Fort Severn, Ontario (Canada) **61** F6
Fort Smith, Arkansas (U.S.) **63** E7
Fort Smith, Northwest Territories (Canada) **61** E3
Fort Wayne, Indiana (U.S.) **63** C8
Fort Worth, Texas (U.S.) **63** E6
Foveaux Strait, New Zealand **149** I9
Foxe Basin, Nunavut (Canada) **61** C6
Fox Glacier, New Zealand **149** H9
France (country), Europe **85** F2
Franceville, Gabon **135** G7
Frankfort, Kentucky (U.S.) **63** D8
Frankfurt, Germany **93** D5
Franz Josef Glacier, New Zealand **149** H9
Franz Josef Land (islands), Russia **109** B5
Fraser (river), British Columbia (Canada) **60** F2
Fraser Island, Australia **149** D8
Fraser Plateau, Canada **54** D2
Fredericton, New Brunswick (Canada) **61** G9
Freetown, Sierra Leone **135** E1

French Guiana, France **71** B6
French Polynesia (islands), France **151** E8
Fresno, California (U.S.) **62** D2
Frisian Islands, Europe **93** C5
Fua Mulaku (island), Maldives **119** I3
Fuji (peak), Japan **113** C11
Fukuoka, Japan **113** D9
Funafuti, Tuvalu **151** E5
Fundy, Bay of, Canada **61** G9
Furneaux Group (islands), Australia **149** G7
Fushun, China **113** C8
Fuzhou, China **113** F8
Fyn (island), Denmark **91** I3

G

Gaalkacyo (Galcaio), Somalia **137** D7
Gabes, Tunisia **133** B6
Gabes, Gulf of, Tunisia **133** B6
Gabon (country), Africa **135** F7
Gaborone, Botswana **139** F5
Gabras, Sudan **137** C3
Galápagos Islands, Ecuador **70** C1
Galati, Romania **97** B7
Galdhøpiggen (peak), Norway **91** E3
Galilee, Sea of, Israel **115** F4
Gambia (country), Africa **135** D1
Gan (island), Maldives **119** I3
Gäncä, Azerbaijan **115** B8
Ganges (river), Asia **119** C4
Ganges, Mouths of the, Bangladesh **119** D7
Gao, Mali **135** C5
Garagum (desert), Turkmenistan **110** D2
Garonne (river), France **93** F3
Garoua, Cameroon **135** D8
Garoua Boulaï, Cameroon **135** E7
Gary, Indiana (U.S.) **63** C8
Gaspé Peninsula, Quebec (Canada) **61** G9
Gaza, Gaza Strip **115** G4
Gaza Strip, Asia **115** G4
Gaziantep, Turkey **115** D5
Gdansk, Poland **94** B3
Gdynia, Poland **94** B3
Geelong, Australia **149** F6
Geeveston, Australia **149** G7
Gemena, Dem. Rep. of the Congo **137** D2
Gemsa, Egypt **133** C10
General Santos, Philippines **121** E8
Geneva, Switzerland **93** F5
Genoa, Italy **93** F6
Geographe Bay, Australia **148** E2
George Town, Malaysia **121** E1
Georgetown, Guyana **79** A3
Georgia (country), Asia **103** D2
Georgia (state), U.S. **63** E9
Geraldton, Australia **148** E1
Germany (country), Europe **85** E4

Getz Ice Shelf, Antarctica **155** F2
Ghadāmis, Libya **133** C6
Ghana (country), Africa **135** E4
Ghardaïa, Algeria **133** B4
Ghāt, Libya **133** D6
Gibraltar (country), United Kingdom **93** I2
Gibson Desert, Australia **148** C3
Gilbert Islands, Kiribati **151** D4
Gisborne, New Zealand **149** F12
Glacier Bay, Alaska (U.S.) **54** C2
Gladstone, Australia **149** D8
Glåma (river), Norway **91** F3
Glasgow, United Kingdom **93** B3
Glorieuses, Îles, France **139** B10
Goba, Ethiopia **137** D6
Gobi (desert), Asia **102** D6
Godavari (river), India **119** E4
Godthåb, *see* Nuuk, Greenland (Denmark) **55** C6
Godwin Austen (peak), *see* K2, Pakistan **119** A4
Goiânia, Brazil **79** E5
Gold Coast, Africa **135** F4
Gold Coast, Australia **149** D8
Golden Bay, New Zealand **149** F10
Gonabad, Iran **117** C7
Gonder, Ethiopia **137** C5
Gongga Shan (peak), China **102** E5
Good Hope, Cape of, South Africa **138** H3
Goondiwindi, Australia **149** D8
Gorakhpur, India **119** C5
Gorē, Ethiopia **137** D5
Gore, New Zealand **149** I9
Gorgan, Iran **117** B6
Gorontalo, Indonesia **123** C6
Götaland (region), Sweden **91** H4
Göteborg, Sweden **91** H3
Gotland (island), Sweden **91** H5
Goulburn, Australia **149** F7
Goulimine, Morocco **132** B2
Governador Valadares, Brazil **79** F6
Grafton, Australia **149** E8
Grahamstown, South Africa **139** H5
Grain Coast, Africa **135** E2
Granada, Nicaragua **65** F7
Gran Chaco (region), South America **81** B3
Grand Bahama Island, Bahamas **67** A2
Grand Canal (river), China **113** D7
Grand Canyon, Arizona (U.S.) **62** D3
Grand Cayman (island), Cayman Islands (U.K.) **67** C2
Grand Junction, Colorado (U.S.) **63** C4
Grand Rapids, Michigan (U.S.) **63** C8
Graz, Austria **93** E7

BACK OF THE BOOK

Great Artesian Basin — Jambi

Great Artesian Basin, Australia **149** D6
Great Australian Bight, Australia **148** E4
Great Barrier Island, New Zealand **149** D11
Great Barrier Reef, Australia **149** B7
Great Basin, U.S. **62** C2
Great Bear Lake, Northwest Territories (Canada) **61** C3
Great Britain (island), United Kingdom **93** C3
Great Dividing Range, Australia **149** C7
Great Eastern Erg (dunes), Algeria **133** C5
Great Falls, Montana (U.S.) **63** A4
Great Inagua Island, Bahamas **67** C4
Great Indian Desert, Asia **119** C3
Great Karroo (range), South Africa **139** H4
Great Plains, North America **54** E3
Great Rift Valley, Africa **126** F6
Great Salt Lake, Utah (U.S.) **62** C3
Great Sandy Desert, Australia **148** C3
Great Slave Lake, Northwest Territories (Canada) **61** D3
Great Victoria Desert, Australia **148** D4
Great Western Erg (dunes), Algeria **133** C4
Great Zimbabwe (ruins), Zimbabwe **139** E6
Greater Antilles (islands), North America **67** C2
Greater Khingan Range, China **113** B7
Greater Sunda Islands, Indonesia **123** D4
Greece (country), Europe **85** G5
Green Bay, Wisconsin (U.S.) **63** B8
Greenland (Kalaallit Nunaat), Denmark **55** A6
Greenland Sea, Atlantic Ocean **54** A6
Greensboro, North Carolina (U.S.) **63** D10
Greenville, Liberia **135** E2
Grenada (country), North America **55** H8
Greymouth, New Zealand **149** G10
Grijalva (river), Mexico **65** E5
Groote Eylandt (island), Australia **149** A5
Groznyy, Russia **99** I5
Guadalajara, Mexico **65** D2
Guadalcanal (island), Solomon Islands **150** E3
Guadalupe Island, Mexico **54** G2
Guadeloupe (island), France **67** C7
Guadiana (river), Europe **93** H2
Guam (island), U.S. **150** C2
Guangzhou (Canton), China **113** F7
Guantánamo, Cuba **67** C3

Guaporé (river), South America **77** G5
Guatemala (country), North America **55** H5
Guayaquil, Ecuador **77** D1
Guiana Highlands, South America **70** B5
Guilin, China **113** F6
Guinea (country), Africa **135** D2
Guinea-Bissau (country), Africa **135** D2
Guinea, Gulf of, Africa **135** F4
Guiyang, China **135** F6
Gujranwala, Pakistan **119** B3
Gulu, Uganda **137** D5
Gunnbjørn (peak), Greenland (Denmark) **54** B6
Guntur, India **119** E5
Gusau, Nigeria **135** D6
Guyana (country), South America **71** A5
Gwalior, India **119** C4
Gwangju, South Korea **113** D9
Gwardafuy, Cape, Somalia **137** C8
Gyor, Hungary **94** E2
Gyumri, Armenia **115** B8

H
Haast, New Zealand **149** H9
Hadramawt (region), Yemen **117** H5
Haifa, Israel **115** F4
Haig, Australia **148** E3
Haikou, China **113** G6
Ha'il, Saudi Arabia **117** E3
Hailar, China **113** B7
Hainan (island), China **113** G6
Haines Junction, Yukon (Canada) **60** D1
Haiphong, Vietnam **121** B3
Haiti (country), North America **55** H7
Halab (Aleppo), Syria **115** D5
Halayeb, Egypt **133** D11
Halifax, Nova Scotia (Canada) **61** G9
Halls Creek, Australia **148** B4
Halmahera (island), Indonesia **123** C8
Hamada de Tinrhert (plateau), Africa **133** C5
Hamadan, Iran **117** C4
Hamath, Syria **115** E5
Hamburg, Germany **93** C6
Hami, China **113** C4
Hamilton, New Zealand **149** E11
Hamilton, Ontario (Canada) **61** H7
Hammerfest, Norway **91** A6
Hangayn Mountains, Mongolia **111** C8
Hangzhou, China **113** E8
Hannover, Germany **93** D6
Hanoi, Vietnam **121** B3
Happy Valley-Goose Bay, Newfoundland & Labrador (Canada) **61** F9
Harare, Zimbabwe **139** D6
Harbin, China **113** B8
Hargeysa, Somalia **137** C7
Harirud (river), Asia **119** A2
Harper, Liberia **135** F3

Harrisburg, Pennsylvania (U.S.) **63** C10
Hartford, Connecticut (U.S.) **63** C11
Hastings, New Zealand **149** F12
Hatay (Antioch), Turkey **115** D4
Hatteras, Cape, North Carolina (U.S.) **63** D11
Hat Yai, Thailand **121** D1
Haugesund, Norway **91** F2
Hauraki Gulf, New Zealand **149** E11
Havana, Cuba **67** B1
Hawai'i (island), Hawai'i (U.S.) **63** G5
Hawai'i (state), U.S. **63** G4
Hawaiian Islands, U.S. **142** A7
Hawf, Yemen **117** G6
Hawke Bay, New Zealand **149** F12
Hayes Peninsula, Greenland (Denmark) **54** B5
Hay River, Northwest Territories (Canada) **61** E3
Hefei, China **113** E7
Heilong Jiang (Amur) (river), Asia **113** A8
Helena, Montana (U.S.) **62** B3
Helmand (river), Afghanistan **118** B1
Helsingborg, Sweden **91** H3
Helsinki, Finland **91** F7
Henderson Island, United Kingdom **151** F9
Hengyang, China **113** F7
Herat, Afghanistan **118** A1
Herlen (river), Mongolia **111** B9
Hermosillo, Mexico **64** B1
Highlands, United Kingdom **84** C2
High Plains, U.S. **54** F3
Hiiumaa (island), Estonia **91** G6
Hilalaye, Somalia **137** D8
Hilo, Hawai'i (U.S.) **63** G5
Himalaya (range), Asia **102** E4
Hindu Kush (range), Asia **119** A3
Hiroshima, Japan **113** D10
Hispaniola (island), North America **67** C4
Hobart, Australia **149** G7
Ho Chi Minh City (Saigon), Vietnam **121** D3
Höfn, Iceland **85** B2
Hofuf, Saudi Arabia **117** E5
Hohhot, China **113** C6
Hokitika, New Zealand **149** G10
Hokkaido (island), Japan **113** B11
Homs, Syria **115** E5
Homyel', Belarus **95** C7
Honduras (country), North America **55** H5
Hong Kong, China **113** G7
Hongshui (river), China **113** F6
Honiara, Solomon Island **150** E3
Honolulu, Hawai'i (U.S.) **63** G4
Honshu (island), Japan **113** C11

Hopetoun, Australia **148** E3
Horlivka, Ukraine **95** E10
Hormuz, Strait of, Asia **117** E6
Horn, Cape, Chile **70** I5
Hotan, China **112** D2
Houston, Texas (U.S.) **63** F6
Hovd, Mongolia **111** C6
Howland Island, U.S. **151** D5
Hrodna, Belarus **95** B5
Huambo, Angola **138** C2
Huancayo, Peru **77** G2
Huánuco, Peru **77** F2
Huascarán, Nevado, Peru **77** F2
Hubli, India **119** F3
Hudson Bay, Canada **61** E6
Hudson Strait, Canada **61** D7
Hue, Vietnam **121** C3
Hughenden, Australia **149** C7
Hungary (country), Europe **85** F5
Hūn, Libya **133** C7
Huntsville, Alabama (U.S.) **63** E8
Huron, Lake, North America **54** E5
Hustai National Park, Mongolia **111** C8
Hyderabad, India **119** E4
Hyderabad, Pakistan **119** C2

I
Iasi, Romania **97** A7
Ibadan, Nigeria **135** E5
Ibagué, Colombia **77** C2
Iberian Peninsula, Europe **84** F1
Ica, Peru **77** G2
Icel (Mersin), Turkey **115** D4
Iceland (country), Europe **85** B2
Idaho (state), U.S. **62** B3
Idaho Falls, Idaho (U.S.) **62** B3
Ife, Nigeria **135** E6
Iferouâne, Niger **135** C6
Igloolik, Nunavut (Canada) **61** C6
Iguazú Falls, South America **70** E6
Iguéla, Gabon **135** G6
Ikaría (island), Greece **97** G7
Illinois (state), U.S. **63** C7
Illizi, Algeria **133** C6
Iloilo, Philippines **121** D7
Īmī, Ethiopia **137** D6
Imperatriz, Brazil **79** C5
Imphal, India **119** D8
I-n-Amenas, Algeria **133** C5
Incheon, South Korea **113** D9
India (country), Asia **103** F4
Indiana (state), U.S. **63** C8
Indianapolis, Indiana (U.S.) **63** C8
Indonesia (country), Asia **103** H6
Indore, India **119** D4
Indus (river), Asia **119** C2
Indus, Mouths of the, Pakistan **119** D2
Ingal, Niger **135** C6
Inhambane, Mozambique **139** E7
Inland Niger Delta, Mali **135** C4
Inongo, Dem. Rep. of the Congo **137** E2

Inner Hebrides (islands), United Kingdom **93** B2
Inner Mongolia, China **113** C6
Innisfail, Australia **149** B7
Innsbruck, Austria **93** E6
I-n-Salah, Algeria **133** C5
Inscription, Cape, Australia **148** D1
International Falls, Minnesota (U.S.) **63** A7
Inuvik, Northwest Territories (Canada) **60** C2
Invercargill, New Zealand **149** I9
Inverness, United Kingdom **85** C2
Ionian Islands, Greece **97** G4
Ionian Sea, Europe **84** G5
Iowa (state), U.S. **63** C7
Iqaluit, Nunavut (Canada) **61** D7
Iquique, Chile **81** A1
Iquitos, Peru **77** E3
Iráklio, Greece **97** H6
Iran (country), Asia **103** E2
Iraq (country), Asia **103** D2
Ireland (island), Europe **85** D2
Ireland (country), Europe **85** D2
Irian Jaya (province), Indonesia **123** C10
Iringa, Tanzania **137** F5
Irish Sea, Europe **84** D2
Irkutsk, Russia **109** F7
Iron Gate Dam, Europe **97** C5
Irrawaddy (river), Myanmar **119** D8
Irtysh (river), Russia **109** E4
Ísafjördur, Iceland **85** A2
Isfahan, Iran **117** C5
Isiro (Paulis), Dem. Rep. of the Congo **137** D3
Iskenderun, Turkey **115** D5
Islamabad, Pakistan **119** B3
Israel (country), Asia **103** D1
Istanbul, Turkey **114** B2
Italy (country), Europe **85** G4
Ivalo, Finland **85** B5
Ivanovo, Russia **99** E4
Ivory Coast (country), see Côte d'Ivoire, Africa **135** F3
Ivujivik, Quebec (Canada) **61** D6
Izhevsk, Russia **99** E6
Izmir, Turkey **114** C1
Izmit, see Kocaeli, Turkey **114** B2

J
Jabalpur, India **119** D4
Jabal Tuwayq (region), Saudi Arabia **117** G4
Jackson, Mississippi (U.S.) **63** E7
Jackson, Mount, Antarctica **155** C2
Jackson Head (cape), New Zealand **149** H9
Jacksonville, Florida (U.S.) **63** F9
Jaffna, Sri Lanka **119** G4
Jaipur, India **119** C4
Jakarta, Indonesia **122** D2
Jamaica (country), North America **55** H6
Jambi, Indonesia **122** C2

James Bay, Canada **61** F6
Jammu, India **119** B4
Jamnagar, India **119** D2
Jamshedpur, India **119** D6
Jan Mayen (island), Norway **84** A3
Japan (country), Asia **103** D8
Japan, Sea of, (East Sea), Asia **102** D7
Jarvis Island, U.S. **151** D7
Java (island), Indonesia **122** D3
Java Sea, Indonesia **123** D4
Jayapura, Indonesia **123** C11
Jebel Marra (peak), Sudan **137** B3
Jebel Toubkal (peak), Morocco **132** B2
Jeddah, Saudi Arabia **117** F2
Jefferson City, Missouri (U.S.) **63** D7
Jelgava, Latvia **91** H7
Jerba Island, Tunisia **133** B6
Jerusalem, Israel **115** G4
Jilin, China **113** B8
Jinan, China **113** D7
Jinja, Uganda **137** E5
Jizan, Saudi Arabia **117** G3
João Pessoa, Brazil **79** D8
Jodhpur, India **119** C3
Joensuu, Finland **91** E8
Johannesburg, South Africa **139** F5
Johnston Atoll, U.S. **151** B6
Johor Baharu, Malaysia **121** F2
Joinvile, Brazil **79** G5
Joinville Island, Antarctica **154** B1
Jönköping, Sweden **91** H4
Jordan (country), Asia **103** D1
Jordan (river), Asia **115** F4
Jos, Nigeria **135** D6
Joseph Bonaparte Gulf, Australia **148** A4
Juan De Nova (island), France **139** D9
Juan Fernández Islands, Chile **70** G3
Juazeiro, Brazil **79** D7
Juba, South Sudan **137** D5
Juiz de Fora, Brazil **79** F6
Juneau, Alaska (U.S.) **62** G3
Juruena (river), Brazil **79** D3
Jutland (region), Denmark **91** H2
Jyväskylä, Finland **91** E7

K

K2 (Godwin Austen) (peak), Pakistan **119** A4
Kaambooni, Somalia **137** E6
Kabala, Sierra Leone **135** D2
Kabul, Afghanistan **119** B2
Kabwe, Zambia **139** C5
Kadugli, Sudan **137** C4
Kaduna, Nigeria **135** D6
Kaédi, Mauritania **135** C2
Kafia Kingi, South Sudan **137** C3
Kahemba, Dem. Rep. of the Congo **137** F2
Kahoʻolawe (island), Hawaiʻi (U.S.) **63** G4
Kaifeng, China **113** D7
Kaikoura, New Zealand **149** G11
Kaipara Harbour, New Zealand **149** E11

Kaitaia, New Zealand **149** D10
Kalaallit Nunaat, *see* Greenland (Denmark) **55** A6
Kalahari Desert, Africa **139** E4
Kalamáta, Greece **85** H5
Kalemie, Dem. Rep. of the Congo **137** F4
Kalgoorlie, Australia **148** E3
Kaliningrad (region), Russia **99** E1
Kalisz, Poland **94** C3
Kaluga, Russia **99** F4
Kama (river), Russia **99** E7
Kamchatka Peninsula, Russia **109** C11
Kamina, Dem. Rep. of the Congo **137** G3
Kampala, Uganda **137** E4
Kamʼyanetsʼ-Podilʼsʼkyy, Ukraine **95** E6
Kananga, Dem. Rep. of the Congo **137** F2
Kandahar, Afghanistan **119** B2
Kandi, Benin **135** D5
Kandy, Sri Lanka **119** G5
Kangaroo Island, Australia **149** F5
Kanin Peninsula, Russia **99** B5
Kankan, Guinea **135** D2
Kano, Nigeria **135** D7
Kanpur, India **119** C5
Kansas (state), U.S. **63** D6
Kansas City, Missouri (U.S.) **63** D7
Kansk, Russia **109** E6
Kanye, Botswana **139** F4
Kaohsiung, Taiwan **113** F8
Kaokoland (region), Namibia **138** D1
Kaolack, Senegal **135** D1
Kapingamarangi Atoll, Federated States of Micronesia **150** D3
Karachi, Pakistan **119** C2
Karakoram Range, Asia **119** B4
Kara Sea, Russia **102** B4
Karbala, Iraq **117** C3
Kariba, Lake, Africa **139** D5
Karlstad, Sweden **91** G4
Karumba, Australia **149** B6
Kasai (river), Africa **137** F2
Kasakh Uplands, Kazakhstan **111** C4
Kashan, Iran **117** C5
Kashi, China **112** C1
Kashmir (region), Asia **103** E4
Kasongo, Dem. Rep. of the Congo **137** F3
Katanga Plateau, Africa **126** G5
Kathmandu, Nepal **119** C6
Katsina, Nigeria **135** D6
Kattegat (strait), Europe **91** H3
Kauaʻi (island), Hawaiʻi (U.S.) **63** F4
Kaunas, Lithuania **91** I7
Kávala, Greece **97** E6
Kayes, Mali **135** D2
Kayseri, Turkey **115** C4
Kazakhstan (country), Asia **103** D3
Kazanʼ, Russia **99** E6

Kebnekaise (peak), Sweden **91** B5
Kédougou, Senegal **135** D2
Keflavík, Iceland **91** A1
Kemʼ, Russia **85** B6
Kemerovo, Russia **109** E5
Kemi, Finland **91** C6
Kenai Peninsula, Alaska (U.S.) **54** C1
Kentucky (state), U.S. **63** D8
Kenya (country), Africa **137** E5
Kenya (peak), Mount, Kenya **137** E6
Kerch, Ukraine **95** G10
Kerikeri, New Zealand **149** D11
Kermadec Islands, New Zealand **151** F5
Kerman, Iran **117** D7
Kermanshah, Iran **117** C4
Khabarovsk, Russia **109** E10
Khaluf, Oman **117** F7
Khamis Mushayt, Saudi Arabia **117** G3
Kharkiv, Ukraine **95** D9
Khartoum, Sudan **137** B5
Khartoum North, Sudan **137** B5
Kherson, Ukraine **95** F8
Khmelʼnytsʼkyy, Ukraine **95** E6
Khorasan (region), Asia **117** C7
Khulna, Bangladesh **119** D7
Khvoy, Iran **117** B4
Kiel, Germany **93** C6
Kielce, Poland **95** D4
Kiev, Ukraine **95** D7
Kiffa, Mauritania **135** C2
Kigali, Rwanda **137** E4
Kigoma, Tanzania **137** F4
Kilimanjaro (peak), Tanzania **137** E6
Kilwa Kivinje, Tanzania **137** G6
Kimberley, South Africa **139** G4
Kimberley Plateau, Australia **142** E2
Kindia, Guinea **135** D2
Kindu, Dem. Rep. of the Congo **137** F3
Kingaroy, Australia **149** D8
King Island, Australia **149** G6
King Sound, Australia **148** B3
King William Island, Nunavut (Canada) **61** C5
Kingman Reef, U.S. **151** C6
Kingston, Jamaica **67** C3
Kingston, Ontario (Canada) **61** H7
Kingston upon Hull, United Kingdom **93** C4
Kingstown, St. Vincent & the Grenadines **67** D7
Kinshasa, Dem. Rep. of the Congo **137** F1
Kiribati (country), Oceania **143** D7
Kiritimati (Christmas Island), Kiribati **151** D7
Kirkenes, Norway **85** A6
Kirkuk, Iraq **117** C3
Kirov, Russia **99** D6
Kirovohrad, Ukraine **95** E8
Kirovsk, Russia **85** B6
Kiruna, Sweden **91** B5

Kisangani, Dem. Rep. of the Congo **137** E3
Kismaayo, Somalia **137** E6
Kisumu, Kenya **137** E5
Kitakyushu, Japan **113** D10
Kitwe, Zambia **139** C5
Kivu, Lake, Africa **137** E4
Kızılırmak (river), Turkey **115** B4
Klaipeda, Lithuania **91** I6
Klarälven (river), Europe **91** F4
Klerksdorp, South Africa **139** F5
Knoxville, Tennessee (U.S.) **63** D9
Knud Rasmussen Land, Greenland (Denmark) **54** A5
Kobe, Japan **113** D10
Kocaeli (Izmit), Turkey **114** B2
Kochi (Cochin), India **119** G4
Kodiak Island, Alaska (U.S.) **54** C1
Kökshetau, Kazakhstan **111** B4
Kola Peninsula, Russia **99** B4
Kolguyev Island, Russia **99** A5
Kolhapur, India **119** E3
Kolkata (Calcutta), India **119** D6
Köln, Germany **93** D5
Kolwezi, Dem. Rep. of the Congo **137** G3
Kolyma (river), Russia **109** B9
Kolyma Range, Russia **109** C10
Kôm Ombo, Egypt **133** C10
Komsomolʼsk na Amure, Russia **109** E10
Konya, Turkey **115** C3
Kópavogur, Iceland **91** A1
Korhogo, Côte dʼIvoire **135** E3
Koro Toro, Chad **137** B2
Kosciuszko, Mount, Australia **149** F7
Kosice, Slovakia **95** E4
Kosovo (country), Europe **97** D4
Kosti, Sudan **137** C4
Kostroma, Russia **99** E4
Koszalin, Poland **94** B2
Kota Baharu, Malaysia **121** E2
Kota Kinabalu, Malaysia **121** E5
Kotka, Finland **91** F7
Kozhikode (Calicut), India **119** G3
Kra, Isthmus of, Asia **119** F9
Kragujevac, Serbia **97** C4
Kraków, Poland **94** D3
Kramatorsʼk, Ukraine **95** E10
Krasnodar, Russia **99** H4
Krasnoyarsk, Russia **109** E6
Kremenchuk, Ukraine **95** E8
Krishna (river), India **119** E4
Kristiansand, Norway **91** G2
Kroonstad, South Africa **139** F5
Kryvyy Rih, Ukraine **95** E8
Kuala Lumpur, Malaysia **121** E2

Kuala Terengganu, Malaysia **121** E2
Kuching, Malaysia **121** F4
Kugluktuk, Nunavut (Canada) **61** C3
Kumasi, Ghana **135** E4
Kunlun Shan (range), China **112** D2
Kunming, China **113** F5
Kuopio, Finland **91** E7
Kupang, Indonesia **123** E6
Kura (river), Asia **115** B8
Kurdistan (region), Asia **117** B3
Kurgan, Russia **109** E4
Kuril Islands, Russia **102** C8
Kursk, Russia **99** F3
Kuskokwim (river), Alaska (U.S.) **54** B1
Kuujjuaq, Quebec (Canada) **61** E8
Kuwait (country), Asia **103** E2
Kuwait, Kuwait **117** D4
Kuzey Anadolu Daglari (range), Turkey **115** B5
Kwango (river), Africa **137** F2
Kyoto, Japan **113** C10
Kyrgyzstan (country), Asia **103** D4
Kyushu (island), Japan **113** D10

L

Laayoune, Western Sahara (Morocco) **132** C1
Labé, Guinea **135** D2
Labrador (region), Newfoundland & Labrador (Canada) **61** E9
Labrador Sea, North America **54** C6
Laccadive Sea, Asia **102** G3
La Ceiba, Honduras **65** F6
Ladoga, Lake, Russia **99** D3
La Esmeralda, Paraguay **81** B3
Laghouat, Algeria **133** B4
Lagos, Nigeria **135** E6
Lagrange, Australia **148** B2
Lahij, Yemen **117** H3
Lahore, Pakistan **119** B3
Lahti, Finland **91** F7
Lake Region, Finland **91** E7
Lakshadweep (islands), India **119** G3
Lamu, Kenya **137** E6
Lanaʼi (island), Hawaiʻi (U.S.) **63** G4
LʼAnse aux Meadows, Newfoundland & Labrador (Canada) **61** F9
Lansing, Michigan (U.S.) **63** C8
Lanzhou, China **113** D5
Laoag, Philippines **121** B7
Laos (country), Asia **103** F6
La Paz, Bolivia **77** H4
La Paz, Mexico **64** C1
Lapland (region), Europe **91** B6
La Plata, Argentina **81** E4
Lappeenranta, Finland **91** F8
Laptev Sea, Russia **102** B5
Laramie, Wyoming (U.S.) **63** C4
Laredo, Texas (U.S.) **63** G5
Lárissa, Greece **97** F5
La Rochelle, France **85** F2

Larsen Ice Shelf — Mek'elē

Larsen Ice Shelf, Antarctica **154** B1
La Serena, Chile **81** D1
Las Vegas, Nevada (U.S.) **62** D2
Latakia, Syria **115** E4
Latvia (country), Europe **85** D5
Launceston, Australia **149** G7
Laurentide Scarp, Canada **54** D6
Lausanne, Switzerland **93** F5
Laverton, Australia **148** D3
Lebanon (country), Asia **103** D1
Leeds, United Kingdom **93** C3
Leeuwin, Cape, Australia **148** F2
Leeward Islands, North America **67** C8
Legnica, Poland **94** C2
Le Havre, France **93** E3
Leipzig, Germany **93** D6
Lena (river), Russia **109** C7
León, Mexico **65** D3
León, Nicaragua **65** F6
Ler, South Sudan **137** C4
Lerwick, United Kingdom **85** C3
Lesbos (Mitilíni) (island), Greece **97** F7
Lesotho (country), Africa **127** H5
Lesser Antilles (islands), North America **67** D6
Lesser Sunda Islands, Asia **123** E5
Lethbridge, Alberta (Canada) **61** G3
Leveque, Cape, Australia **148** B3
Levin, New Zealand **149** F11
Lewiston, Idaho (U.S.) **62** B3
Leyte (island), Philippines **121** D8
Lhasa, China **112** E3
Liberec, Czech Republic **94** D2
Liberia (country), Africa **135** E3
Libreville, Gabon **135** F6
Libya (country), Africa **133** C7
Libyan Desert, Africa **126** C5
Liechtenstein (country), Europe **85** F3
Liepaja, Latvia **91** H6
Ligurian Sea, Europe **93** G6
Likasi, Dem. Rep. of the Congo **137** G4
Lille, France **93** D4
Lilongwe, Malawi **139** C7
Lima, Peru **77** G2
Limerick, Ireland **93** C2
Límnos (island), Greece **97** F6
Limoges, France **85** F2
Limpopo (river), Africa **139** E6
Lincoln, Nebraska (U.S.) **63** C6
Lincoln Sea, North America **54** A5
Lindi, Tanzania **137** G6
Line Islands, Kiribati **151** D7
Linköping, Sweden **91** G4
Linz, Austria **85** F4

Lipetsk, Russia **99** F4
Lisbon, Portugal **93** H1
Lismore, Australia **149** E8
Lithuania (country), Europe **85** D5
Little Cayman (island), United Kingdom **67** C2
Little Rock, Arkansas (U.S.) **63** E7
Liverpool, United Kingdom **93** C3
Livingstone, Zambia **139** D5
Ljubljana, Slovenia **97** B2
Ljusnan (river), Sweden **91** F4
Llanos (region), South America **77** B4
Lobamba, Swaziland **139** F6
Lobito, Angola **138** C1
Łódz, Poland **94** C3
Lofoten (islands), Norway **91** B4
Logan, Mount, Yukon (Canada) **60** D1
Loire (river), France **93** E3
Lokitaung, Kenya **137** D5
Lomami (river), Democratic Republic of the Congo **137** F6
Lombok (island), Indonesia **123** E5
Lomé, Togo **135** E5
London, Ontario (Canada) **61** H7
London, United Kingdom **93** D3
Londonderry, United Kingdom **93** C2
Londrina, Brazil **79** G5
Long Beach, California (U.S.) **62** E2
Long Island, Bahamas **67** B3
Long Island, New York (U.S.) **63** C11
Long Xuyen, Vietnam **121** D3
Longyearbyen, Norway **91** A3
Lopez, Cap, (cape), Gabon **135** F6
Lop Nur (lake), China **112** C3
Lord Howe Island, Australia **142** F4
Los Angeles, California (U.S.) **62** D2
Louangphrabang, Laos **121** B2
Louisiana (state), U.S. **63** F7
Louisville, Kentucky (U.S.) **63** D8
Lower Guinea (region), Africa **126** F4
Lower Hutt, New Zealand **149** G11
Luanda, Angola **138** B1
Lubango, Angola **138** C1
Lubbock, Texas (U.S.) **63** E5
Lublin, Poland **95** D4
Lubumbashi, Dem. Rep. of the Congo **137** G3
Lucknow, India **119** C5
Ludhiana, India **119** B4
Luhans'k, Ukraine **95** E11
Luleå, Sweden **91** D6
Luoyang, China **113** D7
Lusaka, Zambia **139** C5
Luts'k, Ukraine **95** D5
Lützow-Holm Bay, Antarctica **155** A7
Luxembourg (country), Europe **85** E3

Luxembourg, Luxembourg **93** E5
Luxor, Egypt **133** C10
Luzhou, China **113** F5
Luzon (island), Philippines **121** C7
L'viv, Ukraine **95** D5
Lyon, France **93** F5
Lyttelton, New Zealand **149** H10

M

Macapá, Brazil **79** B5
Macau, China **113** G7
Macdonnell Ranges, Australia **148** C4
Macedonia (country), Europe **85** G5
Maceió, Brazil **79** D8
Machala, Ecuador **77** E1
Machu Picchu (ruins), Peru **77** G3
Mackay, Australia **149** C8
Mackenzie (river), Northwest Territories (Canada) **61** D3
Mackenzie King Island, Canada **54** B4
Mackenzie Mountains, Canada **60** D2
Macon, Georgia (U.S.) **63** E9
Madagascar (country), Africa **127** H7
Madeira (river), Brazil **79** C3
Madeira Islands, Portugal **132** A1
Madison, Wisconsin (U.S.) **63** C7
Madras, see Chennai, India **119** F5
Madre de Dios (river), Bolivia **77** G4
Madrid, Spain **93** H2
Madurai, India **119** G4
Magadan, Russia **109** C10
Magdalena (river), Colombia **77** B3
Magdeburg, Germany **93** D6
Magellan, Strait of, Chile **81** I2
Magnitogorsk, Russia **99** F7
Mahajanga, Madagascar **139** C10
Mahia Peninsula, New Zealand **149** F12
Mahilyow, Belarus **95** B7
Maiduguri, Nigeria **135** D7
Maine (state), U.S. **63** A11
Maine, Gulf of, U.S. **54** E6
Majī, Ethiopia **137** D5
Majorca (island), Spain **93** H4
Majuro, Marshall Islands **151** C4
Makassar, Indonesia **123** D5
Makassar Strait, Indonesia **123** C5
Makgadikgadi Pans, Botswana **139** E4
Makhachkala, Russia **99** I6
Makiyivka, Ukraine **95** E10
Makokou, Gabon **135** F7
Makurdi, Nigeria **135** E6
Malabo, Equatorial Guinea **135** F6
Malacca, Malaysia **121** E2
Malacca, Strait of, Asia **122** B1
Málaga, Spain **93** I2
Malakal, South Sudan **137** C4

Malang, Indonesia **123** E4
Malanje, Angola **138** B2
Mälaren (lake), Sweden **91** G5
Malatya, Turkey **115** C5
Malawi (country), Africa **127** G6
Malawi, Lake (Lake Nyasa), Africa **137** G5
Malay Peninsula, Asia **102** G5
Malaysia (country), Asia **103** G6
Malden Island, Kiribati **151** D7
Maldive Islands, Maldives **119** H3
Maldives (country), Asia **103** G3
Male, Maldives **119** H3
Mali (country), Africa **135** D4
Malindi, Kenya **137** F6
Malmö, Sweden **91** I3
Malpelo Island, Colombia **70** B2
Malta (country), Europe **93** I7
Malvinas, Islas, see Falkland Islands, U.K. **81** H4
Mamoré (river), Bolivia **77** H5
Manado, Indonesia **123** C7
Managua, Nicaragua **65** F6
Manama, Bahrain **117** E5
Manaus, Brazil **79** C3
Manchester, United Kingdom **93** C3
Manchurian Plain, China **113** B8
Mandalay, Myanmar **119** D8
Mangalore, India **119** F3
Mangolian Plateau, Mongolia **111** C9
Manicouagan, Réservoir, Quebec (Canada) **61** G4
Manila, Philippines **121** C7
Manitoba (province), Canada **61** F5
Manitoba, Lake, Manitoba (Canada) **61** G4
Mannheim, Germany **93** E5
Manukau, New Zealand **149** E11
Mao, Chad **137** B1
Maoke Mountains, Indonesia **123** C10
Maputo, Mozambique **139** F6
Marabá, Brazil **79** C5
Maracaibo, Venezuela **77** A3
Maracaibo, Lake, Venezuela **70** A3
Maradi, Niger **135** D6
Marajó Island, Brazil **79** C5
Maralal, Kenya **137** E6
Marañón (river), Peru **77** E2
Marble Bar, Australia **148** C2
Marcus (island), see Minami Tori Shima, Japan **150** B3
Mar del Plata, Argentina **81** E4
Mariana Islands, Oceania **142** B3
Maribor, Slovenia **97** B2
Maridi, South Sudan **137** D4
Marie Byrd Land, Antarctica **155** E3
Marie-Galante (island), Guadeloupe (France) **67** C7

Mariupol', Ukraine **95** F10
Marka, Somalia **137** E7
Marmara, Sea of, Turkey **114** B2
Maromokotro (peak), Madagascar **139** C11
Maroua, Cameroon **135** D8
Marquesas Islands, French Polynesia (France) **151** E8
Marquette, Michigan (U.S.) **63** B8
Marrakech, Morocco **132** B2
Marree, Australia **149** D5
Marseille, France **93** G5
Marshall Islands (country), Oceania **143** C5
Martinique (island), France **67** D7
Mary, Turkmenistan **110** E2
Maryborough, Australia **149** D8
Maryland (state), U.S. **63** C10
Marzūq, Libya **133** C7
Maseru, Lesotho **139** G5
Mashhad, Iran **117** B7
Masira (island), Oman **117** F7
Massachusetts (state), U.S. **63** B11
Massif Central, France **93** F4
Masterton, New Zealand **149** G11
Matamoros, Mexico **65** C4
Matterhorn (peak), Europe **93** F5
Maui (island), Hawai'i (U.S.) **63** G5
Mauritania (country, Africa **135** C2
Mauritius (country), Africa **127** H8
Mauritius (island), Mauritius **126** H8
Mawlamyine, Myanmar **119** E9
Mayotte (possession), France **139** C10
Mayumba, Gabon **135** G6
Mazar-e Sharif, Afghanistan **119** A2
Mazatlán, Mexico **65** C2
Mazyr, Belarus **95** C7
Mbabane, Swaziland **139** F6
Mbandaka, Dem. Rep. of the Congo **137** E2
Mbarara, Uganda **137** E4
Mbé, Cameroon **135** E8
Mbeya, Tanzania **137** G5
Mbuji-Mayi (Bakwanga), Dem. Rep. of the Congo **137** F3
McKinley, Mount (Denali), Alaska (U.S.) **62** F2
McMurdo Sound, Antarctica **155** F5
Mead, Lake, U.S. **62** D3
Mecca, Saudi Arabia **117** F2
Medan, Indonesia **122** B1
Medellín, Colombia **77** B2
Medford, Oregon (U.S.) **62** B1
Medicine Hat, Alberta (Canada) **61** G3
Medina, Saudi Arabia **117** E2
Meekatharra, Australia **148** D2
Meerut, India **119** C4
Mēga, Ethiopia **137** D6
Mek'elē, Ethiopia **137** B6

Meknès, Morocco **132** B3
Mekong (river), Asia **102** F6
Melanesia (islands), Oceania
  151 D4
Melbourne, Australia **149** F7
Melekeiok, Palau **150** C1
Melilla, Spain **133** A4
Melitopol', Ukraine **95** F9
Melut, South Sudan **137** C4
Melville Island, Australia
  148 A4
Melville Island, Canada
  61 B4
Melville Peninsula, Nunavut
  (Canada) **61** C6
Memphis, Tennessee (U.S.)
  63 E7
Ménaka, Mali **135** C5
Mendocino, Cape, California
  (U.S.) **62** C1
Mendoza, Argentina **81** D2
Menzies, Australia **148** E3
Merauke, Indonesia **123** D11
Mereeg, Somalia **137** D8
Mérida, Mexico **65** D6
Mérida, Venezuela **77** B4
Merowe, Sudan **137** B4
Mersin, *see* Icel, Turkey
  115 D4
Mesa, Arizona (U.S.) **62** E3
Mesa Verde National Park,
  Colorado (U.S.) **63** D4
Mesopotamia (region), Asia
  102 D2
Messina, Italy **93** H8
Messinia, Gulf of, Greece
  97 H5
Meta (river), Colombia **77** B4
Metz, France **93** E5
Mexicali, Mexico **64** A1
Mexico (country), North
  America **55** G3
Mexico City, Mexico **65** E3
Mexico, Gulf of, North
  America **54** G5
Miami, Florida (U.S.) **63** G10
Mianeh, Iran **117** B4
Michigan (state), U.S. **63** B8
Michigan, Lake, U.S. **63** B8
Micronesia (islands),
  Oceania **150** C3
Midway Islands, U.S. **151** A5
Mikkeli, Finland **91** E7
Milan, Italy **93** F6
Mildura, Australia **149** E6
Milford Sound, New Zealand
  149 H9
Milwaukee, Wisconsin (U.S.)
  63 C8
Minami Tori Shima (Marcus)
  (island), Japan **150** B3
Mindanao (island),
  Philippines **121** D8
Mindoro (island), Philippines
  121 C7
Minicoy (island), India **119**
  G3
Minneapolis, Minnesota
  (U.S.) **63** B7
Minnesota (state), U.S.
  63 B6
Minorca (island), Spain
  93 H4
Minot, North Dakota (U.S.)
  63 A5
Minsk, Belarus **95** B6
Minto, Mount, Antarctica
  155 G5
Mirbat, Oman **117** G6
Mirnyy, Russia **103** C5

Miskolc, Hungary **95** E4
Misool (island), Indonesia
  123 C8
Miṣrātah, Libya **133** B7
Mississippi (river), U.S.
  63 E7
Mississippi (state), U.S.
  63 E8
Mississippi River Delta,
  Louisiana (U.S.) **63** F8
Missouri (river), U.S. **63** C6
Missouri (state), U.S. **63** D7
Mitchell, Mount, North
  Carolina (U.S.) **63** D9
Mitilíni (island), *see* Lesbos,
  Greece **97** F7
Mobile, Alabama (U.S.)
  63 F8
Mobile Bay, Alabama (U.S.)
  63 F8
Moçambique, Mozambique
  139 C8
Moe, Australia **149** F7
Mogadishu, Somalia **137** E7
Mojave Desert, U.S. **62** D2
Moldova (country), Europe
  85 F6
Moloka'i (island), Hawai'i
  (U.S.) **63** G4
Moluccas (islands),
  Indonesia **123** C8
Molucca Sea, Indonesia
  123 C7
Mombasa, Kenya **137** F6
Monaco (country), Europe
  85 G3
Mongolia (country), Asia
  103 D4
Mongu, Zambia **139** C4
Monrovia, Liberia **135** E2
Montana (state), U.S. **63** B4
Monte Bello Islands,
  Australia **148** C1
Montego Bay, Jamaica **67** C3
Montenegro (country),
  Europe **85** G5
Montería, Colombia **77** B2
Monterrey, Mexico **65** C3
Montevideo, Uruguay **81** E4
Montgomery, Alabama (U.S.)
  63 E8
Montpelier, Vermont (U.S.)
  63 B11
Montréal, Quebec (Canada)
  61 G8
Montserrat (island), United
  Kingdom **67** C7
Monywa, Myanmar **119** D8
Moose Jaw, Saskatchewan
  (Canada) **61** G3
Mopti, Mali **135** D4
Moree, Australia **149** E7
Morocco (country), Africa
  132 B3
Moroni, Comoros **139** B9
Morotai (island), Indonesia
  123 B8
Moscow, Russia **99** E4
Moshi, Tanzania **137** F6
Mosquito Cays, Nicaragua
  65 F7
Mosquito Coast, Nicaragua
  65 F7
Mossaka, Congo **137** E1
Mostar, Bosnia &
  Herzegovina **97** D3
Mosul, Iraq **117** B3
Moundou, Chad **137** C1
Mountain Nile (river), South
  Sudan **137** D4

Mount Gambier, Australia
  149 F6
Mount Isa, Australia **149** C6
Mount Magnet, Australia
  148 D2
Mount Maunganui, New
  Zealand **149** E12
Mount Morgan, Australia
  149 D8
Mozambique (country),
  Africa **127** G6
Mozambique Channel, Africa
  126 G7
Mtwara, Tanzania **137** G6
Mubi, Nigeria **135** D7
Muchinga Mountains,
  Zambia **139** B6
Mufulira, Zambia **139** C5
Mullewa, Australia **148** D2
Multan, Pakistan **119** C3
Mumbai (Bombay), India
  119 E4
Munich, Germany **93** E6
Murat (river), Turkey **115** C7
Murcia, Spain **93** I3
Murmansk, Russia **99** A4
Murray (river), Australia
  149 E6
Muscat, Oman **117** F7
Muswellbrook, Australia
  149 E8
Mweka, Dem. Rep. of the
  Congo **137** F3
Mweru, Lake, Africa **137** G3
Myanmar (Burma) (country),
  Asia **103** F5
Myeik, Myanmar **119** F9
Mykolayiv, Ukraine **95** F8
Mysore, India **119** F4

N

Nagasaki, Japan **113** D9
Nagēlē, Ethiopia **137** D6
Nagorno-Karabakh (region),
  Azerbaijan **115** C9
Nagoya, Japan **113** C10
Naha, Japan **113** E9
Nairobi, Kenya **137** E6
Najd (region), Saudi Arabia
  117 E3
Najran, Saudi Arabia **115** G3
Nakhon Ratchasima,
  Thailand **121** C2
Namangan, Uzbekistan
  111 D3
Nam Dinh, Vietnam **121** B3
Namib Desert, Namibia
  138 E2
Namibe, Angola **127** G4
Namibia (country), Africa
  127 H4
Nampo Shoto (islands),
  Japan **102** D8
Nampula, Mozambique
  139 C8
Namsos, Norway **85** B4
Nanchang, China **113** E7
Nanjing, China **113** E8
Nanning, China **113** G6
Nantes, France **93** E3
Napier, New Zealand
  149 F12
Naples, Italy **93** G7
Nara, Mali **135** C3
Narmada (river), India
  119 D4
Narrogin, Australia **148** E2
Narva, Estonia **91** G8
Narvik, Norway **85** B5

Nashville, Tennessee (U.S.)
  63 D8
Nassau, Bahamas **67** B3
Nasser, Lake, Egypt **133** D10
Natal, Brazil **79** D8
Natchez, Mississippi (U.S.)
  63 F7
Natuna Islands, Indonesia
  122 B3
Naturaliste, Cape, Australia
  148 E2
Nauru (country), Oceania
  143 D5
Naxçivan, Azerbaijan **115** C8
Náxos (island), Greece **97** G7
Nay Pyi Taw, Myanmar
  119 E8
Nazwa, Oman **117** F7
Ndélé, Central African Rep.
  137 D2
N'Djamena, Chad **137** C2
Ndola, Zambia **139** C5
Neblina, Pico da, South
  America **79** B2
Nebraska (state), U.S. **63** C5
Negev (region), Israel **115** G4
Negro (river), Argentina **81**
  F2
Negro (river), Brazil **79** B2
Negros (island), Philippines
  121 D7
Neijiang, China **113** E5
Neiva, Colombia **77** C2
Nelson (river), Manitoba
  (Canada) **61** F5
Nelson, New Zealand
  149 G10
Néma, Mauritania **135** C3
Neman (river), Europe **91** I6
Nepal (country), Asia **103** F4
Netherlands (country),
  Europe **85** E3
Neuquén, Argentina **81** F2
Nevada (state), U.S. **62** C2
Newark, New Jersey (U.S.)
  63 C10
New Britain (island), Papua
  New Guinea **150** D3
New Brunswick (province),
  Canada **61** G9
New Caledonia (island),
  France **151** F4
Newcastle, Australia **149** E8
Newcastle, United Kingdom
  93 C3
Newcastle Waters, Australia
  149 B5
New Delhi, India **119** C4
Newfoundland, Island of,
  Newfoundland & Labrador
  (Canada) **61** F10
Newfoundland and Labrador
  (province), Canada **61** E9
New Guinea (island), Asia/
  Oceania **150** D2
New Hampshire (state), U.S.
  63 B11
New Ireland (island), Papua
  New Guinea **150** D3
New Jersey (state), U.S.
  63 C10
New Mexico (state), U.S.
  63 E4
New Orleans, Louisiana
  (U.S.) **63** F8
New Plymouth, New Zealand
  149 F11
New Siberian Islands,
  Russia **109** B7

New South Wales (state),
  Australia **149** E7
New York, New York (U.S.)
  63 C11
New York (state), U.S.
  63 B10
New Zealand (country),
  Oceania **143** G5
Ngaoundéré, Cameroon
  135 E7
Nguigmi, Niger **135** D7
Nha Trang, Vietnam **121** C4
Niagara Falls (waterfall),
  North America **63** B9
Niagara Falls, Ontario
  (Canada) **61** H7
Niamey, Niger **135** D5
Nicaragua (country), North
  America **55** I5
Nicaragua, Lake, Nicaragua
  65 G7
Nice, France **93** G5
Nicobar Islands, India
  119 G8
Nicosia, Cyprus **97** I8
Niger (country), Africa
  135 C6
Niger (river), Africa **135** C4
Niger Delta, Nigeria **135** F6
Nigeria (country), Africa
  135 E6
Niigata, Japan **113** C10
Ni'ihau (island), Hawai'i
  (U.S.) **63** F4
Nile (river), Africa **126** D6
Nile River Delta, Egypt
  133 B10
Nimba, Mont, Guinea
  135 E3
Nineveh (ruins), Iraq **117** B3
Ningbo, China **113** E8
Nioro du Sahel, Mali **135** C3
Nipigon, Lake, Ontario
  (Canada) **61** G6
Nippur (ruins), Iraq **117** C4
Nis, Serbia **97** D5
Nishtun, Yemen **117** H6
Niue (island), New Zealand
  143 E6
Nizhniy Novgorod, Russia
  99 E5
Nizhniy Tagil, Russia **108** E3
Nogáles, Mexico **64** A1
Nola, Central African Rep.
  137 D1
Norfolk, Virginia (U.S.) **63**
  D10
Norfolk Island, Australia
  151 F4
Noril'sk, Russia **109** D6
Normanton, Australia
  149 B6
Norrköping, Sweden **91** G4
Norrland (region), Sweden
  91 D4
Norseman, Australia **148** E3
Northam, Australia **148** E2
North Cape, New Zealand
  149 D10
North Cape, Norway **91** A6
North Carolina (state), U.S.
  63 D10
North China Plain, China
  102 E6
North Dakota (state), U.S.
  63 B5
North East Land (island),
  Norway **91** A3
Northern Cyprus (region),
  Cyprus **97** I8

Northern Dvina — Porpoise Bay

Northern Dvina (river), Russia **99** C5
Northern European Plain, Europe **84** E4
Northern Ireland (country), United Kingdom **93** C2
Northern Mariana Islands, U.S. **150** B2
Northern Territory, Australia **149** B5
North Island, New Zealand **149** E11
North Korea (country), Asia **103** D7
North Land (Severnaya Zemlya) (islands), Russia **109** B6
North Platte (river), U.S. **63** C4
North Saskatchewan (river), Canada **61** F3
North Sea, Europe **84** D3
North Slope, Alaska (U.S.) **62** F2
North Taranaki Bight, New Zealand **149** F11
North West Basin, Australia **142** E1
North West Cape, Australia **148** C1
Northwest Territories, Canada **61** C3
Norvegia, Cape, Antarctica **155** A4
Norway (country), Europe **85** B4
Norwegian Sea, Europe **84** A3
Nottingham, United Kingdom **93** C3
Nouakchott, Mauritania **135** C1
Nouâmrhâr, Mauritania **135** C1
Nouméa, New Caledonia (France) **151** F4
Nova Scotia (province), Canada **61** G9
Novaya Zemlya (island), Russia **109** C4
Novi Sad, Serbia **97** B4
Novokuznetsk, Russia **109** F5
Novosibirsk, Russia **109** E5
Nubia, Lake, Africa **137** A4
Nubian Desert, Sudan **137** A5
Nuevo Laredo, Mexico **65** C3
Nukuʻalofa, Tonga **151** F5
Nullarbor Plain, Australia **148** E4
Nunavut (territory), Canada **61** D5
Nunivak Island, Alaska (U.S.) **54** B1
Nuremberg, Germany **93** E6
Nuuk (Godthåb), Greenland (Denmark) **55** C6
Nyala, Sudan **137** C3
Nzérékoré, Guinea **135** E2

O
Oʻahu (island), Hawaiʻi (U.S.) **63** F4
Oakland, California (U.S.) **62** C1
Oamaru, New Zealand **149** H10
Oaxaca, Mexico **65** E4
Ob (river), Russia **109** D4

Ob, Gulf of, Russia **109** C5
Obo, Central African Rep. **137** D3
Odense, Denmark **91** I3
Oder (river), Europe **84** E4
Odesa, Ukraine **95** F7
Ogbomosho, Nigeria **135** E5
Ogden, Utah (U.S.) **62** C3
Ohio (river), U.S. **63** D8
Ohio (state), U.S. **63** C9
Oka (river), Russia **99** E5
Okavango (river), Africa **138** D3
Okavango Delta, Botswana **139** D4
Okeechobee, Lake, Florida (U.S.) **63** F10
Okhotsk, Sea of, Asia **102** B7
Okinawa (island), Japan **113** E10
Oklahoma (state), U.S. **63** D6
Oklahoma City, Oklahoma (U.S.) **63** E6
Öland (island), Sweden **91** H5
Oleksandriya, Ukraine **95** E8
Olga, Mount, Australia **148** D4
Olsztyn, Poland **95** B4
Olympia (ruins), Greece **97** G5
Olympia, Washington (U.S.) **62** A2
Olympic Peninsula, Washington (U.S.) **54** E2
Olympus (peak), Greece **97** F5
Omaha, Nebraska (U.S.) **63** C6
Oman (country), Asia **103** F2
Oman, Gulf of, Asia **117** E7
Omdurman, Sudan **137** B4
Omsk, Russia **109** E4
Onega, Lake, Russia **99** D4
Onslow, Australia **148** C1
Ontario (province), Canada **61** G6
Ontario, Lake, North America **54** E5
Oodaaq Island, Greenland (Denmark) **54** A5
Oodnadatta, Australia **149** D5
Ooldea, Australia **148** E4
Opole, Poland **94** D3
Oporto, Portugal **93** G1
Oradea, Romania **97** B5
Oral, Kazakhstan **110** B1
Oran, Algeria **133** A4
Orange (river), Africa **138** G3
Orange, Australia **149** E7
Ord (river), Australia **148** B4
Örebro, Sweden **91** G4
Oregon (state), U.S. **62** B2
Orel, Russia **99** F3
Orenburg, Russia **99** F7
Orinoco (river), Venezuela **77** B6
Orizaba, Pico de, Mexico **65** E4
Orkney Islands, United Kingdom **93** A3
Orlando, Florida (U.S.) **63** F10
Orléans, France **93** E4
Örnsköldsvik, Sweden **91** E5
Orsha, Belarus **95** B7
Orsk, Russia **99** F7
Oruro, Bolivia **77** H4
Osaka, Japan **113** D10

Osa Peninsula, Costa Rica **65** G7
Osijek, Croatia **97** B3
Öskemen, Kazakhstan **111** C5
Oslo, Norway **91** F3
Östersund, Sweden **91** E4
Ostrava, Czech Republic **94** D3
Otranto, Strait of, Europe **97** E3
Ottawa (river), Canada **61** G7
Ottawa, Ontario (Canada) **61** H7
Ouadane, Mauritania **135** B2
Ouagadougou, Burkina Faso **135** D3
Ouargla, Algeria **133** B5
Oudtshoorn, South Africa **139** H4
Ouesso, Congo **137** E1
Oujda, Morocco **133** B4
Oulu (river), Finland **91** D7
Oulu, Finland **91** D7
Ounianga Kébir, Chad **137** A3
Outer Hebrides (islands), United Kingdom **93** B2
Oyem, Gabon **135** F7
Ozark Plateau, U.S. **54** F4

P
Padang, Indonesia **122** C1
Paducah, Kentucky (U.S.) **63** D8
Pago Pago, American Samoa (U.S.) **151** E6
Pakistan (country), Asia **103** E3
Palangkaraya, Indonesia **123** C4
Palau (country), Oceania **143** C2
Palawan (island), Philippines **121** D6
Palembang, Indonesia **122** C2
Palermo, Italy **93** H7
Palikir, Federated States of Micronesia **150** C3
Palliser, Cape, New Zealand **149** G11
Palma, Spain **93** H4
Palmas, Cape, Côte d'Ivoire **135** F3
Palmerston North, New Zealand **149** F11
Palmyra Atoll, U.S. **151** C7
Pamirs (range), Tajikistan **111** E4
Pampas (region), Argentina **81** E2
Panama (country), North America **55** H4
Panama City, Panama **65** G8
Panama, Gulf of, Panama **65** G8
Panama, Isthmus of, Panama **54** I6
Panama Canal, Panama **65** G8
Panay (island), Philippines **121** D7
Panié, Mount, New Caledonia (France) **151** F4
Pantanal (region), Brazil **79** E4
Pánuco (river), Mexico **65** D4
Papeete, French Polynesia (France) **151** E8

Papua New Guinea (country), Oceania **143** D3
Paragominas, Brazil **79** C5
Paraguay (country), South America **71** E5
Paraguay (river), South America **70** E5
Parakou, Benin **135** E5
Paramaribo, Suriname **79** A4
Paraná, Argentina **81** D3
Paraná (river), South America **70** F5
Parece Vela (island), Japan **103** E8
Parepare, Indonesia **123** D5
Paris, France **93** E4
Parnaíba, Brazil **79** C7
Parnassus, New Zealand **149** G10
Pärnu, Estonia **91** G7
Parry Channel, Canada **61** B5
Parry Islands, Canada **61** B4
Pasley, Cape, Australia **148** E3
Pasto, Colombia **77** C2
Patagonia (region), Argentina **81** G2
Pathein, Myanmar **119** E8
Patna, India **119** D6
Patos Lagoon, Brazil **79** H4
Pátrai, Greece **97** G5
Patuca (river), Honduras **65** F7
Pavlodar, Kazakhstan **111** B4
Peace (river), Canada **54** D3
Peary Land, Greenland (Denmark) **54** A5
Pec, Serbia **97** D4
Pechenga, Russia **85** A6
Pechora (river), Russia **99** B6
Pechora, Russia **99** B6
Pécs, Hungary **94** F3
Pegasus Bay, New Zealand **149** H10
Peipus, Lake, Europe **91** G8
Pekanbaru, Indonesia **122** C1
Peloponnesus (peninsula), Greece **97** G5
Pelotas, Brazil **79** H4
Pematangsiantar, Indonesia **122** B1
Pemba, Mozambique **139** C8
Pemba Island, Tanzania **137** F6
Pennines, The, (range), United Kingdom **84** D2
Pennsylvania (state), U.S. **63** C9
Penong, Australia **149** E5
Pensacola Mountains, Antarctica **155** C4
Penza, Russia **99** F5
Peoria, Illinois (U.S.) **63** C7
Pereira, Colombia **77** C2
Perm', Russia **99** D7
Persepolis (ruins), Iran **117** D6
Persian Gulf, Asia **117** E5
Perth, Australia **148** E2
Peru (country), South America **71** C3
Peshawar, Pakistan **119** B3
Petra (ruins), Jordan **115** G4
Petropavlovsk, Kazakhstan **111** B4

Petropavlovsk-Kamchatsky, Russia **109** C11
Petrozavodsk, Russia **99** C4
Philadelphia, Pennsylvania (U.S.) **63** C10
Philippine Islands, Philippines **102** F7
Philippines (country), Asia **103** F7
Philippine Sea, Asia **102** F8
Phillip Island, Australia **151** F4
Phnom Penh, Cambodia **121** D3
Phoenix, Arizona (U.S.) **62** E3
Phoenix Islands, Kiribati **151** D6
Picton, New Zealand **149** G11
Pierre, South Dakota (U.S.) **63** B5
Pietermaritzburg, South Africa **139** G6
Pietersburg, see Polokwane, South Africa **139** E5
Pilsen, Czech Republic **94** D1
Pine Creek, Australia **148** A4
Pinsk, Belarus **95** C6
Pinsk Marshes, Belarus **95** C6
Pitcairn Island, United Kingdom **151** F9
Pittsburgh, Pennsylvania (U.S.) **63** C9
Piura, Peru **77** E1
Plate, River, South America **81** E4
Plateau Station, Antarctica **155** C6
Platte (river), U.S. **63** C5
Plenty, Bay of, New Zealand **149** E12
Pleven, Bulgaria **97** D6
Ploiesti, Romania **97** C7
Plovdiv, Bulgaria **97** D6
Plymouth, United Kingdom **93** D3
Po (river), Italy **93** F6
Pocatello, Idaho (U.S.) **62** C3
Podgorica, Montenegro **97** D3
Pohnpei (island), Federated States of Micronesia **150** C3
Poinsett, Cape, Antarctica **155** F9
Pointe-Noire, Congo **137** F1
Poland (country), Europe **85** E5
Polar Plateau, Antarctica **155** D5
Polokwane (Pietersburg), South Africa **139** E5
Poltava, Ukraine **95** D9
Polynesia (islands), Oceania **151** C6
Pondicherry, see Puducherry, India **119** F4
Pontianak, Indonesia **122** C3
Popayán, Colombia **77** C2
Popocatépetl (peak), Mexico **65** E3
Pori, Finland **91** F6
Porirua, New Zealand **149** G11
Porpoise Bay, Antarctica **155** G8

Port Augusta — Sakarya

Port Augusta, Australia **149** E5
Port-au-Prince, Haiti **67** C4
Port Elizabeth, South Africa **139** H4
Port-Gentil, Gabon **135** G6
Port Harcourt, Nigeria **135** E6
Port Hedland, Australia **148** C2
Portland, Maine (U.S.) **63** B11
Portland, Oregon (U.S.) **62** A2
Port Lincoln, Australia **149** E5
Port Louis, Mauritius **127** H8
Port Moresby, Papua New Guinea **150** E2
Porto Alegre, Brazil **79** H5
Port of Spain, Trinidad & Tobago **67** E7
Porto-Novo, Benin **135** F5
Porto Velho, Brazil **79** D2
Portoviejo, Ecuador **77** D1
Port Phillip Bay, Australia **149** F6
Port Pirie, Australia **149** E5
Port Said, Egypt **133** B10
Port Sudan, Sudan **137** A5
Portugal (country), Europe **85** G1
Port Vila, Vanuatu **151** E4
Posadas, Argentina **81** C4
Potiskum, Nigeria **135** D7
Potosí, Bolivia **77** I5
Powell, Lake, U.S. **62** D3
Poza Rica, Mexico **65** D4
Poznan, Poland **94** C3
Prague, Czech Republic **94** D1
Pretoria (Tshwane), South Africa **139** F5
Prince Albert, Saskatchewan (Canada) **61** F4
Prince Charles Island, Nunavut (Canada) **54** C5
Prince Edward Island (province), Canada **61** G9
Prince George, British Columbia (Canada) **60** F2
Prince of Wales Island, Nunavut (Canada) **61** C5
Prince Patrick Island, Northwest Territories (Canada) **61** B4
Prince Rupert, British Columbia (Canada) **60** E1
Príncipe (island), São Tomé & Principe **135** F6
Pristina, Kosovo **97** D4
Prokop'yevsk, Russia **109** F5
Proserpine, Australia **149** C7
Providence, Rhode Island (U.S.) **63** B11
Provo, Utah (U.S.) **62** C3
Prut (river), Europe **95** F7
Prydz Bay, Antarctica **155** C8
Pskov, Russia **99** D2
Pucallpa, Peru **77** F2
Puducherry (Pondicherry), India **119** E4
Puebla, Mexico **65** E4
Pueblo, Colorado (U.S.) **63** D4
Puerto Barrios, Guatemala **65** F6
Puerto Esperanza, Paraguay **81** A4

Puerto La Cruz, Venezuela **77** A5
Puerto Limón, Costa Rica **65** G7
Puerto Montt, Chile **81** F1
Puerto Rico (island), U.S. **54** H7
Puerto Vallarta, Mexico **65** D2
Puncak Jaya (peak), Indonesia **123** D10
Pune, India **119** E3
Punta Arenas, Chile **81** I2
Purus (river), Brazil **79** D2
Putumayo (river), South America **77** D3
Puysegur Point, New Zealand **149** I8
Pweto, Dem. Rep. of the Congo **137** F4
Pyinmana, Myanmar **119** E8
Pyongyang, North Korea **113** C8
Pyrenees (range), Europe **93** G3

Q

Qaidam Basin, China **102** E5
Qalat Bishah, Saudi Arabia **117** G3
Qaraghandy, Kazakhstan **111** C4
Qardho, Somalia **137** C8
Qatar (country), Asia **103** E2
Qattara Depression, Egypt **133** C9
Qazvin, Iran **117** B5
Qeqertarsuaq (island), Greenland (Denmark) **54** B6
Qeshm (island), Iran **117** E6
Qingdao, China **113** D8
Qinghai Hu (lake), China **113** D5
Qiqihar, China **113** B8
Qizilqum (desert), Uzbekistan **110** D2
Qom, Iran **117** C5
Qomsheh, Iran **117** C5
Quchan, Iran **117** B7
Quebec (province), Canada **61** G8
Québec, Quebec (Canada) **61** G8
Queen Charlotte Islands, British Columbia (Canada) **60** E1
Queen Elizabeth Islands, Canada **61** A5
Queen Maud Land, Antarctica **155** B5
Queensland (state), Australia **149** C6
Queenstown, Australia **149** G6
Queenstown, New Zealand **149** H9
Queenstown, South Africa **139** G5
Quelimane, Mozambique **139** D7
Querétaro, Mexico **65** D3
Quetta, Pakistan **119** B2
Quetzaltenango, Guatemala **65** F5
Quezon City, Philippines **121** C7
Qui Nhon, Vietnam **121** C4
Quito, Ecuador **77** D2
Qurayyat, Oman **117** F7

R

Raba, Indonesia **123** E5
Rabat, Morocco **132** A3
Race, Cape, Newfoundland & Labrador (Canada) **61** F10
Rafsanjan, Iran **117** D6
Raga, South Sudan **137** C3
Raipur, India **119** D5
Rajkot, India **119** D2
Rakaia (river), New Zealand **149** F10
Raleigh, North Carolina (U.S.) **63** D10
Ralik Chain (islands), Marshall Islands **151** C4
Rangitaiki (river), New Zealand **149** E12
Rangitata (river), New Zealand **149** H10
Rangoon, see Yangon, Myanmar **119** E8
Rangpur, Bangladesh **119** C7
Rankin Inlet, Nunavut (Canada) **61** E5
Rapa Nui (Easter Island), Chile **151** F11
Rapid City, South Dakota (U.S.) **63** B5
Ras Dejen (peak), Ethiopia **137** C6
Rasht, Iran **117** B5
Ratak Chain (islands), Marshall Islands **151** C4
Ravensthorpe, Australia **148** E2
Rawalpindi, Pakistan **119** B3
Rawlinna, Australia **148** E3
Recife, Brazil **79** D8
Red (river), U.S. **63** E7
Red (river), Vietnam **121** A3
Redding, California (U.S.) **62** C1
Redwood National Park, California (U.S.) **62** B1
Reggane, Algeria **133** C4
Regina, Saskatchewan (Canada) **61** G4
Reindeer Lake, Canada **61** E4
Renk, South Sudan **137** C5
Rennes, France **85** E2
Reno, Nevada (U.S.) **62** C2
Resistencia, Argentina **81** C4
Resita, Romania **97** B5
Resolute, Nunavut (Canada) **61** B5
Réunion (island), France **126** H8
Revillagigedo Islands, Mexico **54** H2
Reykjavík, Iceland **91** A1
Rhine (river), Europe **93** D5
Rhode Island (state), U.S. **63** B11
Rhodes (island), Greece **97** H8
Rhodes, Greece **97** H8
Rhodope Mountains, Bulgaria **97** E6
Rhône (river), France **93** F5
Ribeirão Preto, Brazil **79** F5
Richmond, Virginia (U.S.) **63** D10
Rida, Yemen **117** H4
Riga, Latvia **91** H7
Riga, Gulf of, Latvia **91** H7
Riiser-Larsen Ice Shelf, Antarctica **155** A4

Riiser-Larsen Peninsula, Antarctica **155** A7
Rijeka, Croatia **97** B2
Rimouski, Quebec (Canada) **61** G8
Río Azul (ruins), Guatemala **65** E6
Rio Branco, Brazil **79** D2
Rio Bravo del Norte (river), see Rio Grande, North America **65** B3
Rio de Janeiro, Brazil **79** G6
Río Gallegos, Argentina **81** I2
Rio Grande (river), North America **54** G3
Río Muni (region), Equatorial Guinea **135** F7
Rivera, Uruguay **81** D4
Riverside, California (U.S.) **62** E2
Riviera (region), Europe **84** F3
Rivne, Ukraine **95** D6
Riyadh, Saudi Arabia **117** E4
Rochester, New York (U.S.) **63** B10
Rockall (island), United Kingdom **93** A1
Rockford, Illinois (U.S.) **63** C8
Rockhampton, Australia **149** C8
Rocky Mountains, North America **54** D3
Roma, Australia **149** D7
Romania (country), Europe **85** F5
Rome, Italy **93** G7
Ronne Ice Shelf, Antarctica **155** C3
Roosevelt Island, Antarctica **155** F4
Roraima, Mount, South America **77** C6
Rosario, Argentina **81** D3
Roseau, Dominica **67** C7
Ross Ice Shelf, Antarctica **155** E5
Ross Island, Antarctica **155** F5
Rosso, Mauritania **135** C1
Ross Sea, Antarctica **155** F4
Rostock, Germany **93** C6
Rostov, Russia **99** H4
Roswell, New Mexico (U.S.) **63** D4
Rotorua, New Zealand **149** E11
Rotterdam, Netherlands **93** D4
Rotuma (island), Fiji Islands **151** E5
Rouen, France **93** E4
Rovaniemi, Finland **91** C7
Rovuma (river), Africa **139** B8
Royale, Isle, Michigan (U.S.) **63** A7
Ruapehu, Mount, New Zealand **149** F11
Rubtsovsk, Russia **109** F5
Rukwa, Lake, Tanzania **137** F5
Rumbek, South Sudan **137** D4
Ruse, Bulgaria **97** C7
Russia (country), Europe/Asia **103** C4
Rust'avi, Georgia **115** B8

Rwanda (country), Africa **137** E4
Ryazan', Russia **99** F4
Rybinsk, Russia **99** E4
Rybinsk Reservoir, Russia **99** D4
Ryukyu Islands, Japan **113** E9
Rzeszów, Poland **95** D4

S

Saaremaa (island), Estonia **91** G6
Saba (island), Netherlands Antilles (Netherlands) **67** C6
Sabah (state), Malaysia **121** E6
Sabhā, Libya **133** C7
Sable, Cape, Nova Scotia (Canada) **61** H9
Sable Island, Nova Scotia (Canada) **61** G10
Sabzevar, Iran **117** B7
Sacramento, California (U.S.) **62** C1
Safi, Morocco **132** B2
Sahara (desert), Africa **126** D2
Sahel (region), Africa **126** D3
Saidabad, Iran **117** D6
Saigon, see Ho Chi Minh City, Vietnam **121** D3
St.-Barthélemy (island), France **67** C7
St. Elias Mountains, North America **60** D1
Ste. Marie, Cap, Madagascar **139** F9
St. Eustatius (island), Netherlands Antilles (Netherlands) **67** C7
St. George's, Grenada **67** D7
St. Helena (island), United Kingdom **126** G2
St. John's, Antigua & Barbuda **67** C7
St. John's, Newfoundland & Labrador (Canada) **61** F10
St. Kitts and Nevis (country), North America **55** H8
St. Lawrence (river), North America **61** G8
St. Lawrence, Gulf of, Canada **61** F9
St. Lawrence Island, Alaska (U.S.) **54** A1
Saint-Louis, Senegal **135** C1
St. Lucia (country), North America **55** H8
St. Martin (island), Netherlands Antilles (Netherlands)/France **67** C7
St. Marys, Australia **149** G7
St. Petersburg, Russia **99** D3
St.-Pierre and Miquelon (island), France **61** F10
St. Vincent and the Grenadines (country), North America **55** H8
Saipan (island), Northern Mariana Islands (U.S.) **143** B3
Saipan, Northern Mariana Islands (U.S.) **150** C2
Sajama, Nevado, Bolivia **77** H4
Sakarya (river), Turkey **115** B3

Sakarya — Sudan

Sakarya, Turkey **115** B3
Sakhalin (island), Russia **109** E10
Salalah, Oman **117** G6
Salamanca, Spain **93** G2
Sala-y-Gómez (island), Chile **151** F11
Salem, India **119** F4
Salem, Oregon (U.S.) **62** B1
Salta, Argentina **81** B2
Saltillo, Mexico **65** C3
Salt Lake City, Utah (U.S.) **62** C3
Salto, Uruguay **81** D4
Salton Sea, California (U.S.) **62** E2
Salvador (Bahia), Brazil **79** E7
Salween (river), Asia **102** F5
Salzburg, Austria **93** E7
Samar (island), Philippines **121** C8
Samara, Russia **99** F6
Samarinda, Indonesia **123** C5
Samarqand, Uzbekistan **111** D3
Samoa (country), Oceania **143** E6
Samoa Islands, Oceania **151** E6
Sámso (island), Greece **97** G7
Samsun, Turkey **115** B5
Sanaa, Yemen **117** H3
Sanaga (river), Cameroon **135** E7
San Ambrosio Island, Chile **70** F3
Sanandaj, Iran **117** C4
San Antonio, Texas (U.S.) **63** F6
San Bernardino, California (U.S.) **62** D2
San Cristóbal, Venezuela **77** B3
Sandakan, Malaysia **121** E6
San Diego, California (U.S.) **62** E2
Sandoa, Dem. Rep. of the Congo **137** G2
San Félix Island, Chile **70** F2
San Francisco, California (U.S.) **62** C1
San Jorge, Gulf of, Argentina **81** G2
San Jose, California (U.S.) **62** C1
San José, Costa Rica **65** G7
San José del Guaviare, Colombia **77** C3
San Juan, Argentina **81** D2
San Juan (river), North America **65** G7
San Juan, Puerto Rico **67** C6
San Justo, Argentina **81** E4
Sanliurfa, Turkey **115** D6
San Lucas, Cape, Mexico **64** C1
San Luis Potosí, Mexico **65** D3
San Marino (country), Europe **85** G4
San Matías Gulf, Argentina **81** F3
San Miguel, El Salvador **65** F6
San Miguel de Tucumán, Argentina **81** C2

San Pedro Sula, Honduras **65** F6
San Salvador (island), Bahamas **67** B3
San Salvador, El Salvador **65** F6
Santa Ana, El Salvador **65** F6
Santa Clara, Cuba **67** B2
Santa Cruz, Bolivia **77** H5
Santa Cruz Islands, Solomon Islands **151** E4
Santa Fe, Argentina **81** D3
Santa Fe, New Mexico (U.S.) **63** D4
Santa Maria, Brazil **79** H4
Santa Marta, Colombia **77** A3
Santander, Spain **93** G2
Santarém, Brazil **79** C4
Santiago, Chile **81** D1
Santiago, Dominican Republic **67** C4
Santiago de Cuba, Cuba **67** C3
Santiago del Estero, Argentina **81** C3
Santo Domingo, Dominican Republic **67** C5
Santoríni (island), see Thíra, Greece **97** H6
Santos, Brazil **79** G5
São Francisco (river), Brazil **79** E6
São José do Rio Preto, Brazil **79** F5
São José dos Campos, Brazil **79** G6
São Luís, Brazil **79** C6
São Paulo, Brazil **79** G5
São Tomé (island), São Tomé and Principe **135** F6
São Tomé & Principe (country), Africa **135** F6
Sapporo, Japan **113** B10
Sarajevo, Bosnia & Herzegovina **97** C3
Saransk, Russia **99** F5
Saratov, Russia **99** F5
Sarawak (state), Malaysia **121** F5
Sardinia (island), Italy **93** H6
Sarh, Chad **137** C2
Sari, Iran **117** B5
Saskatchewan (province), Canada **61** F4
Saskatchewan (river), Canada **54** D3
Saskatoon, Saskatchewan (Canada) **61** F3
Satu Mare, Romania **97** A5
Saudi Arabia (country), Asia **103** E1
Sault Ste. Marie, Ontario (Canada) **61** G6
Sava (river), Europe **97** C4
Savannah, Georgia (U.S.) **63** E10
Savannah (river), U.S. **63** E9
Savannakhét, Laos **121** C3
Sawkanah, Libya **133** C7
Scandinivia (region), Europe **84** B5
Schefferville, Quebec (Canada) **61** F8
Scotland (country), United Kingdom **93** B3
Seattle, Washington (U.S.) **62** A2
Ségou, Mali **135** D4
Seine (river), France **93** E4

Selenga (river), Mongolia **111** B8
Selvas (region), Brazil **79** C2
Selwyn Mountains, Yukon (Canada) **60** D2
Semarang, Indonesia **122** D3
Semey, Kazakhstan **111** C5
Sendai, Japan **113** C11
Senegal (country), Africa **135** C2
Sénégal (river), Africa **135** C2
Senyavin Islands, Federated States of Micronesia **150** C3
Seoul, South Korea **113** C9
Sept-Îles, Quebec (Canada) **61** F8
Serbia (country), Europe **85** G5
Serowe, Botswana **139** E5
Sété Cama, Gabon **135** G6
Sétif, Algeria **133** A5
Sevastopol', Ukraine **95** G9
Severn (river), Ontario (Canada) **61** F5
Severnaya Zemlya (islands), see North Land, Russia **109** B6
Severodvinsk, Russia **99** C4
Seville, Spain **93** I2
Seward Peninsula, Alaska (U.S.) **54** B1
Seychelles (country), Africa **127** F8
Sfax, Tunisia **133** B6
Shackleton Ice Shelf, Antarctica **155** E9
Shanghai, China **113** E8
Shantou, China **103** F6
Shark Bay, Australia **148** D1
Shebele (river), Africa **137** D7
Sheffield, United Kingdom **93** C3
Shenyang, China **113** C8
Sherbro Island, Sierra Leone **135** E2
Shetland Islands, United Kingdom **93** A4
Shijiazhuang, China **113** D7
Shikoku (island), Japan **113** D10
Shiraz, Iran **117** D5
Shkodër, Albania **97** D4
Sholapur, India **119** E4
Shott el Jerid (dry salt lake), Tunisia **133** B5
Shreveport, Louisiana (U.S.) **63** E7
Shymkent, Kazakhstan **111** D3
Sialkot, Pakistan **119** B3
Siauliai, Lithuania **91** H7
Siberia (region), Russia **109** D5
Sibiu, Romania **97** B6
Sibu, Malaysia **121** F4
Sichuan Basin, China **102** E6
Sicily (island), Italy **93** I7
Sîdi Barrâni, Egypt **133** B8
Sidon, Lebanon **115** F4
Sidra, Gulf of, Libya **133** B7
Siem Reap, Cambodia **121** C3
Sierra Leone (country), Africa **135** E2
Sierra Madre (range), North America **54** H4

Sierra Madre del Sur (range), Mexico **65** E3
Sierra Madre Occidental (range), Mexico **65** C2
Sierra Madre Oriental (range), Mexico **65** D3
Sierra Morena (range), Spain **93** H2
Sierra Nevada (range), California (U.S.) **62** C2
Sikasso, Mali **135** D3
Sikhote Alin Range, Russia **109** E10
Silet, Algeria **133** D5
Simferopol', Ukraine **95** G9
Simla, India **119** B4
Sinai (region), Egypt **133** B10
Sinai, Mount, Egypt **133** C11
Singapore, Singapore **121** F2
Singapore (country), Asia **103** H6
Sinkiang (region), China **112** C2
Sinop, Turkey **115** B4
Sioux Falls, South Dakota (U.S.) **63** C6
Sittwe, Myanmar **119** D7
Sivas, Turkey **115** C5
Sîwa, Egypt **133** C9
Skagerrak (strait), Europe **91** G2
Skellefteå, Sweden **91** D6
Skien, Norway **91** G3
Skopje, Macedonia **97** D4
Slave (river), Canada **54** D3
Slave Coast (region), Africa **135** F5
Sliven, Bulgaria **97** D7
Slovakia (country), Europe **85** F5
Slovenia (country), Europe **85** F4
Slov''yans'k, Ukraine **95** E10
Smolensk, Russia **99** E3
Snake (river), U.S. **62** B3
Sochi, Russia **99** I4
Society Islands, French Polynesia (France) **117** I6
Sofia, Bulgaria **97** D5
Sokoto, Nigeria **135** D5
Sokhumi, Georgia **115** A6
Solimões (river), see Amazon, South America **79** C2
Solomon Islands, Oceania **150** D3
Solomon Islands (country), Oceania **143** D4
Solomon Sea, Oceania **150** E3
Somali Peninsula, Africa **137** D7
Somalia (country), Africa **137** D7
Somaliland (region), Somalia **137** C7
Somerset Island, Nunavut (Canada) **61** C5
Songea, Tanzania **137** G5
Songkhla, Thailand **121** D1
Sonoran Desert, U.S. **54** F3
Sorong, Indonesia **123** C8
South Africa (country), Africa **127** H5
Southampton, United Kingdom **85** E2
Southampton Island, Nunavut (Canada) **61** D6
South Australia (state), Australia **149** D5

South Carolina (state), U.S. **63** E9
South China Sea, Asia **102** F7
South Dakota (state), U.S. **63** B5
Southern Alps (range), New Zealand **149** H9
Southern Cross, Australia **148** E2
South Georgia (island), United Kingdom **70** I7
South Island, New Zealand **149** H10
South Korea (country), Asia **103** D7
South Magnetic Pole, Antarctica **155** G8
South Orkney Islands, Antarctica **154** A1
South Ossetia (region), Georgia **115** B8
South Pole, Antarctica **155** D5
South Saskatchewan (river), Canada **61** G3
South Shetland Islands, Antarctica **154** A1
South Sudan (country), Africa **137** D4
South Taranaki Bight, New Zealand **149** F11
South West Cape, New Zealand **149** I9
Spain (country), Europe **85** G1
Sparta, Greece **97** G5
Spencer Gulf, Australia **142** F2
Spitsbergen (island), Norway **91** A3
Split, Croatia **97** C2
Spokane, Washington (U.S.) **62** A3
Springfield, Illinois (U.S.) **63** C7
Springfield, Missouri (U.S.) **63** D7
Sri Jayewardenepura Kotte, Sri Lanka **119** G6
Sri Lanka (Ceylon) (country), Asia **103** G4
Srinagar, India **119** B4
St. Louis, Missouri (U.S.) **63** D7
St. Paul, Minnesota (U.S.) **63** B7
St. Petersburg, Florida (U.S.) **63** F9
Stanley, Falkland Islands (U.K.) **81** I4
Stara Zagora, Bulgaria **97** D6
Starbuck Island, Kiribati **151** D7
Stavanger, Norway **91** G2
Stavropol', Russia **99** H4
Steppes, The, Kazakhstan **111** B3
Sterlitamak, Russia **99** F7
Stewart Island, New Zealand **149** I9
Stockholm, Sweden **91** G5
Strasbourg, France **93** E5
Stuttgart, Germany **93** E6
Subotica, Serbia **97** B4
Sucre, Bolivia **77** I5
Sudan (country), Africa **137** B4

Sudbury — United Arab Emirates

Sudbury, Ontario (Canada)
61 G7
Sudd (marsh), South Sudan
137 C4
Suez Canal, Egypt 133 B10
Suez, Gulf of, Egypt 133 B10
Sukhona (river), Russia
99 D5
Sukkur, Pakistan 119 C2
Sula Islands, Indonesia
123 C7
Sulu Archipelago,
Philippines 121 E7
Sulu Sea, Asia 121 D6
Sumatra (island), Indonesia
122 C1
Sumba (island), Indonesia
123 E5
Sumbawa (island), Indonesia
123 E5
Sumqayıt, Azerbaijan
115 B10
Sumy, Ukraine 95 D9
Sundsvall, Sweden 91 E5
Superior, Wisconsin (U.S.)
63 B7
Superior, Lake, North
America 54 E5
Sur, Oman 117 F7
Surabaya, Indonesia 123 D4
Surakarta, Indonesia 122 E3
Surat, India 119 D3
Surgut, Russia 109 E4
Suriname (country), South
America 71 B5
Surt, Libya 133 B7
Suva, Fiji islands 151 E5
Svealand (region), Sweden
91 F4
Sverdrup Islands, Nunavut
(Canada) 61 A5
Swakopmund, Namibia
138 E2
Swaziland (country), Africa
127 H6
Sweden (country), Europe
85 C5
Switzerland (country),
Europe 85 F3
Sydney, Australia 149 E8
Syktyvkar, Russia 99 D6
Syracuse, Italy 93 I8
Syr Darya (river),
Kazakhstan 111 C3
Syria (country), Asia 103 D1
Syrian Desert, Asia 102 D1
Szczecin, Poland 94 B2
Szeged, Hungary 94 F3
Székesfehérvár, Hungary
94 F3

T

Tabelbala, Algeria 132 C4
Tabora, Tanzania 137 F4
Tabriz, Iran 117 B4
Tabuk, Saudi Arabia 117 D1
Tacloban, Philippines 121 D8
Tacoma, Washington (U.S.)
62 A2
Tademaït Plateau, Algeria
133 C4
Taganrog, Russia 99 H4
Tagus (river), Europe 93 H2
Tahat, Mount, Libya 133 D5
Tahiti (island), French
Polynesia (France) 151 E8
Tahoe, Lake, U.S. 62 C2
Tahoua, Niger 135 C6
Tainan, Taiwan 113 F8
Taipei, Taiwan 113 F8

Taitao Peninsula, Chile
70 H4
Taiwan (island), China
102 F7
Taiwan Strait, Asia 113 F8
Taiyuan, China 113 D7
Taizz, Yemen 117 H3
Tajikistan (country), Asia
103 E3
Tajumulco, Volcán,
Guatemala 65 F5
Takapuna, New Zealand
149 E11
Taklimakan Desert, China
112 D2
Talara, Peru 77 E1
Talaud Islands, Indonesia
123 B7
Talbot, Cape, Australia
148 A3
Talca, Chile 81 E1
Taldyqorghan, Kazakhstan
111 D5
Tallahassee, Florida (U.S.)
63 F9
Tallinn, Estonia 91 G7
Tamale, Ghana 135 E4
Tambov, Russia 99 F4
Tampa, Florida (U.S.) 63 F9
Tampere, Finland 91 F6
Tampico, Mexico 65 D4
Tamworth, Australia 149 E8
Tana, Lake, Ethiopia 137 C5
Tanga, Tanzania 137 F6
Tanganyika, Lake, Africa
137 F4
Tangshan, China 113 C7
Tangier, Morocco 132 A3
Tanimbar Islands, Indonesia
123 D8
Tanjungkarang-Telukbetung,
Indonesia 122 D2
Tânout, Niger 135 C6
Tanzania (country), Africa
137 F5
Taormina, Italy 93 H8
Taoudenni (Smeïda), Mali
135 B3
Tapajós (river), Brazil 79 C4
Taranaki, Mount (Mount
Egmont), New Zealand
149 F11
Taranto, Gulf of, Italy 93 H8
Tarawa, Kiribati 151 D4
Taraz, Kazakhstan 111 D3
Tarfaya, Morocco 132 C1
Târgu-Mures, Romania
97 B6
Tarija, Bolivia 77 I5
Tarim (river), China 112 C2
Tarim Basin, China 112 C2
Tarom, Iran 117 D6
Tarsus, Turkey 115 D4
Tartu, Estonia 91 G7
Tashkent, Uzbekistan 111 D3
Tasman Bay, New Zealand
149 G10
Tasmania (state), Australia
149 G7
Tasman Sea, Oceania 142 G4
Taunggyi, Myanmar 119 D8
Taupo, New Zealand 149 F11
Taupo, Lake, New Zealand
149 F11
Tauranga, New Zealand
149 E11
Taurus Mountains, Turkey
115 D3
Taymyr Peninsula, Russia
109 C6

Tbilisi, Georgia 115 B8
Tchibanga, Gabon 135 G7
Te Anau, Lake, New Zealand
149 I9
Techla, Western Sahara
(Morocco) 132 D1
Tegucigalpa, Honduras
65 F6
Tehran, Iran 117 C5
Tehuantepec, Gulf of, Mexico
54 I4
Tehuantepec, Isthmus of,
Mexico 54 H4
Tel Aviv-Yafo, Israel 115 F4
Teles Pires (river), Brazil
79 D4
Temuco, Chile 81 F1
Ténéré (desert), Niger
135 B7
Tennant Creek, Australia
149 C5
Tennessee (river), U.S. 63 E8
Tennessee (state), U.S.
63 D8
Tepic, Mexico 65 D2
Teresina, Brazil 79 C6
Ternate, Indonesia 123 C8
Tessalit, Mali 135 B5
Tete, Mozambique 139 C7
Tetovo, Macedonia 97 D4
Texas (state), U.S. 63 F5
Thailand (country), Asia
103 F5
Thailand, Gulf of, Asia
121 D2
Thames (river), United
Kingdom 93 D3
Thebes (ruins), Egypt
133 C10
The Hague, Netherlands
93 D4
The Pas, Manitoba (Canada)
61 F4
Thessaloníki, Greece 97 E5
Thiès, Senegal 135 C1
Thimphu, Bhutan 119 C7
Thíra (Santoríni) (island),
Greece 97 H6
Thiruvananthapuram
(Trivandrum), India 119 G4
Three Gorges Dam, China
113 E6
Three Kings Islands, New
Zealand 149 D10
Thunder Bay, Ontario
(Canada) 61 G6
Thurston Island, Antarctica
155 E2
Tianjin, China 113 D7
Tian Shan (range), Asia
102 D4
Tibesti Mountains, Chad
137 A2
Tibet (region), China 112 E3
Tibet, Plateau of, China
112 D2
Tidjikdja, Mauritania 135 C2
Tierra del Fuego (island),
South America 81 I2
Tigris (river), Asia 102 D2
Tijuana, Mexico 64 A1
Tikal (ruins), Guatemala 65
E6
Timaru, New Zealand
149 H10
Timimoun, Algeria 133 C4
Timisoara, Romania 97 B5
Timmins, Ontario (Canada)
61 G7
Timor (island), Asia 123 E7

Timor-Leste, see East Timor
(country), Asia 123 E7
Timor Sea, Asia/Australia
123 E7
Tindouf, Algeria 132 C3
Ti-n-Zaouâtene, Algeria
133 E5
Tirana, Albania 97 E3
Tiraspol, Moldova 95 F7
Tirbil, Iraq 117 C2
Tisza (river), Europe 84 F5
Titicaca, Lake, South
America 77 H4
Tmassah, Libya 133 C7
Toamasina, Madagascar
139 D11
Tobruk, Libya 133 B8
Tobseda, Russia 85 A7
Tocantins (river), Brazil
79 D5
Togo (country), Africa 135 E5
Tokar, Sudan 137 B6
Tokelau (islands), New
Zealand 151 E6
Tokyo, Japan 113 C11
Toledo, Ohio (U.S.) 63 C9
Toledo, Spain 93 H2
Toliara, Madagascar 139 E9
Tombouctou (Timbuktu),
Mali 135 C4
Tomini, Gulf of, Indonesia
123 C6
Tomsk, Russia 109 E5
Tonga (country), Oceania
143 E6
Tonga Islands, Tonga 142 E6
Tonkin, Gulf of, Asia 121 B4
Tonle Sap (lake), Cambodia
121 C3
Toowoomba, Australia
149 D8
Topeka, Kansas (U.S.) 63 D6
Torneälven (river), Europe
91 C6
Toronto, Ontario (Canada)
61 H7
Torreón, Mexico 65 C3
Torres Strait, Australia/
Oceania 150 E2
Tórshavn, Denmark 85 B2
Touggourt, Algeria 133 B5
Toulouse, France 93 G4
Toummo, Libya 133 D7
Tours, France 93 E4
Townsville, Australia 149 C7
Towot, South Sudan 137 D5
Toyama, Japan 113 C10
Trabzon, Turkey 115 B6
Transantarctic Mountains,
Antarctica 155 D4
Transylvania (region),
Romania 97 A6
Transylvanian Alps (range),
Romania 97 B6
Trenton, New Jersey (U.S.)
63 C10
Trieste, Italy 93 F7
Trinidad, Bolivia 77 G5
Trinidad (island), Trinidad &
Tobago 54 H8
Trinidad & Tobago (country),
North America 55 H8
Tripoli, Lebanon 115 E4
Tripoli, Libya 133 B7
Tripolitania (region), Libya
133 B6
Trivandrum, see
Thiruvananthapuram,
India 119 G4
Tromsø, Norway 91 A5

Trondheim, Norway 91 E3
Trondheimsfjorden (bay),
Norway 91 E3
Trujillo, Peru 77 F1
Truk Islands, Federated
States of Micronesia
142 C3
Tshwane, see Pretoria, South
Africa 139 F5
Tual, Indonesia 123 D9
Tuamotu Archipelago,
French Polynesia, France
151 E8
Tucson, Arizona (U.S.) 62 E3
Tukangbesi Islands,
Indonesia 123 D6
Tuktoyaktuk, Northwest
Territories (Canada) 60 C2
Tula, Russia 99 F4
Tulcea, Romania 97 C8
Tulsa, Oklahoma (U.S.)
63 D6
Tunis, Tunisia 133 A6
Tunisia (country), Africa
133 A6
Tunja, Colombia 77 B3
Turan Lowland, Asia 110 C2
Turin, Italy 93 F5
Turkana, Lake (Lake Rudolf),
Kenya 137 D5
Turkey (country), Asia/
Europe 103 C1
Turkmenistan (country), Asia
103 D3
Turks Islands, Turks &
Caicos Islands (U.K.)
67 B4
Turku, Finland 91 F6
Turpan Depression, China
112 C3
Tuvalu (country), Oceania
143 D6
Tuz, Lake, Turkey 115 C4
Tver', Russia 99 E4
Tyre, Lebanon 115 F4
Tyrrhenian Sea, Italy 84 G4
Tyumen', Russia 109 E4

U

Ubangi (river), Africa 137 E2
Uberlândia, Brazil 79 F5
Ubon Ratchathani, Thailand
121 C3
Ucayali (river), Peru 77 E2
Udon Thani, Thailand 121 B2
Uele (river), Dem. Rep. of
the Congo 137 D3
Ufa, Russia 99 E7
Uganda (country), Africa
137 E5
Ukraine (country), Europe
85 E6
Ulaanbaatar, Mongolia
111 C9
Ulan Ude, Russia 109 F7
Uluru (Ayers Rock) (peak),
Australia 148 D4
Ul'yanovsk, Russia 99 F6
Umba, Russia 85 B6
Umeå, Sweden 91 D5
Umeälven (river), Sweden
91 D5
Umm al 'Abīd, Libya 133 C7
Unayzah, Saudi Arabia
117 E3
Ungava Bay, Canada 61 E8
Ungava Peninsula, Quebec
(Canada) 61 E7
United Arab Emirates
(country), Asia 103 E2

United Kingdom — Zürich

United Kingdom (country), Europe **85** D2
United States (country), North America **55** F3
Upington, South Africa **138** G3
Upper Guinea (region), Africa **126** E3
Upper Hutt, New Zealand **149** G11
Uppsala, Sweden **91** F5
Ur (ruins), Iraq **117** D4
Ural (river), Europe/Asia **102** C3
Ural Mountains, Europe/Asia **102** C3
Uranium City, Saskatchewan (Canada) **61** E4
Urmia, Iran **117** B4
Urmia, Lake, Iran **117** B4
Uruguay (country), South America **71** G5
Uruguay (river), South America **70** F5
Ürümqi, China **112** C3
Ushuaia, Argentina **81** I2
Ussuriysk, Russia **109** F10
Ust' Ilimsk, Russia **109** E7
Ustyurt Plateau, Asia **110** C1
Usumacinta (river), North America **65** E5
Utah (state), U.S. **62** C3
Utrecht, Netherlands **93** D5
Uxmal (ruins), Mexico **65** D6
Uyuni, Salar de, Bolivia **77** I4
Uzbekistan (country), Asia **103** D3
Uzhhorod, Ukraine **95** E4

V

Vaal (river), South Africa **139** F6
Vaasa, Finland **91** E6
Vadsø, Norway **85** A5
Valdés Peninsula, Argentina **81** F3
Valencia, Spain **93** H3
Valencia, Venezuela **77** A4
Valladolid, Spain **93** G2
Valletta, Malta **93** I7
Valparaíso, Chile **81** D1
Van, Turkey **115** D7
Van, Lake, Turkey **115** C7
Vancouver, British Columbia (Canada) **60** F1
Vancouver Island, British Columbia (Canada) **60** F1
Vänern (lake), Sweden **91** G3
Vanua Levu (island), Fiji Island **151** E5
Vanuatu (country), Oceania **143** E5
Varanasi (Benares), India **119** D5
Varna, Bulgaria **97** D7
Västerås, Sweden **91** G5
Vatican City (country), Europe **85** G4
Vatnajökull (glacier), Iceland **91** A2
Vättern (lake), Sweden **91** G4
Velikiy Novgorod, Russia **99** D3
Venezuela (country), South America **71** A4
Venezuela, Gulf of, South America **77** A4
Venice, Italy **93** F6
Venice, Gulf of, Europe **97** B1

Veracruz, Mexico **65** E4
Verde, Cape, Senegal **126** D1
Verkhoyansk Range, Russia **109** C8
Vermont (state), U.S. **63** B10
Verona, Italy **93** F6
Vesterålen (islands), Norway **91** B4
Vestfjorden (bay), Norway **91** B4
Vesuvius, Mount, Italy **93** G7
Vichy, France **93** F4
Victoria (state), Australia **149** F6
Victoria, British Columbia (Canada) **60** F1
Victoria Island, Canada **61** C4
Victoria, Lake, Africa **137** E5
Victoria Land, Antarctica **155** G6
Victoria Nile (river), Uganda **137** E5
Victory Peak, Asia **111** D5
Vienna, Austria **93** E7
Vientiane, Laos **121** B2
Vietnam (country), Asia **103** F6
Vigo, Spain **93** G1
Vijayawada, India **119** E5
Villahermosa, Mexico **65** E5
Villarrica, Paraguay **81** C4
Vilnius, Lithuania **91** I7
Vinh, Vietnam **121** B3
Vinnytsya, Ukraine **95** E7
Vinson Massif (peak), Antarctica **155** D3
Virgin Islands, North America **67** C6
Virginia (state), U.S. **63** D10
Virginia Beach, Virginia (U.S.) **63** D10
Virunga Mountains, Africa **126** F6
Visby, Sweden **91** H5
Vishakhapatnam, India **119** E5
Vistula (river), Poland **94** B3
Viti Levu (island), Fiji Islands **151** E5
Vitória, Brazil **79** F7
Vitória da Conquista, Brazil **79** E7
Vitsyebsk, Belarus **95** A7
Vladikavkaz, Russia **99** I5
Vladimir, Russia **99** E4
Vladivostok, Russia **109** F10
Vlorë, Albania **97** E4
Volcano Islands, Japan **150** B2
Volga (river), Russia **99** G5
Volgograd, Russia **99** G5
Vologda, Russia **99** D4
Volta, Lake, Ghana **135** E4
Vopnafjördur, Iceland **85** A2
Vorkuta, Russia **99** B7
Voronezh, Russia **99** F4
Vostok Island, French Polynesia (France) **151** E7
Vostok Station, Antarctica **155** E7

W

Wabash (river), U.S. **63** D8
Waco, Texas (U.S.) **63** F6
Wadi Halfa, Sudan **137** A5
Wagga Wagga, Australia **149** F7
Waiau (river), New Zealand **149** I9

Waikato (river), New Zealand **149** E11
Waitaki (river), New Zealand **149** H10
Waitemata, New Zealand **149** E11
Wajir, Kenya **137** E6
Wakatipu, Lake, New Zealand **149** H9
Wake Island, U.S. **151** B4
Walbrzych, Poland **94** D2
Wales (country), United Kingdom **93** D3
Wallaroo, Australia **149** E5
Wallis and Futuna (islands), France **151** E5
Walvis Bay, Namibia **138** E2
Wanaka, New Zealand **149** H9
Wanaka, Lake, New Zealand **149** H9
Wandel Sea, Greenland (Denmark) **54** A5
Wanganui (river), New Zealand **149** F11
Wanganui, New Zealand **149** F11
Warrnambool, Australia **149** F6
Warsaw, Poland **95** C4
Washington, District of Columbia (U.S.) **63** C10
Washington (state), U.S. **62** A2
Waterford, Ireland **93** D2
Wau, South Sudan **137** C4
Webi Shabeelle (river), Africa **135** F5
Weddel Sea, Antarctica **155** B3
Weipa, Australia **149** A6
Welkom, South Africa **139** G5
Wellesley Islands, Australia **149** B6
Wellington, New Zealand **149** G11
Wellington Island, Chile **81** H1
Wessel Islands, Australia **149** A5
West Antarctica, Antarctica **155** E3
West Bank (region), Asia **115** F4
West Cape Howe, Australia **148** F2
Western Australia (state), Australia **148** D2
Western Desert, Egypt **133** C9
Western Dvina (river), Europe **84** D6
Western Ghats (range), India **119** F3
Western Plateau, Australia **142** E1
Western Rift Valley, Africa **137** E4
Western Sahara (Morocco), Africa **132** C1
West Ice Shelf, Antarctica **155** D9
West Indies (islands), North America **54** H7
Westport, New Zealand **149** G10
West Siberian Plain, Russia **109** D5

West Virginia (state), U.S. **63** C9
Whakatane, New Zealand **149** E12
Whangarei, New Zealand **149** D11
Whitehorse, Yukon (Canada) **60** D1
White Nile (river), Africa **137** C5
White Sea, Russia **84** B6
White Volta (river), Africa **135** E4
Whitney, Mount, California (U.S.) **62** D2
Whyalla, Australia **149** E5
Wichita, Kansas (U.S.) **63** D6
Wilhelm, Mount, Papua New Guinea **150** D2
Wilkes Land, Antarctica **155** F8
Wiluna, Australia **148** D2
Windhoek, Namibia **138** E2
Windorah, Australia **149** D6
Windsor, Ontario (Canada) **61** H7
Windward Islands, North America **67** D8
Winnipeg, Manitoba (Canada) **61** G5
Winnipeg, Lake, Manitoba (Canada) **61** F5
Winton, Australia **149** C6
Wisconsin (state), U.S. **63** B7
Wollongong, Australia **149** F8
Wonsan, North Korea **113** C9
Woods, Lake of the, North America **63** A6
Woomera, Australia **149** E5
Worcester, South Africa **138** H3
Wrangel Island, Russia **109** A9
Wroclaw, Poland **94** C2
Wuhan, China **113** E7
Wuwei, China **103** E5
Wyndham, Australia **148** B4
Wyoming (state), U.S. **63** C4

X

Xai-Xai, Mozambique **139** F7
Xiamen, China **113** F8
Xi'an, China **113** E6
Xingu (river), Brazil **79** D4
Xining, China **113** D5
Xuzhou, China **113** D7

Y

Yablonovyy Range, Russia **102** C6
Yakutsk, Russia **109** D8
Yalta, Ukraine **95** G9
Yamal Peninsula, Russia **109** C5
Yamoussoukro, Côte d'Ivoire **135** E3
Yanbu al Bahr, Saudi Arabia **117** E2
Yangon (Rangoon), Myanmar **119** E8
Yangtze (river), China **113** E6
Yangtze Gorges, China **102** E6
Yaoundé, Cameroon **135** F7
Yap Islands, Federated States of Micronesia **150** C1
Yaqui (river), Mexico **64** B1
Yaren, Nauru **151** D4

Yarlung Zangbo (river), China **112** E3
Yaroslavl', Russia **99** E4
Yazd, Iran **117** C6
Yekaterinburg, Russia **108** E3
Yellow (river), China **113** D7
Yellowknife, Northwest Territories (Canada) **61** D3
Yellow Sea, Asia **113** D8
Yellowstone Lake, Wyoming (U.S.) **63** B4
Yellowstone National Park, U.S. **63** B4
Yemen (country), Asia **103** F1
Yenisey (river), Russia **109** D5
Yerevan, Armenia **115** C8
Yevpatoriya, Ukraine **95** G9
Yogyakarta, Indonesia **122** G5
Yokohama, Japan **113** C11
Yola, Nigeria **135** E7
York, Cape, Australia **149** A6
Ysyk-Köl (lake), Kyrgyzstan **111** D4
Yucatán Peninsula, Mexico **65** E6
Yukon (territory), Canada **60** C2
Yukon (river), North America **54** B2
Yukon Plateau, Canada **54** C2
Yuma, Arizona (U.S.) **62** E2
Yumen, China **113** D4
Yuzhno Sakhalinsk, Russia **109** E11

Z

Zabol, Iran **117** D8
Zadar, Croatia **97** C2
Zagreb, Croatia **97** B2
Zagros Mountains, Iran **117** C5
Zahedan, Iran **117** D7
Zambezi (river), Africa **139** D7
Zambia (country), Africa **127** G6
Zamboanga, Philippines **121** E7
Zanjan, Iran **117** B4
Zanzibar, Tanzania **137** F6
Zanzibar Island, Tanzania **137** F6
Zaporizhzhya, Ukraine **95** E9
Zaragoza, Spain **93** G3
Zealand (island), Denmark **91** I3
Zenica, Bosnia & Herzegovina **97** C3
Zhengzhou, China **113** D7
Zhytomyr, Ukraine **95** D7
Zibo, China **113** D7
Ziguinchor, Senegal **135** D1
Zimbabwe (country), Africa **127** G6
Zinder, Niger **135** D7
Zonguldak, Turkey **115** B3
Zouîrat, Mauritania **135** B2
Zufar (region), Oman **117** G6
Zürich, Switzerland **93** E5

Aden, Gulf of — Herdman Seamount

OCEAN FEATURES

A

Aden, Gulf of, Indian Ocean **164** C3
Adriatic Sea, Mediterranean Sea **163** C7
Aegean Sea, Mediterranean Sea **163** D7
Aegir Ridge, Atlantic Ocean **167** E11
Agalega Islands, Indian Ocean **165** E4
Agassiz Fracture Zone, Pacific Ocean **161** H7
Agulhas, Cape, Indian Ocean **164** G1
Agulhas Bank, Atlantic Ocean **163** H7
Agulhas Basin, Indian Ocean **164** H1
Agulhas Seamount, Atlantic Ocean **163** H7
Alaska, Gulf of, Pacific Ocean **161** B6
Aldabra Islands, Indian Ocean **164** E3
Aleutian Basin, Pacific Ocean **161** B4
Aleutian Trench, Pacific Ocean **161** B4
Alexandra Land, Arctic Ocean **167** C7
Alpha Cordillera, Arctic Ocean **167** F5
Amirante Isles, Indian Ocean **164** E3
Amirante Trench, Indian Ocean **164** E3
Amsterdam (island), Indian Ocean **165** G5
Amundsen Gulf, Arctic Ocean **166** H3
Andaman Basin, Indian Ocean **165** C7
Angola Plain, Atlantic Ocean **163** G6
Anjou Islands, Arctic Ocean **166** C3
Arabian Basin, Indian Ocean **165** C4
Arabian Sea, Indian Ocean **165** C4
Arafura Sea, Indian Ocean **165** E11
Argentine Plain, Atlantic Ocean **163** I3
Ascension (island), Atlantic Ocean **163** F5
Ascension Fracture Zone, Atlantic Ocean **163** F5
Atlantic-Indian Ridge, Indian Ocean **164** I1
Atlantis Fracture Zone, Atlantic Ocean **163** D3
Atlantis II Fracture Zone, Indian Ocean **165** G4
Austral Islands, Pacific Ocean **161** G6
Aves Ridge, Atlantic Ocean **163** E2

B

Baffin Bay, Atlantic Ocean **167** H7
Baltic Sea, Atlantic Ocean **163** B7
Banda Sea, Pacific Ocean **160** F1
Barents Plain, Arctic Ocean **167** D7
Barents Sea, Arctic Ocean **167** C8
Barrow Canyon, Arctic Ocean **166** G2
Barrow Strait, Arctic Ocean **167** H6
Baydarata Bay, Arctic Ocean **167** A8
Beata Ridge, Atlantic Ocean **163** E2
Beaufort Sea, Arctic Ocean **166** G3
Beaufort Shelf, Arctic Ocean **166** G2
Beaufort Slope, Arctic Ocean **166** G2
Belgica Bank, Arctic Ocean **167** E8
Bengal, Bay of, Indian Ocean **165** C6
Benham Seamount, Pacific Ocean **165** C10
Bering Sea, Pacific Ocean **160** A4
Bering Strait, Arctic Ocean **166** F1
Bermuda Rise, Atlantic Ocean **163** D2
Bill Baileys Bank, Atlantic Ocean **163** B5
Biscay, Bay of, Atlantic Ocean **163** C5
Biscay Plain, Atlantic Ocean **163** C5
Bjørnøya (island), Arctic Ocean **167** D9
Black Sea, Europe/Asia **163** C7
Blake-Bahama Ridge, Atlantic Ocean **163** D2
Blake Plateau, Atlantic Ocean **163** D1
Bol'shevik Islands, Arctic Ocean **167** B5
Bonin Trench, Pacific Ocean **160** D2
Boothia, Gulf of, Arctic Ocean **167** I6
Boreas Plain, Arctic Ocean **167** E9
Bothnia, Gulf of, Atlantic Ocean **163** B7
Bounty Trough, Pacific Ocean **161** I4
Bouvet (island), Atlantic Ocean **163** I6
Bowers Ridge, Pacific Ocean **161** B4
Broken Ridge, Indian Ocean **165** G7
Buor-Khaya Bay, Arctic Ocean **166** B3
Bylot Island, Arctic Ocean **167** H6

C

Campbell Plateau, Pacific Ocean **160** I3
Campeche Bank, Atlantic Ocean **163** E1
Canada Basin, Arctic Ocean **166** G3
Canada Plain, Arctic Ocean **166** F3
Cape Verde Islands, Atlantic Ocean **163** E4
Cargados Carajos Bank, Indian Ocean **165** E4
Caribbean Sea, Atlantic Ocean **163** E1
Carlsberg Ridge, Indian Ocean **165** D4
Carnegie Ridge, Pacific Ocean **163** F1
Carpentaria, Gulf of, Pacific Ocean **165** E11
Cayman Trench, Atlantic Ocean **163** E1
Cedros Trench, Pacific Ocean **161** D8
Celebes Sea, Pacific Ocean **160** E1
Celtic Sea, Atlantic Ocean **163** C5
Central Pacific Basin, Pacific Ocean **161** E44
Chagos Trench, Indian Ocean **165** E5
Chain Fracture Zone, Atlantic Ocean **163** F5
Challenger Deep, Pacific Ocean **160** E2
Chatham Rise, Pacific Ocean **161** H4
Chaun Bay, Arctic Ocean **166** D1
Chelyuskin, Cape, Arctic Ocean **167** B5
Chesha Bay, Arctic Ocean **167** A9
Chile Basin, Pacific Ocean **161** G9
Chile Rise, Pacific Ocean **161** H9
Chinook Trough, Pacific Ocean **161** C4
Christmas Island, Indian Ocean **165** E8
Chukchi Plain, Arctic Ocean **166** E3
Chukchi Plateau, Arctic Ocean **166** E3
Chukchi Sea, Arctic Ocean **166** E1
Clarion Fracture Zone, Pacific Ocean **161** E7
Clipperton Fracture Zone, Pacific Ocean **161** E7
Coco-De-Mer Seamounts, Indian Ocean **165** D4
Cocos Ridge, Pacific Ocean **161** E9
Columbia Seamount, Atlantic Ocean **163** G4
Comoro Islands, Indian Ocean **164** E3
Congo Canyon, Atlantic Ocean **163** F6
Coral Sea, Pacific Ocean **161** G3
Coral Sea Basin, Pacific Ocean **160** F2
Corner Seamounts, Atlantic Ocean **163** D3
Cornwallis Island, Arctic Ocean **167** H5
Crozet Basin, Indian Ocean **165** H4

Crozet Islands, Indian Ocean **164** H3
Cuvier Plateau, Indian Ocean **165** F8

D

Davis Strait, Atlantic Ocean **163** A2
Demerara Plain, Atlantic Ocean **163** E3
Denmark Strait, Atlantic Ocean **163** A4
Diamantina Fracture Zone, Indian Ocean **165** G8
Diego Garcia (island), Indian Ocean **165** E5
Discovery Tablemount, Atlantic Ocean **163** H6
Disko (island), see Qeqertarsuak, Arctic Ocean **167** H8
Doldrums Fracture Zone, Atlantic Ocean **163** E4
Dumshaf Plain, Atlantic Ocean **163** A6

E

East Caroline Basin, Pacific Ocean **160** E2
East China Sea, Pacific Ocean **160** D1
Easter Fracture Zone, Pacific Ocean **161** G8
East Indiaman Ridge, Indian Ocean **165** F7
East Mariana Basin, Pacific Ocean **160** E2
East Novaya Zemlya Trough, Arctic Ocean **167** B7
East Pacific Rise, Pacific Ocean **161** G8
East Sea, see Japan, Sea of, Pacific Ocean **160** C1
East Siberian Sea, Arctic Ocean **166** D2
Eauripik Rise, Pacific Ocean **165** D11
Egeria Fracture Zone, Indian Ocean **165** F4
Eirik Ridge, Atlantic Ocean **163** B3
Ellef Ringnes Island, Arctic Ocean **167** G5
Eltanin Fracture Zone, Pacific Ocean **161** I6
Emerald Basin, Pacific Ocean **160** I3
Emperor Seamounts, Pacific Ocean **161** C3
Emperor Trough, Pacific Ocean **161** C4
English Channel, Atlantic Ocean **163** C6
Europa (island), Indian Ocean **164** F2
Exmouth Plateau, Indian Ocean **165** F9

F

Falkland Escarpment, Atlantic Ocean **163** I3
Falkland Plateau, Atlantic Ocean **163** I3
Farewell, Cape, Atlantic Ocean **163** B3

Faroe Bank, Atlantic Ocean **163** B5
Faroe-Iceland Ridge, Atlantic Ocean **163** B5
Farquhar Group, Indian Ocean **164** E3
Fiji Islands Plateau, Pacific Ocean **161** G4
Finland, Gulf of, Atlantic Ocean **163** B7
Flemish Cap, Atlantic Ocean **163** C3
Fletcher Plain, Arctic Ocean **167** E5
Flores Sea, Pacific Ocean **165** E9
Foxe Basin, Atlantic Ocean **163** A1
Fram Basin, Arctic Ocean **167** E6
Frio, Cape, Atlantic Ocean **163** G3
Fundy, Bay of, Atlantic Ocean **163** C2

G

Galápagos Fracture Zone, Pacific Ocean **161** F6
Galápagos Rift, Pacific Ocean **161** E9
Galápagos Rise, Pacific Ocean **161** F9
Gambia Plain, Atlantic Ocean **163** E4
Ganges Fan, Indianv **165** C6
Gardar Ridge, Atlantic Ocean **163** B4
George Bligh Bank, Atlantic Ocean **163** B5
George Land, Arctic Ocean **167** C7
Gibraltar, Strait of, Atlantic Ocean **163** D5
Gilbert Islands, Pacific Ocean **161** F3
Gloria Ridge, Atlantic Ocean **163** B3
Graham Bell Island, Arctic Ocean **167** C7
Grand Banks of Newfoundland, Atlantic Ocean **163** C3
Great Australian Bight, Indian Ocean **165** G10
Great Meteor Tablemount, Atlantic Ocean **163** D4
Greenland Fracture Zone, Arctic Ocean **167** E9
Greenland Plain, Arctic Ocean **167** E9
Greenland Sea, Arctic Ocean **167** E9
Guatemala Basin, Pacific Ocean **161** E9
Gusinaya Bank, Arctic Ocean **167** B9

H

Halten Bank, Atlantic **163** A6
Hatteras Plain, Atlantic Ocean **163** D2
Hawaiian Ridge, Pacific Ocean **161** D5
Henrietta Island, Arctic Ocean **166** D3
Herdman Seamount, Atlantic Ocean **163** I6

Hess Rise — Saya de Malha Bank

Hess Rise, Pacific Ocean **161** C4
Hope, Point, Arctic Ocean **166** F1
Hotspur Seamount, Atlantic Ocean **163** G4
Hudson Bay, Atlantic Ocean **163** B1
Hudson Canyon, Atlantic Ocean **163** D2
Humboldt Plain, Pacific Ocean **161** I10

I

Iceland Plateau, Atlantic Ocean **167** F10
Iceland Sea, Atlantic Ocean **163** A5
Imarssuak Seachannel, Atlantic Ocean **163** B3
Indomed Fracture Zone, Indian Ocean **164** H3
Indus Fan, Indian Ocean **165** B4
Investigator Ridge, Indian Ocean **165** E7
Islas Orcadas Rise, Atlantic Ocean **163** I4
Izu Trench, Pacific Ocean **160** D2

J

Jan Mayen Fracture Zone, Arctic Ocean **167** E10
Jan Mayen Ridge, Atlantic Ocean **163** A5
Japan, Sea of, (East Sea), Pacific Ocean **160** C1
Japan Trench, Pacific Ocean **160** C2
Java Ridge, Indian Ocean **165** E8
Java Sea, Pacific Ocean **165** D8
Java Trench, Indian Ocean **165** E8
Jeannette Island, Arctic Ocean **166** D3
Josephine Seamount, Atlantic Ocean **163** D5
Juan De Fuca Ridge, Pacific Ocean **161** B7

K

Kane Fracture Zone, Atlantic Ocean **163** E3
Kara Sea, Arctic Ocean **167** B6
Kerguélen Islands, Indian Ocean **165** I5
Kerguélen Plateau, Indian Ocean **165** I5
Kermadec Trench, Pacific Ocean **161** H4
Kolbeinsey Ridge, Atlantic Ocean **163** A5
Komsomolets Island, Arctic Ocean **167** C5
Kotzebue Sound, Arctic Ocean **166** F1
Krylov Seamount, Atlantic Ocean **163** E4
Kuril Basin, Pacific Ocean **160** C2

Kuril Trench, Pacific Ocean **160** C2
Kyushu-Palau Ridge, Pacific Ocean **160** E1

L

Lancaster Sound, Arctic Ocean **167** H6
Laptev Sea, Arctic Ocean **167** B4
Lau Basin, Pacific Ocean **161** G4
Laurentian Fan, Atlantic Ocean **163** C3
Lau Ridge, Pacific Ocean **161** G4
Lincoln Sea, Arctic Ocean **167** F7
Line Islands, Pacific Ocean **161** E5
Lomonosov Ridge, Arctic Ocean **167** E5
Lord Howe Rise, Pacific Ocean **160** H3
Louisville Ridge, Pacific Ocean **161** H4
Lyakhov Islands, Arctic Ocean **166** C3

M

Macclesfield Bank, Pacific Ocean **165** C9
Mackenzie Trough, Arctic Ocean **166** H3
Macquarie Ridge, Pacific Ocean **160** I3
Madagascar Basin, Indian Ocean **164** F3
Madagascar Plateau, Indian Ocean **164** G3
Magellan, Strait of, Atlantic Ocean **163** I2
Magellan Rise, Pacific Ocean **161** E4
Maine, Gulf of, Atlantic Ocean **163** C2
Makarov Basin, Arctic Ocean **167** E4
Manihiki Plateau, Pacific Ocean **161** F5
Mapmaker Seamounts, Pacific Ocean **161** D3
Mariana Trench, Pacific Ocean **160** E2
Mariana Trough, Pacific Ocean **160** E2
Marquesas Fracture Zone, Pacific Ocean **161** F7
Martin Vaz Islands, Atlantic Ocean **163** G4
Marvin Spur, Arctic Ocean **167** E5
Mascarene Basin, Indian Ocean **165** E4
Mascarene Plain, Indian Ocean **164** F3
Mascarene Plateau, Indian Ocean **165** E4
Mathematicians Seamounts, Pacific Ocean **161** E8
Mauritius Trench, Indian Ocean **165** F4
Maury Seachannel, Atlantic Ocean **163** B4
M'Clintock Channel, Arctic Ocean **167** I5

M'Clure Strait, Arctic Ocean **167** H4
Mediterranean Sea, Europe/Asia/Africa **163** D6
Menard Fracture Zone, Pacific Ocean **161** I8
Mendeleyev Plain, Arctic Ocean **167** E4
Mendeleyev Ridge, Arctic Ocean **167** E4
Mendocino Fracture Zone, Pacific Ocean **161** C6
Meteor Seamount, Atlantic Ocean **163** I6
Mexico, Gulf of, Atlantic Ocean **163** E1
Mexico Basin, Atlantic Ocean **163** E1
Mid-Atlantic Ridge, Atlantic Ocean **163** D4
Middle America Trench, Pacific Ocean **161** E9
Mid-Indian Basin, Indian Ocean **165** E6
Mid-Indian Ridge, Indian Ocean **165** E4
Mid-Pacific Mountains, Pacific Ocean **161** D3
Mississippi Fan, Atlantic Ocean **163** D1
Mohns Ridge, Arctic Ocean **167** E10
Molloy Deep, Arctic Ocean **167** E8
Molokai Fracture Zone, Pacific Ocean **161** D6
Morris Jessup Rise, Arctic Ocean **167** E7
Mozambique Escarpment, Indian Ocean **164** G2
Mozambique Plateau, Indian Ocean **164** G2
Murmansk Rise, Arctic Ocean **167** C8
Murray Fracture Zone, Pacific Ocean **161** D6
Musicians Seamounts, Pacific Ocean **161** D5

N

Nansen Basin, Arctic Ocean **167** C5
Nansen Ridge, Arctic Ocean **167** D6
Nares Plain, Atlantic Ocean **163** E2
Natal Basin, Indian Ocean **164** G2
Naturaliste Plateau, Indian Ocean **165** G8
Nazareth Bank, Indian Ocean **165** E4
Nazca Ridge, Pacific Ocean **161** G9
Necker Ridge, Pacific Ocean **161** D5
New Caledonia Basin, Pacific Ocean **161** G3
New England Seamounts, Atlantic Ocean **163** D2
New Hebrides Trench, Pacific Ocean **161** G4
Nikitin Seamount, Indian Ocean **165** D6
Ninetyeast Ridge, Indian Ocean **165** E7

Norfolk Ridge, Pacific Ocean **161** G3
North Australian Basin, Indian Ocean **165** E9
Northeast Pacific Basin, Pacific Ocean **161** D6
North Fiji Basin, Pacific Ocean **161** G3
North New Hebrides Trench, Pacific Ocean **161** G3
North Sea, Atlantic Ocean **163** B6
Northwest Atlantic Mid-Ocean Canyon, Atlantic Ocean **163** B3
Northwest Hawaiian Ridge, Pacific Ocean **161** D4
Northwest Pacific Basin, Pacific Ocean **161** C3
Northwind Escarpment, Arctic Ocean **166** F3
Northwind Plain, Arctic Ocean **166** F3
Northwind Ridge, Arctic Ocean **166** F3
Norwegian Basin, Atlantic Ocean **167** E11
Norwegian Sea, Atlantic Ocean **163** A6

O

Ob, Gulf of, Arctic Ocean **167** A7
Ob' Bank, Arctic Ocean **167** E8
Ob' Tablemount, Indian Ocean **164** I2
Oceanographer Fracture Zone, Atlantic Ocean **163** D4
October Revolution Island, Arctic Ocean **167** C5
Okhotsk, Sea of, Pacific Ocean **160** B2
Olga Basin, Arctic Ocean **167** D8
Oman, Gulf of, Indian Ocean **165** B4
Orphan Knoll, Atlantic Ocean **163** C3
Osborn Plateau, Indian Ocean **165** E6
Outer Bailey (bank), Atlantic Ocean **163** B5
Owen Fracture Zone, Indian Ocean **165** C4

P

Palau Trench, Pacific Ocean **160** E1
Palawan Trough, Pacific Ocean **165** C9
Panama Basin, Pacific Ocean **161** E10
Paracel Islands, Pacific Ocean **165** C8
Parry Channel, Arctic Ocean **167** H5
Patton Escarpment, Pacific Ocean **161** D8
Pechora Bay, Arctic Ocean **167** A8
Pernambuco Plain, Atlantic Ocean **163** F4
Persian Gulf, Indian Ocean **164** B3

Perth Basin, Indian Ocean **165** G8
Peru Basin, Pacific Ocean **161** F9
Peru-Chile Trench, Pacific Ocean **161** G9
Philippine Basin, Pacific Ocean **165** C10
Philippine Sea, Pacific Ocean **160** D1
Philippine Trench, Pacific Ocean **160** E1
Pico (island), Atlantic Ocean **163** D4
Pioneer Fracture Zone, Pacific Ocean **161** C6
Pole Plain, Arctic Ocean **167** D5
Porcupine Bank, Atlantic Ocean **163** C5
Porcupine Plain, Atlantic Ocean **163** C5
Prince Edward Fracture Zone, Indian Ocean **164** H2
Prince Edward Islands, Indian Ocean **164** H2
Prince Regent Inlet, Arctic Ocean **167** I6
Puerto Rico Trench, Atlantic Ocean **163** E2

Q

Qeqertarsuaq (Disko), Atlantic Ocean **167** H8

R

Ra's al Hadd (cape), Indian Ocean **165** B4
Red Sea, Indian Ocean **164** B2
Researcher Ridge, Atlantic Ocean **163** E3
Reykjanes Ridge, Atlantic Ocean **163** B4
Rio Grande Rise, Atlantic Ocean **163** G4
Rodrigues (island), Indian Ocean **165** F4
Rodrigues Fracture Zone, Indian Ocean **165** F4
Romanche Gap, Atlantic Ocean **163** F5
Røst Bank, Atlantic Ocean **167** D11
Ryukyu Trench, Pacific Ocean **160** D1

S

St. Lawrence, Gulf of, Atlantic Ocean **163** C2
St. Paul (island), Indian Ocean **165** H5
St. Peter and St. Paul Rocks, Atlantic Ocean **163** F4
Sala y Gómez Ridge, Pacific Ocean **161** G9
San Jorge, Gulf of, Atlantic Ocean **163** I2
Santos Plateau, Atlantic Ocean **163** G3
Sargo Plateau, Arctic Ocean **166** E3
Saya de Malha Bank, Indian Ocean **165** E4

Shatskiy Rise — Zhokhova

Shatskiy Rise, Pacific Ocean
161 D3
Shirshov Ridge, Pacific
Ocean **161** B3
Somali Basin, Indian Ocean
164 D3
South Australian Basin,
Indian Ocean **165** G10
South China Sea, Pacific
Ocean **165** C9
Southeast Indian Ridge,
Indian Ocean **165** H7
Southeast Pacific Basin,
Pacific Ocean **161** I9
South Fiji Basin, Pacific
Ocean **161** G4
South Tasman Rise, Pacific
Ocean **160** I2
Southwest Indian Ridge,
Indian Ocean **164** H3
Southwest Pacific Basin,
Pacific Ocean **161** H6
Spitsbergen Bank, Arctic
Ocean **167** D9
Spitsbergen Fracture Zone,
Arctic Ocean **167** E8
Spitzbergen (island), Arctic
Ocean **167** D8
Stocks Seamount, Atlantic
Ocean **163** G4
Sulu Basin, Pacific Ocean
160 E1
Surtsey (island), Atlantic
Ocean **163** B5
Svalbard (island), Arctic
Ocean **167** D8
Svyataya Anna Fan, Arctic
Ocean **167** D6
Svyataya Anna Trough, Arctic
Ocean **167** C6

T
Tasman Plain, Pacific Ocean
160 H2
Tasman Sea, Pacific Ocean
160 H3
Thailand, Gulf of, Pacific
Ocean **165** C8
Tonga Trench, Pacific Ocean
161 G4
Tristan da Cunha Group,
Atlantic Ocean **163** H5
Tufts Plain, Pacific Ocean
161 C6
Tyrrhenian Sea,
Mediterranean **163** D6

U
Udintsev Fracture Zone,
Pacific Ocean **161** I5

V
Valdivia Fracture Zone,
Pacific Ocean **161** H9
Vema Fracture Zone,
Atlantic Ocean **163** E3
Vema Fracture Zone, Indian
Ocean **165** E5
Vema Seamount, Atlantic
Ocean **163** H6
Viscount Melville Sound,
Arctic Ocean **167** H5
Vitória Seamount, Atlantic
Ocean **163** G4

Vityaz Trench, Pacific Ocean
161 F4
Voring Plateau, Atlantic
Ocean **163** A6
Voronin Trough, Arctic Ocean
167 C6

W
Wallaby Plateau, Indian
Ocean **165** F8
Walters Shoal, Indian Ocean
164 G3
Walvis Ridge, Atlantic Ocean
163 G6
Wandel Sea, Arctic Ocean
167 E7
Weber Basin, Pacific Ocean
160 F1
West Caroline Basin, Pacific
Ocean **160** E2
West Mariana Basin, Pacific
Ocean **160** E2
Wharton Basin, Indian Ocean
165 F8
White Sea, Arctic Ocean
167 B10
Wrangel Plain, Arctic Ocean
167 D4
Wüst Seamount, Atlantic
Ocean **163** H5
Wyandot Seamount, Atlantic
Ocean **163** H7
Wyville Thomson Ridge,
Atlantic Ocean **163** B5

Y
Yana, Gulf of, Arctic Ocean
167 B3
Yap Trench, Pacific Ocean
160 E2
Yellow Sea, Pacific Ocean
160 C1
Yenisey Gulf, Arctic Ocean
167 A6
Yermak Plateau, Arctic
Ocean **167** E8

Z
Zanzibar Island, Indian
Ocean **164** E2
Zapiola Ridge, Atlantic
Ocean **163** I3
Zhokhova (island), Arctic
Ocean **166** C3

Illustrations Credits

ISBN 978-0-545-62412-1

Copyright © 2013 by National Geographic Society. All rights reserved. Published by Scholastic Inc., 557 Broadway, New York, NY 10012, by arrangement with National Geographic Society. SCHOLASTIC and associated logos are trademarks and/or registered trademarks of Scholastic Inc.

12 11 10 9 8 7 6 5 4 3   14 15 16 17 18/0

Printed in the U.S.A.   08

First Scholastic printing, September 2013

Published by the National Geographic Society
John M. Fahey, *Chairman of the Board and Chief Executive Officer*
Declan Moore, *Executive Vice President;*
  President, Publishing and Travel
Melina Gerosa Bellows, *Executive Vice President;*
  Chief Creative Officer, Books, Kids, and Family

Prepared by the Book Division
Hector Sierra, *Senior Vice President and General Manager*
Nancy Laties Feresten, *Senior Vice President,*
  Kids Publishing and Media
Jay Sumner, *Director of Photography, Children's Publishing*
Jennifer Emmett, *Vice President, Editorial Director, Children's Books*
Eva Absher-Schantz, *Design Director, Kids Publishing and Media*
R. Gary Colbert, *Production Director*
Jennifer A. Thornton, *Director of Managing Editorial*

Staff for This Book
Priyanka Lamichhane, *Project Editor*
David M. Seager, *Art Director*
Lori Epstein, *Senior Illustrations Editor*
Ariane Szu-Tu, *Editorial Assistant*
Callie Broaddus, *Design Production Assistant*
Hillary Moloney, *Illustrations Assistant*
Carl Mehler, *Director of Maps*
Matthew W. Chwastyk, *Map Project and Production Manager*
Sven M. Dolling, Steven D. Gardner, Thomas L. Gray, Michael McNey, Nicholas P. Rosenbach, Tibor G. Tóth, Gregory Ugiansky, Mapping Specialists, and XNR Productions, *Map Research and Production*
Martha Sharma, *Contributing Writer*
Grace Hill, *Associate Managing Editor*
Joan Gossett, *Production Editor*
Lewis R. Bassford, *Production Manager*
Susan Borke, *Legal and Business Affairs*

Manufacturing and Quality Management
Phillip L. Schlosser, *Senior Vice President*
Chris Brown, *Vice President, NG Book Manufacturing*
George Bounelis, *Vice President, Production Services*
Nicole Elliott, *Manager*
Rachel Faulise, *Manager*
Robert L. Barr, *Manager*